STUDIES OF THE EAST ASIAN INSTITUTE

# Contemporary Japanese Budget Politics

## The East Asian Institute of Columbia University

The East Asian Institute of Columbia University
was established in 1949 to prepare graduate students for
careers dealing with East Asia, and to aid research
and publication on East Asia
during the modern period.
The faculty of the Institute are grateful to the
Ford Foundation and the Rockefeller Foundation
for their financial assistance.

The Studies of the East Asian Institute were
inaugurated in 1962 to bring to a wider public
the results of significant new research
on modern and contemporary East Asia.

# Contemporary Japanese Budget Politics

John Creighton Campbell

University of California Press
Berkeley · Los Angeles · London

University of California Press
Berkeley and Los Angeles, California

University of California Press, Ltd.
London, England

ISBN 0-520-02573-3
Library of Congress Catalog Card Number: 73-85782
Printed in the United States of America

*To my mother and father:*
*Ruth C. Campbell*
*Charles E. Campbell*

# Contents

# List
# of Tables
# and Charts

## Tables

## Charts

# Preface

This book on the Japanese budgeting system as it works today and as it has evolved over twenty years is written within two frames of reference and with two audiences in mind. The first frame of reference is comparative public policy—in particular, the search for variables of political structure and process which help account for what governments do. Granting that budget systems in advanced mixed-economy countries are fundamentally similar, variations are important and can be compared. In fact, it is similarity which highlights differences and allows us to specify their consequences. I have tried to maintain an international perspective throughout the book, and to include comparisons to budgeting elsewhere where appropriate.

The second frame of reference is contemporary Japan, specifically the study of Japanese organizations and governmental process. While certainly both Japanese and Western political scientists have performed valuable research on these themes, because of both the issues they have selected and the rather high level of generality often adopted, our understanding of how Japan's business flows through its governmental system remains quite limited. I suppose I view politics as fundamentally complicated and find most research in this field oversimplified. Without claiming that day-to-day decision making is necessarily the essence of politics, I hope to help fill a significant gap by making sense of the complexity of one process, and then by describing it in a way that conveys both the complexity and the sense.

The idea that I might apply generalizations derived from American budgeting to Japan first glimmered in a course on bureaucratic politics taught by Wallace Sayre, and materialized during conversations with my advisor, James William Morley. In common with so many students in the East Asian Institute at Columbia University, I owe a great deal to Professor Morley's good advice and cheerful support.

While in Japan in 1969-70 and again briefly in 1974, my research was aided by many officials, politicans, reporters and others who found time to talk with me. Unfortunately, by prearrangement they must be nameless. I can however mention with pleasure two good friends and *senpai* — one a journalist, one a scholar — who made my project possible. Ōuchi Yukio of NHK knows everyone in the world of economic policy making and introduced me to many, often actually participating in my interviews. Kojima Akira, then of the Legislative Reference and Research Bureau of the National Diet Library and now on the faculty of Hōsei University, helped in many practical matters, advised at all stages, and offered detailed comments on two complete drafts of the manuscript. Particular thanks also are due to Professor Ishida Takeshi of the Institute

I am grateful for financial support from several sources. Initial preparation and the major field research were carried out as a fellow of the Foreign Area Fellowship Program of the Social Science Research Council and American Council of Learned Societies. The first version of the manuscript was finished thanks to a Ford Foundation Travel and Study Award. Supplementary interviews and other research were performed on a trip to Japan devoted mainly to other purposes, under a grant to the Interuniversity Consortium for Political and Social Research from the Joint Committee on Japanese Studies of the SSRC and ACLS. Finally, support for additional research, many revisions and final preparation of the manuscript came from Japan Foundation funds administered by the Center for Japanese Studies, University of Michigan, and from the East Asian Institute, Columbia University. Naturally, none of these institutions is responsible for my opinions and conclusions, let alone errors and omissions.

Very helpful comments and criticism were received from Thomas J. Anton, Gerald L. Curtis, Michael W. Donnelly, Itō Daiichi, Robert Putnam, Aaron Wildavsky, and especially Haruhiro Fukui, whose detailed as well as broad suggestions, were invaluable. For provision of materials, research assistance and other aid I would like to thank Paul S. Kim, Steven R. Reed, Lester Ross, and particularly John Strate. The manuscript was expertly typed by Barbara Hohol. My colleagues at both the Social Science Research Council and the University of Michigan have always been kinder than necessary.

I have been engaged in this enterprise for eight years, a period of some trauma and despair as well as satisfaction and pleasure. My wife Ruth has gamely borne much of the burden. I am happy to make known my gratitude for her patience, humor and constant stimulation.

# Editorial Notes

Japanese names are written in Japanese order, family name first. Conversions from yen to dollars are approximate and for the sake of consistency over time are figured at the rate of $1 = ¥ 300 throughout even though the official exchange rate was $1 = ¥ 360 in the 1950s and 1960s. For titles and names of organizations, official English equivalents devised by the Japanese government are used—hence for example *ka,* usually called "section," is here translated "division," and the Jichishō, literally Ministry of Local Autonomy, is here the Ministry of Home Affairs (see Japan, Prime Minister's Office, Administrative Management Agency, *Table of Organization of the Government of Japan* [Tokyo: Ministry of Finance Printing Bureau, 1974]). For Liberal Democratic Party titles I follow Haruhiro Fukui's authoritative *Party in Power: The Liberal Democratic Party in Policy-Making* (Berkeley and Los Angeles: University of California Press, 1970).

The following abbreviations are used in the text: MOF—Ministry of Finance; BB—Budget Bureau; MITI—Ministry of International Trade and Industry; EPA—Economic Planning Agency; LDP—Liberal Democratic Party; PARC—Policy Affairs Research Council; FILP—Fiscal Investment and Loan Program. In addition, the following abbreviations of newspapers are used in the footnotes: AS—Asahi Shinbun; MNS—Mainichi Shinbun; NKS—Nihon Keizai Shinbun; SS—Sankei Shinbun; TS—Tokyo Shinbun; YS—Yomiuri Shinbun. For reasons of space many specific citations, particularly those of ordinary newspaper articles, have been omitted. For events prior to 1971 more complete documentation will be found in my unpublished dissertation, "Contemporary Japanese Budget Politics" (Columbia University, Department of Political Science, 1973).

# 1

# Introduction

EVERY GOVERNMENT budgets. Because the activities of government seen as desirable always cost more than the resources available, everywhere — at least among the Western industrialized nations which have been studied — we find the same basic budgeting roles. Spenders in line agencies try to expand their programs. Budgeters cut demands down to fit a sensible total. Politicians trade on the close connections between spending and votes. How these roles are played and how they fit together vary from country to country, of course, but the range is surprisingly narrow.[1] Budgeting approximates a universal function of modern government.

## Themes

This book is not about budgeting in general, but budgeting in particular: how the General Account budget was compiled in Japan during the period 1954-1974. Within the relatively narrow range of variation in budgeting behavior, I have found Japan distinctive in several respects: particularly, in the intimacy of participation by a political party organization; the high proportion of total governmental decision making occupied by budgeting; rapidity of economic and therefore budget growth; the prevalence of budgetary norms related to traditional

---

1. See Aaron Wildavsky, *Budgeting: A Comparative Theory of Budgetary Processes* (Boston: Little, Brown and Company, 1975), which builds upon, as well as his own pioneering *The Politics of the Budgetary Process* (Boston: Little, Brown and Company, 1964), such studies as Hugh Heclo and Aaron Wildavsky, *The Private Government of Public Money* (Berkeley and Los Angeles: University of California Press, 1974); Guy Lord, *The French Budgetary Process* (Berkeley and Los Angeles: University of California Press, 1973); and Thomas J. Anton, *The Politics of State Expenditure in Illinois* (Urbana: University of Illinois Press, 1966).

1

Japanese values; and finally the stability of Japanese public policy outputs over time. These five topics are worth a few words right at the outset.

*Party Role* — The most striking aspect of Japanese politics is that one party has controlled the government for over twenty years, and the most striking aspect of Japanese budgeting, to those familiar with other budget systems, is that the majority party organization intervenes routinely at nearly all stages of the budgetary process. The Liberal Democratic Party's Policy Affairs Research Council (PARC), incorporating a structure of committees parallel to the governmental ministries, has as its major function the review of ministerial budget requests and Finance Ministry drafts to be sure that party interests are sufficiently represented. The final budget negotiation, preceding pro forma approval by the Cabinet before submission to the Diet, is between the finance minister and the top leadership of the LDP. Asked about any deficiencies or anomalies in the budget, a Ministry of Finance official will always lay the blame on overwhelming pressures from the majority party. Politicians everywhere are of course interested in budgets, and it is likely that where, how and to what degree elected officials achieve access to budgetary decision making is an important structural variable differentiating budgetary systems. Apparently unique to Japan is the extent of penetration by a partisan organization as such.

*Budget Primacy* — Less immediately obvious, but nonetheless an important underlying condition of Japanese politics, is the "large space" occupied by the budgetary system. That is to say, if one could somehow define "decisions" so that their numbers could be reliably compared cross-nationally, it would turn out that more decisions were made as part of the budgetary process in Japan than elsewhere.[2] Formal reasons partly explain this phenomenon: the administrative principle has become established that any matter involving governmental expenditure (even when the amount is rather minor, such as the costs of setting up a new office) must be considered first within the budgetary process. Unlike in the United States, appropriations precede authorization — when substantive legislation is also required to establish a program or a new set of regulations, it will be passed by the Cabinet and submitted to the Diet *after* the budget has been settled; such "budget-related bills," as they are called, are often thought of simply as routine implementation of matters already decided. More informal factors too, many of which will be

2. This point by no means implies that the budget occupies an unusually large share of the economy. Quite the opposite: mainly because of low defense and social security spending, Japanese governmental expenditure as a proportion of GNP is by some margin the smallest among comparable nations.

discussed below, have tended to force more and more disputes into the budget process for resolution. The result is that issues which in other countries would be debated and decided in other arenas—arenas with different rules, conferring different advantages on a different array of participants—in Japan are subject to the highly constrained rules of the game characteristic of budgeting. As the perceptive political scientist Itō Daiichi puts it:

What is characteristic of Japan these days is that, while the principle of party government is in force, in actuality, as a result of the parties having lost the capability of policy decision-making, the rules of the budgetary compilation process have, as they stand, necessarily come to substitute for the rules of policy decision-making.[3]

*High Growth*—Because Japanese economic growth has been so rapid— an average of over 10 percent per year even in constant prices through the period studied here—the budget has risen each year by amounts unequalled among advanced nations. For the entire 1954-1974 period, average yearly growth of the General Account budget was 14.4 percent; if figured from the beginning of the supergrowth era, 1961, budget growth averages an astonishing 18.7 percent.[4] Some consequences of such rapid growth are obvious. Since the tax system is progressive, governmental revenues tend to rise still more rapidly, allowing a substantial tax cut each year.[5] Even afterward budgeters have always had a large surplus (in the sense of resources additional to those available in the previous year) to allocate, and accordingly have not had to face the most disagreeable task of budgeting, pruning back or eliminating existing programs to allow expenditures of higher priority. In fact, most often even programs seen as outmoded have actually been able to continue growing, without preventing the rapid expansion of newer or more crucial enterprises. In short, the politics of budgeting less resembles a zero-sum game, where a gain for any participant is matched by a loss to another. Japanese budgeting is more comfortable.

*Balance*—Japanese budgeting takes place in a social and cultural setting quite different from the more or less common heritage of the

---

3. Itō Daiichi, "The Bureaucracy: Its Attitudes and Behavior," *The Developing Economies* 6, 4 (December 1968), 446-467.

4. Averaged yearly growth rates of initial (i.e., before Supplementary Budgets) budgets after Diet passage. Japan, Ministry of Finance, Budget Bureau, Research Division, *Zaisei Tōkei* ("Fiscal Statistics") (Tokyo: Ministry of Finance Printing Bureau), 1970 ed., pp. 28-29; 1974 ed., pp. 28-29.

5. See Joseph Pechman and Keimei Kaizuka, "Taxation," in *Asia's New Giant: How the Japanese Economy Works,* eds. Hugh Patrick and Henry Rosovsky (Washington, D.C.: The Brookings Institution, 1976), pp. 317-382; see esp. Table 5-3, p. 325, for the size of yearly tax cuts.

advanced capitalist countries of the West. Many potentially relevant elements of Japanese tradition might be mentioned: for example, Chie Nakane maintains that a predominantly "vertical" structure of Japanese society, related to the traditional household and rural hamlet, leads to an extraordinary degree of "sectionalism" in government organization, and therefore — as Takeshi Ishida also emphasizes — intense competition among ministries.[6]   However, such competition tends not to be expressed through face-to-face conflict, since Japanese place great value in maintaining "harmony" and in reaching decisions through a process of consensus building, which takes into account the interests of all participants.[7] One effect is a "tendency to retain the existing stability with the least amount of modification [, which requires] sacrifice of a thoroughgoing solution."[8]  All these traits seem to be related to a budgeting norm called "balance" (*baransu*), which though not unique to Japan — it is closely related to the American notion of "fair share" — is unusually prevalent there.[9]  To the extent that budget items (anything from tiny administrative expenditures up to the ministry level) are decided by balance criteria, they are treated equitably, given equal amounts or (more appropriately in Japan's high-growth context) allowed to grow at an equal rate. Balancing is thus the opposite of making clear-cut choices among competing alternatives based on a set of priorities.

*Stability* — Finally, we note that despite the high rate of economic growth, which presumably reflects considerable change in the economic and social environments of policy-making, the "outputs" of the Japanese government have not changed very much. Table 1 displays the percentage change in budget shares occupied by the major functions of government in Japan and the United States during the 1960s.[10] The Japanese budget is much the more stable; in particular, the absence of

6. Chie Nakane, *Japanese Society* (Berkeley and Los Angeles: University of California Press, 1970); and Takeshi Ishida, *Japanese Society* (New York: Random House, 1971), esp. pp. 37-40.

7. E.g., see Nakane, *Society*, pp. 144-45, and for an account of consensus building in a rural village, Richard K. Beardsley et al, eds., *Village Japan* (Chicago: University of Chicago Press, 1959), pp. 354-55.

8. Y. Hideki, "Modern Trends of Western Civilization and Cultural Peculiarities in Japan," in *The Japanese Mind,* ed. Charles A. Moore (Honolulu: East-West Center Press, 1967), p. 58. For remarks on similar phenomena in Japanese society, see Ezra Vogel's introduction to his edited volume, *Modern Japanese Organization and Decision-Making* (Berkeley and Los Angeles: University of California Press, 1975), pp. xxiii-xxiv.

9. For "fair share," see Wildavsky, *Politics*, pp. 16-18. A more complete discussion of "balance" will be found in my "Japanese Budget *Baransu*," in Vogel, *Organization and Decision-Making*, pp. 71-100.

10. A table with more countries is not presented because of comparability problems. However, an informal survey of other budget data indicates that the size of the differences

such rapidly growing policy areas as the American health, education and space fields is notable. Of course, within each of these categories some programs have grown faster than others and new programs have been started—Japanese budgeting was not totally immobilized. At the most general level, however, and at least through this period governmental priorities remained relatively constant.

These five factors are of course not unrelated to one another. For example, the high degree of stability in Japan is perhaps explained by some combination of the other four unusual characteristics. All these matters will be explored from various points of view in the pages below.

# Approach

The research reported here is not based on a very elaborate theoretical structure, and only a few words about concepts are required. My focus is the behavior of complex organizations within the budgetary system, behavior which is constrained by formal and informal role expectations, and which is influenced by changes (in objectives, strategies, strength) of other organizations within the system as well as by changes in several environments outside the system. The organizations which make up the budgetary system are those which play a *direct* role in budgeting: the spending ministries, the Budget Bureau (and some other Ministry of Finance staff), and certain organs of the Liberal Democratic Party. Some individual roles—notably the prime minister, finance minister and top LDP leaders—are also seen as directly participant. The budget system is a subsystem of the more general decision-making system or "governmental system" (which includes the LDP organization), itself a subsystem of the political system (all political roles in the society).

This vocabulary is rather conventional; more original is my division of the budgetary process into three functions. The first is "macrobudgeting," top-down decision making: in practice, this means budgeting at the aggregate level, referring primarily to the determination of the total budget, including estimates of revenue and long-term expenditure trends as well as considerations of economic policy.[11] "Microbudgeting," on the other hand, consists of the thousands—perhaps millions—of individual decisions about programs, personnel, quantities and prices; in short,

---

shown here is not caused by American budgets being unusually changeable; indeed, in an international context American budgets too seem relatively stable, albeit not as stable as the Japanese.

11. In principle, top-down decisions about expenditures on particular programs—e.g., a presidential decision to spend whatever is necessary to go to the moon—should also be included within this category; some examples are discussed in chap. 9.

## TABLE 1
### LONG TERM CHANGE IN BUDGET SHARES
(Unit: Percent)

| JAPAN | | | | UNITED STATES | | | |
|---|---|---|---|---|---|---|---|
| Function | Share 1961–62 | Share 1969–70 | Percent Change | Function | Share 1961–62 | Share 1969–70 | Percent Change |
| National Administration | 7.9 | 6.7 | -15 | National Defense | 47.0 | 41.2 | – 12 |
| Local Governments | 18.9 | 21.4 | 13 | International Affairs and Finance | 3.7 | 1.9 | – 49 |
| National Defense | 8.6 | 7.2 | -16 | Space Research and Technology | 0.9 | 2.0 | 122 |
| Disposition of External Affairs | 1.2 | 0.3 | -75 | Agriculture and Rural Development | 3.6 | 3.2 | – 11 |
| Preservation and Development of Natural Resources | 18.7 | 16.3 | -13 | Natural Resources | 1.6 | 1.2 | – 25 |
| Agriculture, Commerce and Industry | 8.7 | 11.7 | 25 | Commerce and Transportation | 5.0 | 4.4 | – 12 |
| Education and Culture | 12.4 | 11.4 | – 8 | Community Development and Housing | 0.4 | 1.2 | 242 |
| Social Security | 14.5 | 15.8 | 9 | Education and Manpower | 1.3 | 3.5 | 169 |
| Pensions | 5.4 | 3.7 | -32 | Health | 1.0 | 6.3 | 530 |
| National Debt | 2.3 | 3.8 | 65 | Income Security | 20.4 | 20.7 | 2 |
| Reserves | 0.9 | 1.1 | 22 | Veterans Benefits and Services | 5.2 | 4.2 | – 22 |
| Other | 0.5 | 0.5 | 0 | Interest | 7.9 | 8.7 | 10 |
| | | | | General Government | 1.5 | 1.6 | 7 |
| Total | 100.1 | 99.9 | | Total | 99.7 | 100.1 | |

NOTES: For Japan, the postsupplement General Account. For the United States, budget outlays, which include certain lendings and receipts, as well as undistributed governmental transactions (which have also been included in the total, so 2–3 percent double counting is present). "Community Development and Housing" includes sizable loan funds and is not comparable to other figures. Because of errors due to rounding, columns may not add to 100. Numbers were rounded after calculations were complete. The American figures were drawn from one table, so that categories and accounting practices are consistent over time. Ten-year tables are not available for Japan, but budget categories did not change much in this period, and crosschecking among several seven-year tables indicates any technical distortions are quite small. Shares are item budgets divided by total budgets, averaged over two years to dampen the effect of a single unusual year. Percent change is later share minus earlier share, divided by earlier share, times 100.

SOURCES: Japan: *Zaisei Tōkei*, 1970, pp. 32–33; 1974, pp. 32–33. United States: *The Budget of the U.S. Government*, 1972, pp. 61–65.

bottom-up decision making. It seems likely that in all countries these two functions are carried out more or less independently by quite distinct structures (which may or may not be included in the same institutional framework); these structures are usually not difficult to identify and even to understand in some rudimentary way. The mystery of budgeting is that every year, without fail, the final number produced by each process is exactly the same. The two processes therefore have to be linked, but the nature of the linkages—in either theoretical or nuts-and-bolts terms—is not well understood.[12] For lack of a better word, I call the intermediate process between macro- and microbudgeting "integration," and hypothesize that it is carried out in Japan by adjusting allocations or "frameworks" (waku) at the ministerial or broad functional level of aggregation. This tripartite division of the budget process appears throughout the text.

The methodology employed in my research was rather eclectic. One major source was a series of ninety interviews with budget participants and close observers conducted in 1969-70 and 1974. About half those interviewed were officials (ranging from assistant division chief to administrative vice-minister) of the Ministry of Finance and various other ministries; the remainder comprised Liberal Democratic Dietmen (including a few current or former Cabinet Ministers) and their staffs, journalists, representatives of interest groups and others. Several were reinterviewed either immediately or four years later. The interviews were quite unstructured and most lasted an hour (though a few were shorter and some went on for two hours or more); nearly all were conducted in Japanese, tape recorded, and afterward transcribed in English. Interviewees were promised anonymity, and so in the text below identities are generalized and occasionally disguised. My impression, incidentally, was that most who spoke with me were quite candid, and some were amazingly cooperative. One reason may have been that my questions were of the "how" variety—"How does this procedure work?," or "How do you hear about that participant's opinions and take them into account?" Bureaucrats and politicians apparently are rarely asked such questions and find them interesting.[13]

Other important sources are mentioned in the notes and discussed briefly in Appendix C. In comparison with other budget studies, rather

12. However, John P. Crecine has shown the overwhelming importance of fiscal policy in defense budgeting: see e.g. "Fiscal and Organizational Determinants of the Size and Shape of the U.S. Defense Budget," Institute of Public Policy Discussion Paper No. 69, University of Michigan, April 1975 (Mimeographed). Crecine's current research extends this line of analysis to non-defense budgeting.
13. For a discussion of open-ended elite interviewing, see Joel D. Aberbach, James D. Chesney and Bert A. Rockman, "Exploring Elite Political Attitudes: Some Methodological Lessons," Political Methodology 2 (Winter 1975), 1-27.

less use has been made of official documents (such as transcripts of committee hearings), since there are few public records of the more crucial aspects of the process in Japan. More than making up for this lack is the extraordinary quantity and quality of newspaper coverage of budgeting, which I have relied upon extensively. Few analytic studies by political scientists pertaining to budgeting—or indeed, to any governmental decision-making processes—were available to aid in building the foundations of this research. In order to make the budget process intelligible, therefore, I have been forced to make inferences from primary materials about many aspects of government which would already be well understood in many similar countries.

A word about the organization of the book: Budgeting systems are so complicated that one must first comprehend the whole in order to understand any of the parts. The final section of this chapter is therefore a short account of the budget process, intended as a backdrop for the details which follow. Chapters 2 through 6 take up the major budget participants: the spending ministries, the Finance Ministry (busy enough to require two chapters), the LDP, and the several important leadership or individual roles. Most of the budget process is accounted for at appropriate points in these chapters, but its most dramatic stage, the revival negotiations, is given chapter 7 to itself because all the participants interact there. Chapter 8 deals in short compass with "other budgets," processes such as Supplementary Budgets, the Fiscal Investment and Loan Program, Special Accounts and various forms of national planning which are separate from the regular General Account budget process, but too closely connected and important to ignore. Chapter 9 is a dynamic rather than cross-sectional approach to budgeting, examining how the system has evolved over twenty years. For the most part, my conclusions about how the process works are presented at the end of each chapter; the last chapter is an attempt to place contemporary Japanese budget politics into broader international and Japanese contexts.

# An Overview

Here is a preliminary description of how Japanese budgeting works: Under the Constitution, the annual budget is prepared by the Cabinet, but provisions of the Finance Law assign the responsibility of actual preparation to the Ministry of Finance (Ōkurashō; MOF). The process begins shortly after the beginning of each fiscal year on April 1, when the various ministries and other agencies (*Kakushōchō*, which for simplicity's sake we will refer to as "the ministries") begin formulating their budget requests for the following fiscal year. In recent years, MOF regulations have usually required each ministry to limit its request to an amount 25 percent greater than the budget granted in the current year. To fit the demands of its own divisions and bureaus within this limitation, each ministry undergoes a budget miniprocess of its own in the summer months. Requests, which are most often very close to the maximum size permitted, are submitted to the Finance Ministry by August 31, after securing the general agreement of the Liberal Democratic Party (Jiyū Minshutō; LDP)—in particular, that of the appropriate division (*bukai*) of the Policy Affairs Research Council (Seimu Chōsakai, or Seichōkai; PARC).

During the month of September, ministry officials appear at the MOF Budget Bureau (Shukeikyoku) to explain these requests to the budget examiners (*shukeikan*), who ask questions about programs but do not actually negotiate over budget figures. In October and November, examiners and their staffs go over the requests in detail, discussing possible options with the responsible bureau vice-director, the director and other officials. This process is what we term "microbudgeting"; at the same time higher-level MOF officials are discussing the total budget figure, the size of the yearly tax cut and other "macrobudgeting" matters. For about two weeks in early December, the MOF ministerial budget conference (*yosan shōgi*) meets to ratify, and sometimes modify, the draft budget prepared within the Budget Bureau; at time of release (*naiji*) it is called the "Finance Ministry draft" (*Ōkurashō gen'an*). At about the same time, a brief and abstract Budget Compilation Policy (*Yosan Hensei Hōshin*) is drawn up within the Budget Bureau, ratified at the MOF top level, and passed by the Cabinet.

For the most of this period the regular organs of the majority party do not intervene in the compilation process going on within the Finance Ministry, although individual Dietmen will often let their preferences be known (for example, by accompanying groups of petitioners to the Finance Ministry). However, in December the Policy Affairs Research Council's Deliberation Commission (Seisaku Shingikai or Seichō Shingi-ki) draws up the annual LDP Budget Compilation Program (*Yosan Hensei Taikō*). This program is then passed by the party's Executive Council (Sōmukai) and referred to the Cabinet and MOF before the release of the Finance Ministry draft.

The release of the MOF draft—scheduled for mid-December, although more often than not it is postponed into January or later —begins the "revival negotiations" (*fukkatsu sesshō*) period of about a week. During this rather hectic period ministry appeals are heard by progressively higher levels of Finance Ministry officialdom, and small amounts of supplementary funds are doled out. The Liberal Democrats also formulate "political" revival requests through a series of brief divisional hearings followed by reviews at higher levels, which are presented during the penultimate Cabinet-level negotiations or at the final session, one which often has lasted all night, between top officials of the party and government. The resulting budget is then ratified by a meeting of the Cabinet to become the government draft (*Seifu-an*), and is sent on to the Diet for passage.

These are the major institutions, documents and events of Japanese budgeting. Our task now is to explain their meanings, causes and effects.

# 2

# The Ministries

SINCE ONE MUST start somewhere, it is sensible to begin a discussion of Japanese budget politics with the spenders. The ministries do the work of government, and it is their estimates of how much money is needed which become the raw material of budgeting. Ministries are a varied lot: they differ in size, age, traditions, complexity, personnel, tasks performed, relations with clientele groups, and hence in an undefinable characteristic that might be called "personality." In budgeting, each has its own objectives, strategies, and behavior patterns. Still, it makes sense to speak of a "spender's role" in a budgetary system, because so much of the content of that role is imposed, first, by the activities intrinsic to budgeting itself (and therefore common to spenders in all countries), and second, by characteristics of the Japanese budgeting system as a whole.

This chapter begins with a discussion of the internal budgetary process of the ministries, and then turns to relations with the outside world—in particular, the strategies they employ to achieve objectives. The conclusion will assess those objectives. First, as an introduction we should note that there are twelve ministries (shō) in the Japanese government,[1] plus six other budgeting units. Five of these—the Imperial Household, Diet, Courts, Board of Audit and Cabinet—are small and will not be of great concern here; the sixth is the Prime Minister's Office (Sōrifu), an umbrella organization containing several Agencies (chō) that are actually quite independent, in budgeting as in other functions.[2] Several other agencies (Cultural Affairs, Tax Administration, Food, and

1. In the conventional order, they are Justice, Foreign Affairs, Finance, Education, Health and Welfare, Agriculture and Forestry, International Trade and Industry, Transport, Posts and Telecommunications, Labor, Construction and Home Affairs.

2. Chief among them, those headed by a director-general who sits on the Cabinet (as a Minister of State, Kokumu Daijin), are Administrative Management, Defense, Economic Planning, Science and Technology, and Environment.

so forth) are attached to ministries; they are more independent than regular bureaus, but generally are subservient in budgeting, formally and informally.

# Formulating Requests

Before submitting its formal budget requests to the Ministry of Finance on August 31, each ministry must undergo a budget process of its own. Procedures, strategies and calculations closely resemble those of the government-wide process, though since the participants are all members of the same organization their conflicts are more hidden from view.[3]

## Structure and Process

Taking the role of the Ministry of Finance's Budget Bureau within a ministry is the Accounting Division of the Ministerial Secretariat, headed by a director (*Kaikeikachō*) who is the equivalent of the Budget Officer in an American agency. He will be among the ministry's most able officials at that level; rather than an accountant or a budget specialist, he will have had experience in several of the ministry's bureaus, and usually will rise to an even more responsible position after his term of two years or so in this post. As the Budget Bureau deals with ministerial Accounting Divisions, within the ministry the Accounting Division usually deals with the General Affairs (or sometimes First) Division of each bureau. Each General Affairs Division prepares its bureau's request (which may be ratified at a bureau meeting) and passes it along to the Accounting Division in early July. For the next month or so, the Accounting Division holds hearings, and then prepares a draft of the full ministerial request, which is then distributed back to the bureaus. Appeals of cuts are argued in "revival negotiations" with the Accounting Division for about five days. Opportunity to appeal the revision of the next draft is also provided. A final draft, and its voluminous supporting documentation, is then submitted by the Accounting Division to the Ministerial Budget Conference; although a few minor changes in the request may be made at this stage, the major function of this meeting is ratification. After discussions with the appropriate Division (*bukai*) of the LDP Policy Affairs Research Council (described below), the request is ready for submission.

3. Information on the intraministerial budget process is scanty. Along with interview materials, this account depends on an excellent report to the Temporary Administrative Systems Investigative Commission in 1962 by Katō Yoshitarō, later published as "Yosan Hensei ni tsuite: Nōrinshō no Jirei" ("Concerning the Budget Process: The Case of the Ministry of Agriculture and Forestry"), *Keizai to Keizaigaku* 23-24 (August 1968), 231-248. Although administrative structure and process vary among ministries and over time, this account may be taken as roughly typical.

## Ceilings

How does a ministry determine how much to ask for? This problem was much more difficult earlier in our period than later, because in 1961 the MOF began to set a percentage ceiling on budget requests. Table 2 shows the progressive dropping of the ceiling, as well as the total amount requested in each year and the budget for that year as a percentage of the budget of the previous year. In general, agencies whose budgets are mainly for routine administrative functions will often request somewhat below the limit; ministries with larger and more complicated budgets usually hit the ceiling on the nose or miss it by a small fraction of 1 percent.

However, the amount requested at this stage is not an accurate representation of the ministry's complete budget proposal. For one thing, some programs will be left out, and requested later in the fall or even during the revival negotiations. This may be because, for a very complicated, very political, or rapidly changing program, the details or even basic conception may not have been agreed upon within the ministry or with interested outside groups and LDP organs;[4] or the ministry may have decided that more money could be obtained by bypassing routine budget review (as with poorly-justified programs that have strong LDP support). Also, ministry requests commonly do not include full adjustments for inflationary factors, particularly for the inevitable and large rises in personnel costs. Even though public employee salaries rise 10 percent or more each year, budget requests show personnel costs at current salary levels—the adjustment is made later. For a ministry like Education, where personnel costs occupy about one-half the total budget, this factor might in effect allow a raise of five percentage points or more in the request ceiling. Such factors make possible the anomaly for 1972 seen in Table 2, when the budget granted actually exceeded the amount requested.

In some ministries, the ceiling imposed by the Finance Ministry is passed along to the bureaus, formally or informally. One interviewed official said that the Ministry of Education required each bureau to stay within the 125 percent limitation; if this sort of policy were carried out strictly, little actual budgeting would have to be done at the ministerial staff level, since bureau requests could simply be sent along to the MOF after only technical modifications. It is more common, however, for either more lenient limits or none at all to be imposed on the bureaus: each bureau can make some choices among the items proposed by its

4. An example is the Transport Ministry's railroad budget request for 1972, held up until December because the responsible LDP PARC division's endorsement was withheld. Yamamoto Masao, *Keizai Kanryō no Jittai* ("The Reality of the Economic Bureaucrats") (Tokyo: Mainichi Shinbunsha, 1972), pp. 98-100.

## TABLE 2
### Total Budget Requests
(Unit: Percent)

| Budget Year | Request Ceiling | Actual Requests | Actual Budget |
|---|---|---|---|
| 1954 | none | 104 | 3.5 |
| 1955 | none | 90 | – 0.8 |
| 1956 | none | 36 | 3.3 |
| 1957 | none | 70 | 9.9 |
| 1958 | none | 62 | 15.4 |
| 1959 | none | 90 | 8.2 |
| 1960 | none | 48 | 10.6 |
| 1961 | 50 | 48 | 24.4 |
| 1962 | 50 | 40 | 24.3 |
| 1963 | 50 | 38 | 17.4 |
| 1964 | 50 | 35 | 14.2 |
| 1965 | 30 | 26 | 12.4 |
| 1966 | 30 | 25.8 | 17.9 |
| 1967 | 30 | 27.6 | 14.8 |
| 1968 | 25 | 24.2 | 17.5 |
| 1969 | 25 | 22.5 | 15.8 |
| 1970 | 25 | 22.1 | 17.9 |
| 1971 | 25 | 23.3 | 18.4 |
| 1972 | 25 | 21.5 | 21.8 |
| 1973 | 30 | 28.1 | 24.6 |
| 1974 | 25 | 22.4 | 19.7 |

NOTE: All figures are growth rates (percentage increments) from the previous year's total initial budget.

SOURCES: Newspaper accounts and *Zaisei Tōkei*, 1974, pp. 54–55, 189–203.

divisions, and the Accounting Division then reduces or eliminates portions of the bureau requests. To the extent the former pattern is characteristic, the budget shares of the various bureaus within the ministry will tend to remain constant over time; the latter pattern allows more flexibility at the discretion of the central staff.

Such variations are likely to be the product of differences in the power relations between ministry-level officials and the bureaus.[5] In some

5. Such differences have an important effect on American budgeting as well. See "Agency Budgeting," in Jesse Burkhead, *Government Budgeting* (New York: John Wiley and Sons, 1965), pp. 246-277; and Aaron Wildavsky, *The Politics of the Budgetary Process* (Boston: Little, Brown and Company, 1964), pp. 32-35.

ministries, the central staff may be very influential; in others, one or two
bureaus may dominate the rest; in still others, several bureaus may be
equally powerful and pay little attention to ministerial staff. While not
enough data are available to allow specific comparisons, it is often said
that the ministries descended at various times from the prewar Home
Ministry (Health and Welfare, Transport, Labor, Construction and
Home Affairs) tend to have strong central staffs, while others are more
likely to take an "umbrella" form with strong bureaus; in all, however,
the influence of the central staff has probably been increasing over time.[6]

## Criteria

Once requests are received from the bureaus, the Accounting Division
must decide how much should be cut from each item and which of the
new programs requested should be approved for transmittal to the MOF.
It is difficult to know precisely what standards are used in making these
judgments. Ministry of Agriculture and Forestry officials Katō interviewed gave the following list:

1. Accordance with policy, as established in the ministry's basic legislation and
   other guidelines.
2. Accordance with rules on budget itemization, yearly breakdowns, and applicable legislation.
3. Appropriateness of the amount with regard to that of the previous year and
   "balance" with other items.
4. Whether the work proposed seems capable of achievement.
5. Correctness of calculations of unit prices and other budget technicalities.[7]

The most significant of these is likely to be the third. Japanese budgets
exemplify "incrementalism": each year most budget items receive a small
increment of additional funds above what had been received in the
previous year. "Balance" implies that these increments will tend to be of
similar size (in percentage terms) among most items; that is, items will
tend to have similar growth rates. It is probable that "balance" among
bureau budgets is particularly characteristic of ministries with relatively
strong bureaus. A good example is provided by Katō in describing how
the public works portion of the budget is apportioned among the bureaus
of the Agriculture and Forestry Ministry:

Except for disaster reclamation projects, each public works item is adjusted so
that the budgets of the Agricultural Land Bureau, the Forestry Agency and the
Fisheries Agency have equivalent growth rates (from the initial budget of the

6. See Katō, "Yosan Hensei," and Hayashi Yoshio, *Zaiseiron* ("Public Finance") (Tokyo:
Chikuma Shobō, 1968), p. 40.
    7. Katō, "Yosan Hensei," 236.

previous year). Disaster reclamation projects are adjusted restrictively so that the same rate of progress will apply to all.[8]

If bureau budgets are balanced to a large extent, it is likely the Accounting Division will depend on each bureau chief to identify which of his programs are deserving of greatest priority. On the other hand, in more flexible ministries, the central staff may play the larger role in choosing a few programs from among those of all bureaus to be supported more strongly in budget requests, even if this produces markedly higher growth rates for one bureau over another.

## Request Size

An over-hasty critic might observe at this point that given the overall 25 percent ceiling, a ministry would seem to have little room for maneuver in deciding how much to request for individual programs. However, one must consider the structure of a ministry budget. A very high proportion of the total allocation is likely to be taken up by very few enormous programs — unemployment benefits, say, for the Labor Ministry, or school subsidies for the Ministry of Education. These programs are so large and well established that most often the criteria for deciding their budgets are already understood by both ministry and MOF officials; hence, there is little hope for a major expansion and little reason to submit a large request. Room under the ceiling is left, therefore, to request much larger expansions for the smaller programs.

These patterns may be observed in a sample of fifty-three Ministry of Health and Welfare programs, for which a series of figures for the 1970 budget were collected.[9] Requests for the largest three programs, those

8. *Ibid*, 238.

9. In this analysis and several below, a sample of 53 programs requested by the Ministry of Health and Welfare in 1970 is employed. These programs cover approximately one-third of the (1969) budget of that ministry. They were selected on the basis of availability of data, comprising all programs listed in LDP, PARC, Social Affairs Division, "Shōwa 45 Nendo Yosan Fukkatsu Yōkyū Juten Jikō" ("Important Items of Appeals Rerequests for the Fiscal 1970 Budget") (Photoreproduction; n.d. [but about January 27, 1970], 7 pp.). That is, these were the programs singled out by the LDP for attention, a fact which clearly biases the sample; however, these items did closely resemble a larger sample of 179 Welfare Ministry programs — virtually all the programs of that ministry except for a few missing data items — in terms of such indicators as the government draft amount as a percentage of the amount budgeted in 1969 or requested in 1970. The larger sample was compiled by examination of Japan, Ministry of Health and Welfare, "Shōwa 45 Nendo Kōseishō Yosan Yōkyū no Jūten Kōmoku" ("Important Items of the Fiscal 1970 Ministry of Health and Welfare Budget Request") (Mimeo: August 26, 1969, 56 pp.); and "Shōwa 45 Nendo Kōseishō Shokan Yosan'an no Gaiyō" ("Summary of the Fiscal 1970 Ministry of Health and Welfare Jurisdiction Budget Draft") (Mimeo: February 4, 1970, 50 pp.) — the latter was also used, along with official government-wide documents, to find government draft figures. "Items" here means programs which were not further subdivided in the LDP documents, so the sample ranges from quite large programs to quite small subprograms; hence, percentages of the sample cannot be generalized. The primary interest of this dataset lies in discovering how different types of items are treated.

over ¥100 billion (about $350 million) averaged only 18 percent over their 1969 budgets, and these requests were cut only 1.5 percent in the final budget (for the two programs with data available). These three items alone covered 85 percent of the total budget for the sample. Enough margin was thereby created to allow the remaining requests to average more than double their 1969 budgets, and for many new programs to be requested, still within the ceiling.[10] Hence, strategic considerations may still play a part in deciding the size of budget requests.

# Strategies

An ambitious young man, seeking to make his way in the world, might be advised by a kindly uncle to be sure to leave a favorable impression on those who might do him favors, to gather a group of friends and supporters, and to stay alert to take advantage of whatever situations might arise. Ministries, seeking to increase their incomes, follow similar "strategies," defined (by Aaron Wildavsky) as "the links between the intentions and perceptions of budget officials and the political system that imposes restraints and creates opportunities for them."[11] Again following Wildavsky, the three rules recommended above may be termed "confidence," "clientele," and "contingent" budgeting strategies. All seem to be as characteristic of budgeting in Japan as in the United States and elsewhere.

## Confidence

When a line ministry asks the Ministry of Finance for a large increase in a program, the response is likely to be determined partly by the MOF's previous experience with the ministry, the particular program in question, or the man who is asking. If a feeling of trust can be maintained, much detailed argumentation or an expensive application of political pressure may often be avoided. This point is well understood by budgeters everywhere:

If you have the confidence of your subcommittee your life is much easier and you can do your department good; if you don't have confidence you can't accomplish anything and you are always in trouble over this or that. (American bureau official)[12]

10. Specifically, the mean percentage requested increase for the 41 continuing programs in this sample was 135 percent (*above* the 1969 budget); the very high standard deviation of 156 indicates the enormous range.

11. Wildavsky, *Politics*, p. 63.

12. *Ibid.*, p. 74.

When the civil administrator of the budget division has acquired some experience of the ministry for whose estimates he is responsible, he may become less suspicious of that ministry. (an analyst of the French budgetary system)[13]

If the Treasury does not have this kind of confidence in you, it will create all kinds of road blocks and go out of its way to find the cons in your argument. (British permanent secretary)[14]

The man with the money tends to play hard to get and won't give up easily, but if he has confidence in you, you are more likely to receive what you want. (Japanese Accounting Division director)[15]

Confidence is as universal a budgeting medium as money. Somewhat artifically, since it tends to be rather an undifferentiated impression, we may separate the strategies used to build confidence into three facets:

*In the Institution:* — The basic minimum requirement for a Japanese ministry seeking a good reputation with the Ministry of Finance is keeping its figures straight. As a ministerial budget officer noted in an interview, "There is nothing the Budget Bureau likes better than finding an error in a budget request." Or sometimes the audit will turn up a misuse of funds, damaging the ministry's credibility. For example, in 1956, the Defense Agency was accused by the Board of Audit of improper spending, with particular attention given to two flagpoles which were installed and then never used. Later, the MOF said that it would hold the Agency's budget constant for the next year because of loose accounting practices, particularly the large amount of unspent funds it had carried over from year to year. A spokesman noted, "This indicates that our evaluation of Defense Agency requests has been too lenient; so this year it will be done much more carefully."[16] In general, according to a ministerial official, "the MOF definitely does not like to see unused appropriations — it shows their initial calculations were wrong. . . . Since they don't give overly-generous amounts of money, there is no need to prove savings."

To maintain confidence it is helpful to keep the MOF informed of developments even outside the budgetary period. Under the Finance Law, certain changes in budget execution, such as shifting funds from one account to another, require formal approval by the Minister· of

13. Buy Lord, *The French Budgetary Process* (Berkeley and Los Angeles: University of California Press, 1973), p. 144.

14. Hugh Heclo and Aaron Wildavsky, *The Private Government of Public Money* (Berkeley and Los Angeles: University of California Press, 1974), p. 16.

15. Interview by the author in 1970.

16. TS, November 15, 1956; SS, January 13, 1957.

Finance, but the wise official will report his more minor problems as well. Changes in existing policy, even those with no budgetary implications, will often be discussed informally with the examiner, and his advice is always solicited, if not always taken, on major shifts. Such consultations also bring the side benefit of providing clues to the MOF's later attitude when a program does come to face budget scrutiny.

A less tangible component of a ministry's reputation has to do with clientele relations. The MOF, which prides itself on its independence from politics, tends to be somewhat disdainful not only of politicians but of bureaucrats who appear subservient to politicians or interest groups. An examiner was reputed to have said to an official from the Ministry of Transport, "You are no better than your boss, the cab driver."[17] The ministry which occasionally stands up against LDP or interest group pressure to fight for its own policies will gain in respect at the MOF.

*In the Program.* — If the MOF has confidence in the ministry, it may be favorably disposed toward its requests for increases in old programs and new proposals. However, particularly because the budget examiner cannot exhaustively investigate the substance of each request, he must have assurances that the ministry has at least followed proper procedures in drawing up its justifications. Good research, as exemplified in detailed documentation which indicates that the ministry has looked over all the relevant data and considered other alternatives, is helpful. It is also necessary to demonstrate that the proposal has been "fully discussed within the ministry" — that is, that a favorable consensus exists among the officials themselves — and that concerned clientele groups have been consulted and agree. Such agreement is often embodied in a report favoring (or, often enough, formally suggesting) the proposal from an official consultative committee. The ministry must also prove that an expansion or a new program does not infringe on the jurisdiction of another ministry, or if there is some overlap, that the ministries involved have come to some understanding. In other words, good staff work on the part of the ministry is necessary if the MOF is to be confident that a request is sound.

*In the Man.* — Finally, there is the question of personal relationships between the ministry official, especially the Accounting Division director, and the MOF budget examiner and his staff. Budget participants reject the notion that friendship (perhaps dating back to student days at the Tokyo University Faculty of Law) makes any difference in the substance

17. Kusayanagi Daizō, "Ōkurashō Shukeikyoku no Samuraitachi" ("The Samurai of the Ministry of Finance Budget Bureau"), *Bungei Shunju* 46, 12 (November 1968), 229.

of budget negotiations, although personal ties outside of the office may help to smooth discussions. It is, however, extremely important that a good working relationship be maintained. As an examiner put it in an interview, "There has to be mutual trust. When trust is strong, you can make a good budget." Both sides agree on the proper nature of this relationship: two responsible officials, with slightly differing interests but sharing the same fundamental outlook, sitting down to work out mutual problems. "These days, we think about things together, we are more rational. We think together about what programs are needed."

How does the ministerial Accounting Division director maintain this necessary feeling of mutual respect? Probably most importantly, he must project an image of sincerity. An examiner said, "More than anything else, he has to be *shōjiki*"—this word can be translated as honest, upright, square, frank, candid, straightforward. One must always avoid giving an impression of trickery, of glossing over defects or trying to put something over; instead, the examiner must be brought to perceive the problems of the ministry. "If you cheat, you can only do it once; if you make them understand, you will continue to prosper."

As well as being straightforward, the ministry official must also be seen as reliable. If he makes a commitment, it must stick. An examiner commented:

We might say, 'how about half of the amount you requested?,' and he will say, 'that's fine' . . . the matter is decided right there, and he can go back and convince the bureau in his own ministry that made the original request.

A ministerial bureau director noted that once a promise has been made that a given project will be completed in three years, the trustworthy official should not seek an appropriation for the fourth year. The Accounting Division director must even be able to speak for the LDP:

There might be an item where the party wants ¥2 billion, our ministry really wants about ¥1.5 billion, and the MOF is offering ¥1 billion. We have to convince the MOF that if they give us ¥1.5 billion, it will stick. This builds confidence . . . if the estimates are different, it creates problems for the MOF. If we ask for ¥1.5 billion and get it, and then the LDP comes back and asks for still another billion and forces the MOF to finally give in . . . well, their confidence in the man who originally said ¥1.5 billion is gone. After a ministry official has gone through the budget process a couple of times, they will know he is safe.

Finally, the official should have a detailed knowledge of the programs he is requesting, and be able to furnish the examiner with the most useful arguments in their favor that can in turn be used at higher levels within BB. "I must have a very clear conception of the contents of our own programs and how they fit into national policy," said one Accounting Division director, adding that it is disastrous to give an impression of just being out after more money. Accounting Division directors previously have served in several bureaus of their ministries; this and their participation in intraministerial budget reviews usually makes them very familiar with ministry programs.

Not surprisingly, the characteristics needed for an official, a program or a ministry to maintain MOF confidence are very much those of the MOF's own self-image. In this, and in the very qualities projected, Japanese officials closely resemble their American counterparts, who according to Wildavsky try to appear as "masters of detail, hard-working, concise, frank, self-effacing fellows who are devoted to their work."[18] The long-range benefits of a good reputation outweigh short-term payoffs; it helps to turn the potentially conflict-ridden relationship between the seeker after funds and the guardian of the purse strings into one of cooperation.

## Clientele

No matter how confident a Ministry of Finance official may feel about the virtues of the man asking for money or the logic of a newly proposed program, he is unlikely to take a request very seriously until he becomes convinced that the program is needed. A good evidence of need is a demonstration that people — preferably many and influential people — are actively in support; best of all is to show that a program could be pushed through even were the MOF to object. The most important clientele group for any ministry is the Liberal Democratic Party, to be discussed in chapter 5, and many strategies are designed to influence both the LDP and the Ministry of Finance, or the Finance Ministry via the LDP.

Virtually all ministries try, in the normal course of business, to inspire generalized popular support for their activities. Although public information offices as such are rarely encountered on organizational charts, a quick tour through one of the several government publications centers will indicate the enormous quantities of material produced by ministries or, commonly enough, by closely related semiprivate organizations.[19] Most notable are the White Papers published annually by many agencies, which both give accounts of current programs and point out immediate and future problems that will require greater expenditure.[20] More specifically related to budgeting are the "ad balloons" appearing in

18. Wildavsky, *Politics,* p. 74. Compare also the strikingly similar comments by British officials in Heclo and Wildavsky, *Private Government,* pp. 14-18.

19. For example, the monthly magazine *Fainansu,* openly billed as a public relations organ for the Ministry of Finance and edited by the Documents Section of the Secretariat, is published by an organization called the Ōkura Zaimu Kyōkai which is staffed by MOF ex-bureaucrats. Its semi-official status means the journal can accept advertising and publish a wide variety of materials.

20. The most significant of these have been collected and translated since 1969 in the annual *White Papers of Japan* by the Japan Institute of International Affairs.

newspaper articles every summer and early fall, as the ministries leak the more attractive aspects of their new budget requests to generate public enthusiasm. That this practice irritates those responsible for budgeting is indicated by Finance Minister Mizuta's stricture in 1968: "There is a particular need to control the release of publications and reports about new programs being requested, so that an impression that these programs are already government policy is not given."[21]

Despite MOF disapproval, these attempts to generate a favorable climate of public opinion continue, but participants see them as having only a moderate effect in budgeting. For example, the director of a division which investigates water pollution said in a 1970 interview:

Pollution problems have become a popular topic, with many articles in the newspapers and so forth. These serve to focus attention on our work. But we do not have direct connections with the people, which makes things harder. There is no special pressure group support, no group to back up our interests at the Budget Bureau. Sometimes when there is an incident [e.g., people getting sick], the newspapers all write about it and create interest around the country. This is helpful in budgeting . . . it is true our budget growth has been high, but the amount of money is quite low.

Specific publics tend to be more influential than general publics. Even rather small groups of quite ordinary people can be important in cases of programs with narrow application. Every year in Tokyo, the most obvious sign that the budget season has rolled around again is the appearance of "petition groups" (chinjōdan) roaming among government buildings; typically these are residents of some local area come to appeal for a new highway or dam, or representatives of a functional group seeking a subsidy or other benefit. While most often petitioning is taken for granted, such groups will sometimes gain the ear of an important participant—for example, this interviewed Budget Bureau official:

. . . in Japan, buying land is very important. If you are going to build a dam, say, a major factor in the decision is whether or not the local residents oppose the project. Even when cost-benefit analysis indicates the project is sound, if we can't get the land cheaply because of local opposition, the data are meaningless. . . . Since a petition group from the locality itself is generally a good indication of local support, this becomes one source of information for our decision. Also, most public works projects have to be partly paid for by the local government; that is, the residents. A petition group can express their feelings on this, too.

Many ministries, particularly those with major public works programs, will try to stimulate or at least coordinate petition groups, often cooperating with local Dietmen. Although ministries usually are not

21. NKS, July 19, 1968. For a similar remark by an earlier finance minister, see MNS, July 27, 1957.

particularly interested in whether a project goes to one town or another, they hope that the cumulative effect of many such groups will impress MOF budgeters or LDP Dietmen.

In most policy areas, the more specialized and interested publics are represented by organized groups. As in other industrialized nations, many Japanese interest groups are well institutionalized, with full-time professional staffs and elaborate representational structures, and influence over governmental policy making is seen as a primary—sometimes almost sole—function. From a ministry's point of view, very often a minimum requirement for getting a new program or a major program expansion passed will be acquiescence by the relevant interest groups in the field. A common mechanism for obtaining or symbolizing their approval is a report by a public advisory council (most often *shingikai,* also *kondankai* or another term).[22] Each ministry has several such commissions appointed by law, and others more informally constituted, to perform various functions (including resolving conflicts among opposed groups, making sensitive administrative decisions, and developing long-range plans); many are used chiefly to mobilize and demonstrate clientele support. Representatives of groups affected by a ministry's policies will be brought together with "men of learning and experience" (*gakushikikeikensha,* often university professors) and are asked questions about the ministry's programs and plans. Appointments and staff work are controlled by the ministry, often with an eye to excluding or isolating opposition, so unfavorable reports are rare, and in the process of discussion group representatives may well enlist themselves among the supporters of the ministry's plans.

Other tactics available to ministries for mobilizing the influence of organized groups range from merely providing whatever information may be asked for to initiating and managing full-scale pressure campaigns. In the mid-1950s, during an intense controversy over rice prices, many Dietmen received telegrams from local agricultural groups telling them not to bother running for reelection unless prices were raised; it was later revealed that the campaign had been arranged under direct instructions from top Ministry of Agriculture and Forestry officials. In such cases, the relationship between ministry and interest group staffs can become very close: a reporter stationed at the ministry at a time when budget decisions were being announced observed the farmers' representatives sitting about on desks, pulling abacuses out of their pockets to calculate the breakdowns right along with the bureaucrats.

22. For a complete discussion of such bodies, see Ehud Harari, "Japanese Politics of Advice in Comparative Perspective," *Public Policy* 24, 4 (Fall 1974), 537-577. Also, T. J. Pempel, "Bureaucratization of Policy Making in Postwar Japan," *American Journal of Political Science* 18, 4 (November 1974), 647-664, and the special issue on this topic of *Gyōsei Kenkyū Nenpō* for 1969.

In some cases, a given policy area will be unpopulated by well organized interest groups, or by groups favorable to the ministry's objectives. A common response is to take a more or less active hand in getting grassroots organizations started. For example, according to an interviewed official, the Ministry of Education took the lead in setting up associations of educators along a variety of functional lines — principals and other administrators, and teachers of science or another subject — partly because the major teachers' group, the Japan Teachers' Union (*Nikkyōso*), was oriented well to the left, opposed to the ministry, and unlikely to influence the LDP and government positively. At a higher level, the Ministry of Agriculture and Forestry was largely responsible for the formation of the Council to Promote Agricultural Administration (*Nōsei Suishin Kyōgikai*), a "peak association" of many farm groups designed to coordinate their efforts and intensify their impact in influencing governmental policy making, particularly budgeting.

Of course, the ministry adopting this tactic may face Frankenstein's problem — the interest group may aim its pressure at its parent. Organizations do take on lives of their own, and farmers' interests are not identical with bureaucrats' interests. An official in a ministry that lacks strong clientele group support remarked of the Ministry of Agriculture and Forestry:

. . . political power depends on the character of the ministry. But I wonder if this would be desirable or not . . . I wouldn't want too much support. At the Agriculture Ministry, people are forever asking them for things. The political demands are always for the bad things — if the requests were valid, they would be granted without pressure. When political power diverts you from what should be done, it is not welcome.

Such feelings are not just sour grapes; they are often shared even by officials with close interest group ties. An Agriculture official was quoted in a newspaper article as saying of the farm groups:

These guys, who think that their only role is to put on pressure, are actually causing trouble. Since they only think of their own position, they grab more money than is needed by any one group. They just turn away from national needs indifferently. Couldn't they use their power more effectively?[23]

Faced with this problem, a ministry must struggle to maintain its own autonomy, and in particular to protect the sections of its budget not backed by strong clienteles from being overwhelmed. For Agriculture and Forestry, this means obtaining enough funds for programs other than price supports for rice farmers. For the Ministry of Construction, most pressure comes from constituency-sized public works projects. An interviewed official describes one possible defense:

23. YS, December 5, 1965.

Interest groups and Dietmen tend to be strong on highway and river projects; in the end, their weight falls here, first in pressure on us, and then on the MOF . . . since we know this will happen, at the beginning we really push areas like urban development and housing. The highway and river budgets will go up regardless, so we work on the others. If we don't do this, and just ask for everything equally, the budgets for housing, sewers, parks and so forth will be very small. Our strategy is: because it's hard to get, do it first — the Dietmen will take care of the highways.

As implied in this observation, LDP support tends to follow clientele support, because a Dietman's predominant interest lies in attracting votes. Still, some techniques other than working through organized groups are available to gain assistance from politicians. Regular communication with the corresponding Policy Affairs Research Council division and any special committees in the ministry's policy area is a routine requirement. Ministry ex-officials in the Diet, or lacking these perhaps Dietmen who had served as minister or parliamentary vice-minister, are expected to look out for ministry interests, and sometimes a faction chief or other influential leader can be attracted to a particular program. Such channels of influence are more adequately explored in chapter 4; worth mentioning here, however, is the possibility of attracting opposition support. While certainly outside the budget-making system, the opposition parties as such and their individual members are not without influence over the budget. The role that is most important is as potential disrupters of the legislative process and mobilizers of public opinion, if the LDP or the government should propose a policy directly opposed to their interests. Such proposals are not normally introduced through the budget, if only because getting the budget passed by the Diet expeditiously is always a high government priority; but the threat remains in case, for example, a major expansion of defense spending might be contemplated.[24]

This antiestablishmentarian role is not particularly useful to a ministry, but on less controversial matters opposition Dietmen do talk with their LDP colleagues on committees, with the leaders of the majority party and with Ministry of Finance officials; those who have become experts in a particular policy area may be listened to quite attentively.[25] Most common is representation of particularistic constituency interests, perhaps a public works project, but more organized support has also been given for the needs of urban areas (particularly those controlled by

24. For opposition party disruption tactics and their effects, see Hans Baerwald, *Japan's Parliament: An Introduction* (New York: Cambridge University Press, 1974).
25. A good example in the field of public finance itself was Kimura Kihachirō, Socialist member of the Upper House from Takyo until defeated in 1971, and chairman of the Audit Committee of that house.

progressive local governments) and programs in fields like welfare.[26] Furthermore, officials from the Ministry of Finance and other ministers are aware that they may face hostile questions from opposition party Dietmen in Diet committee sessions. One interviewed budget examiner acknowledged that he worried about this possibility during budgeting, and a skillful line ministry official would not find trading on such worries too difficult.

Japanese ministries vary quite widely in their patterns of clientele support. However, it is apparent that the variations depend less on skill in applying these techniques—which can only make the best of a given potential—than on differences in objective circumstances. At one extreme, agricultural ministries in most countries have close ties with farm organizations, who are intensely concerned with increasing the budget for their policy area; at the other, foreign ministries typically find it difficult to inspire interest on the part of anyone except perhaps a few intellectuals. It is sometimes possible in the long run to manipulate these objective circumstances, as by expanding programs in directions that may attract more popular support, but in the context of the yearly budget struggle the margins within which a ministry can affect how much or what kind of support it will receive from organized groups are ordinarily quite narrow.

## Contingent Strategies

Ministries always try to maintain confidence from the MOF and support from clientele. However, particularly when initiating a major program, seeking an unusually large increase or defending some activity which has come under attack, these techniques may not be enough. On such occasions ministries must be ready to grasp any opportunity that comes to hand or any argument which might appeal to other participants. These strategies are hard to categorize neatly, but an array of typical examples will be presented to give a sense of the range available.

*New Proposals.* — Very few programs start big. Almost all are begun with one or another variant of the "camel's nose" strategy (the anecdote of the "camel's nose under the tent" is not widely known in Japan, but there were instant nods of recognition when I told it during several interviews).[27] Perhaps most commonly, a ministry requests only "research

26. Indeed, the Ministry of Health and Welfare has at least been rumored to seek out and coordinate such backing rather actively, even from the Communists. Cf. AS, January 14, 1969.

27. Finance Minister Mizuta said in his first discussion of the 1969 budget process with the Cabinet, "Please avoid the sorts of requests which call for only the tiniest, partial amounts in the first year of a program, but incur heavy burdens for the future." NKS, July 19, 1968,

expenses" (chōsahi) to look into a problem. The MOF is of course well aware of the strategy being used and will resist making the grant, but the ministry (with LDP backing) can argue successfully that the problem (and the interested constituency) are surely important enough for at least a small study. Such a research allocation may continue almost unchanged, or with small incremental raises, for a number of years, until the ministry feels the time is propitious for a quantum leap. The legitimacy accorded by previous MOF recognition, the interest and constituency support built up by the allocation itself, and the more generalized feeling that the problem has been studied enough, are all likely to be helpful when that time is reached.

Some programs, once started, are naturally adapted to incrementalism, slow but steady growth over time. For example, there was considerable political debate before a program of supplying schoolchildren with free textbooks was begun in 1963; initially, only first grade children were covered. However, in the following years, the program was extended one grade at a time without much attention, until the middle school level was reached in 1967 and the MOF again tried to resist.

A ministry will often try to get a "principle" established in the budget, without much concern for the amount of funds granted, or even the formula or rationale of their allocation. In 1970, after the MOF had approved a subsidy for personnel expenses of private universities at a relatively low level and on a differential basis (more money for medical and scientific fields, less for the humanities), rather than the larger and equal distribution favored by the Ministry of Education and the universities themselves, an executive of one of the private university associations commented in an interview that

to an extent this was unavoidable, though we wanted a more general "level-up." The basis of our request was not to obtain a lot of money this year, but to get it decided that the government would support the personnel expenses of private universities. This point had not been established over the past ten and some years, and now it has been. Getting more money is for next year and after.

An interviewed BB official concerned with this policy area maintained that requests for increases would be looked at carefully, and that the MOF would examine how well the universities were using the new money before granting any additional funds, but he seemed resigned to the prospect that this program would rise rather sharply every year until it reached some plausible plateau.

---

evening. Roughly equivalent to "camel's nose" in Japanese is burabura satei, "lingering review." Nihon Keizai Shinbunsha, ed., Yosan wa Dare no Mono ka ("The Budget: Whose is it?") (Tokyo: Nihon Keizai Shinbunsha, 1971), p. 45.

The best way to start a new program, of course, is to make it appear to be an old program. The "contents" (*nakami*) of an old, less desirable program can be changed while its title and description remain about the same. Or when a ministry—or more likely a bureau or division within the ministry—has a program that has outlived its usefulness, it will

> try to think of a new program at about the same amount of money, to request in its place. We don't like to see the amount of the budget go down. . . . This technique is used even when the objectives of the new program have little connection with those of the old one.[28]

*Existing Programs.*—When a ministry wishes to move a program ahead more rapidly than simple cost-of-living increases would allow, it must develop some special arguments. These will usually include some statement of the "merits"—why a program is good, needed, and successful. Occasionally such statements use quantitative data, such as cost-benefit calculations in public works projects, but budget participants do not indicate that these have been terribly important in negotiations with the Finance Ministry (although perhaps more so in intraministerial decisions). In general, the MOF finds difficulty in deciding strictly on "merit" because comparisons among various "merits" are not easy. Ministries therefore seek criteria which give the appearance of objectivity. Many of these show the increase as somehow inevitable, the product of trends beyond the control of the ministry.

The easiest case for a ministry is where there is legislation on the books, or a contract approved and signed, that requires additional expenditure. The latter is common in public works budgeting, where contracts may cover several years. There are laws that all children of certain ages must go to school; if the population in that age group rises, school budgets go up almost automatically. Ministries with heavy administrative workloads can often easily demonstrate a trend that demands more funds: for example, the constantly increasing flow of paper into the National Tax Administration Agency. Here, quantitative work-load data are often used to indicate that more personnel will be needed.

When not absolutely compelled to raise its expenditures, a ministry may well argue that broader trends in its environment will require more money just to maintain the same level of services. An official Ministry of Agriculture and Forestry publication on fisheries is typical. It begins by citing the need for economic growth and improvements in the life of the people, and then says that (1) with the rise in the standard of living, demand for marine products is rising, particularly for the more expensive

28. Interview in 1969 with a division director in the Ministry of Education.

varieties; (2) industrial development is draining the fishing industry's labor force, and (3) pollution and increasing international competition mean that fishermen must seek out new grounds and methods.[29] These trends make life more difficult for the fisheries industry, and so for it to continue providing fish the ministry will need more money.

These cases are relatively straightforward, but environmental trends may also provide opportunities for ministries to pursue more adventurous strategies. The business cycle is the major determinant of the spending climate: journalists noted that the 1963 budget was a good "chance" for the Ministry of Construction, because the government was concerned about economic slowdown, and public works is viewed as the quickest stimulus. The Ministry has tried to play this argument both ways—in 1967, when everyone worried about inflation, its leaders claimed that highway, waterworks, and sewer construction do not stimulate the economy, but rather keep prices down by stabilizing the life of the people. An economic downturn (or impending government policies to cool off a boom) will usually also bring demands from the Health and Welfare and Labor Ministries for funds to ease the impact on low income groups, and from MITI to relieve the distress of small and medium industry.

Such gradual or cyclical trends in the environment bring requests for incremental adjustments of growth; a sudden change may allow demands for large expansions. This is the "crisis" tactic, for which Wildavsky cites the classic example of Sputnik's contribution to American education.[30] Beginning in the later 1960s, incidents of deaths and illness caused by pollution were given wide publicity, and were cited by many ministries seeking new or larger antipollution programs. As a rather extreme example, when Tokyo schoolchildren on playgrounds had been stricken by smog, the Ministry of Education sought funds to move all urban schoolchildren to rural areas for a week at a time. After a great typhoon hit Japan in the fall of 1959, the Construction Ministry demanded new seashore facilities to guard against future occurrences, and also gained its long-sought Flood Control Special Account; the Science and Technology Agency used the opportunity to press for rapid completion of the weather forecasting network. Asked in an interview in 1970 what single factor had been most important in changing the Finance Ministry's policy against subsidizing private university personnel expenses, a Ministry of Education official said

I think it was the campus disputes themselves, over the last year or so, all over the country . . . this was felt even within the Budget Bureau, and the LDP was quite

29. The Ministry of Agriculture and Forestry, "The State of Agriculture, Forestry and Fisheries: 1967-68" (Tokyo: n.d.), pp. 127-28.
30. Wildavsky, *Politics*, pp. 118-123.

worried. There was a kind of "panic." The feeling was that one couldn't simply control the situation with "policy" — there had to be a basic improvement.

It should be noted that the "policy" referred to meant calling in the police, and indeed the violent student uprisings also provided excellent opportunities for the National Police Agency to increase its budget.

*Abstract Criteria.* — Frequently, a ministry will not be able to find a trend in its environment that would justify an increase of the magnitude desired. In such cases, it will often seek some other sort of criterion against which, it will argue, the level of expenditures should be measured. Many of these are designed to appeal to the sense of justice of other budget participants, generalized or specific.

The Constitution offers one set of norms that are often cited. For example, Article 25 says that: "All people have the right to maintain the minimum standards of wholesome and cultured living. In all spheres of life, the State shall use its endeavors for the promotion and extension of social welfare and security, and of public health." The difficulty, of course, is in translating such an injuction into budget figures: the Ministry of Finance and the line ministry tend to choose different criteria of measurement. In the case of the public assistance program, the MOF, while conceding that its budget should go up every year, often maintains that the rise should be no more than the rate of inflation, or perhaps equal to the percentage salary increase granted to public employees. The Ministry of Health and Welfare, on the other hand, believes the Constitution requires that the gap between welfare families and the rest of the population should be narrowed, or at least that the program should keep pace with the growth rate of personal spending. Such debates may vary from year to year, but will usually center on the question of which set of data is most relevant for the program in question.

Somewhat less abstract is the disagreement between the MOF and the Ministry of Education over allocations (on a per student basis) made to universities. An Education Ministry division director said in an interview that "the MOF is usually tough on this item, and wants to give us just an increase of five per cent or so to cover cost increases. We usually compare the proportions of the aid given today with prewar figures, to show that it is much lower now." And even more common than comparisons with prewar figures are arguments that Japanese governmental expenditures for a given program or policy are much lower than their equivalents in other countries. The Ministry of Agriculture and Forestry defends the rice price support system by noting that all industrialized countries subsidize agriculture; the Ministry of Health and Welfare is constantly comparing Japan's social welfare expenditures unfavorably with those of England or Sweden; scientists point to big

American research and development programs. This tactic probably owes its considerable persuasive power to Japan's long history of borrowing from the West and using the United States and Europe as reference models. Even today, some hints of a "what will the Westerners think of us" psychology may be detected in these budgetary tactics, as when before the Olympics (a useful "crisis" for budgetary purposes), not only were funds demanded and granted for highways and other facilities to handle increased tourism, but also for improving Tokyo's parks and sewer system.

*Balance.* — A special but quite common case of using such abstract criteria to justify an increased level of expenditures is a strategy that trades on the high value assigned to "balance," to "fair" treatment of each participant in the budget system. If a ministry can show that its program is equivalent to another program, it will be equipped to argue that their budgets should be the same, or they should get the same budget raise, or their growth rates should be equal. For example, there are a variety of government-financed health insurance plans, and when benefits for one are raised, the Ministry of Health and Welfare will find it easy to claim that the others should receive similar increases. Or, if the formulas for figuring the budget for national universities require a raise, the Ministry of Education will call for increases in support for private universities as well (and perhaps, more tenuously, even for secondary or other schools).

Such "balance" strategies are not limited to the level of individual programs, but can apply to broader policy areas. For example, it was held in the 1950s that giving a smaller increase to social welfare programs than to defense would constitute "remilitarization." In later years, when defense growth was slower, welfare was more often compared by ministry officials to the public works sector on the general grounds that people are more important than things.

Although a ministry will not ordinarily compare the absolute amount of its own organizational budget directly with that of another ministry, a more subtle variant of the "balance" strategy is quite common. This is to stress the ministry's budget "share," or its growth rate in comparison with the budget as a whole.[31] Clearly, this device is most

31. Budgeters elsewhere also pay attention to balance: a British official, asked how he knew what his "proper share" should be, replied: "There were two and only two objective criteria. One, what had happened before. What was our share of total government expenditure last year? Are we doing as well this year? Two, what is the rate of growth of the department compared with the rate shown by others?" Heclo and Wildavsky, *Private Government*, p. 27. (A Japanese official probably would have realized that these two criteria are, in fact, identical.)

useful as a defensive strategy, not in the American sense of protecting programs from absolute budget cuts, but rather the prevention of a relative slippage of position in an era of high economic growth.

The most obvious example is the Ministry of Agriculture and Forestry, which despite strong support from the LDP has been faced with a long-term decline of the importance of agriculture in Japan's economy. In the mid-1950s, when the total budget ceiling was being held constant, the budget allocation for agriculture was actually cut in three consecutive years, and when growth resumed its spokesmen tried to maintain the "10% principle," that one-tenth of the budget should go to agriculture. Ikeda Hayato, newly installed as prime minister at the time of the 1961 budget process, tried to initiate a gradual cutback in the proportion of national resources going to agriculture, but met with vehement protests from the ministry and its supporters in the LDP; in the end, an enormous grant to the rice price control system had to be made during the revival negotiations. Again, the Ministry of Agriculture and Forestry growth rate dropped slightly below that of the budget as a whole in the 1965 MOF draft, and the protest was immediate. Such "share-consciousness" gave this ministry and its supporters a reputation of caring nothing for programs, desiring only to grab as much of the budget as possible regardless of how the money would be spent.[32] Rather similar was the response of the Ministry of Home Affairs to a cut in local taxes scheduled for 1960 (a time when the financial position of local governments, which the ministry represents, was relatively strong): "Losing this tax revenue was like a man getting hit by a car. Even if the victim is wealthy, he still deserves some compensation."[33]

*Strategies for Defense.* — A handy example of how tactics of abstract criteria, including "balance" notions, can effectively substitute for a convincing case on the "merits" is provided by the Defense Agency. Without necessarily implying that this agency has not deserved increasing financial support, it can be said that its spokesmen have had a difficult time in finding justifications for any given level of expenditures. The Self-Defense Forces have never fought, and have no early prospect of fighting. The Constitution and public opinion limit their role to repelling conventional invasion, a function which does not require rapidly rising expenditures. Indeed, fear of a public outcry has prevented the Defense Agency from even naming a hypothetical enemy, so the familiar Pentagon tactic of racing to keep abreast of real or imagined Soviet or

32. Cf. YS, December 5, 1965.
33. NKS, January 1, 1960.

Chinese military advances (i.e., an environmental trend) is not available.[34]

The Defense Agency has accordingly resorted to justifying its budget in terms of the percentage of the total budget or of the gross national product that it occupies. Both proportions have tended to decline slightly over time, a trend that was viewed with alarm by those favoring defense spending. Stressing this calculation allowed the Defense Agency to obscure the fact that its rate of growth (because of high GNP growth) actually caused the budget to double about every six years.

This strategy is "defensive" in the sense that it is aimed at maintaining a current share but cannot be helpful in arguing for faster expansion. Those hoping for a major, nonincremental increase in security expenditures therefore use a different criterion: Japan's low GNP share for defense is compared to those of the United States or Western Europe. They do not imply that Japan should put forward an equivalent military effort because war with these countries is likely; rather, her status as a major nation somehow demands an appropriate share of resources to defense. Arguments that the GNP defense share should be raised from about 1 percent to 2 percent for such abstract reasons are much more commonly heard than claims that, for example, a new weapon system is required for security, or that the mission of the Self-Defense Forces should be extended. After an interview in which this percentage of GNP criterion had been mentioned numbers of times, a Defense Agency official was asked why—he conceded that it had little real meaning, but "it is the only objective indicator available."

All ministries try to use confidence strategies in about the same way (though perhaps with varying success); clientele strategies depend most of all on objective situations beyond a ministry's immediate control. Contingent strategies are more interesting, since it is here that the skill of an individual ministry official may make a real difference in budgetary outcomes. A resourceful entrepreneur will be able to find new justifications for old programs, old justifications for new programs and different justifications in speaking with different participants. The more passive bureaucrat will be willing to take what comes.

## Choosing Strategies: A Short Case Study

The strategies outlined here will most often reinforce each other. The camel's nose ploy may be unworkable unless one has already gained the

---

34. Among many treatments of Japanese defense policy, see John K. Emmerson, *Arms, Yen and Power* (New York: Dunellen, 1971); Fred Greene, *Stresses in U.S.-Japanese Security Relations* (Washington, D.C.: The Brookings Institution, 1975), pp. 5-29, 77-104; and Martin E. Weinstein, *Japan's Postwar Defense Policy* (New York: Columbia University Press, 1971).

confidence of the MOF. When one is stressing the importance of some environmental trend that requires new expenditures, it is helpful when LDP politicians and relevant interest groups share the concern. On the other hand, strategies are also to a degree substitutable: a ministry with weak resources in one area will try to compensate in another. The substitution which comes most readily to mind, as illustrated by the Ministry of Agriculture and Forestry case noted above, is the use of LDP backing to overwhelm MOF suspicions—the principle was aptly summarized by a ministerial Accounting Division director as "when the numbers are weak, turn to the party." Life is more difficult and the need for creativity greater where party and interest group support are lacking. A good example is the Ministry of Labor.[35]

Japan's postwar economic boom was not a boon for the Labor Ministry, in that its major program, unemployment compensation, continuously lessened in importance. The ministry's share of the total budget dropped accordingly: from 1955 to 1970, when the national budget expanded 7.8 times, the Labor share grew only 3.5 times. Although the ministry is generally seen as "liberal" in the context of the Japanese bureaucracy, its natural clientele, the labor unions, are not effective supporters in budgeting, and its programs do not attract much LDP interest. On the business side, the Labor Ministry deals intimately with the Federation of Japanese Employers' Associations (Nikkeiren), but according to officials this organization is little concerned with budgetary matters or with expanding the influence of the ministry. As an official said in an interview, clientele relations are hence rather difficult:

We can't just go along with the unions, or in fact with either side—that's life in the Ministry of Labor, to try to be positive, but to be disliked by both sides. We do work with the unions, but not on the surface—Sōhyō [the General Council of Trade Unions] might announce its opposition to a program, but actually behave passively or even quietly approve. There simply aren't any cases where both sides actively approve . . . on labor standards, if we go too far, management complains; if not far enough, labor complains. This can be very difficult at times.

However, the ministry does the best it can. In the fall of 1969, after many attempts, it finally succeeded in getting both union and business representatives to participate in a single consultative commission (along with scholars and government officials), to exchange opinions on the labor problems of the 1970s (except for the question of income policy, ruled out of order as a precondition for Sōhyō membership). As the official cited above noted, "If they can get together and form a consensus

35. This account is mainly based on interviews with ministry officials and others in 1969-70. The best discussion of the Ministry of Labor in English, though not centered on budgetary matters, is Ehud Harari, *The Politics of Labor Legislation in Japan* (Berkeley and Los Angeles: University of California Press, 1973).

on points of common interest, and then back us up during budgeting, it could be helpful. When we are trying to start a new program, the minister can ask them to deliberate. This helps mold opinion." Then in 1970, the Labor Minister initiated a system he called "administration by dialogue," a series of talks with executives of various industries. He said the primary goal was exchange of information, but added that "if we come to understand the real situation in industry, our persuasiveness in future budget negotiations with the MOF will be strengthened" — presumably, industry's greater understanding of the Labor Ministry might also be helpful.[36]

Lack of clientele backing means lack of much enthusiasm on the part of the LDP, but the ministry tries to compensate here as well. Since neither the Labor Division nor the Labor Problems Investigative Commission in the Policy Affairs Research Council is very active, the ministry turns first to the four Labor ex-officials in the Diet (as of 1970 all four were in the LDP, and two had been vice-ministers before retirement). These politicians can be counted on to represent the ministry's point of view; a degree less helpful are the second line of "old boys," the LDP Dietmen who have served as its minister or parliamentary vice-minister.

The Ministry of Labor has also been noted for its public relations efforts and effective use of newspapers. Officials maintain that the ministry's true constituency is the entire working population, and it therefore has sought publicity for programs with broad popular appeal, such as a policy of increasing ownership of homes and even stocks and bonds by ordinary workers. However, while officials acknowledge that this technique is used as an alternative to partisan support, they say it is not a very effective budgetary tactic: "Public opinion might be raised, bringing a long-term effect, but campaigns for public support and campaigns for Ministry of Finance support do not have much connection. An examiner won't listen much to this sort of thing."

Perhaps partly for general publicity and to impress other budgeting participants, but mostly as an attempt to adjust creatively to an unfavorably changing environment and maintain internal morale, the ministry has aggressively tried to develop new programs. Among the ideas developed for the 1970 and 1971 budget requests were aid to workers handicapped by industrial accidents, information centers on labor market conditions, measures for easing the transition from agricultural to industrial employment, various ways to increase assets held by workers, mechanisms to encourage labor transfers from "wasteful" to labor-short sectors, inspections of factories producing pollution, and aid to the labor ministries of underdeveloped nations.[37] The Ministry of Labor is also

36. NKS, August 12, 1970.
37. See MNS, August 27 and 31, 1969; NKS, May 2, 9, 21, 27, 31 and July 14, 1970.

known for its skill in research. A veteran journalist observed in an interview that "each ministry has a kind of personality, and I see Labor as a ministry that studies very hard. They were among the first to use computers—the Budget Bureau has been positive in encouraging computer use, and cooperated closely with Labor in setting up something like a model case." The ministry has also been in the forefront of other administrative innovations, such as program budgeting techniques. It is known for coming in with expertly justified budget requests. In these and other ways, a ministry creates confidence at the MOF.

No one at the Ministry of Labor would maintain that this assortment of strategies amounts to more than making the best of a bad situation, and its is certainly insufficient to compensate entirely for a negative environmental trend (full employment) and fundamental weaknesses in clientele support. Still, the ministry has had its budgetary successes. For example, in 1970 it was granted major expansions in its programs to increase workers' assets (an early stage in the camel's nose—the program became much bigger in later years), to provide welfare facilities for young workers and women, and for the collection of labor statistics; a new program to assist workers moving from agriculture to industry was also initiated.[38] More generally, both Labor officials and other observers said in interviews that the ministry gets a much friendlier than average respose for its program ideas from the Ministry of Finance. Such victories do not raise aggregate budget statistics very much, but they provide satisfactions for ministry officials and perhaps significantly shape national labor policy.

The limitations of this analysis do not permit a full discussion of the patterns of strategies adopted by Japanese ministries. It would be most interesting to compare the strategies (and successes) of ministries with more or less activist leaders, of old and new ministries, of ministries in areas of expanding public concern and those with declining functions.[39] Equally fascinating would be the question of how strategies and their effectiveness change over time, had we but enough information.

# Conclusions

Readers of the literature on budgeting in other political systems may have noted that little in the discussion above could not be applied, so far as we know, to nearly any industrialized democracy. Examples can be found in

38. *Kuni no Yosan,* 1970, pp. 504-511.
39. For example, the Courts have been particularly passive. YS, December 24, 1965. A narrow-focus attempt at this sort of comparison for the United States is Ira Sharkansky's "Four Agencies and an Appropriations Subcommittee: A Comparative Study of Budget Strategies," *Midwest Journal of Political Science* 9 (1965), 254-281. See particularly Figure II, "Revised Causal Model of Factors Involved in the Assertiveness of an Agency's Budget."

the United States, Great Britain and elsewhere for nearly everything Japanese ministry budgeters do, and conversely most practices of spenders in those countries have their counterparts in Japan. It seems to be the case here that similarities of structure and function are more significant than differences of history or culture in accounting for this subset of budgetary behavior.

However, this is not to say that Japanese ministries are identical to those of the West. The distinctive elements of the various environments within which ministries operate inevitably have their influence; the mixture of strategies chosen, perhaps the "style" adopted in attempting to achieve goals, may be seen as characteristically Japanese. For example, the emphasis given to "balance" is related to elements of the Japanese cultural environment, intertwined with structural characteristics of the budgetary system. These points will be examined from a more general point of view below. However, it is appropriate here to move back a step, widen our focus from the ministry itself, and see how this administrative unit fits into the broader context of the Japanese budgetary system.

If one can imagine for a moment that there exists some definable volume of budgetary decisions, and that some method is devised to determine what portion of each decision is contributed by the several levels of the budgetary system, it would become possible to ascertain the relative weight or influence of each level. Compared with other nations it appears that the ministry level is unusually important in Japanese budgeting.[40] The reasons for the pattern are complex: in part, it is that the ministry organization itself tends to be stronger than elsewhere, but also the competition it faces from other levels is weaker.

One of the most enduring generalizations about Japanese government is that the administrative structure is extremely departmentalized, that "sectionalism" dominates all. Historically, the roots of strong ministerial autonomy date at least as far back as the Meiji period, when ministers were responsible directly to the Emperor.[41] The contemporary Japanese personnel system is both a product of this autonomy and an important factor in its continuing strength: all but two or three officials in each ministry are permanent civil servants, promotion is largely internally controlled, and officials are rapidly rotated among bureaus within one ministry but rarely transfer to another ministry except on a

40. The term "level" is used here because I am not necessarily implying that a minister himself or his staff will predominate. Rather, the point is that more choices are made in the ministerial arena of decision making than, for example, within bureau arenas or a government-wide arena (the cabinet, say, or a finance ministry, or a programmatic party). The term therefore refers to a level of aggregation of decision making. However, it does not mean "the bureaucracy"—each ministry is quite separate.

41. See the various works of Tsuji Kiyoaki, esp. *Nihon Kanryōsei no Kenkyū* ("Studies of the Japanese Bureaucratic System") (rev. ed., Tokyo: Tokyo Daigaku Shuppankai, 1969).

temporary basis.[42] The contrast with other countries is clear-cut. In the United States, interdepartmental transfers are more common but repeated transfers among bureaus atypical, and both political appointees and temporary "in-and-outers" are numerous.[43] In Great Britain, elite civil servants are deliberately shifted from ministry to ministry so that each will gain perspective, facilitating easy communication within the "establishment." French adminstration is dominated by the *grand corps* of civil servants, whose attachment to each other may well outweigh loyalty to the particular organization they serve at the moment. Given such differences it is not surprising that the Japanese official develops unusually strong feelings of psychological attachment to his ministry, an intense "we-they" orientation; nor that horizontal communications among ministries tend to be difficult (while interbureau communication is relatively open). Of course, Japanese ministries are by no means free of internal conflicts over goals, means, personal ambition and budgetary allocations. More than elsewhere, however, these battles will tend to work themselves out within ministerial boundaries so that a relatively unified front can be presented in the outside world.

What of the competition? In France and the United States, albeit in very different fashions, a higher proportion of real decision making seems to take place at the bureau or divisional level; in these more fragmented systems ministries (or departments) appear less able to intervene in the operations of formally inferior agencies. In Great Britain, the ministry-bureau relationship may not differ so markedly from that of Japan, but the quantity of decision making accounted for by "sideways" agreements (between the upper levels of two or more line ministries) or at the Cabinet level is substantially greater. In Japan bureau autonomy, horizontal coordination and "top-down" leadership all are weak; it is the ministry level that fills the vacuum, at least in budgeting.[44]

42. The only data available are from the 1950s, when wartime and Occupation disruptions could still be seen in officials' career patterns. Nonetheless, 71 percent of one sample of higher civil servants both began and ended their careers in the same ministry. However, mobility within the ministry was high: over 70 percent had experience in field offices. See Akira Kubota, *Higher Civil Servants in Postwar Japan* (Princeton: Princeton University Press, 1969), pp. 107, 113.

43. One study found that of American supergrade civil servants in 1963, about half had worked in the same agency or department for their entire careers; but since 40 percent of the total sample had worked in but one bureau, only some 10 percent at all resembled the pattern typical for Japan. Another study of higher civil servants in the early 1960s showed 56 percent serving in only one department but 68 percent in no more than two bureaus; 90 percent had never served outside headquarters in a field office. For citations, see Randall B. Ripley and Grace A. Franklin, *Congress, the Bureaucracy, and Public Policy* (Homewood, Ill.: The Dorsey Press, 1976), p. 30.

44. This discussion, which is based primarily on works on budgeting cited above by Heclo and Wildavsky, Wildavsky, and Lord, ignores both the substantial interministerial variation in all countries (including Japan) and trends over time which have probably led to

While this discussion has concentrated on administrative organization, it should not be taken to mean that bureaucratic actors monopolize decision making in Japan. On the contrary, politicians and interest-group representatives are at least as active in Japan as elsewhere. However, in order to be effective, these actors must intervene in the policy process at the ministry level, rather than above or below it. In fact, over time, quite stable and accepted clusters of actors have developed within each policy area. These may be thought of as policy "subgovernments" made up essentially of one ministry, its corresponding division in the LDP Policy Affairs Research Council, and a number of interest groups.[45] A key point is that the boundaries of each subgovernment are defined by the formal jurisdiction of the ministry, as set forth in its basic legislation. For example, small businesses in a field called "environmental hygiene," including public baths, bars, butchers, dry cleaners and others, all are regulated by the Ministry of Health and Welfare. Their trade organizations are grouped into a "peak association" called the Central Council of National Environmental Hygiene Trade Associations, which is very active politically, and has succeeded in establishing a large loan fund (one of the government corporations) to allow its members to modernize facilities. Other small businesses including fish and bread stores share the same problems as those within the environmental hygiene field, and by objective measure would seem to be eligible to receive such loans, but they are regulated by the Ministry of Agriculture and Forestry (which generally orients itself more toward producers than retailers), and hence are excluded.[46] Even when a group approaches various ministries during the budget season, it will most commonly have close relations with only a single ministry, as is the case with the various groups representing local governments and the Ministry of Home Affairs.

The rather obvious point may be added here that after twenty years of continuous rule by one party, interest groups (with the exception of labor unions and a few others) are unlikely to direct very much attention to the opposition. They frequently enter into quite stable relationships

---

gradual increases in ministry-level influence everywhere. Still, the differences appear large enough to justify even these oversimplifications.

45. For "subgovernments," see Ripley and Franklin, *Congress,* pp. 5-7, or for a very comparable notion called "subsystem," J. Leiper Freeman, *The Political Process: Executive Bureau-Legislative Committee Relations* (rev. ed., New York: Random House, 1965). Note that for many purposes it is helpful also to include the Budget Bureau examiner and his staff specialized in a given policy area in each Japanese subgovernment. Basic works on interest groups in Japan include Ishida Takeshi, *Gendai Soshikiron* ("Contemporary Organization") (Tokyo: Iwanami Shoten, 1961), pp. 65-84; and Masumi Junnosuke, *Gendai Nihon no Seiji Taisei* ("The Political System of Contemporary Japan") (Tokyo: Iwanami Shoten, 1969), pp. 56-88.

46. YS, December 2, 1965.

with groups of Dietmen in the LDP. Taking these factors together, it seems natural that patterns of interest articulation and aggregation in Japan should fit into and reinforce the model of separate subgovernments outlined above. That is, competiton among interest groups, rather than intensifying conflict among political parties, is likely to be reflected in conflict among subgovernments: between ministries in the government and between their allied divisions (and perhaps other groups of interested Dietmen as well) within the LDP.[47]

Patterns of decision making roughly corresponding to this model of policy subgovernments are probably to be found in any industrialized nation. The assertion here—for which supportive evidence will be found throughout the study—is simply that this level is more salient in Japan when accounting for budgetary and other decisions. When one turns to examine relationships *within* each subgovernment, considerable variety is likely to be encountered. In some policy areas, all the active interest groups may nearly agree on goals, while in others questions of priorities may generate intense conflicts; such patterns of consensus or dissensus both reflect and are reflected in the behavior and attitudes of party politicians and functional bureaus within the ministry. Where substantial agreement exists, all will be able to cooperate happily on the goal of maximizing budgets, following the sorts of strategies described earlier in this chapter. On the other hand, in cases where ministry preferences differ markedly from those of many LDP Dietmen or influential clientele groups, ministry officials must play a trickier game. Perhaps by trading upon previously established Ministry of Finance confidence, they will quietly lay greatest stress on their own program preferences, at the same time assuring the clientele that everything possible is being done on their behalf. Occasionally, in such difficult situations, officials may even choose to sacrifice potential financial gains for the sake of protecting their conception of the ministry's mission.

Still, if one were to construct a hierarchy of objectives for Japanese ministries in budgeting, simply maximizing the budget would have to rank first; more often than not other values will be sacrificed to this end. For one thing, even aside from what might be done with money, budget success—as measured by growth rate or budget share—is a key indicator for those inside and outside the organization in evaluating the ability and achievements of the ministry as a whole and particularly its top officials, the minister, vice-minister and deputy vice-minister. The second objective is to put into effect the policy preferences of ministry officials as they may differ from those of interest groups and LDP politicians within the subgovernment, or perhaps from the national leadership or even the

47. Cf. Masumi, *Seiji Taisei,* pp. 56-68.

Ministry of Finance. Conflicts between these two objectives occur most often for ministries with strong party support, such as the Ministries of Construction or Agriculture and Forestry. Finally, a third, independent objective is to satisfy the clientele—interest groups and politicians. Most often, ministry officials will find this objective compatible with maximizing budgets and pursuing their own policy preferences, but when it is not, they will frequently resort to symbolic outputs which give the appearance of following clientele wishes. The Ministry of Finance is often quite ready to cooperate in such deceptions, as by keeping the contents of real negotiations secret.

Each of the policy subgovernments in the Japanese governmental system has a structure and personality of its own. As a matter of central tendency, however, the leading role in each is likely to be taken by the ministry. Bureaucrats, after all, have advantages of expertise, information and financial resources, and they play the game full-time. Moreover, they—in the American bureaucratic politics phrase—"have the action": it is the ministry which normally will draft legislation or draw up and submit budget requests. While the interests and opinions of other subsystem members may never be ignored, the ministry itself will most often predominate.

# 3

# The Ministry of Finance: Microbudgeting

THE SPENDING MINISTRIES propose, the Ministry of Finance disposes. Standing at the center of government activity, the MOF and its Budget Bureau are legally responsible to the Cabinet for preparing the annual budget; less formally, they are responsible to the nation for preserving Japan's financial solvency. If government spending is to be restrained, the job must be done here. Monopolization of the cutting role gives the ministry great power and appropriately high status; its officials are the elite of the elite, respected and resented throughout the government.

As the only full-time budget participant, the Ministry of Finance plays a complex role which deserves two chapters of discussion. This chapter will treat the structure and character of the ministry and the microbudgeting process. In chapter 4 we will take up macrobudgeting and the process which links these two arenas, "integration," followed by an account of the strategies used by the MOF to protect its interests.

## Structure and Staff

The activities of the Ministry of Finance span an enormous range. Its breadth is conveyed by listing the main bureaus: Budget, Tax, Customs and Tariff, Financial, Securities, Banking, International Finance. Some of these have more functions than their names imply: the Financial Bureau administers the national debt, governmental investment, trust funds, national property, loans to local governments and even housing for civil servants; the Securities Bureau is similar to and rather more influential than the American Securities and Exchange Commission; the Banking Bureau supervises the Bank of Japan and controls many aspects

of commercial banking and the insurance industry. Customs Houses,
Regional Finance Bureaus and over 500 District Tax Offices spread the
ministry's net throughout the land. The Mint and the bureau which does
all the government printing are also attached.[1]

Japanese pay much attention to the relative status of organizations,
and Finance would be found at the top of nearly anyone's prestige list of
ministries. It attracts the pick of the yearly crop of university graduates.
More of its officials retire to become elected to the Diet.[2] A higher
proportion of its officials transfer temporarily to other ministries but then
return.[3] Rumor has it, at least, that MOF officials receive the best
apartments in government housing projects, and that they are deferred to
in interministerial meetings.[4] Although the ministry does not exercise all
the general supervisory functions over other government organs once
monopolized by the British Treasury, its budgeting role is naturally a key
factor in its high status; all ministries must be wary of offending the
holder of the purse strings.

## Recruitment

Civil servants in the Japanese national government are divided into three
classifications, of which only the top one, made up entirely of university
graduates, supplies all the top posts. In a normal year, the Ministry of
Finance will recruit 20 to 25 recent graduates for this classification,
following administration of an extremely competitive written examination
and an oral interview. From 1966 to 1974, 194 of the 200 who joined the
ministry at this level were graduates from one of the three major national
universities (Tokyo, Kyoto and Hitotsubashi); indeed, over three-quarters
of the total came from Tokyo University and over half from its Faculty of
Law. By discipline, 134 were trained in law, 61 in economics and only 5
in other fields. Recruitment for the ministry has become more diverse in
recent years, as Table 3 reveals — dividing the nine years covered in half,
we see the proportion from universities other than Tokyo increased from
just over a tenth to just under a third, and those specializing in law

1. A handy guide to governmental organization and functions is Government of Japan,
Prime Minister's Office, Administrative Management Agency, *Table of Organization of the
Government of Japan* (Tokyo: Printing Bureau, Ministry of Finance, 1974).

2. In 1974, seventeen MOF ex-officials served in the Lower House, eight in the Upper
House. Kusayanagi Daizō, "Kanryō Ōkoku ron: Ōkurashō" ("Bureaucratic Kingdom:
Ministry of Finance"), *Bungei Shunjū* 52, 7 (June 1974), 176.

3. Akira Kubota, *Higher Civil Servants in Postwar Japan* (Princeton: Princeton
University Press, 1969), p. 109.

4. Discussions of the personality and prestige of the Ministry of Finance, nearly all based
on impressionistic evidence, will be found in Suzuki Yukio, "Ōkura Kanryō no Shisō" ("The
Thought of Ministry of Finance Bureaucrats"), *Chūō Kōron* 81, 2 (February 1966), 106-123,
and *Keizai Kanryō* ("Economic Bureaucrats") (Tokyo: Nihon Keizai Shinbunsha, 1969);
Amano Hajime, "Ōkurashō Kanryō" ("Ministry of Finance Bureaucrats"), *Chūō Kōron* 84,
10 (October 1969), 241-252; and Kusayanagi, "Kanryō Ōkoku."

dropped from 71 to 63 percent. Still, the conventional wisdom that the MOF is dominated by Tokyo law graduates is hardly refuted by the most recent data.

What may be said of these fledgling Finance bureaucrats? First, that they are all extremely bright. Second, that a majority have received very similar training, and share alumni bonds.[5] Third, that most are generalists, with most of their coursework largely in nontechnical law and traditional political science; the economists may be either "Marxist" or "modern," but are not econometricians. Fourth, that most will be "Finance Ministry types"—organizationally minded, ambitious, willing to devote themselves to working very hard. The sort of applicant the ministry looks for might be represented by this Tōdai Law graduate, who answered a question about why he had selected the MOF with a little speech:

Going through grammar school, middle school, high school, university, I was always the leader. My feeling was that a person like myself must not think only of his own future, but more broadly; he should choose his career so as to be useful to State and Society—that was my motive for joining the Ministry of Finance. Why the Ministry of Finance? Why anywhere else? The reason is, the State runs on money, so through public finance one can be useful to Society.[6]

The type avoided by the MOF is illustrated by an anecdote: In one year an applicant showed up for the entrance examination without a coat and tie, but received the highest score on the written portion. For the interview, he borrowed a coat from another applicant, and performed reasonably. However, he was rejected; an official explained that "he is too individualistic and might have an influence on others."[7]

## Socialization

Once he joins the MOF the young career official begins a quite standardized—more so than in other ministries—sequence of posts which actually amounts to a seven-year training program (see Chart 1). Those undergoing this process often speak of it as an extension of their university experience, with the difference tht they are usually impressed by the degree of responsibility they are expected to take, and by their

5. In Japanese writings on bureaucracy much is made of *gakubatsu*, "school cliques." For a brief account see Kubota, *Higher Civil Servants*, pp. 85-91, 132, 165-68. For interesting views of various organizational problems, see Albert M. Craig, "Functional and Dysfunctional Aspects of Government Bureaucracy," in *Modern Japanese Organization and Decision-Making*, ed. Ezra Vogel (Berkeley and Los Angeles: University of California Press, 1975), pp. 3-32, esp. 11-15, and Chalmers Johnson, "Japan: Who Governs? An Essay on Official Bureaucracy," *Journal of Japanese Studies* 2, 1 (Autumn 1975), pp. 1-28.

6. Said at a discussion for a magazine of first-year employees in various organizations, in 1955. Honda Yasuharu, *Nihon Neokanryō ron* ("The 'New Bureaucrats' of Japan") (Tokyo: Kōdansha, 1975), pp. 83-84.

7. Kusayanagi, "Kanryō Ōkoku," p. 178.

## TABLE 3
### DIVERSITY IN MINISTRY OF FINANCE RECRUITING

#### A. Discipline

|  | Law | | Economics | | Other | | Total | |
|---|---|---|---|---|---|---|---|---|
|  | No. | % | No. | % | No. | % | No. | % |
| 1966–1970 | 70 | 71 | 27 | 28 | 1 | 1 | 98 | 100 |
| 1970–1974 | 64 | 63 | 34 | 33 | 4 | 4 | 102 | 100 |
| Total | 134 | 67 | 61 | 31 | 5 | 3 | 200 | 101 |

#### B. University and Faculty

|  | Tokyo Law | | Tokyo Other Faculties | | Kyoto & Hitotsubashi | | Other Universities | | Total | |
|---|---|---|---|---|---|---|---|---|---|---|
|  | No. | % | No. | % | No. | % | No. | % | No. | % |
| 1966–1970 | 66.5 | 68 | 20.5 | 21 | 10 | 10 | 1 | 1 | 98 | 100 |
| 1970–1974 | 47.5 | 47 | 22.5 | 22 | 28 | 27 | 4 | 4 | 102 | 100 |
| Total | 114 | 57 | 43 | 22 | 38 | 19 | 5 | 3 | 200 | 101 |

NOTE: Since an odd number of years was covered, figures for 1970 were split between the two periods evenly (accounting for the half-people). Percentages may not add to 100 because of rounding.

SOURCE: Japan, Ministry of Finance, "Ōkurashō no Aramashi" ("Outline of the Ministry of Finance"), Mimeo, 1974, p. 46. This is a handout prepared for applicants to the ministry.

participation in the making of important national policies. Even in the second year, the typical official will be serving as a chief clerk with several ordinary employees in his charge, and in the sixth year, at age 27, will have sole responsibility for the district tax office in a small city (a slot usually filled by a much older noncareer official). This job requires frequent discussions on an equal basis with the mayor, police chief and other city influentials, and supervision of perhaps thirty or forty employees.[8] When assigned to the ministry in Tokyo, the young official will frequently be placed in a research or planning post, where he must learn very quickly about some substantive area (balance of payments, capital market operations, local government finances) so that he can

8. Including, often enough, such aspects of a Japanese supervisor's role as officiating at weddings. This point, and the discussion in general, is drawn both from interviews with younger officials and Japan, Ministry of Finance, "Ōkurashō no Aramashi" ("Outline of the Ministry of Finance") (Mimeo, 1974). In 1968 there were 497 district tax offices in Japan, with an average of 85 employees each: Government of Japan, Ministry of Finance, Tax Bureau, *An Outline of Japanese Taxes: 1968* (no publishing information), pp. 214, 219-221. It is likely that young officials became directors of the smaller offices.

contribute to the group discussions in which policy evolves. For the academic stage, following the second year, several officials go to the United States or Europe for both language training and graduate work in economics; a few have managed later to obtain Ph.D. degrees. Those who remain in Japan attend special classes full-time for a year, taught by university professors, on such subjects as quantitative economics, public finance, monetary theory, international economics and welfare economics.

One gains an impression, talking with younger Finance Ministry staff, that this program is an extremely effective mechanism for socialization with regard to substantive and administrative competence, a strong sense of personal responsibility and self-confidence, acceptance of the values of the organization, and loyalty and dedication. In addition, it provides many opportunities for review of the official's achievements and potential by his superiors—the ministry's advice to its applicants concludes its outline of this program with the words: ". . . with endeavor, the path to division chief, bureau chief, and higher office will open."[9]

After this seven or eight year training period, career paths become less standardized, although advancement, as in other Japanese organizations, still proceeds by seniority.[10] Each official considers himself in competition with the other twenty-five or so members of his entering cohort; progressively it will become apparent which of them is still on the "success course" (*shusse kōsu*). The first crucial stage comes when one has spent two or three years in a "junior" division chief post in the home office, after twenty-two or twenty-three years in the ministry—those on the "success course" become directors of key divisions (the Secretarial and General Coordinating Divisions of the Minister's Secretariat; the General Affairs Division of the Budget, Tax, Banking and then Financial and International Finance Bureaus), while others are attached to the Securities or Customs and Tariff Bureaus or the National Tax Administration Agency. The next stop is an important regional post—which region matters—after which one reaches the second crucial stage, appointment as a bureau vice-director (*jichō*), or department director (*buchō*). The top job here is Budget Bureau vice-director, but there are four or five others also included in the "success course." It is from this point on that rivalries become intense. Only one of any "class" may become vice-minister; custom dictates that his classmates (plus any from an older class which did not include a vice-minister) will resign at the time he takes office.

*"Ministry Character"*.—Rivalries and tensions there may be, but among Japanese ministries Finance is famous for unity—the "finance

9. "Ōkurashō no Aramashi," p. 45.
10. This discussion is largely based on Honda, *Neokanryō*, pp. 86-99.

## CHART 1

### STANDARD COURSE FOR ENTERING MINISTRY OF FINANCE OFFICIALS

| Year | Location | Rank | Job | Alternatives |
|---|---|---|---|---|
| First | Home Office | Ordinary Employee | Junior member of a regular division. | |
| Second | Regional Tax Administration Bureau | Chief Clerk | Tax inspector; supervising small staff and making site visits. | Service as a researcher in an attached institute. |
| Third | Home Office | (student) | Training in economic theory. | Overseas study (two years). |
| Fourth | Home Office | Chief Clerk | Heads one section (*kakari*) of a regular division. | |
| Fifth | | | (similar to fourth but probably in a different post) | |
| Sixth | District Tax Office | Director | Supervision of office and liaison with local officials. | |
| Seventh | Home Office | Assistant Division Director | Second level within a regular division. | Service overseas, posting to another agency, etc. |

NOTE: Posts in external organs are lower in status than those with similar titles in the Home Office.

SOURCE: See Table 3.

family" (*Ōkura ikka*) is a term often heard. Tradition has it that ministry officials will not allow feelings of competition to slip into professional sabotage, as has been rumored to happen elsewhere, and that for the most part intrabureaucratic factionalism is not intense.[11] On the other hand, in institutional terms the Ministry of Finance is rather less cohesive than other Japanese ministries: its officials have tended to be more specialized and its bureaus more autonomous and fragmented—"all bureaus no ministry," some say. Policy questions are fought out among the bureaus, with the vice-minister serving as mediator; the resulting compromises will reflect the current balance of power and dissatisfaction will be spread fairly evenly.[12] Emotions sometimes run high in institutional disputes: in one case, when the Budget Bureau tried to convert an annoying small agricultural subsidy into interest free loans, which the Financial Bureau would be stuck with, the aggrieved bureau chief responded in a meeting that "the Budget Bureau is always cleaning up its own garden first and throwing all the garbage into ours."[13]

Still, the ministry manages to hang together, and in particular always presents a united front to outsiders. It is known for protecting its personnel system, so that even high-level promotions are screened from interference by LDP politicians (sometimes including the minister).[14] One would suppose such solidarity is largely explained by the recruitment and socialization processes described above, which select and encourage officials having a sense of mission, organizational loyalty and a consciousness of elite status. Down to the lowest levels, all in the Ministry of Finance see themselves as participating in the great affairs of state: when word comes through the loudspeakers that the budget or some piece of MOF legislation has passed the Diet, every divisional office resounds with cheers.

## The Budget Bureau

Nearly all such characteristics of the Ministry of Finance as a whole are even more true of the Budget Bureau (Shukeikyoku—literally "accounting bureau"), whose officials have been called the "samurai of the

11. For example, the MOF has not been split by a battle like that between the Sahashi and anti-Sahashi camps in the Ministry of International Trade and Industry, although a group of officials originally organized by Ikeda Hayato did predominate for a number of years. See *ibid.*, pp. 92-96, and for MITI, pp. 5-41.

12. Amano, "Ōkurashō Kanryō," pp. 243ff.

13. Kusayanagi Daizō, "Ōkurashō Shukeikyoku no Samuraitachi" ("The Samurai of the Ministry of Finance Budget Bureau"). *Bungei Shunjū* 46, 12 (November 1968), 224. The same author concluded in a later article that the bureau-based "franchise system" has declined in recent years as official careers become less specialized and the ministry-level staff gained in power. "Kanryō Ōkoku," 170-71.

14. Honda, *Neokanryō*, p. 95. While the formal process of appointing top-level officials is straightforward, how they are really selected is rather mysterious. A consensus of current officials at the rank in question and above, plus leading ex-officials, is probably the main determinant.

## CHART 2
## BUDGET BUREAU ORGANIZATION

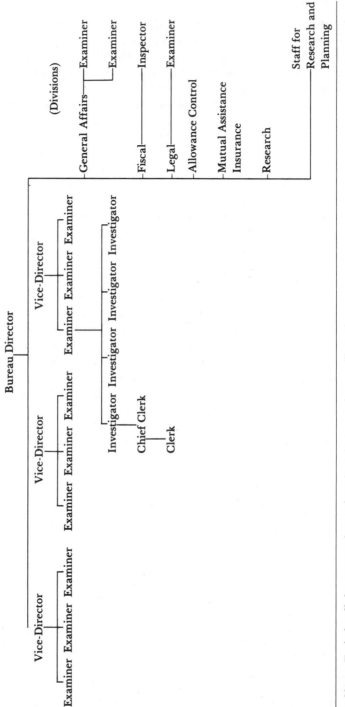

NOTE: Typical staffs for one examiner and one investigator are shown as illustration.

SOURCES: *Bessatsu Ōkura Yōran* (1974 ed.; Tokyo: Ōkura Yōran Shuppansha, 1973), pp. 46–60. Translations are official, and are drawn from Government of Japan, Prime Minister's Office, Administrative Management Agency, "Table of Organization of the Government of Japan, 1973" (Tokyo: Ministry of Finance Printing Bureau, February 28, 1974), p. 54.

Japanese government" or the "elite of the elite."[15] Service in the Budget Bureau is a prerequisite for any younger MOF official hoping to rise in the ministry, and the bureau's director is always a leading candidate for the vice-minister's post.[16] The bureau has its own personality and traditions, and anecdotes. Many could be cited, but we will be content with this example of bureau socialization. A top official of an earlier day, welcoming neophytes into the bureau, told them to remember just three things: "no matter how busy you get, read a book every day, don't catch the clap, and don't borrow from a loan shark." Translation: budgeting officials should master their subjects; avoid becoming intimate with the ministries they review, and never make deals.[17] Budget examiners of an earlier day were famous for taking a high-handed attitude even toward other officials, let alone politicians—the story is told of a vice-minister from a certain ministry who broke a promise not to submit a request; the examiner took him to the finance minister by the scruff of the neck.[18] Line ministry officials today say that the MOF staff has become more polite, but wonder if the essence of the budgeter's role has really changed.

The formal structure of the Budget Bureau is outlined in Chart 2. It may be divided into "staff" and "line" functions. Line functions, the actual review of ministry budget requests, are supervised by the bureau director through the three vice-directors, each responsible for about one-third of the budget. At the end of 1973, the director was in his thirtieth year in the ministry, and the vice-directors had served for twenty-four or twenty-five years.[19] Under each vice-director are three examiners (shukeikan), seen as equal in rank to a division director; their seniority ranged from nineteen to twenty-one years in the ministry. Each examiners's area is in turn divided among three to five subordinates, formally called assistant examiners (shukeikan hosa) but more often known as investigators (shusa).[20] Three to seven officials at the chief clerk (kakari-chō) rank are also included.

15. As well as the citations above, see "Hana no Shukeikan no Kokoroiki" ("The Spirit of the Flowering Examiners"), Zaikai 17, 23 (December 15, 1969), 88-92; and Asahi Shinbun Keizaibu, Keizai Seisaku no Butaiura ("Economic Policy Behind the Scenes") (Tokyo: Asahi Shinbunsha, 1974), pp. 67-68.

16. From 1953 to 1974, nine of the thirteen MOF vice-ministers had directed the BB; conversely, from 1947 to 1968, all seven BB directors had come from the post of deputy vice-minister, and went to the vice ministership afterward. Ōkurashō Hyakunenshi Henshūshitsu, Ōkurashō Jinmeiroku ("Who's Who in the Ministry of Finance") (Tokyo: Ōkura Zaimu Kyōkai, 1973).

17. They are also said to combine an air of amused cynicism with a serious sense of mission. Kusayanagi, "Samuraitachi," 226.

18. Amano, "Ōkurashō Kanryō," 245.

19. Calculated from graduation dates. Bessatsu Ōkura Yōran ("Ministry of Finance Handbook Supplement") (1974 ed.; Tokyo: Ōkura Yōran Shuppansha, 1973), pp. 46-60, for this and the career information below.

20. As is true of assistant division chiefs in all MOF bureaus, this level is staffed either by higher civil servants at an early-middle stage of their careers, or by officials of lower status nearing retirement. The range of seniority among the twenty-one Tokyo University graduates was nine to fifteen years; among the thirteen others, twenty-two to twenty-eight years.

The rest of the Budget Bureau may be seen as performing staff functions, providing technical information to the examiners or dealing with some aspect of the budget as a whole. The division names are fairly self-explanatory; General Affairs is the most important, and includes two officials with examiner status (the Legal Division has one). The Research Division devotes much of its energy to studies of other countries, both patterns of government expenditures and innovations in budgeting techniques — it was the chief enthusiast in the Ministry of Finance for the introduction of program budgeting. The organization of the Budget Bureau has not changed very much in recent years. Perhaps the greatest innovation, if it can be called that, was the creation in August 1973 of a special Staff for Research and Planning, actually one official of examiner status (but junior to the others), reporting directly to the Bureau director, with two assistants and some staff support from the Research Section.[21]

This, in brief, is the formal structure of the Budget Bureau. There also is an informal structure: unwritten role definitions and rules that determine how each component in the decision-making process relates to the others. Some of these less formal characteristics may be mentioned briefly; for example, like the House Appropriations Committee (and the American Bureau of the Budget, or Office of Management and Budget), the Budget Bureau is functionally specialized.[22] Each examiner, with his staff, concentrates on his own precisely delineated area, and does not intervene in the domains of the others except on matters that directly affect his own affairs. This specialization is justified partly on grounds of expertise, since examiners do build up a considerable knowledge of their ministry's operations. However, generally speaking, they are not specially trained in particular policy areas; rather, they rely on hard work and a generalized quality of administrative common sense or feel for "balance" in making decisions.

Sensitive to criticisms that budget examiners are arrogant, and on their own will often casually turn down plans that have been carefully developed by ministerial officials much senior to themselves, the Budget Bureau stresses the amount of supervision of its decision-making process. In an interview when he was MOF vice-minister, Tanimura Hiroshi said

21. The original intention apparently was that this group would produce full-blown policy analysis on major issues; but in its first several months the unit actually was absorbed in writing summaries of recent budgetary actions in a dozen or so policy areas which span two or more examiners' jurisdictions, devoting about two weeks to each. Although the new institution can be viewed as a move in the direction of incorporating independent policy analysis into budgeting, it is clear that a more determined effort would be required before results of much significance could be expected. Based on interviews, May 1974; see also NKS, January 27, 1973.

22. See Richard F. Fenno, Jr., *The Power of the Purse: Appropriations Politics in Congress* (Boston: Little, Brown and Company, 1966), Chaps. 4-5, for informal structures in Congressional appropriations.

It is true that the examiner produces various materials [relating to a ministerial budget request], but he also goes in front of the bureau vice-director or director to explain why he has handled the budget in this way. If he has cut it to zero, he has to explain why, and the decisions and suggestions of the vice-director and director will naturally emerge. To say that the examiner is top man in the Ministry of Finance, or that he decides things on his own, is clearly a mistake.[23]

According to participants, the tone of the various budget conferences is informal and cooperative. The examiner does not simply submit his written recommendations up through channels for decision. Rather, he and the director (or vice-director) communicate face to face, repeatedly talking over how budget problems should be handled. This accounts for the vast amounts of time consumed by meetings. Even in later ministerial conferences, as described by a top MOF official, a typical presentation by the BB director runs something like this: "The bureau tends to think, based on considerations of A and B, that X amount is warranted, but one could also think of this from the perspective of C, in which case Y would be warranted." All at the meeting can contribute an opinion before a decision is made — usually, of course, along the lines originally suggested. Such meetings occupy much of the time of BB officials.

Finally, it is interesting that examiners may become advocates for the ministries they review. A ministrial accounting division director said in an interview, "on the one hand, it is natural for the examiner to be severe toward the side making the request, but with regard to the rest of the bureau, his goal is to increase the budget for his area."[24] Some interviewed examiners denied that such a possibility existed, but a former examiner and upper-level BB official confirmed that

the position of the examiner can be very delicate. Within the bureau, he can become an advocate (*bengoshi*) of his ministry's policies . . . he can be 'infected' by his contacts with the ministry. This can become a problem if he becomes an 'interest representative' . . . and doesn't really analyze the weak points of a budget request.

This official often used the strong word *mazui* (ugly, bad, improper) in referring to such tendencies, indicating that they run counter to a deeply held Bureau norm. This, and direct sanctions like the control by superiors over an examiner's promotions, probably hold the natural development of advocacy in check — in some cases, they produce over-enthusiastic cutters, which is also frowned upon. However, the significance

23. Interview in *Asahi Jaanaru* 9, 49 (November 26, 1967), pp. 46-48, answering a typical attack by former MITI Vice-Minister Sahashi Shigeru in the previous issue, pp. 108-110.

24. Cf. Aaron Wildavsky: "Tough as they may be in cutting the budgets of their agencies, appropriations committee members, once having made their decision, generally defended the agencies against further cuts on the floor." *The Politics of the Budgetary Process* (Boston: Little, Brown and Company, 1964), p. 50.

of this characteristic for the functioning of the budget system is indicated
by the unanimous opinion of interviewed officials in the line ministries that
a smart and competent examiner, who once convinced can argue their
cases effectively within the bureau, is far preferable to one whom they
might be able to fool on occasion.

# Calculations

Ever since the second year of the Meiji period (1869), the central function
of the Ministry of Finance has been its annual review of budget requests
from the other agencies of government. Elaborate statistics are not needed
to indicate how immense this workload has become, as Japan became
modern and the role of its government expanded. Riffling through the
thousand or so pages of *Kuni no Yosan,* already a greatly condensed
summary of the annual budget, gives a sufficient idea of the quantity and
range of decisions which must be made every year.

Or must these decisions be made? — or better, can they? As studies of
budgetary systems elsewhere have exhaustively demonstrated, no budgeting authority is large or intelligent enough to make "rational" decisions on
all the issues which pass before it. In this section, we will see how Japanese
budgeters cope with their problems of complexity, applying techniques not
too different from those of Americans or Englishmen, but with some
interesting wrinkles of their own. This discussion is preceded by a brief
chronological account of the internal BB microbudgeting process.

## *Process*

It takes the Budget Bureau some six months every year to prepare the
national budget, from its preparations in the summer to the publication of
the Ministry of Finance draft in December or January. Two general
principles are followed: first, do the easiest and most routine items first,
leaving the hardest for later; second, do the easy items at the lower levels,
pass the hardest up the ladder to higher levels. These patterns may be
observed in the sequence of decision-making stages.[25]

The formal beginning of the process is the finance minister's budget
call at a Cabinet meeting in late July or early August: he announces the
deadline for requests and the government-wide ceiling, and endorses the
principle of thrift. He and the prime minister also take this opportunity to
comment on fiscal prospects, usually in rather pessimistic terms. However,
Budget Bureau officials are active even earlier. In June, they begin the

25. This account of the BB's internal review process is based largely on an interview with
a BB official. The dates, given as examples, are from a tentative schedule for the 1970
process, which later became delayed. A recent description that differs somewhat is in Ashai
Shinbun Keizaibu, *Butaiura,* pp. 68-74.

"first expenditure estimate" and they participate in early revenue forecasting (both macrobudgeting matters discussed in the next chapter), as
well as getting a start on the most routine budget items.

*Standard Budget.* — The standard budget (*hyōjun yosan*) is a system
for which the Ministry of Finance had great expectations in the earlier
years, but which fell into near insignificance by the late 1960s. This account
was to have been made up of all the routine, unvarying expenses which
could be decided without much argument by technical discussions between
ministry and MOF staff during the summer. A prewar practice, the
standard budget was revived in 1955 (it had been considered impossible
earlier because of sharp inflation) in a cost-cutting context: MOF officials
felt that getting through the nondiscretionary workload before September
would allow all their energies later to be devoted to cutting budgets in the
area where cuts are possible, "policy" expenditures, and thereby aid in
imposing the then current "trillion yen ceiling" on the budget.[26]

The items included in the standard budget have varied considerably
from year to year, making longitudinal comparison difficult. Administrative expenses like government building maintenance were always a major
component, but in the early years items for war-connected pensions, the
national government portion of compulsory education expenses, interest
on the national debt, running expenses of the national universities and
similar items were also included. In 1956, the standard budget amounted
to ¥ 349 billion (about $970 million), or 33.7 percent of the General
Account. However, although the MOF had once hoped that as much as
half of the General Account could be handled routinely through the
standard budget, each year more programs were excluded and reviewed in
the fall along with "policy" expenses. After a decade of high budget
growth, in 1965 the standard budget had risen only to ¥ 401 billion (about
$1.4 billion), 11 percent of the General Account.[27] By 1970, it had fallen
off sharply to ¥ 112 billion ($333 million), a trivial 1.51 percent of the
General Account; even personnel expenses had been excluded, and the
major item (73.5 percent of its total) was *chōhi*, the most routine
administrative costs.[28]

*First Explanations.* — Budget request forms are due on August 31,
and throughout September the officials of the spending ministries troop
over to the Ministry of Finance to explain their needs and hopes. Chief,

26. YS, July 24, 1955.
27. Hayashi Yoshio, *Zaiseiron* ("Public Finance") (Tokyo: Chikuma Shobō, 1968), pp.
128-133.
28. *Kuni no Yosan,* 1970, pp. 885-87. It is not entirely clear why the Standard Budget
system has in effect been abandoned; cf. Hayashi, *Zaiseiron,* p. 130.

clerks talk with assistant division chiefs from the ministries, investigators with division chiefs, examiners only with bureau chiefs or better. No one really negotiates, but the MOF officials do ask a good many pointed questions and often request additional supporting materials. The mood is rather relaxed. In mid-September, the finance minister reports to the Cabinet on the amount requested by each ministry.

*Miscellaneous Expenditures.* — When the explanations are finished, Budget Bureau officials begin their real work; for the next two months they will talk mainly to each other. For review purposes, the budget is divided into two unequal parts. The Miscellaneous Category (*zakken*), which is taken up first, includes most general administrative costs as well as programs which do not fall under one of the Important Items; in recent years it has amounted to about 13 percent of the budget. This category is arranged by ministry.[29] In October the bureau is absorbed in a detailed evaluation of these miscellaneous expenditures. The core of the process is the "Miscellaneous Category bureau meetings" (*zakken kyokugi*) held every morning from October 10 to 22. Here, each examiner explains the overall picture for his ministry, his investigators go into more detail for individual items, and their chief clerks explain the detailed figures and the calculations which back them up. Presiding over these meetings is the responsible vice-director, with the General Affairs Division as staff to assist with calculations, particularly those covering the government as a whole. A vice-director will either accept an examiner's presentation or send it back for more work. These meetings sometimes treat items as small as $250.

*Important Items.* — Simultaneously, several days a week between October 6 and 31, two to three hour meetings are held to discuss the Important Items (*shuyō keihi*, the major functional areas of the budget). These talks, chaired by the BB director, are on a general level, designed to identify problems and gain an overall view, as well as to give examiners a feeling for leadership attitudes. No decisions are made.

Then, in early November come the "second expenditure estimate" (*dainiji suikei*) meetings, in which the finance minister participates. Since the Miscellaneous Category has already been largely determined, and there has been some analysis of the Important Items requests, discussions are quite specific and lead to setting a tentative "framework" (*waku*) for the total budget. This figure, which is kept secret, is compared with the

29. See Appendix B for an explanation of Japanese budget categories. More generally, see Kōno Kazuyuki, *Yosan Seido* ("The Budget System") (Tokyo: Gakuyō Shobō, 1976), esp. pp. 71-82.

revenue estimate being prepared elsewhere in the MOF, and usually turns out to be larger.

In late November the "second Important Items bureau meetings" are held almost daily, to determine specific budget figures for each of the programs included in this budget category. Again each examiner, assisted by his staff, presents his analysis of the budget requests, and then listens to the reactions of the bureau director and vice-directors. During this period the director may also talk over particular problems with the MOF vice-minister, and the minister will receive at least a preliminary briefing. These top officials may also be speaking informally with their counter-parts in other ministries, as well as with top LDP leaders and perhaps influential businessmen. On occasion they may pick up specific ideas and filter them down to the responsible examiner.

Also in late November, the General Affairs Division and other BB officials adjust the various items on a technical level, so that categories like personnel expenses, automobile use, provisions for computerization and so forth are fairly distributed among the ministries—this is called the "unified evaluation" (tōitsu satei). There follows a period for "numerical adjust-ments" (keisū seiri), the checking of figures and their rearrangement into the various classifications required (e.g., from the Important Items to the object base of expenditure).

*Ministry of Finance Draft.* — The "budget ministerial conference" (*yosan shōgi*) begins in early December, lasting perhaps two weeks. Participating are the minister, vice-minister, two parliamentary vice-ministers (sporadically), the deputy vice-minister, chiefs of the Research and Planning, and Documents Division of the Secretariat, the Budget Bureau director and vice-directors (not always present), the examiner responsible for the area under discussion, and sometimes, when needed, members of his staff. Other MOF bureau directors may also participate. These sessions, like the equivalent meetings held in each ministry before budget requests are submitted, primarily serve the function of ratification, although not infrequently items may still be adjusted up or down. The budget ministerial conference also ratifies a draft of the Budget Compilation Policy (*Yosan Hensei Hōshin*), which is then passed by the Cabinet.

Normally in mid-December, although as often as not proceedings become delayed into January, the MOF draft budget is reported to the Cabinet and shown (*naiji*) to ministry officials. As in the September hearings, they come to the Budget Bureau offices, but this time it is their role to listen and ask questions about what the examiners have in mind. Their appeals are made later, after discussions within each ministry and with the PARC divisions; this appeals process, called "revival negotia-tions," is discussed below in chapter 7.

## Information

If the budget may be regarded as an "output" of an information-processing system, it is sensible to ask what the "inputs" are. From what sources does the examiner draw the information which eventually is transmuted into budgetary numbers?

*The Line Ministry.* — Ministry officials are the leading specialists on what needs to be done and the best ways to do them, and the examiner is dependent on them. The raw material for his deliberations are, of course, the budget requests documents themselves. Particularly when a new program or a major expansion of an old one is requested, these will be accompanied by volumes of supporting material, replete with statistics demonstrating that a problem exists and descriptions of how the proposed program will be administered. Reports from one or more ministerial public advisory bodies which purport to examine available alternatives are usually included. In many fields, particularly public works, there will also be previously approved five-year plans of ministry activities to consult.

When he has questions about these written materials, or wishes information they do not contain, the examiner will turn first to the ministry Accounting Division director (or on occasion a higher-ranked ministry-level official), or a bureau director responsible for the activity under question. He may make many such telephone calls every day, but for lengthier discussions, the official will be invited to the MOF offices. An investigator occasionally may call at the ministry to talk to an official at the division director level, but in principle Budget Bureau officials seldom leave their offices.

Interviewed officials provided several examples of such contacts during October and November. In the case of a new program to provide support for the personnel expenses of private universities, finally granted about ¥ 10 billion, there were ten meetings between an investigator and the staff of the responsible Ministry of Education division, and two discussions between the responsible BB vice-director and the Education bureau director. The MOF officials requested more up-to-date statistics on student body size, questioned growth forecasts, asked how giving aid to unworthy schools was to be prevented, sought commitments that the program would not be expanded limitlessly, and generally took a critical attitude toward the ministry's arguments. For a less controversial program at another ministry, an expansion of funds devoted to field studies of water pollution, the examiner's questions centered on three problems: the large boost in the unit price requested for each technical project (justified by very rapid price hikes for the scientific equipment needed); doubts that the section was competent to establish committees of residents to draw up locally applicable environmental standards, as it had no comparable experience; and priorities among the several specific projects requested, since sufficient funds to cover all of them would not be available. These examples indicate that while such discussions usually fall short of actual negotiations (although on occasion the BB might propose an alternative to the requested program, to solicit the ministry's reactions), the range of matters covered may be very broad and extend on occasion beyond strictly fiscal problems.

*Politicians and Concerned Citizens.* — Ministry officials, in meetings like these and even in the September "explanations" of requests, are also the main conduit for the opinions of both interest groups and the majority party to reach the BB. The examiner may ask specifically about these. He also will have direct contacts with LDP politicians — at times a party specialist in his policy area may call on the telephone (though Dietmen are somewhat more likely to speak with the BB director), and individual politicians appear in person, usually with a body of constituents, to argue for a project of special interest. Such low-level pressure is usually little more than a time-consuming nuisance. However, several MOF officials did note in interviews that "petition groups" of citizens occasionally provide useful information, because their perceptions of their own interests may differ from those of the requesting ministry. For example, on one occasion the Ministry of Agriculture and Forestry was emphasizing the need for subsidies to increase the acreage of wet rice fields, partly because they are more expensive than constructing dry fields and accordingly swell the ministry's budget. However, when the petition groups sent around by the ministry were asked directly what their needs were, they replied that dry fields would actually be more valuable.

*Personal Resources.* — Examiners have been known to seek out information on their own. Some may telephone former teachers or friends for information and opinions on problems in their fields. As for more active research, probably the most famous anecdote of budgeting is told of Murakami Kōtarō, later a controversial MOF vice-minister, who when examiner for defense once donned long rubber boots and went down to Tokyo's early morning fish market. In his office later that day, he was able to confront Defense Agency officials with direct evidence that the unit prices requested for purchasing food supplies had been watered.[30] Budget

---

30. This and other Murakami stories may be found in Kusayanagi, "Samuraitachi" and Amano, "Ōkurashō Kanryō."

examiners today relish but rarely emulate this tale; they say that they are far too busy to go out into the field, and so must rely on the truthfulness of the officials from the requesting ministry. However, they are more likely to follow Murakami (reputed to be an expert on Clauswitz and other military classics) in reading up on their field of responsibility.

*The Past Record.* — One would suppose that a very relevant consideration when considering the budget for an ongoing program should be how well it had performed in the past. Line ministry officials recalled that on occasion examiners or investigators had questioned them about their experiences, especially with a newly established program in the previous buget or one for which a sizable increase in financing was asked. However, such queries have been occasional and unsystematic; in general the Budget Bureau apparently either takes program effectiveness for granted, disbelieves that honest responses can be obtained from ministry officials, or has resigned itself to think that, given the realities of LDP or interest group support (especially in an environment of high growth), attempts to abolish outmoded programs would have little chance of success.

There is also little evidence of the Budget Bureau seeking other sources of information on program effectiveness. Asked about this point, several MOF officials noted that the ten Regional Financial Bureaus (*Zaimukyoku*) are sometimes called upon to investigate how past budget allocations have been used. However, it would appear that such inquiries, while not infrequent, have almost always been devoted to whether local governments or other organizations had used their funds illegally, for other than the purposes specified, or if there had been gross waste. They are particularly aimed at disaster reclamation projects. Similarly, the official audit is consulted, but since its figures are both out of date and provide information only on the technical level of illegalities, unspent funds and the like, their usefulness is limited.

The impression I received in interviewing MOF officials was that they feel somewhat defensive about this point, and in fact laments on the quantity of wasteful programs in the Japanese bureaucracy and the MOF's lack of energy in cutting fat are among the most commonly encountered criticisms of the budgetary process. The creation of a new Staff for Research and Planning may be something of a response to such concerns, but until its capabilities for program review are increased substantially, it seems unlikely that the BB will be making very detailed examinations of the effectiveness of governmental programs.[31]

31. According to a mid-1975 personal communication, the Budget Bureau has recently been translating portions of Hugh Heclo and Aaron Wildavsky, *The Private Government of Public Money* (Berkeley and Los Angeles: University of California Press, 1974), and discussing particularly the British Program Analysis and Review (PAR) system, so more innovations in this area perhaps are to be expected.

*Guidelines.* — Another type of information pertinent to the examiner's budget reviewing is guidance passed down from higher levels. One would suppose that he might be instructed to be particularly concerned about new expenditures because of pessimistic economic forecasts, told to emphasize particular programs of high priority, or at least given some sense of how his area fits into the budget as a whole. Perhaps surprisingly, budgeters say that such guidelines are not important in Japan. It seems to be part of the BB system to allow the examiner to take an open-minded approach to ministry requests, at least at first. In some years, a confidential "budget review policy" (*satei hōshin*) may have been issued as instructions to examiners, but the only example of this document to have been made public (for 1959) is limited to detailed rules for cutting 5 or 10 percent from various subsidies and administrative expenses.[32] Several BB officials said in interviews that the examiner never learns what the "framework" will be for his ministry until very late in the process. The preferences and intentions of his superiors are to be imparted during the lengthy conferences described above — he intuits the opinions of the director and vice-director by watching their reactions to his suggestions.

While doubtlessly expressing a general tendency, this insistence on the open-mindedness of examiners is probably a little exaggerated. There are in fact examples of BB leaders issuing instructions, broad or specific, at all stages of the process. The idea that Japanese budgeting is fundamentally bottom-up, based upon detailed evaluation of each individual item, runs deep within the Ministry of Finance and is no small part of the lofty self-image of the budget examiner — which is not to say it might not be partly fictional.

*The Current Budget.* — Conscientious as he may be about studying up on his field, analyzing requests and gathering as much additional data as he can, first and last the examiner will always turn to the budget already in force. Indeed, the forms on which requests are submitted include, for each item, a space for the amount currently being received, and the increment newly requested. This focus is quite natural. In a complex and uncertain environment, nearly the only specific, real information available is how much money is now being spent, and on what — all other inputs tend to be vague and are always debatable.

## Criteria for Decisions

The picture which emerges is an examiner faced with many complicated decisions, armed with more documents than he can read, additional information and advice from the ministry officials who drew up the requests, and a few dribbles of unreliable data from other sources. He

32. Reprinted in Hayashi, *Zaiseiron*, pp. 144-146.

consults continuously with his own assistants, each investigating a portion of the request, and often meets with his superiors to get their reactions to his suggstions. How, then, does he formulate his suggestions; how does he decide that one program should get 5 percent more than the previous year and another 20, or one new proposal be accepted and another rejected?

This question was asked of many officials in the course of interviews, but most gave rather formalistic responses—probably less from an unwillingness to reveal secrets than because the thought processes involved are not easy to unravel. Based on these interviews, a few published accounts and some inferences from studies of budgeting elsewhere, the following tentative account of the considerations which enter into the examiner's decisions is offered.

*The "Book" Answer.* — Over the years traditional formulas for judging expenditures have been developed in the MOF. The economist Kotake Toyoji gave the following list in the mid-1950s:

1. "Logic" (*suji*)—Is the objective worthwhile, and the amount requested appropriate to it? Is the rationale sound?
2. "Framework" (*waku*)—Are there sufficient resources to pay for the program?
3. "Balance" (*baransu*)—How do expenditure levels for the program relate to those of similar, or related, programs?
4. "Timing" (*taimingu*)—When there are many similar requests (such as for dams on ten rivers when there are funds only for five), which should have priority?
5. "Calculations" (*sekisan*)—Are the figures presented by the ministry, particularly for unit price and quantity, accurate and correctly calculated?[33]

Rather similarly but more briefly, a former BB director writing at about the same time mentioned only "balance" and "timing" as the criteria actually used, defining them somewhat more broadly,[34] and these terms also often came up in interviews. Such concepts represent rather conventional budgeting values, and are comparable, for example, to President Johnson's 1966 statement urging program budgeting on the American bureaucracy.[35] And as in the American case, it is clear that such criteria are extremely difficult to put into practice, because the intellectual burden of making such calculations for even a few items, let alone for the enormous number within one examiner's purview, is simply too great.

33. Endō Shōkichi, ed., *Yosan* ("Budget") (Tokyo: Yūhikaku, 1959), pp. 44-45.

34. Kōno Kazuyuki, "Wagakuni ni okeru Yosan Hensei no Kōzō to Katei" ("The Structure and Process of Budget Compilation in Japan"), in *Gyōsei Kanri no Dōkō* ("Trends in Administrative Management"), ed. Nihon Gyōsei Gakkai (Tokyo: Keisō Shobō, 1957), pp. 70-71.

35. "Memorandum from the President to the Heads of Departments and Agencies on the Government-Wide Planning, Programming and Budgeting System, November 17, 1966," reprinted in *Politics, Programs and Budgets: A Reader in Governmental Budgeting*, ed. James W. Davis, Jr. (Englewood Cliffs, N.J.: Prentice-Hall, 1969), pp. 160-61.

*Incrementalism.* — In Japan as in the United States, practical budgeters cope with such difficulties through a collection of techniques and rules of thumb that have been lumped together under the label "incrementalism." The most important of these is incrementalism proper: taking nearly all past decisions for granted and focusing only on marginal changes to meet new conditions. In budgeting, the column on the budget form that shows the difference between the current year's budget and the next year's request is the one examined, and even here programs which are growing at a "normal" rate, determined by inflation or some obvious growth of workload, will be dismissed from further consideration. Most attention is given to new programs or major changes in old ones. This behavior is of course a budgeting constant found around the world, but it may even be more prevalent in Japan — if only because of high GNP and budget growth, there has rarely been a need to scrutinize programs very carefully.

*Simplifying.* — Another technique or style of decision making which minimizes complexity is to treat budgeting "as if it were non-programmatic."[36] Instead of discussing a program in terms of the importance of the problem it is designed to solve, its likely effectiveness, or whether there might be cheaper alternatives, there is a tendency to examine administrative aspects of the request itself. Such behavior is probably as prevalent among Japanese as among American budgeters. For example, a former budget examiner was told during an interview of a device described by Wildavsky: Congressmen dealing with a request for a large and complicated installation in the atomic energy field asked how personnel costs or real estate transactions had been handled — if these seemed properly taken care of, they could be confident that the rest of the program was worthwhile.[37] The Japanese official's immediate response was a startled "They do that in America too?" His impression had been that this technique is natively Japanese, often used in reviewing atomic energy projects in particular.

The Budget Bureau has many ways to transform policy decisions into administrative decisions, most of them encouraged by the line-item budget forms which reduce expenditures to calculations of quantity and unit price. Requests are first examined for errors in calculation. Then, any request for a unit price rise higher than official Economic Planning Agency inflation forecasts (which have proven to be unrealistically low) will be sharply questioned, as indicated by the water pollution case mentioned above. Similarly, on the quantity side a ministry's contention that economic or other environmental trends force an expansion of services will

36. Wildavsky, *Politics,* p. 60.
37. *Ibid.,* pp. 11-12.

be rebutted by saying there is no hard data to support the assertion, and the ministry may well be forced to use current quantity figures (or an average of past figures) in its plans.[38]

*Economizing.* — It is also common for the Budget Bureau to apply simple cost criteria in making complex judgments. As Thomas J. Anton remarked of American state budgeting, "agencies press for expansion using programmatic criteria while budget review officers attempt to negate expansion using financial criteria."[39] Some critics allege that cost cutting is the *only* standard for BB decisions, and while this is an exaggeration, one finds many examples like the following: In 1968, a major controversy arose between the Defense Agency and the MOF over whether the next generation of jet fighter planes, the F4E, should be imported from the United States or manufactured within Japan. Though this question had enormous implications for long range national security policy, trade relations with the United States and so forth, the MOF was said to take its position in opposition to domestic manufacture solely on grounds that importing was cheaper. When it was later shown that auxiliary systems would force the import price up to within ¥200 million of the domestic cost, the MOF changed its mind, again strictly on the narrow grounds that repairs and servicing would be simplified.[40] As well as satisfying objectives of holding spending down, such drastic limitations on the relevant factors to be considered in a decision greatly eases the burden of calculations on the MOF.

*"Balance."* — Another simplifying device is one of the "book" criteria mentioned above: former BB Director and MOF Vice-Minister Kōno Kazuyuki said that an expenditure level for a program is "balanced" when it is appropriate with regard to the levels of similar, or somehow related, programs.[41] Another official said in an interview that balance means a "round budget" (*marui yosan*), one without any "bulges" of too much money for any one program, policy area or organization. These rather vague explanations can be understood more clearly when it is asked what

38. Cf. Hayashi, *Zaiseiron*, p. 127.

39. Thomas J. Anton, "Roles and Symbols in the Determination of State Expenditures," *Midwest Journal of Political Science* 11 (1967), 27-43, reprinted in Davis, ed., *Politics, Programs and Budgets,* pp. 120-133.

40. See "Bōeiryoku Kyōka ni Miru Keizai Kanryō no Ishiki" ("Economic Bureaucrats' Consciousness of Strengthening Defense Power"), *Ekonomisuto* 47, 47 (October 25, 1969), 56-63; and for the more recent and quite similar example of the American F5B versus the Japanese T-2, Yamamoto Masao, *Keizai Kanryō no Jittai* ("The Reality of the Economic Bureaucrats") (Tokyo: Mainichi Shinbunsha, 1972), pp. 118-124. What role bribes by American aerospace companies may have played in such decisions is unknown to me.

41. Kōno, "Kōzō to Katei," pp. 70-71. This section is drawn from my "Japanese Budget *Baransu,*" in *Organization and Decision-Making,* ed. Vogel, pp. 75-77, 89-91.

balance is not: it is not the setting of budgets competitively by assessing the merits of a particular item *as compared with* those of similar or related items. Rather, for balance, two or more items are seen as requiring the *same* level of expenditure *because they are similar,* or related. Or more precisely, how allocations are "balanced" depends on circumstances. Examples of all the following usages may be found — two or more items are viewed as "balanced" when:

1. They receive, or are increased by, the same amount of money;
2. They receive the same amount per unit, such as number of officials or beneficiaries, or square feet of floor space;
3. One receives enough additional funds to cover the burdens imposed upon it by an increase in another;
4. They receive the same percentage raise, or in other words each maintains its share of a total.

The clearest case of "balance" as an aid to calculation is the third item. If a new harbor is being constructed, it requires highways leading to it; these two budget items will be balanced when the road budget is increased enough to cover the costs. Similarly, a budget allocation to increase health insurance payments for hospital costs must be accompanied by provision for more beds, and perhaps more nurses, for these items to be in balance. In effect, setting a total for one item almost automatically determines the budget for another.

Balancing routine administrative expenses is also relatively straightforward: examples include salaries, many unit prices, building maintenance, numbers of government cars per one hundred employees, and so forth, all established on a government-wide basis so that ministries will not be treated "unfairly." However, balancing administrative expenses often extends beyond those that are obviously routine, as in the provision for computers or allotments for travel, where it could be argued that needs of ministries vary widely. Reflecting on this problem in an interview, an examiner recalled that

travel expenses were needed for an international economic meeting to Bangkok; here, we balance so that, for example, the Ministry of Construction will not have a full delegation and the Ministry of Agriculture and Forestry only half that number. This is checked with great care . . . it is not a matter of policy questions . . . we really pay attention to this extremely routine work of maintaining balance. This is traditionally what has controlled most thinking about budgeting in Japan.

Though in the example given, it might be that far more construction than agricultural specialists should have been sent, such a judgment would require an investigation of the meeting's substance by the examiner, and would irritate Agriculture Ministry officials. It is easier to be equitable.

Such considerations extend beyond administrative to policy expenses. Particularly when expenditures within a single budget category are allocated to different ministries or among different programs, there will be a tendency to have them grow at similar rates. An accounting division director from a ministry concerned with public works commented:

If the total budget for public works goes up about 10 percent, the public works budget of each individual ministry should also get a 10 percent hike. Unless there is some special reason, they won't sharply cut or raise only our ministry's public works budget [share].

Partly in order to maintain balance, public works are handled by a specialized budget examiner. This is not true of the Promotion of Science and Technology budget, but as a former BB director noted, similar considerations prevail:

To some extent, a standard is set (*medo o tsukeru*) for Promotion of Science and Technology, for example, that it should go up 15 percent next year. The various examiners then keep this in mind while reviewing their ministry's budgets. The system is used because of the fear of an unbalance—for example, among the three BB vice-directors, one might be enthusiastic about science, so this budget [for the ministries in his purview] would go up 20 percent, while another with no interest would keep it down to 10 percent.[42]

Even when programs are not formally related by budgeting categories, any shared characteristics will be taken as a justification for balancing. An example cited by Kōno Kazuyuki is the so-called "postwar settlement," compensation for war veterans and their families, A-bomb victims, landlords expropriated in the land reform, repatriates with property expropriated during wartime residence abroad, and the like. The repatriates case in 1967 was extremely difficult for the Finance Ministry not only because of intense political pressures, but also in that property records were chaotic, and there were no obvious guidelines for deciding how much compensation should be given. Accordingly, the MOF held to a position that the grant should be balanced with earlier payments to equivalent claimants, and these precedents were cited in its proposals on the amount of payments to individuals or households, the total burden on the budget, methods of payment, and a formula to adjust for inflation.[43]

To the extent an examiner can determine the budget level for an item by precedent, or by tying it to another item, he need not analyze the detailed justifications provided by the ministry, or seek out other sources of information. Of course, he must still have found the appropriate precedent or other item to balance against—it is this talent which is meant, perhaps,

42. A 1970 interview. Note such standard-setting contradicts the BB custom of not giving "guidelines" to examiners, mentioned above.
43. Kōno, "Kōzō to Katei," pp. 70-71; MNS, March 3, 1967; and AS, April 12, 1967.

when a budget examiner is complimented for his finely tuned sense of balance.

*Relegating Decisions.* — In attempting to avoid hard choices on the basis of program criteria, an even simpler method than applying administrative, financial, or balance calculations is to defer to someone else. If an examiner has confidence in the judgment of the officials of his counterpart ministry, who after all both know more about their own policy area and have the responsibility for carrying out policies once they are approved, he can safely leave many marginal decisions in their hands. Indeed, it would be dangerous not to take their opinions into account, since a ministry which is severely dissatisfied with budgetary results has the potential for disrupting the budget process at a later stage; and more subtly, the BB is dependent on good relations with the ministries for information and other necessities. Even more directly, the preferences of the Liberal Democratic Party, and particularly those of the members who specialize in a particular policy area, cannot be ignored, since the approval of the party-controlled Cabinet and Diet is needed before the budget is passed. In general, agreement of other participants is one of the fundamental criteria of any budgetary system.[44]

Even in the September "explanations" of ministry requests, participants report, budget examiners and their staffs often seek clues from ministry officials about their own preferences and those of the corresponding LDP Policy Affairs Research Council division. Such priorities are nowhere included on budget request forms or their supplementary documentation, and indeed are almost never stated publicly, to prevent the proponents of programs not rated highly from learning of the slight. During the October and November period of full scale budget review, BB queries to the ministries often center on such points. The level of officialdom consulted depends on how broad a matter is in question. If ten public works projects of a certain type have been requested when funds are available for only five, a division or bureau chief may be able to indicate which five are preferred, and their choices will normally be respected by the BB unless some specific reason to the contrary appears (most commonly, it seems, when the project has been highly rated solely to satisfy political pressures on the ministry). For more general questions, relating to which major program of the ministry should grow more rapidly, the vice-minister or other ministry-level staff must be consulted (perhaps by the BB director or a vice-director).

The nature of these consultations varies considerably, all the way from the ministry in effect receiving a sum to allocate as it likes, to a subtly raised eyebrow or brief smile by a ministry official while explaining his

44. Cf. Wildavsky, *Politics,* esp. pp. 152-156.

budget that indicates to the examiner that a given request is not altogether serious. Indeed, ministry (and party) preferences may be a dominant factor in budget decisions even when no such consultation has taken place. Two BB officials mentioned in interviews that phrases often used in budget conferences by an examiner, explaining his recommendations to a superior, are "they probably will accept something like this," "they can put up with (*gaman*) that," or "this will go." When an examiner knows his ministry and its officials well enough, he is able to draw such conclusions entirely on his own.

*Nothing New.* — Finally, as a special case of these various aids to calculation, the handling of requests for new programs may be mentioned. The intellectual burdens of making such choices are always greater because the decisions cannot be incremental, and so at the stage of budget review the BB uses a radical simplifying device: it rejects virtually all of them. Some more or less plausible reason is usually found in each case. For example, a new activity is likely to have some relation to the programs of another ministry, in which case the MOF will say it "overlaps with existing organs"; or it may be proposed at once by several ministries, and be rejected because "the interests of the various ministries have not been coordinated." If the proposal contradicts some applicable public works, defense, or economic plan, it will be rejected almost automatically.[45] General rules against the proliferation of new administrative organs, government corporations and subsidies are often cited. The proposal to begin subsidies of private university personnel expenses in 1970 mentioned above was initially rejected by the MOF partly on the grounds that no recommendation from an appropriate advisory committee had been made ("discussions within the Ministry of Education are not complete"), and even constitutional issues were raised briefly.[46] However, reasons like these are not absolutely required — when none are apparent, the MOF will say simply that it does not have enough funds.

# Conclusions

In this chapter we have seen how Ministry of Finance budgeters approach their problems of complexity. The analyst of budgeting faces similar problems: so many factors seem to bear upon budget decisions that if he wishes to move from description to rigorous analysis, both sophisticated techniques and large quantitites of detailed and accurate data are

45. Cf. MNS, August 12, 1964; NKS, December 24, 1964; AS, February 17, 1967. Some cynics allege that these are the only times the MOF ever uses such plans.

46. AS, October 21, 1969; *Asahi Evening News,* November 6, 1969. Somewhat exceptionally, this program came to be approved before the MOF draft.

required. Neither resource was available in this research. However, the sample of fifty-three Ministry of Health and Welfare programs requested in 1970 (mentioned in the previous chapter) offers some tentative answers to a series of questions about how Budget Bureau officials decide on budgetary allocations.[47]

First of all, was the "nothing new" strategy actually used? Yes: of the eleven newly requested items in the sample, all but one were turned down at the MOF draft stage. Second, which of the two major pieces of information available—the amount of the 1969 budget or the 1970 request—is most relied upon by BB officials in writing the MOF draft? The answer, clearly, is the amount in the 1969 budget. Inspection of histograms reveals that for three-quarters of the forty-one cases for which we have needed data, the MOF draft figure is either somewhat below (eight cases), equal to (two cases) or no more than 25 percent above (seventeen cases) the 1969 budget figures. The amount requested in the summer does not seem to have a direct effect: percentage cuts from the request distribute almost evenly from 0 to 85 percent among continuing programs (and those will small cuts are those for which the percentage request was small—that is, those close to the 1969 budget). The simple correlation between the MOF draft and the 1969 budget is .9950, and between the summer request and the MOF draft a significantly lower .9287.[48]

Third, given that the Budget Bureau's calculations were based on the 1969 budget, how much did it offer? On the average, the amount of the current budget was raised about 23 percent in the MOF draft among the items which received raises. However, there was considerable variation in the percentage raises granted: the standard deviation here was 18 percentage points.

Fourth, what might explain this variation? To some extent the "strength" of the request (its percentage increase over the current budget) does have an effect at this secondary level. For example, the programs for which the Welfare Ministry had relatively modest expectations—defined as those for which a less-than-40-percent increase was demanded—were raised an average of only 8.4 percent over the current budget in the MOF draft. By contrast, the programs for which the ministry had great expectations, those with a more-than-40-percent requested increase, received an average 14.9 percent raise. Regression analysis provides another angle on this question: some 15 percent of the variation in the percentage rise over the current budget is statistically explained by the size of the request in percentage terms.

47. See chap. 2, n. 9.
48. These correlations and those reported below are based on a subsample of forty-eight cases selected by eliminating items larger than ¥10 billion in 1969, since these much larger datapoints tend to inflate all correlations. As commonly true of time series budget data, multicolinearity is very high, complicating analysis considerably.

While we should not draw sweeping conclusions from such a small and perhaps unrepresentative sample, we are comforted to learn that the inferences from available data which are possible are not inconsistent with the more impressionistic analysis above. It is unsurprising that nearly all new requests are rejected at this stage, that budget officials use the previous year's allocation as the base from which to calculate MOF draft amounts, and that in those calculations the strength of the ministry's request is taken into some account. It is also not surprising that the range of decisions made by examiners is quite broad and only in small measure can be explained by mechanical rules. That is, some 85 percent of the variation in the percentage raise (for this sample) is caused by other factors, presumably including differences in LDP pressure, informal ministry preferences, and the informed judgments of the budget examiner.

The importance of this last factor should not be taken lightly. On the one hand, clearly it is not true that, as Finance Ministry leaders in their more complacent moments have been heard to claim, in budgeting they "settle things by rationally and scientifically placing them in an order of preference."[49] This ideal of budgeting has been attained nowhere in the world, certainly not in Japan; the burdens of "rational" decision making are so great that simplifying devices of the sort described above are indispensable. On the other hand, Budget Bureau examiners are not mere paper-shufflers who produce budgets by adding and subtracting numbers in accordance with simple-minded rules of thumb. A great many quite real and quite difficult decisions are left after all these rules have been applied.

In the course of this research I had many conversations with Budget Bureau officials, and as well as recognizing their obvious talent and competence, I was impressed by the specialized knowledge of policy matters they had acquired. Moreover, it seemed to me that many exemplified the model of the "generalist" public official, combining a degree of idealism regarding the need for government action in the public interest with a mature sense for administrative and political feasibility, and most of all the difficult-to-determine quality of "balance." Examiners do discuss the substance of programs with line ministry officials. If they view a program as wasteful or misguided, they will suggest improvements or do their best to resist pressures for its adoption, but they will also work within the MOF to gain support for programs seen as having laudable ends and practical means. Both sides of the budgetary coin—the routinized workings of the system and the officials who find space within it for effective action—must be seen to understand the microbudgeting role of the Ministry of Finance Budget Bureau.

49. Vice-Minister Tanimura Hiroshi in the *Asahi Jaanaru* interview cited in n. 23 above.

# 4

# The Ministry of Finance: Macrobudgeting

WERE IT not for scarcity, budgets could be compiled solely from the bottom up, adding together the amounts each program or agency "needs" to reach a total budget figure. Unfortunately, there is never enough money to cover all these needs. Moreover, in the modern world government expenditures have come to play a crucial role in the regulation of the entire national economy. Hence "macrobudgeting" or top-down decisions on the size and perhaps the composition of the national budget are necessary. Macrobudgeting decisions take place in a different arena and under different rules than the microbudgeting process described above.[1] Over time, macrobudgeting has received increasing emphasis in Japan and the rules of the game have tended to change: while earlier, the essential budgeting problem was perceived as squeezing expenditures into a total determined by available tax revenues, today more complex economic considerations have come to the fore.

## Decision Making

When one first asks an MOF official how the size of the budget is decided, the process summarized in Chart 3 will be outlined. First, it is said, the Economic Planning Agency estimates the growth in Gross National Product for the following year, based on analyses of domestic and international economic conditions. The MOF then derives an estimate of

1. For accounts of macrobudgeting processes elsewhere, see Lawrence C. Pierce, *The Politics of Fiscal Policy Formation* (Pacific Palisades, Calif.: Goodyear Publishing, 1971), and Hugh Heclo and Aaron Wildavsky, *The Private Government of Public Money* (Berkeley and Los Angeles: University of California Press, 1974), pp. 171-181.

## CHART 3
### IDEALIZED MACROBUDGETING
### DECISION MAKING PROCESS

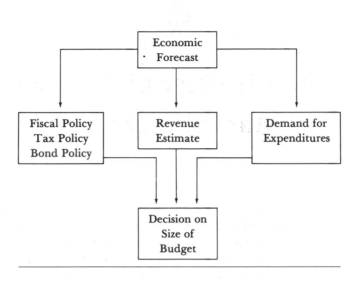

revenues at current tax rates from this figure. Tax rates are reduced in accordance with the long-range principle that the tax burden should not exceed 20 percent of national income. Consideration is given to the quantity of necessary expenditures. A decision is made on how fiscal policy should affect economic conditions in the following year, and the size of the bond issue (the budget deficit) is fixed keeping in mind the principle that the "bond-dependence ratio" should be reduced each year if possible. Therefore, the final number, the figure for the total size of the budget, emerges from a series of objective, technical, economic decisions. Such is the idealized macrobudgeting process in Japan.

In the real world, however, the process is neither so straightforward nor so objective. Each of these decisions is subject to various pressures and emerges only after complicated negotiations and adjustments.

*Forecasting Economic Growth.* —Budgeters must work from assumptions about the state of the economy in the coming year, both because tax revenues vary with the level of economic activity and in order to make intelligent decisions about whether the budget should stimulate or dampen the business cycle. Although estimates for specific economic sectors (business investment, housing, consumer spending) have received increased attention in Japan recently, the key index of interest is growth in GNP, officially estimated each year in the Economic Planning Agency's Economic Forecast (*Keizai Mitōshi*), which is reported to the Cabinet either just before or on the same day as the MOF draft budget. This document usually includes the following items, with estimates presented for both the current and following fiscal years: gross national product; real growth; nominal growth; private capital formation in plant and equipment, inventory, and housing; personal expenditure; the mining-manufacturing index; wholesale and retail price indices; balance of payments; exports, and imports. Notably absent are any figures for governmental finance, such as public investment or the government purchase of goods and services account. These figures clearly are required for an estimate of national income accounts, and thus must be used internally within the EPA, but they are not reported because pressure from the Ministry of Finance has prevented advance specification of any figures which might constrain budget decisions.

All these indicators, and particularly the GNP growth forecast itself, bear directly on the interests of institutions. The three most involved, because of their direct economic role and because they themselves share control of the EPA, are the MOF, the Ministry of International Trade and Industry, and the so-called "agency economists" of the EPA itself.[2] These three groups each have internally conflicting interests with regard to growth estimates. The "agency economists" are concerned with their professional reputations for accurate forecasting, which given the historical record provides an incentive for higher estimates, but the EPA's institutional goal of controlling inflation argues for lower estimates so as not to encourage business expectations. The typical interest of the Ministry of International Trade and Industry, in keeping with the "full speed ahead" ideology it maintained until recently, has been for higher growth estimates to encourage high industrial investment. On the other hand, in some situations it has pushed for lower growth rate forecasts, as when it wishes to raise its budgets for aid to small or medium industry, or more significantly when trying to "rationalize" and extend its control over some sector of industry (through a "depression cartel," requiring pessimism about production).

The Ministry of Finance traditionally has held out for lower growth forecasts, because it fears that if growth and therefore revenue estimates are high ministries will be encouraged to ask for more and more funds. However, if a growth rate is too low, it may not produce enough revenue to

2. For a good short account of the EPA power structure, see "Keikichō Tekunokuraato no Ishiki to Kōdō" ("Thought and Behavior of EPA Technocrats"), *Tōyō Keizai* (July 25, 1970), 31-35.

cover necessary expenditures, thus leading to pressures for deficit spending or to a budget that grows much faster than GNP and so appears too stimulatory.[3] In such cases the MOF may favor a higher estimate.

When all three participants are pursuing their "normal" goals, as has probably been true more often than not, MITI will be calling for the highest growth forecast, the MOF the lowest, and the "agency economists" (in early negotiations) somewhere in between; the final decision will lie between the positions of the MOF and EPA economists. But exceptions are frequent enough: in 1973, according to an MOF official interviewed in 1974, MITI urged a low forecast because it wished to introduce regulations to restrain oil consumption and it thought this plan would be workable only when the economic outlook was gloomy. The MOF, on the other hand, was faced with enormous obligatory expenditure increases and was concerned that the budget not *appear* inflationary in a time of rapidly rising prices; accordingly, it pressed for a higher economic growth figure than appeared realistic to economists.[4] Whatever the positions taken, the annual debate is carried out initially among the secretariat research divisions of each institution, as well as among their representatives within the EPA, and is often resolved by negotiations at the vice-ministerial or ministerial level.

Such institutional rivalries are not the only "political" influences on the growth forecast. At times it has been subject to foreign policy considerations — in 1962, Japan was attempting to secure a loan from the International Monetary Fund to cover a balance of payments deficit, and the EPA's forecast was dropped from an anticipated 6.4 percent to 5.4 percent in less than a month. Asked why, EPA Director-General Fujiyama Aiichiro replied "it is important that we be in a position to gain the approval of the IMF for Japan's fiscal situation"; in other words, to make it appear that growth, and inflation would slow, even though underlying economic policies changed not a bit.[5] Prime ministers have also been known to interfere. Anticipating political difficulties, EPA economists were quoted before the 1972 LDP presidential election that if conservative Fukuda Takeo won (and therefore became prime minister), the growth rate for 1973 would be forecast at 8 percent, but if expansionist Tanaka were successful 10 percent would be required.[6] In 1974, three draft forecasts were written at the working levels, and the prime minister,

3. Early in the 1963 budget process, MOF economists thought that growth would be around 5 percent, but the ministry argued for an 8 percent rate to forestall LDP demands for issuing deficit bonds. NKS, August 25, 1962, evening.

4. The result — a forecast of 12.9 percent nominal growth for fiscal 1974 — turned out to be higher than actual performance.

5. AS, December 5, 1961, evening.

6. NKS, July 10, 1972. Tanaka won, and the forecast was 10.7 percent.

finance minister and LDP Policy Affairs Research Council chairman met to choose among them.[7]

These examples indicate that even though the economic forecast is presented every year, with considerable fanfare, as the product of impartial and expert economic analysis, it actually results from the complicated interplay of political and institutional interests. If this is the case, how can such an "irrational" figure become the basis for rational budgetary decision making, as in estimating governmental revenues? The answer, in brief, is that it cannot.

*Revenue Estimating.* —Even leaving political considerations aside, the Economic Planning Agency's official economic forecast cannot determine MOF revenue estimates because it comes too late, at the time when all the important fiscal decisions have already been made. The MOF actually begins its revenue forecasting in the summer, as a component of its first trial estimate of the entire budget. However, the figures produced at this stage are guesses based on extrapolation of trends rather than calculations from detailed data. The real revenue estimation process begins in the early fall. Three sorts of information are required: economic forecasts, accumulated experience, and up-to-date details of current economic performance in various sectors and its effect on actual collections.

The economic forecasts come from the Research and Planning Division of the MOF's own Secretariat. This body keeps in touch with those doing parallel research in the Economic Planning Agency and elsewhere, but its estimates, which are not made public, often differ.[8] MOF economic forecasts depend heavily on the corporate reports on the first half of the fiscal year (April-September), which are quite volatile, so much of the research is concentrated in November when these materials become available.

The Japanese ability to translate economic growth figures into revenue estimates has been celebrated by outsiders. Correspondents from the British *Economist*, who wrote admiringly of the Japanese fiscal system in 1962, saw the MOF reckoning that

for every 0.1 per cent of the agreed target rate for growth in national income the Japanese reckon that they can expect a stated amount of extra tax revenue on the basis of existing tax rates. Thus with a target growth rate of 5.4 per cent in the fiscal year 1962, they reckoned on nearly ¥500 million in extra revenue; and by the rules of the budget balancing act precisely that sum—together with the

7. NKS, December 14, 1973.
8. Hayashi Yoshio, *Zaiseiron* ("Public Finance") (Tokyo: Chikuma Shobō, 1968), p. 140. However, the MOF and EPA figures cannot be so out of line that the MOF's revenue estimate becomes incongruous with the official forecast.

surplus of tax revenue carried over from the previous year—is then assumed to be available for deliberate increases in government expenditure or for new tax reliefs.[9]

While not completely unperceptive, this account is somewhat misleading, in that the "stated amount of extra tax revenue" that can be expected from each point of economic growth actually varies a good deal from year to year: "tax revenue elasticity" (*zeishū danseichi*) averaged 1.33 from 1959 to 1968, but varied widely between extremes of 0.89 and 1.74 during that period.[10] Thus the calculation of additional revenue from economic growth figures is not an automatic application of a rule of thumb, but requires exhaustive research into each tax category. This function is performed primarily by the Tax Bureau in the MOF, while nontax revenues are estimated by the Budget Bureau.[11] The EPA does not participate in revenue estimating. The complications of the research required, and the MOF monopoly over this function, mean that no other participant can credibly challenge Finance's revenue figures.[12]

On the other hand, the process is not necessarily completely technical and objective. Indeed, the very complications and economic uncertainties of revenue estimating allow many opportunities for political considerations to be inserted. Though participants outside the Finance Ministry lack sufficient information for effective intervention, the amount of the revenue forecast has often been subject to organizational debate within the MOF itself. The Tax Bureau tends to give lower estimates than thought desirable by the Budget Bureau, and the National Tax Administration Agency, responsible for actually collecting taxes, is usually most conservative of all. Since deficit financing began in 1965, the Financial Bureau and Banking Bureau have also entered into this decision, trying to keep the bond issue as low as possible. As well as organizational interests, strategic considerations are also taken into account by the MOF leadership—for example, in the early 1960s, the MOF estimated revenues higher than it would normally think prudent in order to satisfy strong LDP spending pressures which otherwise, it was feared, might be transformed into demands for deficit financing.[13] At such times, it is announced with some fanfare that

9. The articles were published as a book: *Economist Correspondents Consider Japan* (London: Gerald Duckworth & Co., 1963), pp. 32-33.

10. *Fainansu* 3, 7 (October 1967), 9; Nihon Keizai Shinbunsha, ed., *Yosan wa Dare no Mono ka* ("The Budget: Whose is it?") (Tokyo: Nihon Keizai Shinbunsha, 1971), pp. 80-83; for estimates, Joseph Pechman and Keimei Kaizuka, "Taxation," in *Asia's New Giant: How the Japanese Economy Works,* eds. Hugh Patrick and Henry Rosovsky (Washington, D. C.: The Brookings Institution, 1976), p. 347.

11. For details, see Hayashi, *Zaiseiron,* pp. 133-142.

12. Cf. Nihon Keizai Shinbunsha, ed., *Yosan wa Dare no Mono ka,* pp. 81-83.

13. According to a former Tax Bureau official interviewed in 1968, his bureau had been forced by the Budget Bureau to raise its pessimistic forecasts in October 1964, so that expenditures would not have to be cut to the point of stimulating demands for bonds. That time, revenues did not run ahead of forecasts, and a fiscal crisis resulted.

the MOF is making a "full" estimate of revenues, although in other more normal years, an admission that the estimate is less than full is never heard. In general, the MOF is widely reputed to deliberately underestimate revenues — a pattern which may be common to all budgeting authorities.[14]

*Taxes and Bonds.* — In Japanese macrobudgeting, the most common decision sequence has been to determine the amount of the tax cut after the "natural" increase in revenues has been calculated. Exceptionally, in the late 1950s tax cuts themselves were the focus of political slogans from early in the process ("¥ 100 billion tax cut, ¥ 100 billion for programs" in 1957; "¥ 80 billion tax cut and the establishment of a national pension" in 1959). More often, the initiative on the size and composition of the annual tax cut is taken by the Tax Bureau, working through its advisory organ, the Tax System Investigatory Commission (*Zeisei Chōsakai*), although the BB and the MOF leadership also have a voice. As noted, the long-range principle in force for virtually the entire postwar era has been to maintain the governmental share (all levels) of national income at about 20 percent. This stricture was violated by the enormous Tanaka era budgets of 1972-73, when the ratio rose as high as 20.7 percent, but the figure fell again to 19.9 percent (estimated) in 1974.[15] Both the size and the composition of the tax cut varies from year to year, to meet short-run policy objectives such as relieving the burdens of the middle class, or encouraging industrial investment or exports.

Tax policy, of course, is a highly political issue in most countries, and in Japan all political parties and many interest groups frequently call for large cuts in the taxes affecting their constituencies. There have been two chief exceptions. One is the groups representing local governments, who oppose any tax changes that would reduce either the taxes collected locally or those redistributed by the national government under the local allocation formula. The other, interestingly enough, is the LDP. While the ruling party too has often demanded tax relief, usually for middle income groups and sometimes special constituencies of voters, it has not infrequently argued in the opposite direction. This peculiar pattern has been particularly evident near elections or at other times when political pressures are high. Examples can be found (for the 1957, 1958, 1961 and 1962 budgets) of the MOF either reducing or eliminating an anticipated tax cut under LDP pressure, and in one case the gasoline tax was actually raised.[16] In the 1971 budget, strong pressures from LDP Dietmen interested in increasing highway and railroad construction expenditures

14. See Donald Gerwin, "Toward a Theory of Public Budgetary Decision Making," *Administrative Science Quarterly* (March 1969), 35.
15. Estimated figures for post-supplement budgets, from Pechman and Kaizuka, "Taxation," p. 324.
16. NKS, November 16, 1956, January 14, 1958, and December 15, 1961; AS, January 19, 1961, evening, and December 7, 1961.

forced a new automobile tax over the extreme objections of the Ministry of
Finance.[17] Such behavior, which reverses Anthony Downs' proposition that
political parties will press for lower than optimum public spending because
benefits of programs are less tangible than taxes, indicates that the LDP
tends to be more concerned with having sufficient funds to expand
programs aimed at specific clientele groups than with the reactions of
citizens en masse.[18]

   Before 1966, the process described above was sufficient to determine
the total size of the budget, but in 1965 (in a Supplementary Budget) and
then from the initial budget of 1966, part of governmental expenditures
came to be financed through deficit bonds. As we will see in chapter 9, the
avoidance of deficit financing had long been a major Finance Ministry
objective, shaping many of its strategies, until the change in policy had
been forced by a revenue crisis. However, once accomplished, this change
was fully accepted by the MOF and the rest of the budget system — no one
called for eliminating bonds after the crisis had passed. The MOF merely
tried to establish a ceiling and enunciated a policy of each year reducing
the "bond dependence ratio," the proportion of the budget financed by
bonds: Finance Minister Fukuda, in 1966, announced that this ratio (then
at 16.9 percent) should be reduced to 14-15 percent by 1971, and 10
percent in 1976.[19] The MOF succeeded in overfulfilling this plan, reducing
the ratio (and even the absolute amount of deficit financing) after 1967
down to 4.5 percent in the initial 1971 budget. However, the enormous
1971 Supplementary Budget, passed in a time of economic slowdown,
pushed the bond dependence ratio back up to 11.9 percent, and it rose
further to 15.2 percent in 1972 before declining again to 11.9 and then
12.6 percent in 1973-74.[20] The decision on the size of the annual bond issue
is made late in the budget process, simultaneously with final determination
of the tax cut.

   *Fiscal Policy.* — If these are the mechanisms for making macrobudgeting decisions, what is the content of those decisions? What objectives have
been pursued by the Ministry of Finance? This book is not a work on public
finance, and a lengthy discussion of the role of the government in the

   17. Journalists said the MOF believed the tax was premature, in that considerable time
would be required to gain approval from carowners. Nihon Keizai Shinbunsha, ed, *Yosan wa
Dare no Mono ka,* p. 110.
   18. Cf. Anthony Downs, "Why the Government Budget is Too Small in a Democracy,"
*World Politics* 12 (1960), 541-563.
   19. AS, October 27, 1966.
   20. Newspaper accounts and Japan, Ministry of Finance, Budget Bureau, Research
Division, *Zaisei Tōkei* ("Fiscal Statistics") (Tokyo: Ministry of Finance Printing Bureau), 1974
ed., p. 14. The 1971-72 figures are from the Audit; 1973, post-Supplement; 1974, initial
budget. In most years the actual amount of bonds issued is lowered during execution of the
budget.

national economy would not be appropriate.[21] However, the considerations which bear on MOF decisions, the criteria it takes into account in determining the size and broad composition of the budget, are directly relevant to our concerns. In particular, we are interested in the rules or guidelines provided by fiscal policy that govern yearly budgetary decisions.

It has sometimes been maintained that Japan has really had no fiscal policy. The 1970 OECD economic survey of Japan reported that "Japan's experience with a conscious and active use of fiscal policy is relatively recent. Until the 1965 recession, demand management had relied almost exclusively on monetary instruments."[22] This remark refers to Japan avoiding deficit finance until that time, but is also true in the sense that the fiscal considerations which American and European governments take into account in making budget decisions had not been important in the Japanese process. The first factor changed in 1965; the second, by and large, did not:

. . . in view of the weak response of the economy to monetary relaxation in 1965, the authorities resorted progressively to reflationary budget policies: intentional "deficit spending," speeding up of public works, and tax cuts. However, since full employment levels have been restored, the main aim was to keep the effects of public finance neutral with the burden of arresting inflationary tendencies again failling primarily on monetary policies.[23]

That is, considerations of fiscal policy, as it is construed in the United States and elsewhere, have not ordinarily played an important part in the yearly process of budget making. Although "the availability and quality of basic economic statistics are generally good in Japan," the OECD Survey points out that "there seems to be a lack of some requirements, useful for the formulation of efficient fiscal policy and for adequate budget analysis."[24] The decision makers do not even have the data to make fiscal decisions—with Japan's sophisticated statisticians, this lacuna is clearly because they do not perceive a need for them. In fact, the EPA does prepare estimates that bear on these matters, but they are neither published nor used in budgeting. When the American budget is announced by the president, newspaper headlines concentrate on the estimated surplus or deficit in the national government cash account. The corresponding estimate is not mentioned at all in even the most detailed newspaper coverage of the Japanese budget, and indeed considerable searching is required to find even after-the-fact figures for earlier years.

21. See Gardner Ackley and Hiromitsu Ishi, "Fiscal, Monetary and Related Policies," *New Giant*, eds. Patrick and Rosovsky, pp. 153-247.
22. Organization for Economic Cooperation and Development, *Japan* (OECD Economic Surveys), July 1970, p. 53.
23. *Ibid.*
24. *Ibid.*, p. 55.

Asked about such criticisms, Ministry of Finance spokesmen have sometimes replied — a bit testily — that Japan indeed has a fiscal policy but that its objectives are different, and rather more worthwhile. In a 1970 interview, one of the ministry's leading financial experts noted first that monetary policy has proven more effective and certainly quicker to apply than fiscal policy for short-term demand management, and went on to say that

fiscal policy is more related to longer-term considerations. . . . I think our economists are better, in the sense that they have grasped the real issue. The most important point is the size of government expenditures, determined primarily by the size of the budget; this is the "government demand" element of GNP. . . . Many say our fiscal policy is very conservative, doesn't have enough imagination and so forth, but I think it is very sound because . . . it has been used to promote growth over a long period.

While this argument probably has merit, more to the present point is, what are the implications of this conception of fiscal policy for yearly budgeting decisions? That establishing a set of relatively clear-cut decision rules is an important function of fiscal policy is emphasized by Jesse Burkhead, who characterizes the classic "balanced budget" rule of earlier American budgeting as providing

an easily understood rule to guide the transfer of resources from the private to the public sector. . . . there is no doubt that budget-balancing, particularly annual budget-balancing, has a definite and precise character which is lacking in any other available guide to fiscal policy. . . . Moreover, budget-balancing is a practical guide for policy-making officials, who can roughly gauge the amount of taxation which the community can stand and then trim expenditures to fit the revenue.[25]

The Japanese too held to the balanced budget until 1965, but in a rapidly growing economy, and with the flexibility of revenue forecasting described above, this principle did not provide decision-making rules of the clarity indicated by Burkhead. The "20 percent rule" of governmental expenditures within national income, and the principle of reducing the "bond dependence ratio" to some posited ideal level, may be seen as additional simplifiers or reducers of decision-making costs in this same sense (as well as dikes against pressure for spending). However, another rule is still more important. It holds that the most important effect of the budget on economic conditions stems from the relationship of budget growth to economic growth. Precisely, the annual budget is held to be fiscally neutral if it grows at the same rate as estimated GNP. If its growth

25. Jesse Burkhead, *Government Budgeting* (New York: John Wiley and Sons, 1965), p. 450.

rate is lower than GNP, it is called deflationary or restrictive. A growth rate higher than GNP means the budget is stimulatory.

The economic justification for this criterion, which received extensive MOF-generated publicity particularly in the 1960s, does not seem to lie in the same theoretical area as Keynsian thinking on public finance, which stresses the impact of governmental deficits or surpluses on the utilization of productive resources.[26] The revenue side is not taken into account in this decision-making rule, which implies instead either that a larger government sector in the economy increases economic activity, or that, more dynamically, an expansion in the government sector from one level to another will stimulate the economy in the short run no matter how it is financed.

Regardless of whether or not this hypothesis is correct in terms of economic theory, such guidelines may still be an effective tool of economic regulation. This is because, as Hugh Patrick points out,

> government tax and expenditure policy can affect the level of private spending both directly and indirectly. In addition to the direct multiplier effect on total aggregate demand, the indirect effect in Japan on private, and especially business, expectations is also quite strong. Changes in the amount of tax cuts, government general account expenditures, and the government investment and loan program are the three main indicators to which business expectations respond.[27]

Specifically, perhaps due to the MOF's annual publicity campaign, it appeared that businessmen react most to the budget-GNP growth relationship. If, in response to a policy the government calls "restrictive," businessmen cut back on investment plans, or if they step up their plans after a "stimulatory" policy is announced, the resultant effect on the economy might well be that called for even if there were no direct economic impact of the policy whatsoever.

There is evidence that the MOF takes these indirect effects rather more seriously than it does the budget-GNP growth comparison itself. Particularly in the late 1960s it often manipulated definitions in order to show a budget as "neutral" when it would actually appear to be stimulatory under the usual formula. In both 1968 and 1969, when attempts were being made to eliminate supplementary budgets, the final, post-Supplementary Budget, instead of the more usual initial budget, was taken as the basis for the growth calculation. Then for the 1970 budget, when the forecast growth in nominal GNP was 15.8 percent and the General

26. For a brief nontechnical account of the development of public finance theory, see *ibid.*, chap. 17.

27. Hugh Patrick, "Cyclical Instability and Fiscal-Monetary Policy in Postwar Japan," in *The State and Economic Enterprise in Japan,* ed. William W. Lockwood (Princeton, N.J.: Princeton University Press, 1965), p. 598.

Account was set to grow by 17.95 percent, the MOF argued that total spending minus the allocation going to local governments was a more valid measure, and that since this was to rise only 15.7 percent (and moreover government purchases of goods and services in the national General Account would grow less than 15 percent), the budget was actually restrictive in effect. This logic is not persuasive, and the intent of such arguments clearly lies more in public relations than substance.

The MOF has also gone beyond mere verbal devices in its efforts to convince business that budgets are not inflationary. On many occasions, budget accounting formats have been adjusted to this end. For example, the Japanese financial system includes over forty Special Accounts, established for reasons of efficiency and convenience, which often combine revenues from fees or other miscellaneous sources with contributions from the General Account.[28] This means that if certain functions can be switched from the General Account to a Special Account (perhaps newly created), its miscellaneous revenues will no longer be counted as part of general revenues, and only the portion of the Special Account covered by tax revenues is included in the expenditure totals used in figuring the budget-GNP growth comparison. There are several cases where the creation of Special Accounts has had this effect, perhaps simply as a byproduct; they include changes in the handling of national schools and car registration in 1964, and of the coal industry in 1967. In at least two cases, however, it appears that the impact on the budget-GNP growth comparison was the sole or major motive. For the 1968 budget, moving ¥14.1 billion in revenues from the General Account into the National Hospitals Special Account brought the budget growth rate (figured from the 1967 post-Supplementary Budget) from 12.1 to 11.8 percent—forecast GNP growth was 12.1 percent, so this allowed the MOF to call the budget "restrictive." In the following year, the functions of the National Property Special Consolidation Fund were enlarged to include ¥5 billion that previously had been included in the General Account. This brought total expenditures down sufficiently to make the budget growth rate equal 14.4 percent, precisely the same as the GNP growth estimate and therefore "neutral."[29] These adjustments, clearly, have no economic effect beyond the psychological, since only governmental bookkeeping practices, not real public sector revenues or expenditures, have been modified. This point indicates that the MOF (in the late 1960s) did not itself feel constrained to stay within the GNP growth guideline in determining the total size of the budget, but thought it important that others, particularly businessmen, get the impression that the old standards were inviolate.[30]

28. See chap. 8.

29. Respectively, NKS, January 1, 1968, and AS, January 7, 1969.

30. Readers familiar with the American budgetary record will recall similar efforts to maintain a fictional balanced budget. See, e.g., the *Business Week* article, "$40 Billion the

The use of the budget-GNP growth comparison as the major indicator of the economic effects of the budget began in the accelerated growth years of the early 1960s, as a more dynamic criterion for macrobudgeting decisions than simply holding down expenditures to match revenues. Budgets could be characterized as neutral or only moderately stimulative even when they were expanded enormously. However, the original formulation became more difficult to apply after deficit financing was begun: so long as taxes made up nearly all budget revenues, and the tax burden was held approximately constant by adjusting the rates every year, budgets naturally grew at about the same rate as the economy. From 1966, however, bond sales were added on top of tax revenues, which continued at just under 20 percent of national income, and budgets accordingly grew more quickly than GNP. But the MOF was reluctant to give up its benchmark, and so was forced to resort to the new justifications and gimmicks described above. As these became more tortured, the formulation itself apparently was seen as less useful, and so received much less publicity in the early 1970s.

American budgeters have sometimes tried to replace the outmoded balanced budget ideology with the "full employment budget" concept, invoked to throw a cloak of respectability over large budgets (and perhaps to provide some decisional guidelines). Japan to date has been unable to develop a successor to the budget-GNP growth comparison. The 1972 budget was avowedly stimulatory, and so presented no problems of justification, but Tanaka's record breaking 1973 budget (up 24.6 percent) actually came on an economic upswing, a time of strong inflationary pressures, and left MOF spokesmen on the defensive. Toward the end of the process Finance Minister Aichi Kiichi indicated that the MOF had held the totals down "as much as possible" and therefore the budget was not really inflationary.[31] Aichi's statements were not accorded much credibility, but in the following year, Fukuda Takeo's appointment as finance minister in the midst of the oil crisis was followed by an all-out cost-cutting campaign; his claim that the resulting 1974 budget was sharply restrictive was accepted by both political and business circles, despite the fact that, at 19.7 percent, budget growth was well ahead of the projected GNP nominal growth rate of 12.9 percent.

In fact, whatever its aggregate effect on the economy, the 1974 budget did display a more selective use of fiscal policy tools than had been evident in the past. Public works expenditures—normally about one-fifth of the budget, and the most directly stimulative category—were unprecedently held to zero growth, which in such inflationary times meant a sizable real

Budget Leaves Out," reprinted in *Politics, Programs and Budgets: A Reader in Governmental Budgeting,* ed. James W. Davis, Jr. (Englewood Cliffs, N.J.: Prentice-Hall, 1969), pp. 16-18.

31. E.g., NKS, January 8, evening, and 10, evening, 1973.

cut. Still, whether or not the MOF maintained this pattern of applying fiscal instruments more flexibly to the tasks of economic management, the need for some understandable rule of thumb to allow judgments on an appropriate size for the total budget will continue to be felt, and recent pleas that a budget is restrictive because everyone tried as hard as he could are likely to be found inadequate.

*Expenditure Estimates.* —Having examined the revenue side and economic policy considerations, there remains one component of the decision on total size: how much has to be spent? Much of the answer, of course, must come from microbudgeting, the detailed analysis of each government program. But these results come late; some tentative macro-budgeting estimates are needed early in the process to guide Budget Bureau leaders (to establish the MOF's "attitude," as budgeters put it), so they can properly react to proposals from examiners. This process, called the "first expenditure estimate" (*daiichiji suikei*) takes place over two months beginning in June, and is based completely on projections of past trends plus more or less intelligent guesses about changes. The spending ministries are not consulted at all; the process is entirely contained within the Budget Bureau.

The calculation begins by taking the budget of the previous year essentially for granted. Then, the "natural expenditure increase" (*tozenzo keihi*) is added—this is the amount of additional expenditure required by law or contract. It is distinguished from "policy expenditures" (*seisakuhi*), the term for spending which is formally within budgetary discretion. A table used by the MOF in the summer of 1969, translated as Table 4, indicates how the MOF views this calculation.

In this table, the 9210 figure on the "total" line represents the difference between the 1969 and 1968 General Account budget, and the 15.8 percent growth figure just below is the growth rate of the budget for 1969. Of this, 12.0 percentage points represent "natural," unavoidable increases, and only 3.8 percentage points, ¥225.6 billion (or about three-quarters of a billion dollars), were available for all new programs or discretionary increases in old programs. (These figures, however, are distorted by the "borrowing" of ¥69 billion by the MOF from the Local Allocation Tax account, a sum which was then applied to "policy" expenditures.) The MOF gave this table some publicity to underline its difficulties with fixed expenditures; the 1970 budget would have to grow by 13.6 percent, it said, even if no new funds whatsoever were allocated.

The most oppressive fact of life for Japanese budgeters is that these "natural expenditure increases," over the long term, have tended to expand more rapidly than have revenues. Table 5 shows the actual or estimated increase in fixed expenditures as a percentage of the total

TABLE 4
"NATURAL" AND "POLICY" INCREASES
(Units: 100 Million Yen; Percent)

| Category | | 1968 to 1969 | | 1969 to 1970 |
| | Natural | Policy | Total | Natural (Est.) |
|---|---|---|---|---|
| **General Section** | | | | |
| National Debt | 776 | 0 | 776 | 500 |
| Local Allocation | 3100 | – 690 | 2410 | 4000 |
| Foodstuffs Control | | | | |
|   Special Account | 0 | 537 | 537 | 0 |
| Salaries | 1140 | 435 | 1575 | 1630 |
| Other | 1492 | 480 | 1972 | 2020 |
|   Subtotal | 6508 | 762 | 7270 | 8150 |
| Percentage of Previous | | | | |
| Year's Total Budget | 11.2 | 1.3 | 12.5 | 12.1 |
| **Investment Section** | | | | |
| Public Works | 397 | 960 | 1357 | 940 |
| Other Facilities | 17 | 73 | 90 | 20 |
| Disbursements | 32 | 461 | 493 | 30 |
|   Subtotal | 446 | 1494 | 1940 | 990 |
| Percentage of Previous | | | | |
| Year's Total Budget | 0.8 | 2.5 | 3.3 | 1.5 |
| Total | 6954 | 2256 | 9210 | 9140 |
| Percentage of Previous | | | | |
| Year's Total Budget | 12.0 | 3.8 | 15.8 | 13.6 |

SOURCE: Report to the Zaisei Seido Shingikai by the Ministry of Finance, September 24, 1969. Printed in NKS, September 25, 1969.

expenditure growth for the years 1964-1974; in Column D the amount left over for "policy" expenditures is listed. The great growth in fixed expenditures in 1968 was the incentive for the MOF's "break fiscal rigidification movement" in that year.[32]

However, "policy" expenditures does not mean that the entire amount is available for new programs. The MOF sometimes uses the term "semi-natural increases" for new expenditures in areas like public works which are not legally required, but realistically have to be made. For 1969, this

32. See chap. 9. It seems possible that the figure for fixed expenditures in that year was somewhat inflated since it was released as part of a public relations campaign, although the calculations appear quite straightforward.

## TABLE 5
### GROWTH OF FIXED EXPENDITURES
(Units: 100 Million Yen; Percent)

| Budget Year | A<br>Total Increase in Budget | B<br>Natural Expenditure Increase | C<br>B/A (%) | D<br>"Policy" Expenditures ( = A − B) |
|---|---|---|---|---|
| 1964 | 4054 | 1793 | 55.8 | 2261 |
| 1965 | 4027 | 2155 | 53.5 | 1872 |
| 1966 | 6562 | 2406 | 36.7 | 4156 |
| 1967 | 6366 | 3709 | 58.3 | 2657 |
| 1968 | 8677 | 6781 | 78.1 | 1896 |
| 1969 | 9210 | 6954 | 75.5 | 2256 |
| 1970 | 12102 | 9140[a] | 76.0 | 2962 |
| 1971 | 14646 | 10300[a] | 70.0 | 4346 |
| 1972 | 20534 | 13900[b] | 68.0 | 6634 |
| 1973 | 28164 | 17500[a] | 62.0 | 10664 |
| 1974 | 28153 | 22000[a] | 78.0 | 6153 |

NOTES: [a]Estimates made during budget process.
[b]This estimate is inferred indirectly and may not be accurate.

SOURCES: Column A: *Zaisei Tōkei*, 1974, pp. 194-203 (initial budgets). Column B: 1964-68—Watari Akira, "Tenkanki ni tatsu Zaisei" ("Public Finance in a Period of Conversion"), *Fainansu* 3, 7 (October 1967), 12; 1969-70—NKS, September 25, 1969; 1971—NKS, September 23, 1970; 1972—AS, November 9, 1971; 1973—NKS, December 9, 1972; 1974—NKS, September 1, 1973.

category was estimated at ¥170-180 billion, meaning that the total of the two categories for that year amounted to over ¥870 billion. Finally, guesses are made about what other new expenditures will be required. Examiners and their staffs are responsible for these, and their information comes from general knowledge, newspaper articles about ministry intentions, existing long-term expenditure plans and, again, simple projections of past trends; actual budget requests from the spending ministries are not received until later, and ministry officials are not consulted in this process either formally or informally.

Two sorts of information are generated here. One is the agency by agency (or Important Item by Important Item) breakdown of projected expenditures, providing initial guesses for each that might be used later in the microbudgeting process.[33] The other, the sum of all these, is a

33. It has been claimed that these estimates usually turn out to resemble the final draft of the budget very closely, and moreover that investigators (assistant examiners) are rated on the basis of their predictive ability—if the estimates are off, superiors will think they have

short-term expenditure projection for the entire budget, which is compared with revenues estimates to estimate the "budgetary gap." All of these estimates are kept very secret: if spending ministries come to know the amounts forecast for them, they could regard these as an assured floor and throw their energies into raising them; similarly, a high figure for the total budget would encourage the LDP to try to get even more for favored projects. If it thought the results were to become public, the MOF would inevitably distort its analysis to suit the strategic needs of the moment, and the procedure would become useless as a basis for real planning.

Such secrecy has made reliable information on these "first expenditure estimates" difficult to come by, but according to interviewed MOF officials, its practice began in the 1950s, and in the early 1960s projected revenues and expenditures were generally in balance and also turned out to be fairly accurate in the aggregate. Later in the decade, however, the "gap" widened. One official recalled that in 1970, the estimated rise in expenditures over 1969 was about ¥1.5 trillion, leaving a gap of nearly ¥300 billion (about $1 billion) over anticipated new revenues. Such an outcome will alert decision makers that difficult choices are required before final macrobudgeting decisions can be made. A similar process using much harder data, the "second expenditure estimate meetings," takes place in early November.

*Deciding the Size of the Budget.* — The "ideal model" which began this discussion of macrobudgeting conveys an impression that the total budget figure is the mechanical result of several technical estimating procedures. We have seen in the preceding sections that several of these component procedures are less objective and more political than purported, and so their results could hardly be aggregated into a "rational" final decision. But even if this were not so, even if correct and noncontroversial information were available on all these points, picking the number would still not be easy. For one thing, the policy implications of one component might contradict those of another — a common example is in an economic boom, when revenue forecasts will be high while fiscal policy will call for moderation. For another, many value choices will remain; a high or low budget will favor some participants and interested outsiders and thwart others. The Ministry of Finance is thus faced with a complex decision in both intellectual and political terms.

Readers of the literature on decision making will be able to predict the behavior of the MOF in this uncertain and difficult environment.[34] Instead

---

"poor judgment." Asahi Shinbun Keizaibu, *Keizai Seisaku no Butaiura* ("Economic Policy Behind the Scenes") (Tokyo: Asahi Shinbunsha, 1974), p. 70. This account appears exaggerated to me.

34. Most notably, see David Braybrooke and Charles E. Lindblom, *A Strategy of Decision* (New York: The Free Press, 1963).

of attempting to make a once-and-for-all decision at the very end of the budgetary process, it begins each process with a very tentative judgment on the size of the budget, and modifies it progressively in response to new information, reactions from other participants, and changing strategic calculations.

The MOF's first guess about the size of the coming budget is leaked to the press, in a rather offhand manner, in July or August. Most often the figure itself is accompanied by no details or justifications — feedback is desired, but not specific debates — as simply a tentative, target ceiling based on fiscal and revenue considerations (with data supplied by planning divisions in the Budget and Tax Bureaus and the Secretariat). In reality, however, rather more assumptions have to be built into this estimate for it to be realistic. Pressure from the natural expenditure increase does vary, some tax cut will occur, the level of the bond issue will probably not be the same as in the current year; all these will be factors in the final decision on the final budget. Still, rather than taking such factors into account systematically, it appears that the MOF leadership depends more on a shrewd assessment of what the market will bear; of what number, based on past experience, will be high enough not to arouse anger and possibly retailiation from politicians (and not to appear ridiculous later on, thereby throwing the ministry's acumen into doubt), but low enough to satisfy the MOF's objective of keeping expenditures as low as possible. Enough margin for upward revision in response to pressure must always be left.

Table 6 compares these early guesses with final budget totals (that is, the budget as approved by the Cabinet, before supplements later in the year) for the 1954-1974 period. The first observation to be made is that with few exceptions the MOF has "underestimated" the final budget. The second is that the "error," particularly in recent years, generally runs under 4 percent and sometimes less. In explaining such "success," one must disregard the possibility that the MOF is unusually good at economic analysis — even if more elaborate estimating procedures were followed, the necessary data are simply not available so soon. Rather, the two main possibilities are these: that the ministry has so much power in the budgeting process that, once having made up its mind, it will carry its preference against all opposition; or that the MOF is unusually good at *political* analysis, and is able to weigh the pressures incurred in macro-budgeting each year with considerable accuracy.[35] Both explanations have merit, though the latter appears closer to reality at least for the more recent years. Of course, while small in percentage terms, 2 percent of the

---

35. However, the good guess of 1974 is really a bad guess: the MOF expected a higher budget in the summer but reversed its field late in the process. Similar if not as dramatic events have occurred in other years as well; see chap. 9.

TABLE 6
MINISTRY OF FINANCE SUMMER BUDGET ESTIMATES
(Units: Trillion Yen; Percent)

| Budget Year | Date of Estimate | Estimate | Budget (Government Draft) | Percentage of Error |
|---|---|---|---|---|
| 1954 | August 12 | 1.0 | 0.9950[a] | – 0.005 |
| 1955 | June 21 | 0.99 | 0.9996[a] | 0.1 |
| 1956 | July 6 | 1.04 | 1.0349 | – 0.005 |
| 1957 | July 22 | 1.1 | 1.1375 | 3.4 |
| 1958 | August 24 | 1.2 | 1.3121 | 9.3 |
| 1959[b] | — | — | 1.4192 | — |
| 1960 | August 21 | 1.45 | 1.5696 | 8.3 |
| 1961 | July 4 | 1.8 | 1.9528 | 8.5 |
| 1962 | July 22 | 2.2 | 2.4268 | 10.3 |
| 1963 | July 23 | 2.75 | 2.8500 | 3.6 |
| 1964 | July 14 | 3.15 | 3.2554 | 3.4 |
| 1965 | July 12 | 3.6 | 3.6581 | 1.6 |
| 1966 | August 14 | 4.0 | 4.3142 | 7.9 |
| 1967 | August 29 | 4.9 | 4.9509 | 1.0 |
| 1968 | July 28 | 5.6 | 5.8185 | 3.9 |
| 1969 | August 13 | 6.5 | 6.7395 | 3.7 |
| 1970 | August 3 | 7.7 | 7.9498 | 3.2 |
| 1971 | July 20 | 9.2 | 9.4143 | 2.3 |
| 1972[c] | September 1 | 11.3 | 11.4705[a] | 1.5 |
| 1973 | August 21 | 14.0 | 14.2840 | 2.0 |
| 1974 | August 10 | 17.14 | 17.0994 | – 0.002 |

NOTES: [a]Later modified slightly in the Diet.
[b]None found.
[c]Earliest announcement found, except for a general statement "above 11 trillion yen" by the finance minister on July 26.

SOURCE: Newspaper articles on the date indicated or one day later, in the year previous to the budget year.

1973 budget still amounts to nearly a billion dollars, and as a portion of nonobligatory budget expenditures such percentages are quite significant.

As budgeting progresses during the fall, new economic information is received, and political pressure builds up from the ministries and LDP Dietmen to establish or expand programs. The MOF in most years responds by moving up its budget estimate little by little—this movement in the 1969 budget process is typical. From ¥6.5 trillion estimated on August 13 1968, the figure was moved up to 6.6 on September 1 (confirmed again on November 24), 6.7 on December 7 and 6.74 on

December 30. If spending pressure is very intense, perhaps bringing talk of some radical change in financial custom, the figure can be moved up more rapidly and to a higher final figure, with economic growth or revenue estimates also pushed up to appropriate levels. This strategy was particularly evident in the years prior to 1966, when the threat of deficit financing was feared by MOF officials, but in one case it backfired: overoptimistic revenue estimates for 1965 led to actual shortfalls later in the fiscal year, which had to be covered by resorting to deficit financing for the first time.

Considered most hazardous by the MOF is lowering a budget estimate once offered. For the 1967 budget, the estimate had been raised to ¥5 trillion in November, but the process became delayed and a change in economic conditions brought fears of overstimulation. Some called for a reduction in budget size, but an MOF spokesman replied that "to attempt to reduce budget size after it has already been announced would not be acceptable to the requesting side, and bring on heightened competition for funds which will make the attempt counter-productive."[36] On occasion, as for the 1974 budget, estimates can be reduced midway through the process, but an unusual degree of consensus among budgetary participants on the direness of the economic situation is required.

The real macrobudgeting decisional process—or at least a more real version than the "ideal" process shown in Chart 3—can be abstracted as in the flow chart in Chart 4. Here one finds, instead of one, clear-cut "decision," a lengthy series of adjustments in response to various signals from the environment. None of the subprocesses is entirely scientific or objective, untouched by "political" considerations. Which is not to say, on the other hand, that macrobudgeting is dominated by party politicians: actually, despite some highly publicized intraparty debates over fiscal policy, influences from outside the Finance Ministry are usually indirect. A superior strategic position, particularly in its control of information, allows the Finance Ministry to retain the initiative in macrobudgeting decisions.

# Integration

How do microbudgeting and macrobudgeting fit together? We have seen that tentative decisions are made on the level of spending for each individual program without taking the overall budget picture very much into account. On the other hand, the figure for the total budget is decided with rather little consideration for spending needs. Nonetheless, the two

---

36. AS, February 14, 1967. See also AS, February 7, 1967. The final budget was ¥ 4.95 trillion, but the reduction was a "technical" one occasioned by the creation of a Special Account for aid to the coal industry.

## CHART 4
### ACTUAL MACROBUDGETING DECISION MAKING PROCESS

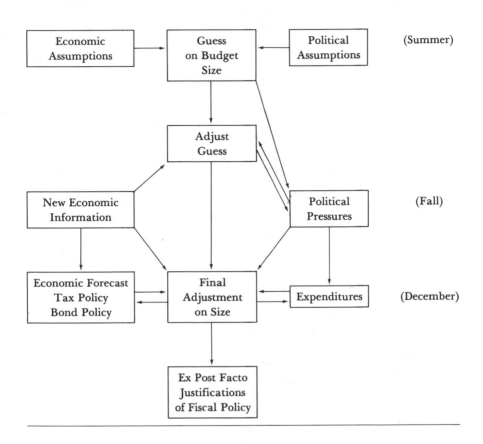

processes produce identical numbers at the end. What is the interface between these two decision-making processes?[37]

Plainly, answering this question requires an investigation of a level of budgetary decision making which lies between review of individual programs and the sorts of macroeconomic (and macropolitical) choices described in the previous section. Appropriately enough, it turns out that

37. This question has considerable theoretical relevance, since it is closely related to recent studies of American budgeting which argue that, contrary to the predictions of the incrementalist model, temporal variation at the subagency level is quite high; still largely unexplored is the problem of how these varying programs aggregate to stable agency

these decisions are made at the level of organization in between the budget examiner, who takes the lead in microbudgeting, and the finance minister, who dominates macrobudgeting; chiefly responsible are the Budget Bureau director and his three vice-directors. Their unit of analysis is the middle level of aggregation, either ministry or Important Item budgets.[38] We could answer this question if we could discover how the budgets for ministries, or for Important Items, are determined every year.

Unfortunately, this critical problem seems to be the single most mysterious area of budgetary politics to both the outside analyst and those who themselves participate in budgeting. Divergent answers can be found in published materials and in interviews with participants to such problems as when the "framework" for each ministry or Important Item is actually determined (early in the fall, to the very end of the process); whether it represents the aggregate of "bottom-up" microbudgeting decisions or a "top-down" comprehensive view; or the extent to which this level of aggregation absorbs the attention of decision makers. However, it is possible to make a few statements about this process with some confidence, based partly on a priori reasoning.

First, the importance accorded the Important Item and ministry breakdowns by those inside and outside the budget process indicates that key participants must keep them in mind at all stages of budgeting. Second, within the budget process, doubtless these "frameworks" take shape by a process of gradual adjustment akin to that described above for the total size of the budget. However, there is evidence to indicate that the critical stage is the "second expenditure estimate" meetings in early November. At this time the conclusions of the summer "first expenditure estimate" have beem reexamined in the light of ministry requests, fairly good revenue estimates have become available, and the detailed discussions on the Miscellaneous Category and at least preliminary discussions of the Important Items are finished with. In these meetings the Budget Bureau director and vice-directors, aided by examiners and their staffs, sit

---

allocations. See for example John R. Gist, "Mandatory Expenditures and the Defense Sector: Theory of Budgetary Incrementalism," *Sage Professional Papers in American Politics 1,* 04-020 (1974); Arnold Kanter, "Congress and the Defense Budget: 1960-1970," *American Political Science Review* 66, 1 (March 1972), 129-43; Peter B. Natchez and Irwin C. Bupp, "Policy and Priority in the Budgetary Process," *ibid.* 67, 3 (September 1973), 951-963; and John Wanat, "Bases of Budgetary Incrementalism," *ibid.* 68, 3 (September 1974), 1221-28. A rejoinder is Aaron Wildavsky, "On Incrementalism: Or, Yes, Virginia, There is no Magic Size for an Increment," University of California, Berkeley, Graduate School of Public Policy Working Paper No. 36 (mimeo; September 1975); see esp. pp. 36-37.

38. The Important Item (*shuyō keihi*) budget classification is a semifunctional arrangement of expenditures into such categories as social security, education, public works and so forth. Appendix A is an example; this and other breakdowns are discussed in Appendix B. MOF officials indicate the Important Item budget is usually referred to in discussions of "policy" matters, and the ministerial classification when "bureaucratic" considerations intrude.

down to explain to the finance minister what the likely shape of the budget will be. The figures for ministries and Important Items produced here (which of course are kept secret) may well be changed at the margin later in the process, but they do provide a base line in a more concrete fashion than is possible in earlier estimates.

Third, the kinds of information which are relevant to decision making here include the following: the absolute amounts, shares and growth rates of each item in the current year; the overall budget picture; the presence of any unusual large-scale spending requirements among the programs which comprise an item; and any applicable policies on priorities or "national goals," long-run or short-run. Perhaps a reading of political conditions within the LDP which might bear on expenditure allocations will also be taken into account. Probably all bear on these decisions in proportions that vary from year to year and from item to item; it would be pointless to list examples.

Fourth, it is reasonable to infer that in the absence of compelling incentives among the latter factors, it is the share occupied by an item (or a ministry) in the current year that will provide a decision-making "base" which then may be modified in the light of other circumstances. That is, under "normal" conditions, other things being equal, the Budget Bureau will tend to give a ministry or item the same share it had earlier, or — another way of saying the same thing — allow it to grow at the same rate as other items.

*Balance* — This last point is of course closely related to the notion of "balance" discussed at several junctures above. There are many indications that Finance Ministry officials are very aware of the significance of balance norms in the integration process — as one noted in an interview "there is nothing a ministry likes less than a 'share-down' in its budget." Budgeters try to avoid exciting the partisans of a particular policy area, by treating ministries evenhandedly unless extremely convicing reasons for cutting are available. In talking with MOF officials, one often hears such statements as "we think that public works and social security should be kept in some sort of balance . . . it is very difficult to lower the shares of public works or social security" (a Budget Bureau director), or "if it appears that the public works budget is going to go up 15 percent and social security only 12 percent, well, we will think that the latter should be brought up a bit" (a division director in the Budget Bureau). Even *raising* a budget item too much can be risky, since demands will follow that all somehow similar programs should also be hiked to preserve balance, and the ultimate result might be a general "level-up" affecting the entire budget. Maintaining budget shares in their established patterns is seen as much the safest course.

To the extent that such considerations are important in decision making, balance will tend to override variations in political support and even in obligatory spending. For example, during the 1960s the Budget Bureau was plagued by the rapid growth of the rice price subsidy and the government contribution to health insurance costs, caused in both cases by a combination of objective factors and intense support from the LDP. From 1960 to 1970, the deficit in the Food Control Special Account made up from the General Account (i.e., ordinary tax revenues) rose from only 0.7 percent of the total budget to 4.5 percent; in the same period, health insurance costs rose from a 3.6 to a 7.1 percent share. Attempts to restrain these programs were ineffective. However, when the ministry budget breakdown is examined, one sees that the Ministry of Agriculture and Forestry share rose only from 9.4 to 10.5 percent in those years, and the Ministry of Health and Welfare from 10.1 to 13.4 percent. Since each program is contained within the budget of its respective ministry, this means that the rest of the Agriculture Ministry's functions actually declined in budget share, from 8.7 to 6.0 percent. Remaining Welfare Ministry functions fell from 6.5 to 6.3 percent of the total budget (a smaller decline, but perhaps more significant in light of the consensus that Japanese welfare programs should be "catching up" with the West during the 1960s).[39]

Operationally, as explained by an Agriculture Ministry official in 1970,

it is a fact that the Foodstuffs Control item has expanded, and this has put pressure [*appaku*] on the rest of our budget . . . the examiner sometimes says it makes the rest of our budget "difficult."

In a 1974 interview, a Ministry of Finance agriculture specialist agreed:

. . . if the Food Control account went up quickly, and the rest of the agriculture budget also grew quickly, it might be all right in theory, but in reality the other ministries would protest. So their other items are cut a bit — or rather, they don't grow as fast. This is a problem that must be faced by the Ministry of Agriculture and Forestry: given a certain amount of money, should most of it be eaten up by one program?

In other words, the practice of setting a basic framework for a ministry (or policy area) on the basis of its past share gives the MOF a certain amount of leverage in forcing the spending ministries to restrain overly expensive

---

39. Shares calculated from *Zaisei Tōkei*, 1970, pp. 65-66; *Kuni no Yosan*, 1970, p. 888; and unpublished tables prepared by the Budget Bureau, August 1969. By 1973, the rice budget was up to 5.3 percent with the total for the ministry at 11.4, so remaining agriculture programs accounted for 6.1 percent of the General Account. Health insurance was up to 7.4 percent in 1973, but other welfare programs also grew to occupy another 6.9 percent. *Zaisei Tōkei*, 1974, pp. 29, 66, 218-19.

programs.[40] Somewhat similarly, even in less extreme cases the Budget Bureau will customarily ask any ministry (or perhaps bureau or even division) requesting a new program to sacrifice an older one—"scrap and build" is the phrase used. Depending on circumstances, then, the fact that Japanese budget participants tend to think in terms of balance considerations can be of strategic advantage to the Ministry of Finance.

*Proportionality.* — As has been noted, balance notions are not unique to Japan—"fair share," much the same thing, is quite significant in at least American and British budgeting. Is there systematic evidence that this norm is unusually prevalent in Japan? It would be difficult to answer this question at the microbudgeting level of aggregation, but sufficiently comparable statistics for the integration level are available. One would expect balance to be associated with relatively stable budget shares for ministries from year to year, which is readily measured. Table 7 presents this information for Japan and the United States. Results for the two countries are similar enough to indicate that both operate within the same budgeting frame of reference—in neither country do budget shares jump around wildly—but just as clearly, Japan is the more stable. Table 8 is a condensed form of the same sort of data for four countries, and again, Japanese ministry budget shares fluctuate the least. At least within this small sample, Japan does seem the most "balanced."

Of course, this sort of analysis is hardly definitive proof that short-run budget stability is caused by a "cultural" factor like balance. Other explanations are certainly possible. Since rapid economic growth is a notable Japanese characteristic, an obvious thought would be that high growth (of GNP, or the budget) causes stability. The logic here might be that large yearly surpluses, by easing the necessity to make hard priority decisions, will encourage budgeters to minimize dissatisfaction by spreading benefits around evenly, thereby equalizing ministry growth rates.[41] Aaron Wildavsky advances a slightly more complex version of this hypothesis, based on comparisons among the four countries of Table 8.[42] If

40. A typical ministry response, incidentally, is not to question the logic of using a "framework," but rather to argue that the program in question should be considered part of a *different* framework (*betsuwaku*)—in the case above, to view rice supports as part of either welfare or anti-inflation policy. According to the quoted official, the MOF replied that rice subsidies made even less sense in those frameworks.

41. For precisely this argument in some detail, see my dissertation, "Contemporary Japanese Budget Politics" (Columbia University, 1973), pp. 366-68 and *passim*.

42. Aaron Wildavsky, *Budgeting: A Comparative Theory of Budgetary Processes* (Boston: Little, Brown, 1975), pp. 232-245. Proportionality is seen as related directly to wealth, economic growth and the proportion of low-visibility taxes, and inversely to the amount tax rates had recently been increased. However, since all these factors influence budgeting by increasing public support for spending, the formulation can legitimately be simplified by taking budget growth itself as the proximate independent variable; this simplification weakens but does not demolish the evidence Wildavsky presents for his argument.

## TABLE 7
## AVERAGE YEARLY CHANGE-IN-SHARE, JAPAN AND U.S.
### (Unit: Percent)

| JAPAN, 1961–1970 | | | | UNITED STATES, 1959–1968 | | | |
|---|---|---|---|---|---|---|---|
| Agency | Average | Average (highest excluded) | Share (1970) | Agency | Average | Average (highest excluded) | Share (1968) |
| **The Twelve Most Stable Agencies** | | | | | | | |
| Transport | 2.3 | 1.8 | 2.3 | Defense (military) | 3.1 | 2.5 | 53.4 |
| Education | 2.5 | 2.3 | 10.6 | Commerce | 4.9 | 3.9 | 1.3 |
| Prime Minister's Office[a] | 2.9 | 1.9 | 15.4 | Justice | 5.5 | 5.1 | 0.3 |
| Home Affairs[a] | 3.0 | 2.6 | 21.2 | Treasury | 5.9 | 5.1 | 11.2 |
| Courts | 4.1 | 3.3 | 0.6 | Veterans Administration | 6.3 | 5.8 | 4.5 |
| Health and Welfare | 4.2 | 3.4 | 11.2 | Judiciary | 6.4 | 4.7 | 0.2 |
| Construction | 4.3 | 3.1 | 11.2 | Atomic Energy Commission | 7.0 | 5.6 | 1.7 |
| Justice | 4.6 | 3.9 | 1.2 | Legislative | 7.5 | 6.5 | 0.2 |
| Foreign Affairs | 4.6 | 4.0 | 0.6 | General Services Administration | 7.9 | 4.4 | 0.5 |
| Posts and Telecommunications | 5.0 | 4.4 | 0.1 | Defense (civilian) | 8.2 | 6.7 | 1.1 |
| Diet | 6.2 | 5.4 | 0.2 | Agriculture | 9.2 | 8.0 | 4.5 |
| Labor | 6.8 | 6.2 | 1.5 | Health, Education, and Welfare | 9.8 | 7.6 | 8.7 |
| **The Six Largest Agencies** | | | | | | | |
| Home Affairs[a] | 3.0 | 2.6 | 21.2 | Defense (military) | 3.1 | 2.5 | 53.5 |
| Prime Minister's Office[a] | 2.9 | 1.9 | 15.4 | Treasury | 5.9 | 5.1 | 11.2 |
| Health and Welfare | 4.2 | 3.4 | 13.4 | HEW | 9.8 | 7.2 | 8.7 |
| Construction | 4.3 | 3.1 | 11.2 | Veterans Administration | 6.3 | 5.8 | 4.5 |
| Agriculture and Forestry | 8.8 | 7.8 | 10.7 | Agriculture | 9.2 | 8.0 | 4.5 |
| Education | 2.5 | 2.3 | 10.6 | National Aeronautics and Space Administration[b] | 46.4 | 33.7 | 3.9 |

NOTES: If an item's budget in a given year is "a" and in the following year "b," and the total budgets for those years A and B, then the item's budget shares will be a/A and b/B, and its "change-in-share" will be b/B divided by a/A or bA/aB. This figure is then multiplied by 100 to put it in percentage terms. Its deviation is its amount either above or below 100 (which represents the growth of the total). The deviations for each item are then averaged over time. The middle columns leave out the year of greatest deviation for each item to lessen the possibility of one extraordinary occurrence (such as the gain or loss of a bureau) distorting the average.

Both sets of figures represent the "executive budget" before it is sent to the legislature, not actual expenditures. Accounting principles differ, particularly in recording governmental receipts and intragovernmental expenditures. Therefore, the two sets are not strictly comparable. The time periods differ because of the availability of statistics. Although these qualifications do not invalidate the points made in the text, this table must not be used for other purposes, such as comparisons of expenditures in particular sectors.

ᵃ1962–1970.      ᵇ1961–1968.

SOURCE: For Japan, unpublished MOF tables for initial budgets. For the United States, U.S. Bureau of the Budget, *The Budget of the United States Government*, Fiscal Years 1958–1963; and U.S. Bureau of the Budget or Office of Management and Budgeting, *The Budget in Brief*, Fiscal Years 1964–1968.

TABLE 8

DISTRIBUTION OF YEARLY CHANGE-IN-SHARE, FOUR NATIONS

(Unit: Percent)

|               | Period      | 0–5%  | 5–10% | 10–15% | 15–20% | Over 20% | Total |
|---------------|-------------|-------|-------|--------|--------|----------|-------|
| Japan         | 1961–1970   | 57.1  | 19.2  | 13.6   | 5.0    | 5.6      | 100.5 |
| France        | 1960–1969   | 49.5  | 25.7  | 12.4   | 0.0    | 12.4     | 100.0 |
| United States | 1959–1968   | 37.4  | 29.7  | 14.2   | 9.0    | 9.7      | 100.0 |
| Great Britain | 1960–1970   | 16.9  | 34.9  | 14.1   | 14.1   | 19.8     | 99.8  |

NOTES: Based on the same formula as in Table 7, but absolute percentage deviations are arranged in a percentage frequency distribution. Rows may not add to 100 because of rounding in original table.

SOURCE: Aaron Wildavsky, *Budgeting* (Boston: Little, Brown and Company, 1975), p. 242. A typographical error in the published table was corrected in a personal communication from the author.

a conclusion were warranted that "proportionality" — Wildavsky's term for short-run stability of budget shares — is simply accounted for by growth, the need for a special "Japanese" explanation would be obviated.

However, further investigation throws doubt on this attractive proposition. Preliminary results of a study of fourteen Communist and capitalist national budgets in the 1950s reveals no positive relationship between budget or GNP growth and proportionality — in fact, if the Communist countries are taken separately, there is a strong *inverse* relationship.[43] Moreover, a longitudinal analysis of Japanese budget shares, 1956-1974, revealed that budgets tended to be least proportional in years of highest budget growth.[44] More research is required before the precise relationship (if any) between these two variables can be specified; in any case, it seems not to be one of direct causality.

With the most attractive alternative hypothesis rejected, our confidence that balance norms represent an important factor in helping to account for high proportionality in Japan is considerably strengthened.

43. This investigation rests on data laboriously compiled by Frederick W. Pryor; see his renowned *Public Expenditures in Communist and Capitalist Nations* (London: Allen and Unwin, 1968). For the entire sample there is no correlation between budget growth and average yearly change-in-share scores (high scores indicate low proportionality). For the eight Communist countries alone, the correlation coefficient is .672.

44. When the dataset is divided by using a dummy variable to distinguish low-growth (1956-59) and high-growth (1961-1974) periods, regressing weighted change-in-share scores against yearly budget growth produces a multiple correlation coefficient of .689. (Because of an administrative change, the change-in-share score for 1960 is unusable.) A similar longitudinal analysis of Pryor's fourteen nations also indicates an inverse (though weak) relationship between growth and proportionality.

# Strategies

In chapter 2, a list was presented of the strategies used by the line ministries to increase expenditures on their programs. Most of these devices belong to the microbudgeting arena; the corresponding responses from the Ministry of Finance are the "calculations" described in the section on budgeting criteria in the preceding chapter. The Finance Ministry's interests, however, are considerably broader than item-by-item tactical maneuvering. In particular, as is clear from the description of the macrobudgeting process above, the MOF's most crucial concern is controlling the total size of the budget. The ministry therefore has developed certain techniques — one is tempted to call them "macrostrategies" — designed to give it a measure of control over other participants in the macrobudgeting arena. Many of these are designed to prevent the occurrence most feared by the MOF: a build-up of enthusiasm for higher spending among the ministries and within the LDP which gathers so much momentum it is impossible to stop, and wrecks any possibility of maintaining a "sound" fiscal policy. I suspect that budgeting authorities in other countries have similar concerns and have adopted comparable strategies on occasion — the principle of Treasury secrecy in Great Britain is surely one such example — but existing research on budget politics has not focused on this topic.

*Pace.* The Finance Ministry always pays close attention to the budget schedule. It is concerned that nonbudgetary events might disrupt the smooth flow of the process, often by stimulating the ministries or the LDP into making stronger demands than otherwise. Chief among these events are Cabinet changes, Diet sessions, holidays and elections.

It has been the custom for Japanese prime ministers to reshuffle their Cabinets relatively often, and particularly under Satō changeovers frequently occurred in November or December, during the budget process.[45] The MOF resists having the outgoing Cabinet make any sort of budget policy statements during the fall, since the new Cabinet will not find them binding. It also declines to discuss even rather pressing budget issues with high level ministry officials under these conditions, since any concession made would be regarded as a minimum figure once the new minister arrived, and he might feel impelled to go his predecessor one better to impress his own officials. Similar considerations apply to some

---

45. Of the twenty-five Cabinet reshuffles between the appointment of the First Hatoyama Cabinet in 1954 and the Third Satō Cabinet in January 1970, nine occurred during November or December; three more were in January or February, following elections, before the government draft had been approved.

extent with top party officers, who are often rotated after a Cabinet reshuffle.

Diet sessions present different problems. An extraordinary session of the Diet will often extend into the second or third week in December, a time when the Cabinet Budget Policy, the LDP Budget Compilation Program and even the MOF draft budget may be scheduled. Not only does the flurry of activity to get last-minute bills passed absorb the time of budget participants, but the MOF worries that publicizing budget issues in that sensitive period will bring comment and criticism from the opposition parties, perhaps even forcing testimony on delicate problems by the prime minister or finance minister before a Diet committee. Calls for more spending on programs from the opposition might well be echoed by ministries and LDP Dietmen, and in any case such politicization of the process would not work to the MOF's advantage. Therefore, it will try to postpone budget actions until after the session is finished. For example, at the end of the 1963 budget process, the Diet session had been extended farther than had been anticipated into December. The finance minister, Tanaka Kakuei, broke a current precedent by deferring Cabinet approval of the Economic Forecast and Basic Policy for Budget Compilation until the same day the MOF draft was reported to the Cabinet, the day after the Diet had recessed. Similarly, he prevailed upon the LDP leadership to postpone its Budget Compilation Program.

An annual event which nearly always causes concern is New Year, the major holiday of the year in Japan, which lasts for almost the entire first week of January. A long Diet session or other delaying factors will more often than not make it questionable whether the government draft can be approved before this break, but the MOF (with the cooperation of the party leadership) places a high premium on speed. Its worry is not merely about losing time or momentum; rather, the assumption, probably correct, is that any time Dietmen get a chance to talk to constituents they will promise more budget benefits. Mizuta Mikio, finance minister in 1961, outlined the strategy clearly:

Over New Year's, facing an Upper House election, the members of the Diet . . . will be returning to their election districts. Therefore, if the budget process is allowed to go into next year, after the Dietmen have come back to Tokyo, the budget will be harder to control. So the leadership too is very emphatic on completion within the year.[46]

The MOF succeeded in finishing the budget within the year only seven times from 1954 to 1974 (the budgets for 1959, the four years 1962-65, 1972 and 1974). When it cannot, even when the delays are such that only

46. NKS, November 14, 1961.

two or three days are lost, it never releases the MOF draft before the New Year break and interrupts the revival negotiations for a week. If this were done, Dietmen would have specific MOF cuts to discuss with their constituents, and their enthusiasm would be increased even more. The draft is therefore not reported to the Cabinet until after the break, on January 6 or 7, with the government draft following a week or so later.

General elections scheduled during budget time present similar but more severe problems. As Mizuta's remark above implies, it is generally believed that any impending election will increase budget demands from Dietmen, and from ministries banking on their support.[47] Such pressure would be at its worst if the election were scheduled immediately after the MOF draft, when all the items which failed to be approved or expanded would be fresh in the minds of constituents and interest groups. Partly for this reason, and also because of the delays in the process that would be incurred, elections were not scheduled during the budgeting period until the Satō administration, when this consideration was overridden by other political factors. General elections were held in January 1967 and December 1969 and 1972, causing substantial delays; only the vaguest of policy statements were enunciated before the interruption. In 1970, the MOF also carefully failed to mention its planned hike in corporation taxes until after the campaign, in order not to irritate the LDP (which would be concerned about effects on big business contributions).[48] Incidentally, it might be thought that budget compilation immediately following a general election would be more difficult than usual, after so many campaign promises had been given, but such is not the case. All agree with the Dietman who said in an interview that "because all the Dietmen are in office already, things go pretty smoothly." Politicians apparently do not worry that unfulfilled promises will be remembered by the following election.

Budget scheduling also is influenced in more subtle ways, by the MOF's reading of the LDP's "mood" or other shifts in the political situation. Most important is that the process move along at what journalists call the "MOF's pace"; that is, that the initiative does not pass to the LDP or some strong politician. The historical account in chapter 9 gives ample indication that the Finance Ministry's worries on this account are not without foundation.

*Discretion.* — A general principle for MOF officials is to be as close-mouthed as possible, particularly regarding budgets for individual

---

47. It should be noted that an attempt to correlate the timing of elections with variations in size and composition of budgets, including the composition of public works, with and without time lags, revealed no relationship whatsoever. Elections may heat up the budget process but do not have a noticeable substantive effect.

48. This according to two interviews, with a journalist and an MOF official.

programs or broad policy areas. The reason is simple: as a BB official put it in 1966, "if a final budget draft were to be proposed in the beginning, things which were supposed to be settled would become unsettled."[49] Any realistic figure mentioned by the MOF early in the process would immediately become a floor for further negotiations. On the other hand, the MOF fears that if it came forward with a tactically low figure as a bargaining position, the ministry concerned and the LDP would be stimulated to redouble their pressure. It is far safer to say nothing, and this rule is usually followed.

Occasionally, the MOF will wish to test the reaction of budget participants to a proposal. The commonest tactic is to leak its position to the press without attribution—rather than specific budget figures, the leak will most often pertain to either a denial of a newly requested program or a conceptual reformulation. For example, when the Ministry of Education requested government support for private university personnel costs in the 1970 budget, unattributed stories appeared in the press reporting MOF objections that such payments were unconstitutional and that the plan had not been fully discussed within the Education Ministry. After strong reactions from university circles, a new MOF notion surfaced that payments should be differentiated by field, instead of made evenly across the board as requested. This position proved acceptable and was adopted.

Though the MOF usually reserves its definite decisions until the end of the process, for either the MOF draft or the revival negotiations, it sometimes is concerned that political support for an unusually popular program will build up to an explosive point, perhaps infecting supporters of other programs. In such cases, a favorable decision may be given early. An example is the approval of a Flood Control Special Account in November 1960, after long MOF opposition; this concession was explicitly viewed as a means to satisfy LDP desires and thereby cool down the rest of the budget process. The danger here, of course, is that after winning one battle the party might be encouraged to turn to increasing its pressure on another budget request.

Another exception to this principle was described above: it is normal for the Finance Ministry to issue, and then revise, its rather strategic guess on the total size of the budget from early in the process. Its other macrobudgeting estimates—aggregate expenditures, revenue growth—are usually kept close to the chest, since details can often be challenged more credibly than an overall figure with unknown components. However, when revenue stringency or pressure from fixed expenditures is unusually strong and the MOF believes a case must be made against the LDP or the line

49. Quoted in Funago Masamichi, "Yosan Hensei no Butaiura" ("Behind the Scenes at Budget Compilation"), *Fainansu* 1, 4 (March 1966), 25-26.

ministries, such figures, often backed by detailed statistics, may be released. One example is the report on the high natural increase in expenditures for 1970 reproduced as Table 4 above; another, on a larger scale, is the entire "break fiscal rigidification campaign" of the 1968 budget process, when the MOF actively tried to convince the public that a fiscal crisis was in the making. But in general, the ministry finds the dangers of talking too much outweighing the benefits of participating in debates, and remains silent.

*Inhibiting Other Participants.* —Not only does the MOF prefer discretion for itself. The journalist Suzuki Yukio, the most perceptive among regular observers of Japanese budgeting, noted

one budgetary tactic used by the "Finance bureaucrats." . . . Whenever something comes up that is related to finances, be it a speech by the prime minister or the rhetorical slogans in an LDP Budget Compilation Program, they will interfere through preconsultations to ensure that no specific details are included, and that the already abstract statements are made even more general.[50]

Several examples are cited elsewhere: domination of the revenue estimating process and the prevention of EPA publication of government sector forecasts; blocking the use of year-by-year totals in public works five-year plans; attempts (less often successful) to prevent the line ministries from releasing "ad balloons" for newly requested programs in the early fall.

A further example of this central MOF strategy is its handling of the yearly Budget Compilation Policy (*Yosan Hensei Hōshin*), which is nominally the most authoritative statement of general budget policy (in that it is passed by the Cabinet). Over the years, there have been attempts by powerful politicians—Kōno Ichirō was the most active—to turn this document into an instrument for Cabinet control of budgeting. The MOF resisted these attempts successfully. With few exceptions, each year the Basic Policy is prepared within the Budget Bureau and sent over to the Cabinet only for ratification; its provisions are kept vague and general; and its passage is delayed until just before, or the same time as, the MOF draft budget is released. Through this and more informal means, the Cabinet is thus precluded from making any official pronouncements on the budget which might tie the hands of the Ministry of Finance.

In interviews, several MOF officials said that one of the great peculiarities of the Japanese budget system was that policy guidance to the "working level" came only after the process has been nearly completed, and was worded in such abstract terms that it could be of little use. They maintained that this absence of direction causes difficulties for the MOF, and blamed it on the irrationalities of the Japanese political system. The

50. Suzuki Yukio, *Keizai Kanryō* ("Economic Bureaucrats") (Tokyo: Nihon Keizai Shinbunsha, 1969), p. 139.

observation may be correct, but obscures the point that precisely this pattern has been a consistent strategic objective of the MOF itself.

*Prenegotiation.* — It was noted above that, in an effort to moderate budget demands, the MOF occasionally makes program concessions early in the process. More frequently, top MOF officials will prenegotiate budget issues with other participants, including Cabinet ministers, administrative vice-ministers, and the party leadership. Though related, these two tactics are distinct: it is possible to make concessions unilaterally, without prenegotiation; and more frequently the MOF may talk matters over with no intention of giving up any ground.

Strategically, the choice for the Finance Ministry each year is whether it should write an "independent" (*dokuji no*) draft budget, one which either imposes the MOF's own ideas on the budget problems of the year or leaves them open for discussion in the appeals negotiations, or whether it should try to talk over problems before drawing up the draft. The choice has varied from year to year, with various factors coming into play; a trend over time may also be discerned. In the late 1950s, the MOF tended to be fairly independent, and in 1960 Finance Minister Satō Eisaku ran into severe difficulties by not talking enough with party leaders. The 1962 budget, on the other hand, saw the most elaborate prenegotiation strategy of the period. Facing the difficult situation of large revenue estimates and a perceived need for fiscal restraint, Finance Minister Mizuta tried to arrange detailed talks with both Cabinet ministers and party figures. As it turned out, each group resented his talking with the other and the meetings became simply pro forma chats (and the MOF was forced in the end to grant several major concessions).[51]

After this failure in 1962, the strategy of extensive and relatively formal prenegotiations fell into disuse, but the MOF did not return to an "independent" posture. Most commonly, the finance minister has held informal and often unannounced talks with influential participants, and then consulted formally with the one or two ministers whose budgets presented unusual problems. This technique allows some defusing of opposition and satisfaction of desires to be consulted, without bringing on potentially hazardous arguments — occasionally, an actual budget problem may even be solved. In the party-dominated 1973 budget process, Finance Minister Aichi did negotiate with ministry and LDP leaders quite extensively — granting nearly everything asked on occasion — but in 1974 Fukuda Takeo reasserted MOF prerogatives and met with leaders only to gain agreement on the need for stringency.[52]

51. Interesting newspaper articles on this point will be found in AS, January 3 and December 29, 1957; December 31, 1959, and December 3, 10, 16, 19, 19 evening and 29, 1961; NKS, December 15, 1959, and December 14 and 18, 1961.
52. NKS, December 29 and 30, 1972; January 5, and December 20, 1973.

*"Pillars"*. — Another MOF strategy may be mentioned briefly, though it is no longer very significant. In the late 1950s, the political leadership (with at least tacit approval from MOF) liked to announce the "pillars" (*hashira*) of the budget, a few items which would be particularly emphasized that year to give the budget "character." The most famous slogan was the "¥100 billion tax cut, ¥100 billion for programs" policy for the 1957 budget, which began the era of high budget growth. Such slogans were not official and not decided by some formal process; they were just mentioned as "pillars" by one or another participant during the process. In following years, they included such items as "people's life," small business, highways, science and technology, pensions, physical education, schools, harbors, and the establishment of a national pension plan.

At first glance, these would appear to be devices for promoting higher budgets, but they soon became more of an MOF strategy than one useful to ministries or the party. This was revealed in the 1960 budget process, which had been marked by an early debate over which "pillars" should be chosen until a massive typhoon caused great damage in early October. The MOF (and the then allied LDP leadership) seized the opportunity with some relief and made disaster reclamation into the key budget slogan; major expenditures would be required anyway, so this could be used to give the budget "character." In the early 1960s, the most commonly mentioned themes were such broad policy areas as public works, welfare, education and so forth, where expenditures would be bound to rise in any case (for example, most of the rise in the education budget in this period is explained simply by social factors: the postwar baby boom and the larger percentage of students going into higher education). "Emphasizing" a program on which money would have to be spent anyway presents an illusion of policy choice, and gives the MOF a rationale for turning down other proposals by arguing that discretionary resources must be used on the "pillars." However, in this watered-down form, the technique proved to be of little value, and was not as often mentioned in later years.

*Cost-Cutting Campaigns*. — The Finance Ministry shares with budget authorities elsewhere an attachment to administrative virtues like thrift and efficiency, and from time to time engages in direct efforts to control expenditures.[53] Sharp reductions have sometimes occurred in response to sudden unfavorable shifts in the economy during the budget compilation process, as for the 1954 and 1974 budgets, or later during the execution stage. More commonly, the MOF has moved against specific categories of administrative expenditures, as by trying to reduce the number of

53. For a good general discussion of budget-cutting strategies see Aaron Wildavsky, *The Politics of the Budgetary Process* (Boston: Little, Brown and Company, 1964), p. 102-108, 148. For more details on various Japanese efforts to cut costs, see my dissertation, pp. 177-186.

governmental corporations, public advisory bodies, government employ-ees, or—most often—grants-in-aid to local governments and other institutions.[54]

One might expect that major cost-cutting campaigns would come in years when revenues are shortest, so that savings from fixed expenditures could be applied to higher priority programs. However, a look at the record at least for the decade of the 1960s reveals little attention to administrative costs in such stringent years as 1965 and 1968, while paradoxically the years when attacks on fixed expenditures were most publicized were two of great budget growth, 1962 and 1966. The former came during a boom, the latter in the midst of economic recovery from recession through pump-priming, meaning that, in both years, the MOF had much less than its usual difficulty in finding resources to meet budget demands. Nonetheless in 1962, throughout the early budget process and again around the time of the Finance Ministry draft, great publicity was given to administrative economies—a special twenty-item "budget review guideline" was prescribed.[55] In 1966, it was after the decision to turn to deficit spending that the MOF began announcing various formulas for rationalizing fixed costs, and it even took the unprecedented step of rechecking its already compiled "Standard Budget" to see if further administrative savings could be found.[56] Never before, or since, had Finance officials talked so much about rationalizing and cutting fixed administrative expenditures, and as journalists pointed out at the time, their motive was clearly that the traditional ceiling provided by the revenue forecast could not serve its usual function, and the prospect of a big antirecession budget was stimulating unusually strong demands from the ministries and LDP.

Actual savings from such campaigns were minor: in 1966, the MOF reported to the Diet that ¥9.128 billion had been cut from administrative costs, plus ¥9.49 billion from grants-in-aid. This total of about $50 million was only 0.004 percent of the budget that year, and of course overall expenditures in both categories rose substantially (over ¥170 billion in grants-in-aid alone), since only reductions in existing items were counted without reference to new or expanded items.[57] Still, the success or

54. The grants-in-aid (usually *hojokin,* though many terms are used) which receive the most notice are highly particularistic benefits with intense backing from Dietmen, but of course, as in other advanced countries, such transfers of resources support much of the vital work of government. Between 1960 and 1970 the share of the General Account devoted to grants-in-aid of various sorts fluctuated between about 26 and 29 percent, but it rose to over 32 percent in the 1970s. See *Zaisei Tokei,* 1974, pp. 36-37.

55. See MNS, August 24 evening, 1961; NKS, September 9, and December 2, 19 evening, 20 and 29, 1961; and AS, December 15 evening and 29, 1961.

56. NKS, September 10, 16, 17 evening and 25.

57. NKS, February 9, 1966.

failure of an antispending campaign should not be measured by the amount of money actually cut, since administrative savings were not the real objective. The Finance Ministry was tryng to establish a psychological "economy mood" in order to reduce the force of demands from ministries and party. Its cost-cutting drives occurred in years when resources were ample because that was when the strategy was most needed; when revenues are short in reality, the intensity of demands diminishes naturally and MOF propaganda campaigns are superfluous.

*Program Budgeting.* — Which is not to say that Finance officials were unconcerned about rising expenditures. The massive "break fiscal rigidification campaign" of 1968 was a real if ultimately unsuccessful attack on the burdens of fixed costs. The late 1960s were years of budgetary innovation, when the MOF assumed an active stance, and it is completely unsurprising that in the aftermath of the antirigidification effort budgeters should look toward the planning-programming-budget-ing-system, or PPBS. These stark Roman initials stood out boldly in Japanese newspapers throughout the 1969 and 1970 budget periods (translation into Japanese was difficult, because no good equivalents for the terms "program" and "system" exist, and the English acronym received wide enough circulation to be recognized by the man on the street). Teams of officials went off to Washington, D.C., and Santa Monica, California; American books and articles were translated and published; and works by newly created Japanese experts began to appear on such topics as whether PPBS is a management or a budgeting tool, the relationship of program structures to crosswalks, and the virtues of scientific rationality.

Within the government, research on PPBS was initiated by the Economic Planning Agency, which is not a direct participant in budgeting but has had long experience in the application of sophisticated methodologies to economic planning. A Systems Analysis Investigation Office was established in the EPA, with a staff of twenty officials drawn from various ministries and agencies. It was hoped that they would be able to carry back new insights and techniques to their own organizations; but so as not to be left behind, eleven ministries and agencies also asked for grants in the 1969 budget to start their own PPBS research. Several contracted with private economic research institutes for special studies. The Research Division of the Budget Bureau assigned several young officials to look into applications of PPBS to the Japanese process, and its director, Kaneko Tarō, spoke and wrote widely on the topic.[58] The MOF's publicity organ *Fainansu* carried many articles on PPBS beginning in June

58. He also edited *PPBS no Kisochishiki* ("Basic Knowledge of PPBS") (Tokyo: Kinyū Zaisei Jijō Kenkyūkai, 1969).

1968.[59] The Fiscal Systems Council was asked to comment, and obligingly produced reports calling for rapid implementation of the new system.

What was the introduction of PPBS expected to accomplish? The question is difficult to answer precisely: most of the voluminous Japanese literature is devoted to theoretical issues, the success of American reforms, and the peculiarities of the Japanese fiscal system that make PPBS difficult to implement. In general, the Finance Ministry's interest stemmed from its concern with the problems of fiscal rigidification. If the resources available for new public purposes become more limited, more attention must be paid to efficient use of these resources, and waste in fixed expenses must be eliminated. It was hoped that PPBS could aid in the specification of national goals and in choosing among possible alternative programs to achieve those goals most efficiently. Reassessments of old activities would create space for new ones. One problem frequently noted was the overlaps and gaps created by dividing responsibility for a broad policy among several ministries—fragmented anti-inflation measures, environmental policy, and transportation were seen as demonstrating the weaknesses of the Japanese government in adapting to changing conditions, due in part to ministry "sectionalism." PPBS was thought to offer an incentive to the ministries, hitherto lacking, for comprehensive planning and attention to questions of efficiency, rather than concentrating only on raising their own budgets.[60]

Another leitmotif heard in most discussions of the topic was the hope that PPBS could eliminate or at least reduce "political influences" on budgeting. Early news stories that represented Finance Ministry views are typical: ". . . if the MOF advances development of this method, it hopes to limit budget acquisition by political pressure, which is becoming a major factor in fiscal rigidity, and allow more rational budget compilation"; and "[PPBS should be implemented] in order to eliminate the bargaining of pressure groups mixed up in budget compilation."[61] Finance officials consistently viewed LDP and interest group intervention in the budget process as wasteful and "irrational"; such interventions had become common because "no means were available that could establish whether an expenditure was valid or not by comparing costs and benefits."[62] In other words, it was hoped that PPBS could provide the MOF (or a line ministry) with the means to demonstrate that its policy preferences were superior to those urged by the LDP or an interest group. Or the new system might at

59. See particularly the series of seven technical articles beginning in February 1970 and listed in *Fainansu* 7, 9 (December 1970).
60. See, e.g., NKS, April 14, 1970, for MOF views; April 16, 1970, for a report on a PPBS symposium; and the editorial on April 19, 1970. Also, *Yosan wa Dare no Mono ka*, pp. 160-183, and appropriate chapters in nearly all books on public finance published since 1968.
61. NKS, April 10, 1968; and AS, September 29, 1968; see also the citations above.
62. NKS, May 14, 1970.

least furnish more effective bargaining ploys—one senior MOF official joked in an interview that PPBS "sounds so sophisticated that no one will dare to challenge it." The words "rational" and "scientific" were nearly always used in conjunction with PPBS: MOF officials seemed to have in mind a utopia of orderly and efficient planning and policy making, where politicians might play some role in establishing the goals of the nation, but would not get in the way of those responsible for the real work.

Despite such high hopes, PPBS never penetrated very deeply into the actual workings of the Japanese budgetary system. Program analysis was carried out only in the temporary ministry research units, not by line officials, and did not find its way into real budgetary negotiations. When I raised the topic in interviews during 1970, several scholars and journalists, as well as MOF officials connected with the Budget Bureau Research Division, were enthusiastic about PPBS, but most others, including budget examiners, were guarded and perhaps a bit cynical.[63] No LDP politician could be found who was apprehensive about the threat from PPBS, though a few thought that scientific policy making was the wave of the future and the party too should be developing think-tanks to keep up. By 1974, nothing more than vague hopes that PPBS would become possible sometime in the future were heard. If a very Japanese sort of witticism may be attempted, the number of books, articles, meetings and symposia devoted to the subject suggest that the major effect of PPBS in Japan has been to "Promote the Prosperity of Budget Specialists."

*Structural Reform.* —With the "break fiscal rigidification movement" a failure, and PPBS offering little hope of immediate relief, in the early 1970s the Finance Ministry turned to a new approach to the problem of fixed expenditures. This was called (in a series of reports from the Fiscal Systems Council) the "structural reform of public finance" (*zaiseitaishitsu kaizen*), and had its theoretical justification in the "benefit principle" (*juekisha futan gensoku*).[64] In brief, the benefit principle holds that when a governmental program serves one group in society, its costs should be borne (wholly or in large part) by that group rather than the population as

63. Quite similar was the American experience, as recalled by Larry O'Brian: "The advocates of PPBS succeeded in winning over Charlie Schultze and the President, but they failed to win over the Office of Budget Review and many of the key BOB examiners with whom each agency had to deal. . . . Thus, while one group within the BOB was caught up in what often seemed like a religious crusade to implement PPBS, those who dealt directly with our appropriations requests carried on business as usual." Stanley P. Botner, "Four Years of PPBS: An Appraisal," *Public Administration Review*, 30, 4 (July-August 1970), 423-431.

64. See the December 19, 1970, report of the Council reprinted in *Fainansu* 6, 11 (February 1971), 87-89, as well as AS, October 29, and NKS, December 14, 1971. For the history of the "benefit approach" as contrasted with the "ability to pay approach" in Western economic thought, see Richard I. Musgrave, *The Theory of Public Finance* (New York: McGraw-Hill, 1959), pp. 61-89.

a whole. As well as being a generally attractive notion to fiscal conservatives, this principle appealed to MOF officials because it offered a rationale for attacking the "three k's"—rice (*kome*) price subsidies, the National Railroads (*kokutetsu*), and national health insurance (*kenpo*). These three programs had been growing at a rate much higher than the budget as a whole through the 1960s, and had become a severe headache to the Finance Ministry. For the National Railroad and health insurance, the benefit principle meant increasing direct payments for goods and services (in particular, railroad fares and prescription drugs); for rice it dictated a return to the market by phasing out artificially maintained producers' prices as well as encouraging farmers to reduce rice production.

Although closely related to some elements of the earlier "break fiscal rigidification movement," the "structural reform" effort was conducted with less fanfare and on a more selective and gradual basis than that all-out, comprehensive campaign. It began in 1970 with sharp criticism of the rice program and a series of long negotiations among the MOF, the LDP leadership (particularly Secretary-General Tanaka Kakuei), the PARC Agriculture Division, the Ministry of Agriculture and Forestry, and, less directly, the major concerned interest groups. These culminated in a plan devised at the very end of the 1970 revival negotiations to refrain from raising the producers' price, thereby reducing the incentive to grow rice, and at the same time to offer financial benefits to farmers who would convert their paddy land to other uses. The plan was therefore very costly in the short run—the Agriculture Ministry's budget share in 1970 was the highest since 1953—but was aimed at putting a ceiling on future increases. Indeed, the transfer from the General Account to the Foodstuffs Control Special Account increased only moderately through the initial budget of 1973, so that its share declined steadily.

Encouraged by even this degree of success, the Finance Ministry turned its attention to the other two "k's." The dilemma of the railroads was that major capital expenditures were needed to modernize and replace equipment, ordinary revenues had become inadequate to cover even operating expenses, fares were hard to raise in a period of inflation, and—as an added burden—many kilometers of rural railroads made uneconomic by population losses and the growth of motor transport could not be phased out because of political pressure from local LDP Dietmen, causing substantial deficits. As with the rice problem, a series of complicated negotiations in the 1972 budget period made it apparent that the only hope for long-term improvements lay in a reformulation of the railroad financial structure, requiring considerable funds.[65] The health insurance problem was even more intractable. Here, interest groups

---

65. The capital account of the Japan National Railroads, which included a subsidy of operating expenses, rose by 42.5 percent in 1972; the contribution from the General Account

(particularly the Japan Medical Association) had mobilized the Liberal Democrats to compel constant increases in medical costs, but a more generalized concern for voters' reactions had led the party also to oppose raising national health insurance premiums or the fees charged directly for services. As a result, support from the General Account had risen from about a 6.5 percent share in the mid-1960s to over 7.5 percent in 1970, and then dropped only to 7.4 percent in 1972 and 1973.[66] Despite several attempts, the MOF could not get an effective campaign against this program started; more generally, "structural reform" and the benefit principle had not become the solution to the fixed expenditures dilemma hoped for by Finance officials.

The varied array of antispending strategies outlined here — some aimed at specific programs, others at an overall mood; some relying upon scientific rationality, others on traditional Japanese nuances — were all attempts by the Ministry of Finance to cope with a difficult environment, one in which nearly all the other participants are eager to see larger budgets. In any given year, the results of the budget process will mostly depend on a set of objective circumstances. To some real extent, however, the success or failure of the Finance Ministry in reaching its ends depends upon the delicate strategic skills of its officials.

# Conclusions

What are the ends these strategies serve? In the conclusions to chapter 2, it was hypothesized that officials of the spending ministries pursue a hierarchy of objectives in budgeting; maximizing budgets is primary, but obtaining their own policy preferences and satisfying clientele groups are also important. An examination of Ministry of Finance budgeting behavior over the years leads us to infer a somewhat more complex hierarchy of objectives, which is listed here in a loosely estimated order of priority:

1. Protection of the ministry's autonomy, elite status and jurisdictional boundaries.
2. Pursuing correct fiscal policies for given economic conditions.
3. Minimizing the size of the total budget in the current year.
4. Getting the budget finished smoothly and in due time.
5. Preserving "balance."
6. Achieving a desirable policy mix in accordance with national priorities.
7. Avoiding future expansions of expenditures.
8. Eliminating wasteful spending and obsolete programs.

---

jumped from ¥ 3.5 billion to ¥ 65.5 billion (and in the following year to ¥ 195 billion). *Zaisei Tōkei,* 1974, p. 151. Subsidies to this program are difficult to calculate because many come from Fiscal Investment and Loan Program accounts.

66. The percentages are shares of the General Account. *Zaisei Tōkei,* 1974, pp. 26-27.

This list is rather tentative, and it is impossible to assign very precise weightings except to note that the first three are taken very seriously, and the last two rarely are important motives in actual budget behavior (though they may be proclaimed as goals by Finance spokesmen from time to time).

If this enumeration approximates reality, and if it is juxtaposed with the list earlier proposed for the line ministries, some light is shed on the nature of the pivotal budgeting relationship, that between these two participants. Most often, the MOF and the line ministries have been seen as confronting each other—as an LDP Dietman once said, "the work of budgeting looks a lot like a baseball game. Against the defense, the MOF who is holding on to the purse strings, the various ministries come to bat one by one, working so hard just for a single run."[67] When the objectives of the line ministry are characterized as simply increasing its own budget, and that of the MOF as minimizing spending, such sports images (of a "zero-sum game," one might say) seem appropriate, and the relationship between the ministries and the MOF will be essentially characterized as confrontation.

However, when the more complex goal structure of each side is taken into account, these conflictive elements are placed in a broader perspective. Though the first ministerial objective, to maximize budgets, must be opposed by the MOF, the secondary (perhaps sometimes primary) goal of implementing the ministry's own policy preferences is often viewed quite sympathetically. A budget examiner will usually agree more with the ideas of his ministerial counterparts than with those of an interest group or the LDP (though it is true that occasionally the examiner will have contradictory policy ideas of his own). Further, the MOF may have no objection to a ministry pursuing its third goal, that of satisfying clientele groups, particularly when the payoff is symbolic rather than monetary. Finance officials often cooperate by, for example, keeping real negotiations secret so that the ministry can safely take different postures publicly and privately.

Then looking at the Finance Ministry's objectives, it is only the third and, rather unimportantly, the last three which are fundamentally incompatible with ministry interests. While other bureaucrats are often heard to carp about MOF elite status and privileges, they neither threaten nor are really threatened by them. Ministries rarely object to the Finance Ministry's "pace," except that occasionally during the revival negotiations one may try to delay the process in order to win a point; the MOF's more usual confrontations here are with the LDP. As for "balance" on the one hand and "desirable policy mix" on the other, a ministry's views will

67. AS, December 7, 1957.

depend on where it stands. If it feels its programs are regarded favorably enough to be beneficially treated in a priority-based budget, it will argue for optimization. An early example is the 1954 budget, when Prime Minister Yoshida ordered a 10 percent across-the-board cutback late in the process, and MITI protested vehemently. It said that even the previous year's budget had been too *sōbanateki* ("tips for all" — the pejorative word for "balance"), and so instead of using that as a basis for cuts, public works and agriculture should be reduced selectively to allow increases for industrial investment.[68] On the other hand, the Ministry of Agriculture and Forestry case cited in chapter 2 is sufficient evidence that a ministry which is worried that its programs might come under attack will hold out for a "fair share" of the budget, without much consideration of program.

We have already seen many instances of amiable ministry-MOF relations, and this discussion indicates that many major interests of the two are not directly in conflict. A conclusion that this relationship is in reality more harmonious than journalistic accounts indicate would seem to be well justified. There are struggles, to be sure, for payoffs that might be either real or symbolic, but the conflict is overshadowed by cooperation.

To some extent, this point applies throughout the period under study, but a decided trend away from conflict and toward more cooperation may also be discerned. In part, normal processes of routinization provide the explanation. However, a contributing specific factor is a lessening of the MOF's own concern with what can be called "policy."

This assertion requires precise definition. Ministry of Finance leaders do, of course, worry about the great issues — preserving the mixed growth economy, the relationship of Japan and the United States, new problems like pollution, and so forth — and indeed participate in building the consensus that animates Japanese policy making at this broad level. However, there is no special role for the MOF here. At the opposite extreme, the Budget Bureau is professionally concerned with routine administrative matters: seeing that laws and regulations are not violated by the ministries in implementing programs, and that expenditures are allocated fairly and spent correctly. In between, in the middle range of policy, the MOF feels directly responsible for economic questions, such as fiscal and monetary policy, banking practices and international economic relations. In these areas it strives to monopolize decisions.

But left out of this list are many other "middle-ground" policy questions, those which make up the great bulk of budgetary decision making. Though individual officials might have opinions to contribute, the Finance Ministry has no institutional stake in, for example, what program is most effective in meeting the problems of handicapped

68. MNS, December 24, 1953.

children, or whether it is more important to aid these children or old people (or perhaps instead to build another highway). Here the MOF usually has no particular expertise nor, more importantly, much direct interest. More and more its tendency has been to respond mechanically, with an administrative formula or a rule of thumb; to use cost criteria for policy judgments; to relegate a choice to ministry or party; or simply to do the same things as last year. For these reasons, in this broad middle ground — precisely the areas which most concern the line ministries — the budget process has become less and less conflictive. Some historical evidence to back up this observation will be found in chapter 9.

# 5

# The Liberal Democratic Party

THERE IS NO formal reason why the Japanese budget could not be compiled solely by officials. The majority party is needed only to assure its passage in the Cabinet and the Diet. However, the necessity of party approval at these two final stages, together with the strong perceived relationship between budgetary allocations and electoral fortunes, provide both interest and opportunity for LDP intervention in nearly all stages of the budget process.

The conventional norm for the role of the majority party in budgeting, as frequently expressed in newspaper editorials, is that it should establish the broad policy objectives to be met through the budget, functioning as something of a commission on national goals. Details of the budget should be left to administrative hands. This norm is fulfilled formalistically in the process leading up to the annual LDP Budget Compilation Program, but in reality, such general goal identification is not of major significance. To determine how the party actually affects the budget, each level of the LDP's complex organization must be examined. The individual Dietman will be discussed first, followed by informal intraparty groups, the subunits of the Policy Affairs Research Council, the deliberating bodies which aggregate party opinions, and the famous LDP factions. The party leadership, including the president-prime minister, will be treated in the following chapter.

## Backbenchers

As in all democratic political systems, the Japanese legislator believes his first duty is to be re-elected, which means he must please his constituents. Residents of each election district want their fair share, or a bit more, of the bridges, highways, dams, sewers, schools and welfare facilities built with central government aid. They expect their Dietman to get the funds for them, and some will visit Tokyo in "petition groups" to encourage him. Much of any Dietman's time is taken up by meeting with these groups and handling their requests. A newly elected Dietman, Ozawa Ichirō, said that "my energy is now devoted to two things: handling requests from my constituency and learning how the Diet works. If people say that even after they ask me for something, nothing happens, I would soon be departing."[1] The obligation to service constituents' interests extends even to the most senior party figures: Fukuda Takeo was famous for meeting with local groups at his house every morning at breakfast, and only afterward beginning his duties as finance minister or LDP secretary-general.[2]

The budget grants sought by such local groups are frequently matters of line ministry rather than MOF choice. A Dietman will often lead a delegation to meet the appropriate division or bureau director of the Construction or Transport Ministry, impressing upon him the urgency of the demand. Afterward they proceed to the Finance Ministry for a brief talk with the Budget Bureau director, a vice-director or an examiner; even when the allocation desired is not within MOF competence, it is believed that such accumulated pressures will help raise the total appropriation for that category of projects. From the Dietman's point of view, all such demonstrations of his interest, and his ability to command the time of busy officials, can only add to his local reputation. To the MOF official, of course, responding to such petitioning appears as a waste of time, borne somewhat grudgingly, but he will feel that granting at least a brief meeting may help prevent the build-up of anti-MOF sentiment among LDP Dietmen, which might later rebound as intensified pressure on the budget.

Dietmen respond to constituency requests primarily in their own interests, not to benefit the party as a whole. However, the ability to serve local areas is no small component of the LDP's more generalized appeal, especially when contrasted with the ineffectuality of the opposition parties. Note the celebrated campaign speech in January 1971 by Justice Minister Kobayashi Takeji, supporting the LDP candidate for the governorship of Shizuoka, Takeyama Yutarō:

Now let me tell you why you should vote for Mr. Takeyama from a slightly different angle from those of the previous speakers. As you know the Government decided the 1971 budget on December 31 last year. To us members of the LDP, the months of October, November and December are the busiest season. We receive many petitions and demands from you. And it is the responsibility of

1. Asahi Shinbunsha, ed., *Jimintō: Hoshu Kenryoku no Kōzō* ("The Liberal Democratic Party: Structure of Conservative Power") (Tokyo: Asahi Shinbunsha, 1970), p. 18.
2. *Asahi Jaanaru* 8, 5 (January 30, 1966), 18-22. Tanaka Kakuei, when secretary-general, claimed to see at least 400 people on a busy morning. YS, December 10, 1965.

us members of the ruling party, the LDP and the Government, to have these wishes of yours incorporated into the budget. For this reason, we LDP Dietmen have no time to return to our constituencies. In other words, we are working closely with the Government in preparing the budget without sleep and without rest. During this time, what are the gentlemen of the opposition parties doing? I suppose they are back home to keep their feet warm or taking a nap. That is to say, the gentlemen of the opposition have nothing to do with the preparation of the budget. . . . The Diet is a place where people make a lot of noise, but it is powerless as far as budget-making is concerned. . . .

It is absolutely necessary for the central government to move tax money from a rich place to a poor place. If this is the case, every prefecture, city, town and village must count on the central government. This can't be helped. And if this is the case, the Government run by us, the LDP, would naturally be willing to accommodate the wishes of LDP mayors. But it is absolutely impossible for us to give aid to the strengthening of an opposition party.[3]

Kobayashi came under sharp criticism for demeaning the Constitutional role of the Diet, and quickly resigned. Whether or not his claim is completely accurate is difficult to prove: local areas governed by opposition parties perhaps are not greatly disadvantaged in the allocation of central government funds, though they may lose some marginal appropriations, and opposition Dietmen have also been known to petition successfully for local interests.[4] But it is clear that the aggregate of many small favors delivered to many areas over the years has helped to maintain LDP strength.

All Dietmen present petitions, but some are more successful than others. Political power and access are probably the major determinants. Residents of Fukuda Takeo's district in Gumma Prefecture were said never to worry about getting the public works projects they wanted — "just ask Governor Fukuda" was their slogan. Membership and particularly chairmanship of the appropriate Diet standing committee increase a Dietman's influence with a ministry, since its bills can easily be slowed in passage or shelved.[5] Local residents will expect that a Dietman with a special relationship to a ministry, such as former service as an official, parliamentary vice-minister or minister, will be able to secure unusual favors within its jurisdiction. Such expectations may force the Dietman to balance conflicting pressures: when Murayama Tatsuo was serving as parliamentary vice-minister in the Ministry of Transport, he rebuffed a group seeking funds to rebuild railroad stations in his home district by

3. Translated by Kiyoaki Murata. "The Consequence of Truth," *Japan Times,* February 10, 1971.

4. There is unfortunately little reliable information on either of these important points, although current research on urban politics nearing publication by Ronald Aqua of Cornell University will shed some light. Also see Terry Edward MacDougall, "Political Opposition and Local Government in Japan" (Unpublished Ph.D. Dissertation, Yale University, 1975).

5. Asahi Shinbunsha, *Jimintō,* pp. 28-29.

explaining the difficult fiscal situation of the Japan National Railroads. The petition group was annoyed, but an MOF bureau director commented afterward that Murayama "is a man whose understanding goes beyond the interests of his election district" — an expression of confidence that might well be helpful in later budget appeals.[6] Moreover, when a Dietman successfully goes to bat for a ministry request at the Ministry of Finance during the budget process, he is likely to receive a warm welcome when he approaches the ministry at the time individual project allocations are decided.[7]

Such requests individually have little effect on the character of the budget, since typically they refer to choosing a project within a program rather than enlarging the program's size, but they do provide a constant level of pressure for expenditure categories most closely tied to constituent interests: public works, grants-in-aid to local governments, pensions and so forth. Moreover, within a given budget category, LDP pressure may introduce a bias among *types* of programs that is deplored by more "objective" participants like the Budget Bureau: for example, it has been said that among public works, the high level of expenditures for agricultural water control is due to such projects being small enough to fit within a single election district.

The degree of rank-and-file pressure varies with the political situation, increasing particularly when elections are near. However, it appears that such surges of pressure are usually kept within bounds by the party leadership: as noted above, budget statistics reveal no consistent relationship between either the total size of the budget or grants to politically popular programs and the scheduling of elections. Rather, pressure from below seems to become an important factor in the budget process mainly when the party leadership is divided. Under such conditions, the party's budget policies have sometimes even been thrown open to debate in an assembly of all LDP Diet members, resulting in extra-strong formal spending demands.

## Unofficial Groups

The individual Dietman, unless he occupies an unusually strategic position, is too small a target for the national interest group to worry much about — he is seen as a "lone ship." It is more efficient to deal with groups of supporters.[8] The most rudimentary grouping of Dietmen is sometimes called a "tribe" (*zoku*), referring to numbers of LDP members who get together only at budget time to press for greater expenditures in some

6. *Ibid.*, pp. 24-25.
7. Cf. *ibid.*, pp. 130-32.
8. Such party bodies are the "mother ships." AS, December 27, 1964.

policy area. The prototype is the "public works tribe," which apparently first coalesced in 1956 when Tanaka Kakuei led a walkout of Dietmen from a not sufficiently positive Policy Deliberation Council meeting.[9] It remains the most active, but "tribes" in the agriculture, pensions and other fields are also frequently mentioned.

A degree more organized, although lacking the status of official party organs, are "Dietmen's leagues" (*Giin renmei*, or *dōmei*), which are sponsored by an interest group and, depending on the strategy being followed, may be restricted to LDP members or also include opposition Dietmen. In some cases, such as in agriculture, such leagues exist over a long period and are active as one component of a stable ministry-LDP-interest group "subgovernment." Other leagues are organized for one or a few years to support a one-time-only demand, such as those for compensation to former landlords expropriated during the land reform, or to postwar overseas repatriates. Another example is the league formed to support the establishment of a new financial agency to benefit "environmental hygiene" businesses.[10]

Such leagues often enroll a clear majority of LDP Dietmen as members, and sometimes nearly all join up.[11] An individual Dietman will probably belong to dozens. They are not an inordinate demand on his time, however, since often the sole requirement of membership is the inscription of his name on a list, and appearance for fifteen minutes or so at the annual convention of the sponsoring interest group. If he has a greater interest in the objectives of the league, he might be asked to take part in budget-time petitioning, but this is not required.

Few Dietmen see participation in such leagues as having much positive benefit beyond providing one more opportunity to show his face before constituents. The sponsoring interest group can rarely be counted upon for campaign contributions, and the leagues' catholic membership means that election day support is likely to be minor (since the candidate's LDP opponents within his multimember district may well also belong). On the other hand, the costs of joining are minimal, and Dietmen do not wish to incur the displeasure of voter-based organizations. They fear that if they refuse to enroll, a movement might be started against them in their home districts. A senior LDP Dietman said of the National Federation of

9. MNS, January 20, 1956.

10. See Haruhiro Fukui, "Compensating Former Landowners," *Party in Power: The Liberal Democratic Party in Policy-Making* (Berkeley and Los Angeles: University of California Press, 1970), pp. 173-197; John Creighton Campbell, "Compensation for Repatriates," in *Policymaking in Contemporary Japan,* ed. T.J. Pempel (Ithaca, N.Y.: Cornell University Press, forthcoming); "Yosan to Atsuryoku" ("Budget and Pressure"), YS, December 1 and 2, 1965; and Asahi Shinbunsha, *Jimintō,* pp. 137-140.

11. A league to support higher war-related pensions in the 1966 budget actually enrolled nearly the entire Diet, regardless of party. AS, January 11, 1966.

Repatriated Groups, and its associated Dietman's League for Handling the Overseas Property Problem: "I know their demands are thinly justified. But they have a lot of active power, if only because they worked together overseas. If you are their friend, you're safe, but I would be afraid of making an enemy of people with such high-handed characters. If I opposed them, they would be bound to tear up my constituency."[12]

Within the legislative process, the ultimate threat of such a league is the introduction of a Members' Bill (a bill not sponsored by the Cabinet); particularly when opposition Dietmen are included or allied, a league's membership alone would seem to be sufficient to assure passage. Though often mentioned, such threats rarely materialize. One reason is intraparty discipline in the LDP, which discourages such independence; another is the fact that active espousal of an actual bill, likely to be generally unpopular, may well bring more unfavorable publicity than mere participation in a league. Also, it is very often true that the demands of a league will be impossibly large. In the repatriates case, for example, the League for Handling the Overseas Property Problem was on record as supporting an appropriation of ¥600 billion (over $2 billion); Dietmen were willing to endorse this demand, at least in a pro forma way, but it is questionable if many really thought such a large grant would be justified. In actual decision making, a league is not well suited to performing the necessary function of cutting down an interest group's raw demands to more manageable proportions, for three reasons: it is too large for flexibility; its members are too close to local interest group activity, and thus sensitive to charges that they have "betrayed" the original demands; and, since the group has no official status, there is no assurance that any conclusions reached would be taken seriously by other participants.

Rather than unilaterally forcing a decision on its own, or taking an important role in the final process of compromise, leagues are important as one among several pressure-generating mechanisms. They can be particularly influential at the earlier stage of an interest group's strategy, when procedural rather than substantive objectives are being sought, as when asking for the appointment of an official party body (usually a special committee or investigative commission within the Policy Affairs Research Council) to decide how a problem should be handled. It is difficult for the leadership to reject a request for more reflection or information-gathering when it is backed even passively by a substantial portion of the party. Such a committee is smaller and more flexible than a league, is once removed from immediate interest group demands, and by its official status within the party has a legitimate claim for attention; hence it can play a more direct role in actual negotiations for a grant.

12. AS, February 22, 1967.

Other sorts of backbencher organizations in the LDP are worth a mention. The institutionalized intraparty factions are discussed below. In the 1950s and 1960s, several opinion groups formed around ideological causes (China policy, constitutional revision), but these rarely were salient for budgeting.[13] In July 1973, about thirty younger, "new right" conservative LDP Dietmen led by Ishihara Shintarō formed a new association called the "Seirankai," an event widely heralded as the birth of more ideological and policy-relevant factional patterns within the conservative party.[14] Its objectives included income redistribution, sympathy for the disadvantaged, and particularly a stronger defense effort, and the group did for a time attempt to have its views reflected in governmental expenditures, with some success. However, the Seirankai (and the more liberal group which soon sprang up to oppose it, the Hirakawakai) faded in notoriety after its first year or so, and at time of writing it appears doubtful that organized intraparty conflicts on broad policy issues will have much impact on Japanese budgeting.

The Dietmen's leagues described here are truly "bottom-up" phenomena. They represent the interests of LDP backbenchers and outside pressure groups, not the party as a whole. Accordingly, the leadership of the LDP often views them with mild distaste, as an occasional threat and continual nuisance, requiring time and political resources to keep under control

# The Policy Affairs Research Council

The Policy Affairs Research Council is a large and complex organization; though comprised only of Dietmen, its total "membership," the sum of the members of each of its constituent bodies, is much higher than the total number of LDP Dietmen because each serves on several concurrently. It is made up of a chairman (one of the party's "big four"); several vice-chairmen; the Policy Deliberation Commission (*Seisaku Shingikai* or *Seichō Shingikai*) of fifteen-twenty members; seventeen divisions (*bukai*) that correspond to government agencies; and numerous investigative commissions (*chōsakai*) and special committees (*tokubetsu iinkai*) established for particular problems or policy areas.[15] Of concern in this section are the lower-level PARC organs; the Deliberation Commission will be discussed below.

13. Cf. Fukui, *Party in Power,* pp. 198-262.

14. See J. Victor Koschmann, "Hawks on the Defensive: The Seirankai," *Japan Interpreter* 8, 4 (Winter 1974), 467-477, and citations therein.

15. In 1972 there were five vice-chairmen, nineteen members of the Policy Deliberation Commission, twenty-four investigative commissions, and thirty-three special committees.

*Committees.* — The investigative commissions and special committees, which can be only vaguely distinguished by function (and so henceforth will both be called "committees"), are perhaps most often reflections of the universal political tactic expressed in this jingle by Geoffrey Parsons:

If you're pestered by critics and hounded by faction,
To take some precipitate, positive action,
The proper procedure, take my advice, is,
Appoint a Commission and stave off the crisis.[16]

Within this general definition, several types of committees may be distinguished. Some stem from ideological pressures or otherwise have little to do with budgeting — those on Constitutional Revision, Foreign Relations, and (military) Base Problems are examples. Of the remainder, some, as in the repatriates case, are responses to an interest group's demand for governmental support; the appointment of such a committee is the next stage after a Dietmen's league in the group's budget strategy, and itself signifies that a "foothold" (*ashigakari*) has been attained which probably will lead to eventual formal party support. Such committees will have little connection with a government ministry; the repatriates' cause, for example, was at best supported only lukewarmly by the responsible agency (the Prime Minister's Office).

Most committees, however, are more directly related to the work of ministries and therefore overlap or conflict with the regular PARC divisions. One such type is supposed to be devoted to more fundamental or long-range issues within the ministry's policy area, while the division is absorbed in more routine business: an example is the Educational System Investigative Commission. Others are the converse, taking up only one part of the ministry's function. As is true of the Highway Investigative Commission and the Water Control Special Committee (both concerned with the Construction Ministry), these are often intensely interested in budgets, offering the many Dietmen promoting more public works spending another channel for pressure besides the division. These two committees included fifteen chairmen and vice-chairmen, and the incumbents of these posts invariably mention them in their election résumés.

---

Yamamoto Masao, *Keizai Kanryō no Jittai* ("The Reality of the Economic Bureaucrats") (Tokyo: Mainichi Shinbunsha, 1972), p. 108. For more detailed information see Jiyū Minshutō, "Seimu Chōsakai Meibo," ("Policy Affairs Research Council Membership List"), published irregularly; the June 21, 1969 edition was consulted. At that time there were fifteen divisions. More complete discussions of the PARC will be found in Fukui, *Party in Power*, pp. 83-89; and Nathaniel B. Thayer, *How the Conservatives Rule Japan* (Princeton, N.J.: Princeton University Press, 1969), pp. 207-236.

16. From "Royal Commission," *Punch*, August 24, 1955. Quoted in Harold Seidman, *Politics, Position and Power* (New York: Oxford University Press, 1970), p. 23.

Other committees are established when the LDP wishes to appear active (to the public or to an interest group) in a policy area that overlaps the functions of several ministries: of the nineteen committees created in 1971-72, those with this character included the Comprehensive Transportation, "70s Problems," Comprehensive Energy, and Land Problems Investigative Commissions and the Youth Policy, Aged Policy, Traffic Safety, International Cultural Exchange, Rural Village Industrialization Policy, and Population Increase Policy Special Committees. Party spokesmen sometimes assert that such committees take an active role in fighting ministerial sectionalism and resolving conflicts among participating interests, but such functions are probably exceptional; it is more likely that each will simply press for more expenditures or other government activity in its own area.

The most interesting type of committee is established in competition with, or as a counterweight to, one of the regular divisions. An example is the Medical Care Basic Problems Investigative Commission. Ostensibly appointed to take a long-term view of the health insurance program, which ranks in Ministry of Finance eyes along with rice price supports and the maintenance of outmoded railroad lines as one of the most wasteful drains on the treasury, this committee actually functions as the voice of the Japan Medical Association within the LDP. In the annual debates over medical insurance, the Ministry of Health and Welfare argues that medical costs to patients should be kept low, both by making up deficits through General Account contributions and by holding down the fees paid to doctors. Divisions routinely support their ministries and the Social Affairs Division does generally share this Welfare viewpoint, albeit without much enthusiasm. The JMA, however, is a powerful interest group well represented both directly and indirectly in the LPD, and its view that medical fees should be raised each year (through treasury financing and increased direct charges to patients) is articulated by the Investigative Commission, and indeed often prevails.[17]

*Divisions.* — The PARC divisions are the most important party representatives in the ministry-LDP-interest group alliances which we term "subgovernments," the basic elements of Japanese budgetary politics. Each ministry has a single corresponding division (except the Ministry of Agriculture and Forestry, which has one for agriculture and forestry, and another for fisheries); the Prime Minister's Office and the Defense Agency are also represented. Each has a chairman and (usually) three vice-chairmen; total membership varies from 44 (Foreign Relations) to 155

17. An excellent account of the politics of medical care is William E. Steslicke, *Doctors in Politics: The Political Life of the Japan Medical Association* (New York: Praeger, 1973).

(Agriculture-Forestry), averaging 72.[18] Relative size is a good indication of the political attractiveness of each policy area, because membership is partly assigned (all LDP members of Diet standing committees sit on corresponding divisions) and partly voluntary. The Construction and the Transportation Divisions follow Agriculture-Forestry in popularity. The Financial Division corresponds to the Ministry of Finance but usually concerns itself with banking, monetary policies, and other nonbudgeting functions of the ministry — actually, the expenditure budget is the single most important concern of the divisional structure as a whole, rather than that of a single body. Divisions meet fairly regularly, but most intensively when budget negotiations are active (perhaps twice a week in the early fall, every day during the appeals negotiations).[19]

As Thayer points out, although political journalists often speculate on whether it is bureaucrats or politicians who are really in the saddle in the ministry-division relationship, seeing the two sides as antagonistic is misleading.[20] They are most often very cooperative and mutually supportive. Close relations are encouraged by the number of ex-bureaucrats within the LDP (between one-fourth and one-third of conservative Dietmen, depending on definitions), since "old boys" of a ministry tend to continue their specialization by affiliating with its corresponding division, and as members their expertise and good relations with current officials help make them disproportionately influential.[21] Probably even more important, however, are the ties which develop naturally among men who work together over time, built on a foundation of shared interests. Each side can perform many favors for the other.

For the division member, the ministry is a source of information and technical aid, as when he has an idea he wishes to have drafted into a bill. It controls low-level budgetary decisions that may be very important to his constituents, such as where certain projects may be located. If he has larger scale policy ideas, convincing upper-level ministry officials of their worth may be the surest road to implementation. On the other hand, for the ministry official, divisional backing is often a necessary and occasionally a sufficient condition for obtaining approval of a budget request, as well as for legislation or other policy objectives (although their handling may differ in detail from the process described here). Also, division members may be important in the future career of the individual official, both for promotion within the ministry and in obtaining a postretirement position.[22]

18. Figures as of 1969, from Jiyū Minshutō, "Seimu Chōsakai Meibo."
19. Thayer, *Conservatives,* p. 216.
20. *Ibid.,* pp. 225-26.
21. See Asahi Shinbunsha, *Jimintō,* p. 124.
22. There are many descriptions of this relationship. See particularly Nihon Keizai Shinbunsha, ed., *Yosan wa Dare no Mono ka* ("The Budget: Whose is it?") (Tokyo Nihon

In general, the relationship between a ministry and its corresponding PARC division is not dissimilar to that between an American executive department or bureau and a Congressional legislative — not appropriations — committee. In both cases, the members tend to support the agency's program, and serve as its representatives in the larger "legislative" body. Division members, particularly the chairman, will be consulted before all important ministry actions, and communication will be frequent throughout the year. Unlike American legislative committees, however, PARC divisions have an institutionalized role in the budget process.

*Advice and Consent.* — In the late summer or early fall, after a ministry has drafted its budget requests, top officials will appear before the appropriate division to explain their plans and hear advice from the members. For example, the Ministry of Education's hearings in 1970 lasted three days, from August 26 to 28. Since this is a vacation period for Dietmen, when most return to their home districts, attendance is spotty, but most of the important members show up. For the ministry, the Accounting Division director and usually the deputy vice-minister carry the main load of exposition, assisted by bureau directors discussing their own programs. Attention is focused on new programs or unusually large increases requested for old programs. Questions asked by the Dietmen are usually supportive, designed to bring out strong points rather than probe for weaknesses, but differences between bureaucrat and politician will sometimes emerge.

These differences are likely to be of perspective or emphasis, the division tending to favor aspects of the ministry's program which are most closely related to constituency or pressure group interests. For example, at least in the early 1960s, there was a running debate between the Ministry of International Trade and Industry and the PARC Commerce and Industry Division over whether more of the budget should be aimed at promoting exports (the ministry's preference) or at modernizing small and medium industry (the division's demand). The dispute reflected MITI's big business orientation and the importance accorded small business interest groups by the LDP.[23] In public works, both the Construction and Transport Ministries and the MOF have tended to favor large projects, as reflecting their views of Japan's economic needs (and also perhaps the influence of

Keizai Shinbunsha, 1971), pp. 103-125; and Masumi Junnosuke, "Jiyū Minshutō no Soshiki to Kinō" ("The Liberal Democratic Party: Organization and Function") in *Nihon Seiji Gakkai Nenpō* ("The Annals of the Japanese Political Science Association") (Tokyo: Iwanami Shoten, 1967), pp. 34-77 and esp. 66ff. It has been observed similarly for the United States that "a congenial agency can do as much for the 'right' members of Congress as members of Congress can do for the agency." Herbert Kaufman, *Are Government Organizations Immortal?* (Washington, D.C.: The Brookings Institution, 1976), p. 6.

23. See NKS, December 25, 1961, and December 3, 1963.

engineers—who seem to prefer technically ambitious endeavors—within these two line ministries). The divisions or committees concerned, on the other hand, usually are more interested in smaller projects, particularly water control and local roads, which directly benefit a particular local government or group. Such disputes are most often worked out by compromise rather easily, because the problems are concerned with how money should be divided, rather than two exclusive ideological positions; they are typically handled within the division and ministry rather than drawing intervention from the party leadership (unless the interests of another ministry, and therefore another division, are involved).

The division will also hear interest group representatives at about the same time, separately from the ministerial hearings. A Budget Bureau representative, usually the director, may attend some of these hearings, particularly if an anticipated thorny budget problem is to be discussed.

The effect of the fall hearings is somewhat unclear. Some Ministry of Finance informants, and some published sources, maintain that ministry requests are very often revised afterward, nearly always upwards.[24] Interviewed ministry budget officers, however, indicate that this happens very rarely. Likely division reactions may be anticipated to some extent when drawing up the requests, but suggestions at the hearings themselves that a particular item be raised will probably draw the response that since the MOF would never accept a larger figure, revision would be pointless. If the prepared requests already add up to the prescribed ceiling figure, any raise would require cutting another program, which is very difficult after ministerial consensus has already been reached.

In any case, the most significant output of these hearings appears to be the rough and informal idea of specific PARC divisional priorities which emerges. One source indicates that a copy of each ministry's request summary, marked with symbols indicating the programs of greatest interest, is given to the MOF in mid or late September.[25] If so, the document apparently is not seen by the examiner, and probably is not too important. The major channel of communication from the division to the Budget Bureau is via the ministry. Ministry officials gain a sense of PARC division preferences either from the contents and tone of questions asked and opinions expressed at the hearings themselves, or from discussions or a report after the hearings and later deliberations. In their September meetings with the budget examiner, these officials will indicate informally which programs seem to be strongly backed by the LDP; the examiner may himself ask questions designed to reveal the party's attitude (for example,

24. Nihon Keizai Shinbunsha, *Yosan wa Dare no Mono ka,* p. 105.
25. *Ibid.,* pp. 105-106.

with regard to these programs backed more strongly by the ministry than by the party). Later inquiries from the Budget Bureau to the ministry, in the course of internal budget compilation, may also center on such concerns.

During these fall months, the division itself does not routinely participate in the budget process. At most, if the ministry runs into unusual difficulties at the MOF, the division chairman may be asked to help by calling the finance minister, the BB director, or sometimes the examiner. However, there have been more significant exceptions: for the 1972 budget, in which the financing of the national railroad system was perhaps the most critical problem, the PARC's Transportation, Local Finance, and Fiscal Divisions could not agree on a long-term plan, and without party approval a budget request could not be filed on schedule in the early fall. Not until December did leaders of the three divisions manage even to get together to discuss the issue (in a semiformal National Railways Reconstruction Problem Discussion Group). Perceiving that actual decision-making authority in this case had passed from the National Railways and the Ministry of Transport, the Budget Bureau entered into direct talks with the LPD's Transportation Division during the budget preparation period, and came to agreement on a plan — one which incorporated several MOF policies, including the "beneficiary principle" of sharp fare hikes — even in the absence of a formal budget request (which was not submitted until an hour or so before the release of the Finance Ministry draft in Janury).[26] But such behavior is still regarded as unorthodox, and generally speaking the Budget Bureau tries to avoid much intervention by the LDP in microbudgeting matters until after the MOF draft. This example is also exceptional in the degree of policy initiative displayed by the divisions. More often, divisions simply react to ministry proposals; indeed, rather than specifically rank-ordering programs, the Dietmen most often simply will be enthusiastic about one, and very enthusiastic about another.

Many LDP members have called for more effective party inputs into the budget process at the divisional level. However, the divisions usually are dependent on the documentation and arguments provided by the sponsoring ministry, or sometimes by an interest group. Assistance from the party's tiny professional staff is minimal.[27] Many Dietmen build up substantial experience with a ministry's work — leading division members may continue for decades, while both ministry officials and budget examiners rotate every two years or so — but the many demands on their

26. Yamamoto, *Keizai Kanryō no Jittai,* pp. 98-100.
27. This staff is too small to be significant: Thayer, *Conservatives,* p. 216.

time and that of their personal staffs preclude even much analysis of ministry materials, let alone independent investigations.[28] Even if divisional members were sufficiently motivated to take a critical look at agency operations, and were willing to risk the resentment of affected ministry or interest group requesters, their informational resources would prevent any but the most superficial objections.

The motivational aspect, however, may be the most important. Perhaps as another consequence of high-growth budgeting, at no time in the postwar Japanese Diet has there been significant pressure for "cheap government."[29] Both the LDP and the opposition parties have tended to call for more spending on nearly all governmental programs, almost never asking for reductions; the marginal benefits in support gained by increasing particularistic programs apparently outweigh more generalized concerns about taxes.[30] An LDP Dietman, speaking of the grant to former landlords in 1965, expressed this thinking well: "This is a bill that doesn't hurt anyone. Those who got the money are happy, and grateful to us Dietmen. As for the ordinary citizens, the grant is in bonds [rather than cash], so it won't hurt them right away."[31] The strong cutting bias of the House Appropriations Committee in the United States, according to Richard Fenno, stems directly from the goals and expectations of the House as a whole.[32] It is thus not surprising that in Japan, where such expectations are lacking, that the divisions should follow the lead of the ministries and call for more spending. The most common characterization of the division is a "cheering section" (ōendan), sitting on the sidelines and applauding each move of its ministry as it battles with the MOF.

## Aggregating Mechanisms

Divisional participation in budgeting is "fragmented," to use Wildavsky's term: each division considers only its own policy area, with little or no attention to relationships with other policies or the "national interest." Most of the division's influence is within its own subgovernment, on the ministry's requests or on the budget decisions taken by the corresponding

28. Each Dietman serves on an average of eight PARC Divisions and Committees, accordig to Fukui, Party in Power, p. 86.

29. An interviewed MOF official ascribed this lack to Japan's never having undergone a "people's revolution," which would have created a feeling among citizens that "the government is something we made ourselves."

30. The progressive parties do of course demand reductions in the defense budget and industrial subsidies, but interestingly not in agriculture or small business expenditures, since they hope to pick up votes there. For example, see Amano Hajime, "Ōkurashō Kanryō" ("Ministry of Finance Bureaucrats") Chūō Kōron 84, 10 (October 1969), 241-252.

31. "Yosan to Atsuryoku," YS, December 5, 1965.

32. Richard F. Fenno, Jr., The Power of the Purse: Appropriations Politics in Congress (Boston: Little, Brown and Company, 1966), esp. pp. 8-17.

examiner. However, as the governing party, the LDP also feels a responsibility for broad national policy as expressed through the budget.

The two bodies formally charged with formulating and approving party policy from this national point of view are the Policy Deliberation Commission, of fifteen to twenty members, and the Executive Council (*Sōmukai*), with thirty members. Although these two organs are distinct, their budgeting functions are quite similar.[33] In addition, other integrating bodies have at times been given substantial budget roles: a conference of all divisional chairmen, the PARC vice-chairmen group, and especially formed units like the Important Policy Consultative Committee or the Basic Policy Discussion Group.

*The Budget Compilation Program.* — The major formal LDP document on the budget is the party's Budget Compilation Program (*Yosan Hensei Taikō,* at times referred to as the Basic Policy for Budget Compilation, *Yosan Hensei Kihon Hoshin,* although properly speaking this term means the first part only). Originally this policy statement was intended to be a programmatic guide for the government's budget compilation, specific as to priorities if not actual budget figures, and prepared early enough in the fall to have a real impact. However, this attempt at party control of the budgetary process failed — the program has been quite general and vague, and since 1961 has been released only shortly before the publication of the MOF draft.[34]

The size, form and even contents of the Program remain rather constant from year to year. That of 1970 is typical. The first section is the seven point "Basic Policy" (*Kihon Hōshin*), which may be summarized except for Item 5, on expenditures:

1. Growth without inflation; lowering the bond ratio.
2. Various tax reductions.
3. "Efforts" to eliminate the factors causing Supplementary Budgets.
4. Price stability.
5. "While continuing to work toward the repletion of social capital, necessary resources for important policies concerned with comprehensive agriculture, promotion of small and medium industry, environmental and traffic safety measures and others will be provided, and reductions will be realistically planned for allocations of lower priority."
6. "Strict control" of governmental organizations and employees.
7. "Healthy management" of local government.

33. See the more complete discussions of structure and function of these bodies in Thayer, *Conservatives,* pp. 254-267; and Fukui, *Party in Power,* pp. 89-92.

34. The period between release of the two documents varied from two to five days, except when the MOF draft had been delayed into January. Then the custom is for the Program to be released just before the New Year break, and the MOF draft just afterward.

The second part, entitled "Important Policies" (*Jūten Shisaku*), is over ten times the size of the first part. There are 14 major headings, such as "The Renovation of Education and the Promotion of Science and Technology" and "The Modernization of Small and Medium Industry." These are followed by several items or items and subitems; the total number of entries, those not further subdivided, is 116. As one example, under the heading "Promotion of Agriculture, Forestry and Fishing," Item 3 is "Promotion of Fishing," and one of its three subitems reads:

Along with accelerating fishing harbor construction, seashore preservation works, and repair and construction of roads to fishing harbors, the establishment of large-scale underwater rocky areas for fishing, the development of new fishing grounds and structural reform works for coastal fishing will be systematically promoted.

Not all subitems or items are quite this broad, but it will be appreciated that 116 entries of this nature can easily cover a great deal.[35]

One interesting aspect of this document is that although it is a budgetary policy, actual money figures are very rarely used. There have been a few exceptions, mainly in those cases when the MOF and the party have already agreed, before the Program is prepared, on a budget ceiling, the size of the tax cut or the proportion of the budget to be covered by deficit financing. These negotiated figures may then be included in Part One, but Part Two, dealing with expenditure programs, almost never includes actual figures. Three major reasons for this peculiar omission may be advanced: first, the Ministry of Finance has consistently and actively opposed the use of projected budget figures by any other budget participant; second, the informational and technical resources of the PARC are not sufficient to draw up what would in effect by its own budget; third, if figures were attached, the budget requests of the ministries (and the divisions) would either have to be cut, arousing resentment, or else all these figures would add up to a total much higher than available revenues—embarrassing to the party, and still leaving the actual budgeting decisions up to the MOF.

A second aspect of note is the scope of the program, which spans nearly the full range of governmental activities and calls for increases in each. There is little attempt at systematic setting of priorities: a few broad areas are singled out for mention in Item 5 of Part 1, but they are not a plausible list of the nation's, the government's or even the party's main interests for 1970. Neither traffic safety nor pollution received any further party notice that year, small business and social capital appeared to get the

35. Jiyū Minshutō, "Shōwa 45 Nendo Yosan Hensei Taikō" ("Fiscal Year 1970 Budget Compilation Program"), undated pamphlet. The text is also reproduced in *Kuni no Yosan*, 1970, pp. 888-892.

same attention as in other years, and the appeal for "reductions in allocations of lower priority" may be seen as gratuitous. The order of the "shopping list" in Part Two is not completely meaningless, but it is not possible to extract from it a specific idea of LDP intentions. The indiscriminate use of vague words like "stress," "strengthen" and "complete" add to the confusion.

These characteristics of the Budget Compilation Program flow naturally from the process which produces it, and, more generally, the nature of the party organization itself. The document is drawn up by the Policy Deliberation Commission and then ratified, sometimes after amendments, by the Executive Board. As noted above, both bodies are supposed to take a "national" view, rising above parochial interests. However, when the Deliberation Commission draws up the Program in a series of meetings in December, it relies almost totally on information provided by the lower levels of the Policy Board (primarily the divisions, although committees may also participate either by working up joint recommendations with a division or by filing a separate draft). Both written materials and oral testimony from the divisions are received; these are based on the hearings held in late summer or in more detailed discussions with ministry officials held in November or earlier. Other Dietmen and Cabinet ministers may appear. The Commission boils down the masses of material into the document described above, which is then passed (usually in a brief session) by the Executive Board. From there, the program is sent on to the Cabinet and the Ministry of Finance, where nothing in particular is done with it.

Much detail is not available on the operations of the Commission at this stage; it is safe to say that, whatever its role may be in other types of legislation, these December meetings are not the forum for thoughtful and far-reaching discussions of national goals and the policies to implement them, nor for searching examinations of existing or proposed programs to see if they are vital or even desirable. As for the divisions, scarcity of time and information is sufficient to explain such lack of consideration, but just as important has been the unwillingness of upper-level party bodies to offend those below. Each divison has set forth its recommendations, and to ignore these would amount to a statement that a division's favorite programs are not important, or not as important as some other programs. Such harsh official judgments by the party would anger ministries, interest groups and voters, who would tend to blame division members or their other representatives within the LDP for insufficient vigor.

Party sources report that the only time a divisional recommendation is likely to be rejected at either the Deliberation Commission or Executive Board level is when it runs directly against the interests of either a very influential party leader or a major segment of party opinion. This sometimes occurs. However, many budgeting problems can be "solved," in the sense of satisfying interested contenders, by simply recommending more money for both sides, and this course is often adopted. More intractable are disputes between subgovernments: jurisdictional arguments about which ministry (and division) is to be responsible for a new program, or whether one ministry's expanded program should be allowed to encroach on another's territory. Political observers sometimes say that these disputes are most often solved through the LDP; however, if such conflict resolution does occur during the budgetary process, there is little evidence to suggest that the drawing up of the Budget Compilation Program is very helpful. The Program more often ignores or glosses over such confrontations.

In this connection, Haruhiro Fukui maintains that the Executive Council is more susceptible to interest groups, within and outside the party, than is the Deliberation Commission. Particulary in budgeting, this pattern is said to lead to the frequent overruling of Commission recommendations.[36] Since the Commission's draft is not usually published, direct comparisons of the two documents are difficult, but cases of these recomendations being dropped at the Executive Council level appear to be rare. More often, the rank order and sometimes the wording of some recommendations will be changed, and it is common for a few more items to be added on by the Council. For example, for the 1968 Program the amendments by the Executive Board amounted to adding a call for a "comprehensive energy policy," new mentions of defense and military base problems, and slightly more stress on housing and highways.[37]

Finally, the most important point about the Budget Compilation Program is that it has virtually no effect in the actual budget process. It is decided and published immediately before release of the Ministry of Finance draft budget, which at that point has been all but decided and is undergoing final MOF ratifiction. The appeals negotiation period is yet to come, of course, but what is needed for that process is not a broad statement of goals and suggestions but specific reactions to the cuts made by the MOF.[38] The fact that the document will never be used naturally conditions the process which produces it: Deliberation Commission and Executive Council members have little motive to be specific, or to cut requests back to realistic limits, when such difficult and painful labor would have so little payoff.

What, then, is the function of the Program? As with some other highly publicized aspects of Japanese budgeting, it is mostly symbolic. Ministry and interest group representatives are given an opportunity to tell the

36. Fukui, *Party in Power*, p. 91.
37. AS, December 28, 1967.
38. The appeals process, which is more significant, will be described in chap. 7.

governing party what they need, and Dietmen gain a feeling of participating in party decisions and being listened to by the leadership. The party goes on record as supporting a variety of proposals, at least some of which would be attractive to any voter. If these are not finally carried out, clearly the fault would lie not with the Liberal Democrats, but with the Ministry of Finance.

*Other Policy Organs.* — The LDP leaders well realize that the cost of such symbolic gratification is a loss of real influence in budgetary decision making, and they have sought at various times to institute new organizational forms, insulated from the normal process, to come up with more implementable recommendations. Rather than being dependent on the divisions, such bodies are intended to meet with government officials and Cabinet ministers, and their reports are to be prepared early enough to guide the MOF. In 1956, a special Budget Subcommittee (*Yosan Shōiinkai*) of the Policy Board met for four afternoons in September with EPA officials, monetary experts from the Bank of Japan, private economic commentators, and MOF administrative and parliamentary vice-ministers and bureau directors. For the 1958 budget, a similar group was called the Important Policy Advisory Committee (*Jūyō Seisaku Shimon'iinkai*). During both the 1961 and 1964 budget processes, the contemporary Policy Board chairmen, Fukuda Takeo and Miki Takeo, called for the Policy Deliberation Commission to discuss budgetary matters without reference to the divisions; for 1964, the Commission held several meetings in August. In 1968, a new body called the Basic Policies Discussion Council (*Kihon Seisaku Kondandai*) was established, chaired by the Policy Board chairman and with thirty-nine (in 1969) senior and experienced members. It met in the October-November period during the 1969 and 1970 budget processes. However, by its second year, familiar patterns reappeared — several of its nine sessions were devoted to testimony by divisional chairmen. Then, for the 1971 budget, an attempt at better insulation was made by beginning meetings of the Discussion Council as early as June, and by adopting a topical approach (sessions on the economic and fiscal situation; "salary man" problems including urban programs, land use and inflation; tax reform; education; and agriculture) instead of a ministry-by-ministry review. These meetings too apparently had little or no effect on the actual budget.

That such bodies were created so frequently indicates that the majority party hoped for a more effective voice in budgeting. That they failed just as frequently is due to two reasons: the Ministry of Finance was not particularly eager to receive real, rather than symbolic, policy guidance; and the LDP itself was unable to liberate itself from internal pressures and accustomed styles of decision making.

Other innovations aimed at increasing the party's voice in budgeting at the aggregate, "national" level have been proposed from time to time. In the 1960s, Tanaka Kakuei and others suggested establishing a research institute or think-tank, including experts from outside the party. An interviewed Policy Board veteran said that more professional staff should be attached to the Deliberation Commission, and party leaders often emphasize that only the most experienced and able Dietmen be appointed to the Commission and that they should take their work very seriously. Clearly, frequent reiteration of such points demonstrates that the LDP is dissatisfied with its effectiveness, and also that it has been unable to develop the necessary institutional means for formulating and implementing broad policy alternatives. Most fundamentally, perhaps the party has underestimated the difficulties of budgetary decision making at anything above a piecemeal basis.

# Factions

This discussion of LDP roles in budgeting has proceeded so far without much mention of the word "faction" (ha, or habatsu), a surprising omission to the reader familiar with typical writing on the Japanese party system. Robert Ward, for example, writes that "in fact, it is in some ways more accurate to view [the LDP] as a loose coalition of factions united for purposes of campaign and legislative strategy, rather than as a unified national party." Scalapino and Masumi maintain that "the faction, reflective of the cultural roots of Japanese society and the nature of all Japanese organization, has occupied the vital center of the political process."[39]

Neither of these observations is incorrect, but the significance given to factions must vary considerably depending on both the subject and era under investigation. Factions dominate appointments to Cabinet and party posts, most importantly in the selection of the president of the party (who automatically becomes prime minister). They are important in the distribution of party funds, and sometimes in intraparty ideological disputes. There are many cases of factions taking the key role in policy making, particularly major foreign policy decisions.[40] On the other hand, they are rarely very influential in more routine policy making processes. Also, the influence of factions has tended to decline over the years, though with ups and downs; they are most active at politically unsettled times, and

39. Robert E. Ward, Japan's Political System (Englewood Cliffs, N.J.: Prentice-Hall, 1967), p. 65; Robert A. Scalapino and Junnosuke Masumi, Parties and Politics in Contemporary Japan (Berkeley: University of California Press, 1963), p. 149.
40. See Haruhiro Fukui, "Studies in Policymaking: A Review of the Literature," in Policymaking, ed. Pempel.

Japanese politics generally was quieting down between the mid-1950s and the early 1970s. Donald Hellman, in his analysis of the peace agreement with the Soviet Union in 1956, speaks of the "tight intermingling of the *ha* conflicts with foreign policy making," and concludes that "government policy eventually was determined as much by the *habatsu* maneuvers as by international considerations."[41] This assessment is in sharp contrast with the picture presented in this study of budgetary decision making due to differences both of era (1955-56, the period of conservative party union, was a high point of factional activity) and of the kinds of policy making under discussion.

Factions in the LDP are informal groups of Dietmen, held together by ties of political convenience, money, and personal relations, and normally led by a potential (or current) party president. Their number fluctuates: in 1974, there were five main factions, having thirty-eight to eighty-nine members, and four with twenty or fewer members.[42] Since nearly all LDP Dietmen belong to factions, and since many appointments are awarded at least partly on a factional basis (including those to the Cabinet, the Policy Deliberation Council, the Executive Council, PARC vice-chairmen, and so forth), it is inevitable that there are many points of contact between factionalism and the budget process. However, the question of most interest here is, what direct role do the factions as institutions play, or what difference would it make to budgeting if they did not exist?

In general, the degree of direct factional intervention into the budget process in a given year is determined not by the kinds or intensity of budget issues current, but by the intensity of factional strife already present, brought on by other factors. Most often such strife has occurred when the party presidency has been in doubt. The most extreme disruption of the budgetary process by factions was in 1960, when the government draft was delayed for many days by pressures which arose from intraparty maneuvering to remove Prime Minister Kishi from office. Even in the considerably more placid years of the late 1960s the occasion of a coming presidential election produced factional debate over budget issues. Anti-mainstream factions sought to distinguish their positions from the mainstream on all major issues, including macrobudgeting questions, and criticize the budgetary actions of the prime minister and finance minister.[43] Most often, in a bid for backbencher support, the antimainstream will call for more spending, to be financed by more generous

41. Donald C. Hellman, *Japanese Foreign Policy and Domestic Politics* (Berkeley and Los Angeles: University of California Press, 1969), pp. 73, 154.

42. *Seiji Handobukku* (April 1974), 194-200. Good discussions of factional structure and functioning may be found in the works cited above, as well as writings by Watanabe Tsuneo, e.g. *Habatsu to Tatōka Jidai* ("Factions and the Era of Multipartisanship") (Tokyo: Sekkasha, 1967).

43. For example, see AS, December 2, 1966; NKS, November 15, 1968; and AS, November 20, 1968.

growth estimates or a larger bond issue.[44] Such debates receive much publicity in the newspapers, but as a retired MOF elder statesman said in an interview:

If the "opposition party" within the LDP happens to have a great deal of power, the Ministry of Finance might feel that its opinions should be taken into account. However, in general, it would be very rare for this to have much effect.

A rather more significant, though still marginal, impact of factionalism on budgeting works through the pattern of appointments to party and government posts. When the prime minister, finance minister, secretary-general and PARC chairman are of the same or allied factions, criticism is more likely to be abstract and less likely to disturb the actual budget process. It is rare for any of the first three of these posts to be held by any but a mainstream politician, but the PARC chairman sometimes is (or becomes) opposed to the mainstream. For the 1966 budget, Maeo Shigesaburō occupied this post and sharply disagreed with the position taken by Prime Minister Satō and Finance Minister Fukuda on the size of the new bond issue. In 1973 PARC Chairman Kuraishi Tadao of the opposition Fukuda faction effectively undercut the budgetary demands of Hashimoto Tomisaburō, the secretary-general and senior member of the Tanaka faction. In a magazine interview, Mizuta Mikio, who has served five terms as finance minister, was asked about his secrets for budget compilation, and answered in part:

. . . one hopes that the LDP PARC chairman and the finance minister will be of the same faction. Situations which have to be cleaned up between the government and the party are always coming along, and if these two men are not in complete accord they cannot be handled skillfully. There are cases where because the finance minister and the PARC chairman came from different factions, the budget could not be completed on schedule and was carried over into the next year.[45]

That common factional affiliation makes communication among politicians easier was indicated by a senior politician, asked in an interview if it were to the advantage of a Cabinet minister to be in the same faction as the finance minister during the final budget negotiations. He replied that it is hard to say whether more funds would be granted than otherwise, or rather if the finance minister would simply have an easier time convincing the minister to moderate his demands. But, in either case, the negotiations would not take as long.

44. An early example is NKS, December 14, 1960. See also NKS, November 2, 1965, and October 13 and November 15, 1968; and AS, December 2, 1966 and November 20, 1968.
45. Reprinted in Asahi Shinbun Keizaibu, *Keizai Seisaku no Butaiura* ("Economic Policy Behind the Scenes") (Tokyo: Asahi Shinbunsha, 1974), p. 78.

Another form of factional participation in budgeting is seen in cases where a faction takes on some attributes of an interest group representative. Kōno Ichirō's faction was well known as sympathetic to agricultural and particularly fishery interests, and was active in intraparty movements to secure more funds for the Ministry of Agriculture and Forestry. The Satō faction has sometimes taken positions favorable to the Ministry of Transport, stemming from its leader's earlier service in the forerunner of that ministry. In a somewhat different sense, the Ōhira Masayoshi (earlier Maeo) faction, which includes many ex-MOF officials, has sometimes supported restrictive Finance Ministry positions against party voices calling for more spending; this was notably true in the 1968 budget process, when the MOF was in the midst of its "antifiscal rigidification campaign," and was greatly aided by Ōhira as Policy Board chairman.[46]

Leaders of the larger factions, of course, are individually influential politicians, and the support of one of them for a budget proposal is always helpful and sometimes crucial. Tradition has it that an LDP elder such as Kawashima Shōjirō (a partisan of many causes) could simply walk up to the finance minister at any stage of the budget process and hand him a piece of paper, on which would be written a number and a couple of characters identifying a program. This number would then inevitably appear in the final draft of the budget. Whether or not such occurrences are common, however, it is clear that unlike the 1950s, by the mid-1960s summit meetings of top faction leaders were no longer being called to settle or ratify tough budget decisions.[47] The impacts of factional alliances and disputes on budgeting seem to be either rhetorical or largely procedural, smoothing or complicating budget compilation without influencing actual contents very much. As a former finance minister said in an interview, "factions don't really touch the budget any more."

# Conclusions

A recent journalistic survey of the Japanese budget system concludes that "in deciding the contents of the budget, the power of the Liberal Democratic Party is great. Even up against the 'Finance bureaucrats' . . . it stands supreme."[48] Can this judgment be sustained? Does the LDP dominate Japanese budgeting?

The question is a complicated one, and unfortunately is obscured by the fact that nearly everyone involved with Japanese budgeting finds it in his interest to magnify the role played by the majority party. The line

46. See NKS, December 30, 1967, and January 18, 1968 evening.
47. Cf. AS, December 17, 1958, for the earlier pattern.
48. Nihon Keizai Shinbunsha, *Yosan wa Dare no Mono ka,* p. 106.

ministries are able to explain gaps and deficiencies in their programs by citing a lack of enthusiasm from Dietmen. Ministry of Finance officials blame the LDP for preventing shifts of resources away from wasteful, outmoded and "backward-looking" policy areas. Journalists find "political interference" a dependable source of picturesque copy. LDP leaders and members also like to think of themselves as influential and surely wish to convince interest groups and constituents of their efficacy in obtaining financial benefits. Even the objective scholarly observer will tend to play up the role of the majority party, because its direct participation in decision making is one of the most distinctive features of the Japanese budgetary system. We must therefore try to define the locus and impact of LDP participation in the budgetary system as precisely as we can. First, what sort of role does the LDP play in budgeting? Second, what has been the impact of its participation at our three levels of aggregation — microbudgeting, macrobudgeting and integration? Third, how has the party influenced the budget system itself and the way it makes decisions?

What role does the LDP play? One might imagine at least three possible functions for a governing political party in budgeting. First, it might — as newspaper editorialists advise — formulate general principles and priorities to be carried out through the budget, leaving the details to bureaucrats. Second, it might formulate a relatively specific blueprint of budgetary allocations. Third, it might simply throw its weight behind a few programs of greatest clientele appeal.

The Liberal Democrats try to do all three, but the significance of the first two turns out to be more rhetorical than real. The Basic Policy for Budget Compilation, the first part of the Budget Compilation Program, is supposed to establish fundamental principles, but it is couched in such abstract language that very little policy direction can be inferred. Its short list of purported priority expenditures (Item 5 in the translation above) is not a plausible ordering of top government priorities, nor a highlighting of new or controversial programs, nor even a demand for the LDP's special interests (since several of these, such as pensions, are not included, and items like pollution or traffic safety received no further attention from the party). Clearly the Basic Policy is aimed almost entirely at public consumption, not real influence.

The second part of this document, Important Policies, resembles a blueprint for the budget. It is both wide-ranging and very detailed. However, it contains neither a rank-ordering of preferences nor projected budget figures attached to the recommendations; in effect, expansion of nearly everything the government does or might do is called for. This portion too is essentially a public relations effort, though intended more for special publics — bureaucrats, Dietmen and interest groups — than the public as a whole. Anyone who is interested in some specific government program will find encouragement on this shopping list. The Budget Compilation Program is a formal, authoritative statement of the party's intentions, produced after consultation with interested groups and due deliberation by the appropriate party bodies. However, it is virtually unusable, and unused.

We are therefore left with the third function, that of representing a clientele — or rather, several clienteles. Evidence is ample that the LDP tries hard to serve the groups to which it feels beholden. Individual Dietmen petition for projects in their home districts; "leagues" and other informal groupings mobilize the party's energy behind the demands of various organized groups; PARC divisions press both their corresponding ministries and the Ministry of Finance to support programs with political payoffs. As we shall see in chapter 7, the LDP has even found a mechanism for aggregating these various interests during the revival negotiations period, through a process that is more systematic at least than the empty Budget Compilation Program procedure detailed above. Nearly all LDP participation in budgeting is to such particularistic ends; "comprehensive" decision making is beyond its means and apparently not sufficiently appealing to warrent much real — as opposed to symbolic — attention.

If the party's critical role is that of representation of clientele groups, broadly or narrowly conceived, how has its exercise of that role affected budget outputs? The answer at the microbudgeting level is straightforward: in the selection of projects, sites and even programs from among alternatives, the influence of LDP Dietmen has often been crucial. Decisions of this sort are most often made within the boundaries of a policy "subgovernment," with no one other than ministry officials, interest group representatives, a few LDP specialists and perhaps one budget examiner participating or even interested. Though it is the ministry which usually takes the initiative within a subgovernment, there are many opportunities for a politician to assert his preferences, and still more often LDP opinion will be taken into account by anticipation, as when ministry officials prepare their annual budget requests with the necessity for PARC divisional hearings in mind.

However, these highly specific pressures for spending have not aggregated to influence the annual decision on the total size of the budget very much — that is, the occasions when such pressures have had more than marginal influence have been rather rare. In general, over the long term, total government expenditures have been governed by the "20 percent rule." Vagaries of forecasting allow considerable year-to-year flexibility in the application of this rule, but as we observed in chapter 4, the Finance Ministry has most often succeeded in maintaining nearly all decisions in this area under its own control. Typically the MOF's summer estimate of the total size allows for a gradual increase through the fall (amounting to perhaps 1-3 percent) to accommodate political pressures; if these prove more difficult to cope with than expected, perhaps another half-percent or so will be added. In other words, "representational" LDP pressure is very nearly a constant. It can be predicted with considerable accuracy and discounted in advance.[49] So long as the MOF was willing to allow the yearly budget growth rate to be high enough to provide substantial increments for the party's favorite programs—a stricture which, given the economic conditions of the time, usually was not out of line with Finance Ministry intentions—the inherent contradiction between intense majority party spending pressures and MOF control over the budget's size did not lead to confrontation. The Liberal Democrats could leave macrobudgeting largely undisturbed, except for rhetorical flourishes during presidential elections, because its immediate interests were not engaged.

High influence at the micro level, low influence at the macro level—here as elsewhere, when we turn to "integration," the answer lies in between, and also is harder to explicate. Our hypothetical question might be phrased: "To what extent would budget allocation patterns (shares at the ministry or Important Item level) differ if the LDP were not an important budget participant?" On one hand, somewhat as in macro-budgeting, it appears that the Finance Ministry does establish an informal "framework" for each ministry or policy area during its internal budget review process, one which may well allow for later expansion when political pressures develop. Clearly here the LDP cannot—as it might in microbudgeting—push through a demand that the budget share of some major category be raised by five percentage points. On the other hand, evidence is plentiful that party demands fall disproportionally in certain policy areas, notably agriculture, public works, veterans' pensions and the like, and that the MOF has been forced to respond to such demands; surely the uneven distribution of LDP support across Important Items or ministries must have had some effect on allocation patterns.

In my view, the most accurate characterization of the LDP impact at this level is to say that although the party usually does not intervene directly into "integrative" decision making (unlike microbudgeting), still the MOF's anticipations of party reactions are influential in framework-setting and do significantly "distort" budget priorities away from MOF preferences (unlike macrobudgeting). Were it not for the particular patterns of LDP clientele support, the budget shares allocated to rice price supports, to war-widows' benefits, to certain kinds of public works (rural

49. As will be seen in chap. 9, the instances when the MOF's basic "framework" for the budget was pushed up under pressure—in particular, 1961 and 1973—were brought about less by party rank-and-file activity than by an interventionist prime minister (even though the *contents* of the increment so produced mostly reflected particularistic backbencher demands).

highways, water conservation), to doctors' fees, to the maintenance of many rural railroad lines, would doubtlessly be substantially lower. More government resources would have flowed into what the MOF views as "forward-looking" areas. Although oddly enough the LDP would appear to have much less *short-term* impact at the integration level than in either micro- or macrobudgeting—year-to-year fluctuations in budget shares do not often seem to be caused by changes in party pressure, but rather are stimulated by environmental events or actions at the "leadership" level treated in the next chapter—in the longer run it is here that the impact of the party has been most significant.

If these are the effects of majority party participation on budget outputs at our three levels of aggregation, what can be said of the impact on the budget process itself? For example, how has the LDP affected the "responsiveness" of the Japanese budget system, its ability to respond to changes in its environment? Or a related question, does the LDP encourage "innovation" through the budget system? Asked in 1970 about what difference the LDP makes in budgeting, the staff director for one of the party's top leaders replied:

After a policy line has been set in a given direction, anyone can ride on it. In agriculture, the bureaucrats are awfully good at riding along on the old policy, like a locomotive driver. But when it comes to changing direction, they can't do it, they are conservative. This is because of organizations. There are all the various bureaus concerned with rice, but almost none for, say, dairy farming. Now till today the rice policy has been o.k., so all these connected bureaucrats have been o.k. But for dairy farming . . . they don't have the people needed. So because of their organization, they can't start something new. The party, on the other hand, doesn't have to worry about the organizations tied up with rice, and instead asks what is the problem for the people, what did they ask for in the election? So the party can become the engine to change policy.

When it was pointed out that considerable support for rice farmers existed within the LDP, he went on:

It is clear, from economic theory, that rather than promoting agriculture, it should now be cut back. But this can't be done too quickly: if there is a very violent change, there will be social unrest and political confusion. So there has to be a "speed-down," and this too is a party function. . . . a new mechanism is needed for change, and the party can do this. If run by bureaucrats, policies would either be stagnant or else subject to big changes based just on theory. The party has to check both tendencies, to maintain the middle of the road.

This LDP official is suggesting that the party has two somewhat contradictory functions: stimulating change, and moderating the unfortunate consequences of change. In both respects the party is seen as more responsive, more in touch with social trends and problems than the conservative and rather remote bureaucracy. It is true that examples can be found of party "dynamism," to use a favorite word of Tanaka Kakuei, the politician most noted for constantly producing new ideas and forcing them on a recalcitrant bureaucracy. Indeed, many associated with the LDP mention topics like pollution, urbanization and price inflation which do not fall within the jurisdiction of any one ministry, where they think the party should play an innovative and leading role. However, at least when budget processes over several years are examined, the number of actual initiatives seems not to measure up to statements of intentions. Much of the party's weight has been thrown on the side of the status quo, protecting programs and ministries which the Ministry of Finance, for one, would prefer to cut back. In such efforts, the LDP has indeed been responsive to the needs and hopes of some segments of the population, but not necessarily well equipped to cope with new problems caused by rapid social and economic change.

All of these conclusions about the Liberal Democratic Party—that its major function has been representation of specific clienteles, that its influence has been largest in microbudgeting but most significant (with regard to the impact of government policy on society) at the level of integration, that its net effect on the budgetary process has been to diminish responsiveness—are based on evidence from a period of high economic growth. High growth tends to minimize disagreement between party and Finance Ministry over the total size of the budget, and creates enough "slack"—revenue surpluses—so that party demands can be granted without depriving programs which others might see as more vital. A question arises, then, as to whether the substantial degree of success the LDP has achieved in carrying out its representation function has in large part been due to high growth; whether benefits provided to the party and its clients have in effect been luxuries which might be dispensed with under conditions of greater scarcity. Would the LDP be as influential in a period of economic stagnation?

We lack the appropriate period to make the test. The closest approximation is probably 1974, when economic policy dictated stringency; it is indeed interesting that the ministries which were the biggest relative losers in that year were Transport, Agriculture and Forestry, and Construction, in years past the three most favored by the LDP.[50] Of

50. Based on change-in-share from the 1973 post-Supplement budget to the 1974 initial budget, the most appropriate measure for this test. Data from Japan, Ministry of Finance, Budget Bureau, Research Division, *Zaisei Tōkei* ("Fiscal Statistics") (Tokyo: Ministry of Finance Printing Bureau, 1974), p. 66. Relative "winners" were Finance and Health and Welfare. Economic changes influenced the 1974 budget in several ways other than via political pressures—in particular, the high rate of inflation meant some categories (social security benefits, for example) virtually had to rise sharply, while public works is always the easiest category to cut—so this fact must be interpreted with caution.

course, the fact that in one year an economic crisis could be used by a skillful and powerful finance minister to cow the LDP into submission need not imply that over an extended period of deprivation the party would be willing to retire from the field. We might in fact predict that scarcity would lead to increased conflict among the chief political actors, conflict in which a majority party would have substantial resources. It does seem likely, in any case, that the very distinctive patterns of LDP influence we have described here are in large measure peculiar to a high-growth environment. However, if the economy were to settle into a long-term decline, it is unlikely the Liberal Democrats would remain in majority control long enough for us to discover the exact nature of this relationship.

# 6

# Leadership Roles

IN PREVIOUS CHAPTERS we have focused on the roles and behavior of large organizations and their components in budgeting. Here we turn to individuals, those at the top of budgetary institutions. However, the behavior of these leaders should not be seen as stemming solely from their individual goals, personalities and capabilities; much of it is constrained by expectations which have developed among other participants (and indeed in their own minds) about what sorts of behavior are appropriate for a particular role. For each role we seek to discover the contents of these expectations, how much scope for individual variations they allow, and finally how such variations affect the budget process and budgets themselves.

One good method for investigating such topics would be to survey a sizable cross-section of budget participants, asking what each thinks of his own and other roles.[1] However, although the findings here are based in part on interviews, the resources available did not allow quite so systematic an approach. Instead, it is assumed that roles may be inferred from behavior: we study how occupants of these elite positions have participated in budgeting, the effects of their participation, and the reactions of other actors. Since twenty-one budget cycles have been examined (though of course complete information is available for none), it is not surprising that fairly stable patterns of behavior can be discovered; in general, these patterns have been taken as defining the boundaries of a role unless other participants perceive an action as outrageous or unusual. This method obviously depends heavily on the judgment of the analyst. Still, I am confident that the most important aspects of these elite roles are described with reasonable accuracy.

1. An excellent example is Richard F. Fenno, Jr.'s, *The Power of the Purse: Appropriations Politics in Congress* (Boston: Little, Brown and Company, 1966).

The positions included among budgeting leaders, as defined here, are the top officers of the majority party, the Cabinet (as an institution, as well as the roles of individual members), the finance minister, the prime minister, and finally—because so many writers have posited for them a dominant role in Japanese decision making—big businessmen.[2]

# The Party "Big Four"

The leadership of the LDP—the term refers generally to the "big four" posts of secretary-general, PARC chairman, Executive Council chairman and vice-president[3]—participates in several phases of budgeting, though it is most active in the revival negotiations process described in the next chapter. Its nominal role is to represent the interests of the party: the Executive Council is for most matters the authoritative decision-making body, but it functions as a legislative chamber and is too unwieldy, for example, to take part in negotiations with the Ministry of Finance. Hence Council decisions are entrusted to the party executive for implementation. The leadership will usually be given some flexibility in interpreting the party's mandate, and indeed in many situations is allowed to formulate the party's position on its own.

In many years, the first intervention in the budget process by the leadership occurs in the fall, on those occasions when the party has come up with official or semi-official budget recommendations. Occasionally these have covered a range of major issues, but more often they refer to just one or two questions, such as the amount of the tax cut or the establishment and size of a new public works five-year plan. The secretary-general, the PARC chairman, or the entire big four will discuss the pronouncement with the finance minister (sometimes accompanied by the Budget Bureau director or other MOF officials), perhaps securing an early agreement or at least impressing the MOF with the strength of the party's interest. More informally, the party leadership participates in macrobudgeting discussions that lead to decisions on the total size of the budget, the portion to be covered by deficit bonds, and so forth. Such discussions are

2. Other definitions are of course possible: if one were analyzing the entire Japanese political system, virtually everyone who participates in budgeting would be a member of the leadership or "elite"; and as noted in chap. 3, Japanese journalists often refer to Budget Bureau officials as an "elite within an elite," based on their superior qualifications and the fact that they review the work of officials in other ministries.

3. When no vice-president is appointed, this group is the "big three." The secretary-general is the key post for nearly all purposes, but in budget affairs the PARC chairman is also quite prominent. For general discussions of the leadership, see Nathaniel B. Thayer, *How the Conservatives Rule Japan* (Princeton, N.J.: Princeton University Press, 1969), esp. pp. 295-96, and Haruhiro Fukui, *Party in Power: The Liberal Democratic Party in Policy-Making* (Berkeley and Los Angeles: University of California Press, 1970), pp. 93-95.

not peculiar to the budget process; they are characteristic of the normal flow of important policy making for all areas.

On his own initiative, the finance minister may also consult with the party leadership at various points during the process to gain approval or understanding of MOF positions. The pattern of such consultations varies with the strategy being followed by the Finance minister. A common occasion is immediately before the publication of the MOF draft, when a finance minister may seek to negotiate with both Cabinet ministers and the leadership to solve a few of the outstanding budgetary issues before the beginning of the appeals negotiations. However, the party's formal Budget Compilation Program, after its passage by the Executive Council, is not taken up by the leadership as a basis for negotiation. It is simply sent on to the Cabinet and the MOF for their reference, as is appropriate for such a vague and all-encompassing document.

In these negotiations, or simply in statements made to the general public, the leadership will ordinarily be passing along demands from LDP members for more spending, on some specific item or in the budget as a whole. A quite explicit example is a demand by then PARC Chairman Tanaka Kakuei in early December 1961: "With the Upper House election coming up, at least ¥ 100 billion of new funds in the 1962 budget is needed to settle the intraparty situation."[4] That is to say, he warns that pressures within the party are so intense, that unless this amount of money (about one-third billion dollars) is made available for new programs, dissatisfaction and resentment will run so high that the budget process will be seriously disrupted. The Ministry of Finance frequently takes such threats quite seriously.

Such interventions by the leadership are fairly common. However, if the secretary-general and PARC chairman were to see their only responsibility as pursuing every possible advantage for the party, budgets would never be finished. Most often, party leaders play the broker's role, balancing-off demands from the rank-and-file or various groups within the party, which are frequently quite extreme, against the willingness of other participants to go along. For example, during the 1966 budget process PARC Chairman Akagi Munenori observed that "we had been saying ¥ 300 billion" as a recommended tax cut, "but talk like this causes difficulties for [Finance Minister] Fukuda, so now we are just making it 'at least ¥ 200 billion.'"[5]

While this brokerage role might be seen as that of practical political technicians, LDP leaders, like politicians elsewhere, also like to think of themselves as statesmen "looking beyond parochial interests to national

4. AS, December 7, 1961.
5. An interview in *Ekonomisuto* 43, 54 (December 21, 1955), 46-49.

needs," as a PARC vice-chairman put it in an interview. They come to feel a responsibility for the contents of the budget, and particularly for facilitating and smoothing budget procedures. Many of the meetings they hold with the finance minister and the prime minister are devoted to schedule making and agenda setting. Moreover, on several occasions the leadership has actively cooperated in the Finance Ministry's "pace" strategies by adjusting party schedules to suit MOF convenience. In 1963, the MOF gained LDP agreement for a delay in the release of the party's Budget Compilation Program because the Diet was then in session; it was feared that opposition party reactions might disrupt the Diet, delay adjournment, and confuse budgeting. In the previous year, the party had been planning an early Compilation Program in November, but Finance Minister Mizuta asked that it be postponed or at least made vague and general "so that differences of opinion between government and party will not come out into the open," and Secretary-General Tanaka agreed.[6] Many such cases are on record and indicate the leadership's strong concern for keeping the process flowing at an even pace, toward an early and relatively quiet solution.

The threat of disruption that worries both the MOF and the LDP leadership comes, of course, from the lower levels of the party. It is feared that given the opportunity, backbenchers as individuals or interest groupings centered around the divisions will try to protract the budget process and hold out for more money. Though such disruptions had not occurred to an appreciable extent in later years, several precedents from the late 1950s and early 1960s remind participants that the threat is a real one. That the major responsibility for the containment of internal pressures is taken by the leadership (including the president) is partly by default, in that no other party organ has the necessary authority, incentive, sensitivity and flexibility to be effective.[7]

Some positive strategies can be identified. Most basic is the extension of a sense of participation to all, perhaps the major function of the elaborate division-Deliberation Commission-Executive Council process described in the previous chapter. Even if a Dietman's pet project is not finally included in the budget, nor even strongly recommended by the leadership, his resentment will be minimized when he has had an opportunity to take part in party decision making (and in any case, most such desires are at least nominally recognized at the PARC Deliberation Commission level). More specific inducements are also available: in the

6. AS, December 3, 1961.
7. This pattern was established after protracted negotiations in the first year of budgeting under the LDP, 1956, when responsibility was finally handed over to the big three as the only possible way for the party to control itself. MNS, January 20, 1956.

turbulent 1956 process, party dissatisfactions were finally quieted down enough for Cabinet passage of the budget by granting a last minute billion yen as "pocket money" or "intraparty adjustment funds." It is not that this money went directly to rebellious Dietmen; rather, the MOF allowed the party leadership to allocate the extra amount in tiny parcels among projects close to the hearts (and electoral interests) of the Dietmen. While this tactic did not reappear quite so openly in later years, flexible use of pork barrel funds continued to be an important leadership resource.

Whether the "representation" role or the "responsible" role is emphasized by any particular group of leaders in a given year will vary with personality, factional ties, current economic and political conditions, and the strategy being followed by the Finance Ministry. For example, in 1960 and other years the MOF's "independent" position of minimizing consultations with the leadership stimulated them to respond with stronger demands. On the other hand, of particular importance in the two extreme cases of "responsibility," 1968 and 1974, was the presence in the LDP leadership of ex-Ministry of Finance officials; a journalist pointed out in a discussion of the MOF's antirigidification campaign for the 1968 budget, "rather than negotiating with the Finance Ministry on the basis of party demands, Secretary-General Fukuda and PARC Chairman Ōhira played the role of repressing party demands, as if they were representatives of the MOF."[8] In 1974, the fact that Finance Minister Fukuda, Prime Minister Tanaka and PARC Chairman Mizuta Mikio all had long experience as finance minister — they were actually the only three occupants of that post from the first Ikeda Cabinet in 1960 until Tanaka's first Cabinet in 1972 — was not unrelated to the MOF's success in obtaining near consensus on the need for a restrictive budget. Of course, if the leadership pays too much attention to its "statesman" role and does not represent the views of the rank-and-file sufficiently, it runs the risk of incurring resentment which may later erupt either directly in the budget process or indirectly over some other policy dispute or perhaps in the next party election.

On some occasions the LDP leadership will try to take on other than these two functions, such as attempts at comprehensive policy planning — Tanaka Kakuei showed tendencies in this direction during his several terms as secretary-general — or initiation and support of specific programs. For example, Secretary-General Hashimoto Tomisaburō tried to insert a new public corporation for developing residential land into the 1973 budget at the last minute, but was rebuffed. Such activist conceptions of leadership seem not to be among the expectations attached to the role of the LDP leadership.

8. AS, December 27, 1967.

# The Cabinet

Constitutionally, the Cabinet occupies a paramount position in budgeting; under Article 73 it has the responsibility to "Prepare the budget, and present it to the Diet."[9] However, the Finance Law of 1947 delegates the budgeting function to the finance minister. Today, the Cabinet's direct functions are mainly two: ratification of the government draft of the budget, usually at an early hour of the morning after final compromises have been worked out between the finance minister and the LDP leadership; and passage of the official Basic Policy for the Budget (*Yosan Hensei Hōshin*) every year.[10]

This is given wide distribution as the most authoritative statement of government intentions toward the budget, but a review of the series reveals little variation from year to year. The 1970 version is typical, having a twenty-two-line introduction, mentioning general budget principles as they relate to the economy, followed by seven brief items: the size of the budget; tax reform; the bond issue; expenditure policy (divided into three subitems — endorsement of "comprehensive budgeting," a list of fourteen programs or policy areas to be stressed, and a statement on the rice price problem); administrative reforms; flexibility in execution; and local finance. Actual figures are included only in the tax cut and bond issue items. In length it is about one-fifth the printed size of the LPD's Budget Compilation Program, but it is similar in its vagueness of tone.

In the 1950s this instrument was viewed by some politicians as a potentially effective device for asserting Cabinet control over the budget. The Cabinet had set policies early in the budget cycle during the Occupation period, and though no formal action had been taken in 1953 and 1954, for the 1955, 1956, and 1957 budgets efforts were made to develop plans, including budget figures, which could then be imposed on the Finance Ministry.[11] Complicated maneuvering by the MOF prevented this from happening in each of the three years: the document came to be prepared almost completely within the MOF, rather than through Cabinet mechanisms, with just minor last-minute amendments by the Cabinet; the

9. Note also Art. 86: "The Cabinet shall prepare and submit to the Diet for its consideration and decision a budget for each fiscal year"; it is also given authority to make expenditures from the reserve fund (Art. 87) and is charged with reporting functions (Arts. 90, 91).

10. A literal translation of the title would be "Budget Compilation Policy". It may be found in many annual budget-related publications, including *Kuni no Yusan,* and a short English version appears in *The Budget in Brief.*

11. See Kōno Kazuyuki, "Wagakuni ni okeru Yosan Hensei no Kōzō to Katei" ("The Structure and Process of Budget Compilation in Japan"), in *Gyōsei Kanri no Dōkō* ("Trends in Administrative Management"), ed. Nihon Gyōsei Gakkai (Tokyo: Keisō Shobō, 1957), pp. 68-69.

language was general, with only those figures already decided by the MOF (for total size, tax cut, and so forth) included; and it was approved by the Cabinet immediately before the release of the MOF draft, thereby negating any chance of influencing the basic budget process. For 1957, even the total size figure, which in earlier years had been included as part of the MOF's strategy for holding down spending, was eliminated on the specific urging of Finance Minister Ikeda—he said there was no need to cause any unnecessary arguments between the Finance Ministry and the Cabinet or party while the budget was still in the drafting stage. Any problems could be left until later.[12] In later years, with a few exceptions, this devitalized form of the Basic Policy for the Budget became accepted as normal; it is just one tactic, and not a particularly important one, for providing a screen of formal approval for MOF control of budgetary policy.[13]

Most other attempts to assert Cabinet prerogatives have been the products of individual rather than institutional ambition. That is, on those occasions when the Cabinet has sought to enlarge its authority, behind the scenes one finds a powerful politician seeking an independent base for influence. Usually it was Kōno Ichirō. Throughout his career, in large ways and small, Kōno tried to diminish the budgeting role of *both* the Ministry of Finance, as by attempting to transfer the Budget Bureau to Cabinet control, and the LPD organization, as seen in this typical complaint (when he was Construction Minister in 1962):

In budget compilation, it is natural to respect the opinions of the governing party, but these should be referred to the Cabinet, through the secretary-general, and discussed at Cabinet meetings. It is peculiar to learn from newspaper reports that even various ministry matters have been decided between the Finance Minister and the LDP PARC chairman.[14]

This plea went unheeded, of course, and the LDP continued to talk directly with the MOF and to ignore the Cabinet.

Which is not to say that the Cabinet plays no budget role whatsoever. In difficult financial times, the Ministry of Finance frequently feels a need for high-level discussions of broad economic issues, and supports the convening of an informal Cabinet-level subcommittee (often called the "Economic Ministers Discussion Group," *Keizai Kakuryō Kondankai*) during the fall. It does not normally reach binding decisions, but can be

12. YS, January 8, 1957.
13. The exceptions in fact came in years when the MOF itself was particularly concerned about spending pressures and had need of theoretically binding Cabinet strictures. Thus in 1958 and 1968, somewhat more specific policies were passed, earlier in the budget process.
14. AS, December 10, 1962, evening. In a similar statement as Agriculture Minister in 1961, Kōno noted increasing party and interest group "interference" and called for the Cabinet to "take responsibility." NKS, December 5, 1961, evening.

helpful in building consensus. More dramatically, near the end of the 1968 budget process it was announced that budget issues would be settled in an impressive one-day "Budget Plenary Discussion Group" (*Yosan Zentai Kondankai*), where the Cabinet as a body would meet with the LDP leadership and work out exact figures for all the major budget categories. As it happened, however, by a week later this meeting had been watered down to a general discussion of the economy and nonspecific questions and answers on budget items — unsurprisingly, Finance Minister Mizuta thought it had been a great success, because everyone had gotten his complaints aired and MOF plans were left undisturbed.[15]

Why is it the Cabinet has never managed to convert formal into real authority? Fundamentally, because it is more an aggregation than a real institution: its membership turns over every year or so (sometimes every six months), and ministers are normally much more concerned with their individual political affairs than with advancing the Cabinet as such. The budgeting game is played among powerful, enduring organizations — the Ministry of Finance, line ministries, the LDP — which use the Cabinet only occasionally as an arena for their disputes.

*Ministers.* — If collectively the Cabinet is not an important budgetary actor, individual ministers have often assumed prominent parts. The minister who wishes to rise above the rather minimal role expectations attached to his post has two possible directions open to him. The first is to achieve influence over his own ministry. The Japanese norm is for a minister to be dominated by his subordinate officials, if only because he might be on hand barely long enough to find his way around the building, but if a politician has long had an intimate connection with a ministry, or alternatively, if he has a strong personality and definite ideas he wishes to put into practice, he may make a substantial impact on policies and internal processes. His chances are highest when officials are already split by some factional or policy dispute, allowing a minister to play one side off against another. Prominent examples of activist ministers include Kōno, again, in the Ministry of Agriculture and Forestry, and more recently Nakasone Yasuhiro as Director-General of the Defense Agency; both were able to insert several of their own ideas into ministry programs and to an extent shape long-run policies.[16] A more typical illustration of how a

15. AS, December 19, and 29, 1967. Opposition from the LDP was also important in killing the original plan, avowedly for a rather unusual reason: "We are worried that referring these matters to discussion by all will leave the impression of denigrating the budget compilation authority of the finance minister and MOF." NKS, December 22, 1967.

16. Forthcoming dissertations at Columbia University by Michael W. Donnelly and Norman Levin will throw light on the influence of, respectively, Kōno within the Agriculture Ministry and Nakasone within the Defense Agency.

minister may influence his ministry is provided by Nohara Masakatsu, a senior but not extraordinarily distinguished politician with a speciality primarily in agricultural matters, who was named Minister of Labor in 1970. The ministry quickly requested funds and established a special division to look into the labor force implications of the new "comprehensive agriculture policy."[17]

The second possible direction is to seek influence within the wider budget system. Naturally, ministry officials welcome the appointment of prominent or powerful politicians as ministers because they believe such influence will bring larger budgets, at least on the margin in the final negotiations. Some ministers, however, have used the Cabinet as a forum to gain a voice in more general budgetary decision making. The heads of the Ministry of International Trade and Industry and the Economic Planning Agency have institutional roles in economic policy making, and on occasion will insert themselves into areas regarded by the Ministry of Finance as its own domain. More subtly, the post of director-general of the Administrative Management Agency has sometimes become prominent, when it is filled by someone like Kōno or Fukuda Takeo. Fukuda, in the unprecedentedly expansive 1973 budget year, appeared in newspapers regularly with statements that new agencies or government corporations would not be approved, and he often went on to make a few comments on the dangers of inflation and large budgets. Later, he actually took part in the final budget negotiations.[18]

Such cases are rather exceptional. In fact, Kōno and Fukuda, and perhaps Tanaka Kakuei, are probably the only politicians in recent years who have been able to carry their reputations and influence with them almost continuously from job to job. More commonly, even if he is not completely faceless, a Cabinet minister will rise into view for one budget cycle, when his ministry is engaged in some current controversy, and then disappear again into some party or Diet post.

# Finance Ministers

Finance ministers are of course always in the news, dealing with budgets or any other issue connected with the economy. This post is probably next only to the prime minister in public exposure and reputation for power.[19]

17. Interview with a journalist, June 1970.

18. The Administrative Management Agency is charged with reviewing requests for new organizations. See NKS, January 15 and 16, 1973.

19. It is next to the prime minister also in the sense that Prime Ministers Ishibashi, Ikeda, Satō, and Tanaka all had been finance minister previous to attaining the top job; indeed, the post is often called a prerequisite, and we might note that Miki was elected party president and prime minister in 1974 only because of a deadlock between Fukuda and Ōhira, both ex-MOF officials with experience as finance minister.

While there is no need to explain his preeminence, it is interesting to ask how much and what kind of influence the finance minister as an individual has over the budget, and how much variation, based on differences in objectives or style, is permitted in the performance of his role.

Most finance ministers do not take a very direct part in the micro-budgeting process. During the fall, the Budget Bureau director will consult with the minister about particularly difficult or highly political budget items, and the heads of other ministries may wish to speak with him when they face unusual difficulties. At the Budget Ministerial Conference in December, he will listen to detailed reviews of the draft budget from the examiners for about two weeks, and will intervene with suggestions from time to time. Sometimes a minister, particularly a relatively inexperienced one, will be personally interested in some program or policy area: for example, in the 1950s both Ichimanda and Ikeda declared their concern for the problem of housing—Ichimanda managed to raise this allocation over Budget Bureau opposition even in the exceedingly tight 1955 budget, and Ikeda in the 1957 budget actually granted more than the Ministry of Construction had requested for this category. Fukuda was in his fifth month in office in October 1966 when he announced he would give traffic safety special attention in the 1967 budget—one supposes the public appeal and low cost of this program enhanced its attractiveness to him. On a somewhat larger scale, it was continuously rumored in the early 1970s that the rivalry between Fukuda and Tanaka for the post-Satō premiership had led Fukuda to become relatively generous with budget funds in fulfilling requests from LDP Dietmen likely to be influential in the party election. Still, intervention by the finance minister in the business of program review is usually rather insignificant.

In macrobudgeting, on the other hand, it is the finance minister himself who makes the key decisions, though of course he relies on the advice of others and must also balance off a good many political pressures. From midsummer until the publication of the MOF draft in December or January, the minister spends much of his time consulting on economic prospects and the revenue forecast, the size of the tax cut and bond issue, and how large the total budget should be. He is most responsible for devising and implementing strategies for attaining MOF goals; for example, deciding how large or small the first guess on the total budget should be, and when it should be moved up, based on his reading of the political situation. More so than in microbudgeting, the minister's own economic beliefs and preferences (together with those of the prime minister) may well be significant in macrobudgeting decisions.

Somewhat analogously to the LDP leadership, the finance minister must also serve as a go-between and mediator, representing the views of his own organization to the outside world, and transmitting opinions and

## TABLE 9
### FINANCE MINISTERS, 1954-1974

| | a.<br>Years of<br>Service | b.<br>First<br>Appointed | c.<br>Last left<br>Post | d.<br>Served<br>Under | e.<br>Earlier<br>Career | f.<br>Fiscal<br>Policy | g.<br>Strength<br>in LDP | h.<br>Strategy<br>to LDP | i.<br>Influence<br>in MOF |
|---|---|---|---|---|---|---|---|---|---|
| Ichimanda Hisato[a] | 3 | 3/54 | 6/58 | Hatoyama<br>Kishi | Bank of<br>Japan | Conser-<br>vative | None | Independent | Low |
| Ikeda Hayato[b] | 4½ | (2/49)<br>3/56 | 7/57 | (Yoshida)<br>Ishibashi<br>Kishi | MOF | Expan-<br>sionary | High | Independent | High,<br>Intimate |
| Satō Eisaku | 2 | 6/58 | 7/60 | Kishi | Trans.<br>Min. | ? | High | Consult,<br>Manipulate | Medium |
| Mizuta Mikio | 5 | 7/60 | 7/72 | Ikeda<br>Satō | Busi-<br>nessman | Expan-<br>sionary | Medium | Consult | Medium |
| Tanaka Kakuei | 3 | 7/62 | 6/65 | Ikeda<br>Satō | Poli-<br>tician | Expan-<br>sionary | High | Consult | High, Manip-<br>ulatory |
| Fukuda Takeo | 5 | 6/65 | 11/74 | Satō<br>Tanaka | MOF | Conser-<br>vative | High | Fairly<br>Independent | High,<br>Intimate |
| Ueki Kōshirō | ½ | 7/72 | 12/72 | Tanaka | MOF | Expan-<br>sionary | Medium | Consult | Low? |
| Aichi Kiichi[c] | ½ | 12/72 | 11/73 | Tanaka | MOF | ? | Medium | Give in | Low? |

NOTES: [a]Not a Diet member when first appointed.   [b]First served before period covered.   [c]Died in office.

SOURCES: Columns a-e, Ōkurashō Hyakunenshi Henshūshitsu, eds., Ōkurashō Jinmeiroku (Tokyo: Ōkura Zaimu Kyōkai, 1973), and newspapers. Columns f-i are the author's estimates.

pressures from the ministries, the party and perhaps big business and other interest groups to the officials. He must be negative toward spending demands but yet conciliatory. If he appears too generous, he may not receive cooperation from his subordinates; if he takes traditional MOF positions on many issues, demands from the party will be unsatisfied and the budget process may be disrupted. Asked about his part in budgeting during a magazine interview, Mizuta Mikio emphasized the need for liaison with the party:

It is often said that the finance minister just rides on the backs of MOF officials, but actually he plays an important role in budget review decisions. The finance minister takes the summaries of budget reviews that the officials report to him, and from the middle of November or so quietly gets in touch with the party leadership and passes along some rough approximations. If he doesn't give them this sort of sense [of the budget], a real budget review is impossible. Budgeting can be awfully tough anyway, but if you misread the attitude of the party, when you get down to the end you may be stuck with revising the whole basic budget compilation policy.[20]

The politically skillful finance minister will be able to handle the ambiguities of this role without much trouble, but amateurs—Ichimanda in the mid-1950s is perhaps the best example—will be left in difficult straits.[21]

    Anecdotes and examples of how finance ministers have dealt with various situations over the years will be found scattered through chapter 9, but it is also possible to offer a few slightly more systematic comments. A glance at Table 9 reveals that most finance ministers in this period have been men of some stature. Ex-bureaucrats have predominated, half of these from the Ministry of Finance (including two Budget Bureau directors); even the "politicians" are known as "policy-wise" (seisaku-tsū). Time in office tends to be rather longer than for other ministerial posts. Most finance ministers, when out of office and speaking in the abstract, have favored rather positive fiscal policies, but such beliefs are likely to be seen as incongruent role expectations, particularly as defined by permanent MOF officials. Mizuta was severely criticized (anonymously) by his subordinates during the 1961 budget process, which he began by mooting the possibility of issuing deficit bonds, and concluded in a flourish of generous concessions to LDP demands.[22] Much later, in response to an

20. Asahi Shinbun Keizaibu, *Keizai Seisaku no Butaiura* ("Economic Policy Behind the Scenes") (Tokyo: Asahi Shinbunsha, 1974), p. 78.
21. As a top Budget Bureau official said anonymously after Ichimanda's mishandling of the turbulent 1956 budget process, "A minister who cannot hold back the party and Cabinet is no use. If the finance minister cannot perform like a vice-prime minister, our jobs are hopeless." TS, July 27, 1956.
22. NKS, July 21, 1960; AS, July 27, 1960; and esp. analysis in NKS, July 30, 1960; MNS, January 19, 1961.

interviewer's comment that "You are a positivist in fiscal policy, but in actual budget compilation you seem to be on the restrictive side as often as not . . .," he recalled

that was the irony of the time; I was there when the economy had to be cooled down. Besides, in Ikeda's time, if I just went along agreeably with someone of such strong will we would never be able to settle the budget, I thought, so I wound up trying to pull in on the reins.[23]

It is inevitably the MOF's role in the budget system to be negative, and its chief cannot contradict this norm too often, too publicly or too radically.

A finance minister who is unusually influential within the ministry, because he is held in great esteem by officials and because he has acquired a detailed knowledge of its workings, perhaps has more freedom of action and opinion. Ikeda Hayato and Tanaka Kakuei retained many of their expansionist tendencies while serving in this post. Ikeda had been MOF vice-minister in 1947 (his background was in the Tax Bureau), and always maintained exceptionally close ties with the ministry; his influence was perpetuated into the 1970s through the so-called Shinseki Club, made up of his protegés, which dominated most top-level appointments.[24] Tanaka's influence, on the other hand, rested upon his great power within the LDP (including his obvious future prospects) and his deliberate attempts to win friends among the officials; respect for his abilities and talent also played a part. Still, he was generally regarded as an outsider—the comparison with Fukuda Takeo drawn by a senior Budget Bureau official in a 1974 interview is instructive:

Fukuda has a certain sense of mission, and he assumes that others in the Ministry of Finance do too; there is a relationship of trust. Tanaka has a sense of mission, but he makes deals with the officials. For example, when the Budget Bureau is working very hard, there is a custom of seniors (*senpai*) buying dinner for the officials. . . . Fukuda doesn't do this sort of thing much; he doesn't feel the need for it, believing that others think the way he does. Tanaka does it a lot. Fukuda thinks we will all pitch in together, Tanaka gives presents of fruit . . . Fukuda is one of us . . . while opinions vary within the MOF, I have more respect for Fukuda . . . not just money, but heart.

Fukuda Takeo is perhaps the prototypical MOF insider; his background is in the Budget Bureau, and his appearance of taking his principles seriously, coupled with a noncommital style often leavened by dead-pan

23. Asahi Shinbun Keizaibu, *Butaiura,* p. 79.
24. Honda Yasuharu, *Nihon Neokanryō ron* ("The 'New Bureaucrats' of Japan") (Tokyo: Kōdansha, 1975), pp. 93-95. The name "Shinsekikai" is derived from alternate readings of the first characters of the names of its founders, Morinaga Teiichirō (vice-minister, 1957-59) and Ishino Shin'ichi (vice-minister, 1963-65).

wit, is congenial to many officials.[25] And of course his opinions on fiscal matters are relatively conservative.

Influence within the MOF is one of the attributes important in determining how successful a finance minister will be in reaching his objectives, which, as well as implementing his own policy ideas, will include smooth management of the budget process and of course enhancement of his personal reputation and future career prospects. Other relevant individual attributes are his influence within the LDP, his intellectual capacity and willingness to work very hard, and to some extent even his reputation among the public. Experience also seems to be an important factor in this job: new finance ministers seem to have more difficulties, and are more likely to be criticized by other budget participants and journalists, than those who have had a chance to learn the substance of their responsibilities and how to conduct themselves. A recent example is the 1973 budget, handled initially by Ueki and in the last stages by Aichi; although both were once MOF officials, more importantly they were first-time finance ministers. The enormous concessions to party pressure (including even allocations larger than the original requests) as well as the confusion in negotiations among the MOF, ministries and party, were widely ascribed to Aichi's short tenure and lack of skill.[26] In general, most examples of "unconventional" finance minister behavior seem to occur early in their terms, though it is hard to guess whether ministers soon become completely socialized into their role, or alternatively whether they might simply learn to do unconventional things in ways which do not attract the attention of newspaper reporters.

Certain situational variables may also affect a finance minister's success. One is economic: it is easiest to appear effective when little money is available and everyone knows it; hardest when for fiscal reasons one wants to spend little but others are thinking expansively. Another is political: pressure for programs will always come from the party, but it will be somewhat more intense near elections, and will be much more intense and will often take the form of personal attacks and even semi-organized movements against the finance minister when the LDP is in the midst of factional disputes, as when the party presidency is in doubt. Another factor of considerable importance is the nature of his relationship with the prime

25. Stories are still told of Fukuda's exploits when he was the examiner in charge of Army budgets in the 1930's, including the time a military train stopped so he could fish from a bridge, and when General Tōjō apologized after hitching a ride on Fukuda's airplane in Manchuria. He also has been credited with single-handedly bringing down the Katayama Cabinet when Budget Bureau director in 1948. Cf. *ibid.*, pp. 100-101 and Chalmers Johnson, "Japan: Who Governs? An Essay on Official Bureaucracy," *Journal of Japanese Studies* 2, 1 (Autumn, 1975), 9.

26. It was further pointed out that the LDP secretary-general and PARC chairman were also neophytes. NKS, December 30, 1972; January 15 and 16, 1973.

minister, one which may vary from subordination to equality, from friendship to emnity.[27] Whatever his personal traits, the finance minister's strategies and the reception they get will be largely determined by such situational variables.

# Prime Ministers

The prime minister stands at the head of both groups of leaders considered in this chapter: he is president of the Liberal Democratic Party and constitutionally the head of the Cabinet. Unfortunately, while the institution of the prime ministership is of course touched upon in many articles and books on Japanese politics, there is no consensus among scholars on the actual powers of the office: some emphasize that nearly every important issue will be touched by his powers, while others point to severe constraints on how his influence can be exercised.[28] We can perhaps contribute to this discussion in a small way by outlining his functions in budgeting. What expectations are attached to this role, and how much scope is allowed to individual incumbents? It is possible to identify six major functions, of which three have to do with policy and three with process. These will be taken up individually.

*Policy Climate.* — Prime ministers, like American presidents, are prone to establish policy goals for their administrations, which if achieved will give their terms an air of success and will afterward be associated with their names in the history books. Sometimes these goals are proclaimed before he is elected, but others may not be identified until an attractive issue presents itself while in office. Without too much oversimplification, these are the chief examples: for Yoshida Shigeru (prime minister until the end of 1954), the peace treaty with the United States; Hatoyama Ichirō (1954-1956), normalization of relations with the Soviet Union; Kishi Nobusuke (1957-1960), the Mutual Security Treaty with the U.S.; Satō Eisaku (1964-1972), normalization of relations with South Korea and the reversion of Okinawa; Tanaka Kakuei (1972-1974), normalization of relations with China and "restructuring of the Japanese archipelago."[29] One immediately notes how little most of these objectives have to do with budgeting; with two exceptions, they all lie in the foreign policy realm.

27. Haruhiro Fukui, in a personal communication, suggests that this factor accounts for much of the difference in effectiveness between Aichi and Fukuda in 1973-74—Fukuda was Tanaka's equal, while Aichi was clearly subordinate.
28. Curiously enough, there is (to my knowledge) no systematic study of this office in the postwar years; *Sōri Daijin* ("Prime Minister"), ed. Yomiuri Shinbun Seijibu (Tokyo: Yomiuri Shinbunsha, 1971) has a promising title but turns out to be another anecdotal "power elite" study.
29. Ishibashi Tanzan is omitted, since he served only two months in 1956-57.

And in fact, Japanese prime ministers have rarely brought a comprehensive, systematic policy perspective to bear on budgeting. The two partial exceptions were Ikeda and Tanaka, and these were also the two prime ministers most active within the budget process since Yoshida.[30]

*Macrobudgeting.* — Prime ministers are always prominent participants in the macrobudgeting consultations which go on throughout the fall. Fiscal policy is too important a component of economic policy, and economic policy too large a government responsibility, for them to leave this task to others. Still, their degrees of active influence have varied, depending upon individual expertise and interest and whether or not economic conditions seem to demand some change in policy. Ikeda, a financial expert himself, was in large measure personally responsible for developing and implementing the conscious high-growth policies of the 1960s. Not only did he personally make the major macrobudgeting decisions, sometimes after calling Tax Bureau officials into his office to discuss their estimates in detail, but he actively proselytized for his expansionist views within the government and outside. For instance, in November 1961 he said on television, "Next year, when the GNP may go over 17 trillion yen, the movement of some one or two hundred billion yen in or out of the budget has almost no influence" — a heretical statement for an ex-MOF official.[31] Satō took a direct part in deciding to begin deficit financing in 1965-66, but this policy change, compared to the income doubling scheme, was less a deliberately planned new direction than a forced response to an immediate fiscal crisis.

The interaction of individual objectives and style with economic conditions is well seen in Tanaka's term. His first budget was 1973, and he personally intervened at every stage, with the acquiescence of his relatively weak finance ministers, to be sure that the budget would be expansive in all respects. However, though he began the 1974 process on the same tack, when inflation and the oil crisis made a more restrictive budget necessary he appointed a powerful and conservative finance minister, Fukuda Takeo, and kept his hands off the budget almost entirely.

*Microbudgeting.* — Prime ministers have their pet projects and often use their positions to insert them into budgets. An example is the 1970 proposal to build a Tōkai Nature Path, a sort of Adirondack Trail, which

---

30. Yoshida Shigeru is an exception to almost any general propositions about prime ministers; his "one-man rule", nurtured under the Occupation, is unique in postwar history. A forthcoming biography by John Dower should throw more light on his term of office.

31. AS, November 23, 1961. Ikeda's positive tendencies are well expressed in his remark on the 1961 budget: "For myself, rather than dividing three eggs among four people, I prefer to produce six eggs." The Socialists responded that all eggs seemed to be gathered by big business. AS, November 24, 1960.

had picked up considerable newspaper attention. The MOF intially turned the proposal down, as is usual with new programs, but Prime Minister Satō reacted publicly that he thought such a trail would be a wonderful idea. The program was approved in the vice-ministerial negotiations.[32] Such endorsements of programs usually fall into one of two groups: items so small that they have little financial significance, such as the nature trail, and questions with quite obvious solutions but on which formal decisions have not yet been reached. The pattern which has become the norm is for the prime minister not to commit himself openly one way or the other on programs of any higher degree of controversiality, perhaps because his other roles are viewed as more important and might be compromised if he did.

On larger policy allocations prime ministers may become involved in a rather allusive manner. For example, Satō's reference to "the resolution to defend one's country with his own hands" in a 1967 Diet speech apparently was taken by Finance Ministry officials as a hint they should not be quite so severe in reviewing the Defense Agency's 1968 requests.[33] In that same relatively tight budget year, Satō expressed his interest in the housing problem to some MOF officials late in the process, and their reaction was perhaps typical of the significance of such interventions: the total number of private housing units slated to receive government aid was raised from 490,000 to 500,000. More often than not, the responses of the budgeting system to attempts by prime ministers to change allocation patterns will be more symbolic than real. To cite one last Satō example, just after he was first elected many were talking of the new "coloring" he would give his first budget, that for 1965, since he had been extremely critical of Ikeda's economic and social ideas. In the end, no more than the slightest Satō tint could be discerned — the LDP and Cabinet budget policy documents were slightly amended, and the tax cut increased somewhat, but reporters could find very little in actual budget expenditures which seemed to reflect Satō's expressed priorities.[34]

In general, a pattern had become accepted in the 1960s that prime ministers might intervene from time to time in expenditure decisions but would most often stand off. Tanaka, however, broke the pattern. His voice was heard at all stages and all levels of the 1973 budget process. A pastiche of quotations by a number of officials from the Ministry of Finance and other ministries asked in 1974 about Tanaka's impact may convey an adequate impression of his style. Some compared him with Satō:

32. *Asahi Evening News,* January 12, 1970; *Mainichi Daily News,* January 28, 1970; MNS, January 30, 1970.

33. NKS, December 18, 1967. As it happens, the defense budget did do rather better than usual in 1968.

34. AS, December 2, 17; NKS, December 18, 20, 1964.

Satō never liked revolutionary change; when an issue came up, there would be many opinions in the LDP, but he would wait until a consensus had emerged, and then step in to give direction. . . . Tanaka when he first became Prime Minister was called the "computerized bull-dozer," with lots of ideas coming out all the time.

Formally, the role hasn't changed—the prime minister has always had powers of approval and so forth—but the personality has changed . . . Satō would look a situation over and then finally, *paa to,* come in. Tanaka would come out *pon-pon* with whatever is in his head.[35]

Satō was better at following administrative rules; Tanaka is more of a party man . . . it seems to me he tells you what to do—"right now," "regardless"—maybe a little too often.

## What sorts of programs interested him most?

. . . he wants to pour more concrete: a "mothers' center," a "children's center," a "workers' center" in every prefecture and every town in the nation. . . . He likes railroads, too, especially the bullet train.

Tanaka himself is something of a "public works specialist," so he has lots of opinions here.

## What are his basic motives? Does the "restructuring of the archipelago" represent a comprehensive, long-range policy view?

In the Finance Ministry, you'll get an argument over that.

In theory, the restructuring idea was a long-range plan, but in reality just *pon-pon.*

Tanaka was elected as LDP president after a long struggle with Fukuda, and he owed many debts to the leaders of other factions, which he has to pay back. This is why the 1973 budget was so inflationary.

. . . in the United States in the 19th century, you called it "pork barrel" . . .

## What has been the impact of Tanaka's initiatives?

Even when we officials disagree, when the prime minister really wants something he usually gets it.

This sort of prime ministerial activity can be a good thing—it is hard to get anything accomplished through the bureaucracy, and when the problem is broad one ministry can't handle it. This system gives more direction.

35. As is evident, these two onomatopoeias mean, respectively, "suddenly" or "all at once," and "rapid-fire."

In some cases, Tanaka's ideas may have contributed, but his "timing" isn't very good . . . he can cause a good deal of confusion.

The timing problem . . . the economic tide was so strong, moving to high tide anyway, and he added more pressure to make it a flood.

How did Tanaka bring his ideas to the attention of the bureaucracy? In part, through personal interventions — he would occasionally call division directors on the telephone, or bring some junior officials into his office for a discussion. Or he might mention his interest in some project to a Cabinet minister, who would be expected to stir things up in his own ministry. However, more often he worked through the more-or-less formal channels of his staff.[36] For small matters he would send an official confidential secretary — one was a Finance Ministry official at the division chief level — to ask questions or convey orders. He might charge one of the Cabinet councillors, or even the head of the Cabinet Councillors' Office, with running a series of conferences of bureau directors from ministries involved in some policy problem until a compromise solution could be worked out. For weighty affairs the director-general of the Prime Minister's Office, or the chief Cabinet secretary or a deputy, would take the lead. Such devices had all been used before; it was the frequency and intensity of their use which made 1973 such a distinctive budget year.

After the fiscal crisis, 1974 was distinctive in the opposite direction. Tanaka intervened even less extensively than earlier prime ministers: "he became a silent man," said an interviewed official, "it must have been very hard for him." The case of the 1973 budget was sufficient to demonstrate that a Japanese prime minister could, if he wished, take an activist role in budget making; but the association (in the minds of nearly all observers) of Tanaka's spending initiatives with inflation and economic problems perhaps lessened the probability of the more traditional, passive pattern being broken again in the near future.

36. The topic of the size, characteristics and functions of the prime minister's staff badly needs more research. The chief Cabinet secretary and the director-general of the Prime Minister's Office, both Cabinet-level posts, are his chief spokesmen on the government side, similar in some respects to the secretary-general on the party side. These officials have deputies, and many members of the Secretariats under them may also be regarded as the staff of the prime minister. Overlap of functions and even personnel between these two bodies leads to some administrative confusion: see Okabe Shirō, *Gyōsei Kanri* ("Public Administration") (Tokyo: Yuhikaku, 1967), pp. 88-110, 126-29. The principal grouping is the Cabinet Councillors' Office, made up of seventeen officials on temporary assignment from their ministries, charged with "the coordination necessary for keeping integration of the policies of administrative offices such as the coordination of important matters for decision by Cabinet Meetings." Cabinet Law of 1947, as amended, Article 14-2 (3), trans. in Administrative Management Agency, *The Government of Japan*, p. 118. In recent years there have been many proposals to beef up the prime minister's staff, as by adding academic or business experts from outside the bureaucracy, but so far these have had the same success as most suggestions for administrative reform in Japan.

*Process Management.* — With the possible exception of Tanaka, most of the public utterances of prime ministers during the budget season have had little to do with either great economic issues or small program issues; they are devoted to matters of schedule and agenda. The prime minister's authority is thought needed to nail down important deadlines — the release of the MOF draft budget, the final MOF-LDP negotiations — and to limit the scope of topics which may be brought up at each stage. He is also occasionally called upon to make final decisions on matters of controversy; however, this function rarely offers him much chance to influence policy choices, since he cannot determine the issues which come to him, and he is usually able only to pick some compromise point between the positions already reached by the contending parties. Even this limited role has declined notably since the late 1950s and early 1960s.[37] More significant today is his mediation role: as the only person to hold important party and government posts simultaneously, he carries the most important messages back and forth and continually reads the moods and opinions of all participants, alert for potential disputes which threaten to derail the smooth progress of the budget. The commonest characterization of his function is to "achieve harmony" (*chōsei suru*) among contending participants.

*Backing Up the Finance Minister.* — The tradition that the prime minister should take a conservative position on fiscal issues apparently was established before the period of this study; in any case, Yoshida was most stern in his admonitions to the ministries to pare down their requests and spend as little as possible. Most prime ministers have followed suit — the normal expectation is well summarized in this 1960 *Asahi Shinbun* editorial:

Since in budget compilation the various cabinet ministers and the majority party leadership are out to secure their individual requests and argue for increasing the budget, it is very likely the finance minister will be left in a completely isolated position. If at that time he is not strongly supported by the prime minister, it becomes very hard for him to maintain his policies.[38]

This norm was violated most openly by Hatoyama in the 1956 budget process — he said "the task of cutting budgets is assigned to the Finance Minister; for myself, I will submit requests."[39] The result was a budgetary

37. Tanaka again was exceptional, sometimes picking up on disputes earlier in the process. He even chose to make the final decision on the producers' rice price for 1973 himself, a politically loaded decision most prime ministers do their best to avoid. Still, even in this case, according to an MOF agriculture specialist, the usual negotiations probably would have produced the identical decision.

38. AS, January 5, 1960.

39. TS, September 17, 1955.

debacle for Finance Minister Ichimanda, an event seen as reflecting poorly upon Hatoyama's ability to control the policy-making process. By two years later, however, the same finance minister could remark of another prime minister, "to fail in next year's budget compilation would be fatal for the Kishi cabinet, so he will back me up strongly," an expectation that was fulfilled in that and most succeeding years.[40] In Cabinet meetings through the summer and fall, prime ministers will second and frequently expand upon the finance minister's warnings of fiscal dangers and calls for economies, even when behind the scenes they may themselves be working to push up MOF estimates. Ikeda and Tanaka are again the partial exceptions, but even they often went on record in favor of Finance Ministry positions.

*Controlling the Party.*—Finally and probably most importantly, the prime minister, as the key figure in the LDP leadership, must protect the process and contents of the budget from onslaughts from Dietmen and party factions. The prime minister exercises this responsibility in part by employing some of the techniques described above in the section on the LDP leadership, but more crucial is the control which flows almost naturally from his command of the broader political scene. Speaking of the American president, Richard Neustadt says it is "reputation" that counts: the "dominant tone" of appraisals by other participants in regard to his tenacity and effectiveness in pursuing objectives, based on the past record.[41] Just as is true in Washington, the probability of disruption drops when a politician expects that a lack of cooperation will be followed by immediate or future costs. When the prime minister is weak, as was true of Hatoyama and Ishibashi in the mid-1950s and of Kishi in 1960, both factions and intraparty interest groups seize the opportunity to pick up budget grants and at the same time embarrass their leader. Satō Eisaku (with the frequent assistance of Tanaka Kakuei as his secretary-general) was perhaps the most skillful at manipulating party groups to maintain himself firmly in control, but in 1971 and 1972, when his reputation slipped and the end of his regime was in sight, budget pressures again became intense.

*Crucial but Passive.*—Taking all of these considerations into account, what general conclusions can be drawn about the role of the prime minister in budgeting? First, that it is quite important. It will be evident in chapter 9 that variations in the direction and effectiveness of prime

40. Ichimanda quoted in NKS, October 23, 1957.
41. Richard Neustadt, *Presidential Power* (New York: John Wiley & Sons, 1960), pp. 60ff.

ministerial policies have been a major factor in determining at least the smoothness of the budget process from year to year, and probably in budget size and contents as well. That is, although other things are never equal, it is probably true that budgeting will be more placid and budgets will be smaller (and perhaps less "political" in content) when the prime minister:

—is pursuing overall policy goals which are not budget related,

—takes a relatively conservative view of macrobudgeting issues,

—refrains from much intervention in microbudgeting,

—is skillful at mediation and knowing when to speak up to keep the process moving,

—is steadfast in support of the finance minister,

—dominates the LDP.

Certainly it is more true than for any of the other leadership participants that changing the prime minister may well change the shape of the budget appreciably. The reason is not only that his potential impact is so great; actually the finance minister's part is at least as large. Most significant is that—although expectations certainly have developed about what positions he should take—his role boundaries are broader, he has greater scope for improvisation, to decide for himself how he will participate. There has clearly been more variation in the prime minister's budgeting behavior than in that of any other participants.

Having said this, the second major conclusion is that the Japanese prime minister is ordinarily much less active in budgeting than other chief executives, at least the American and French presidents and the British prime minister. This point is quite obvious for all three "policy" functions—comprehensive policy making, fiscal policy and macrobudgeting decisions, initiation of or choices among specific programs—where he simply does not intervene as often or as effectively. Perhaps the prime minister's role is as crucial as the others' on the "process" side, but even here we note it is played for the most part quite passively. He must maintain support for the finance minister and control over the party, and then react deftly to whatever events may occur during the process. As a senior MOF official remarked in an interview, the Japanese prime minister is most effective when least seen.

# Big Businessmen

A widely held conception of Japanese decision making is that "the governing process is essentially the joint effort of big business, party government and the bureaucracy."[42] The phrases "limited pluralism" and "Japan Incorporated" are recent expressions of this notion that Japan is dominated by a three-element "power elite" knit together by mutual advantage.[43] If one accepts this view and the proposition that budgeting is a central process in domestic decision making, it would seem to follow that this power elite should control budgeting; we have seen so far that the budget process is dominated by government officials and Liberal Democratic Party Dietmen. It is natural then to ask, what is the role of big business?

Reviewing various modes of possible business participation in budgeting, we note first that individual firms and their associations may act as interest groups and attempt to raise allocations for programs that benefit them. The most glaring example is the continuing attempt by Mitsubishi Heavy Industries, Japan's largest defense contractor, to raise the proportion of GNP devoted to defense.[44] The shipping industry is said to work through, particularly, ex-Transport Ministry officials in the LDP for port construction. The example most often mentioned, when budget participants were asked in interviews about business participation, is general contractors, who not only compete for specific public works contracts but lobby through trade associations for large expenditures in highway and other construction categories. It is difficult to gauge how effective such pressure has been, to know how large defense or ports or public works expenditures would be in its absence.

If one looked beyond the General Account expenditure budget to examine the politics of revenue collections, one would find business groups competing fervently for "special tax measures" (*sozei tokubetsu sochi*) to encourage imports, exports, technological development and so forth — it was reported that 143 of these measures in 1970 were worth about a billion dollars in tax exemptions.[45] More generally, "peak" business groups have lobbied for reductions or against increases in the corporate income tax. Business firms may also benefit directly by subsidies from Fiscal Investment

42. Chitoshi Yanaga, *Big Business in Japanese Politics* (New Haven: Yale University Press, 1968), p. viii.

43. Haruhiro Fukui, "Economic Planning in Postwar Japan: A Case Study in Policy Making," *Asian Survey* 12, 4 (April 1972), 327-348; Eugene J. Kaplan, *Japan: The Government-Business Relationship* (Washington, D.C.: U.S. Department of Commerce, February 1972).

44. This firm also dominates the Defense Production Committee of Keidanren (the Federation of Economic Organizations, the leading "peak" business interest group), which actively lobbies for increased defense spending. See the critical discussion in Jon Halliday and Gavan McCormack, *Japanese Imperialism Today: "Co-prosperity in Greater East Asia"* (Middlesex, England: Penguin Books, 1973), pp. 107-118, and citations therein. Strictly speaking, such pressure usually does not bear directly on the budget process itself, since the major decisions are taken when formulating the five-year defense plans.

45. Nihon Keizai Shinbunsha, ed., *Yosan wa Dare no Mono ka* ("The Budget: Whose is it?") Tokyo: Nihon Keizai Shinbunsha, 1971), pp. 149-153.

and Loan Program expenditures and those of various Special Budgets and governmental corporations and funds (described briefly in chapter 8). The major banks are interested and active in monetary policy and the specifics of governmental bond financing.

Such examples could be multiplied, but they rather beg the question of whether big business — the Japanese term is *zaikai*, financial circles — in some sense "controls" the budgeting process. If it did, one would expect to find a degree of consensus among business leaders with regard to budgeting issues, communication of business views to those with direct responsibility for budgets, and reflections of those views in budgetary outputs. While the possibility of surreptitious decisions and communication cannot be altogether rejected, the research for this study — somewhat to the surprise of the author — uncovered very little evidence that business leaders as a group formulated views on budgeting issues or communicated them to party or government leaders.[46] Moreover, while some budgetary allocations favor business, others clearly do not — Japan's enormous agricultural subsidies are an obvious example. It is true that formally (through Keidanren) and probably also informally, *zaikai* members do formulate opinions on such questions as whether the economic effect of the budget should be stimulatory or deflationary, and the finance minister does meet with these leaders to discuss such issues. This channel may be important in macrobudgeting decision making. However, for what it is worth, no interviewed budget participant or close observer responded affirmatively when asked if these opinions had much influence. Moreover, none of the many articles and books that deal with budgeting claim that big business takes a major part; in fact, Suzuki Yukio, author of a book on the "power elite" which does focus on the importance of the *zaikai* in politics generally, concludes in another work that "it is normal for the major problems of budget allocation to be controlled by political pressures, unconnected with the opinions of big business."[47]

There is little reason to suppose, then, that very many of the decisions made during the Japanese budgetary process are heavily influenced by the preferences of big businessmen. But to think that the question ends here would be naive — one need not be deeply familiar with the literature on

46. A somewhat parallel line of argument, though not addressing budgeting, will be found in Gerald L. Curtis, "Big Business and Political Influence in Japan," in *Modern Japanese Organization and Decision-Making,* ed. Ezra Vogel (Berkeley and Los Angeles: University of California Press, 1975), pp. 33-70.

47. Suzuki Yukio, *Keizai Kanryō* ("Economic Bureaucrats") (Tokyo: Nihon Keizai Shinbunsha, 1969), p. 176. The other book referred to is *Gendai Nihon no Kenryoku Eriito: Sei-Zaikai Shihaisha no Shisō to Kōdō* ("The Contemporary Japanese Power Elite: Thought and Behavior of the Political-Financial Rulers") (Tokyo: Banchō Shobō, 1967). See also Philip Tresize and Suzuki Yukio, "Politics, Government and Economic Growth," in *Asia's New Giant: How the Japanese Economy Works,* eds. Hugh Patrick and Henry Rosovsky (Washington, D.C.: The Brookings Institution, 1976), pp. 753-811.

"nondecision-making" to realize that decisions never made, alternatives never considered, are at least as important as observable processes and pattenrs of influence in understanding how a political system works.[48] Through the entire postwar period, at least until very recently, the Japanese government had been dominated by men who agree on a fundamental policy goal, rapid economic growth achieved through the development of large-scale private industry. Although the era of major direct subsidies to industry from the General Account had for the most part passed by the mid-1950s, ever since then the underpinnings of budget policy have clearly been structured in favor of a high rate of private investment and building the infrastructure for industrial expansion. Observance of the "20 percent rule" to restrict the proportion of national income flowing through the government, the low (by international standards) level of expenditure in "unproductive" areas such as social transfer payments and defense, and the very high investment in public works (much of it to support industry, directly or indirectly) represent the continuation of policies begun long ago to support long-term growth, which of course serves in the first instance to benefit big business.

In the context of any year's budget process, such policies are determined by "nondecisions": they are rarely seriously debated or even thought about, and for the most part continue as nearly unconscious assumptions. In this environment there is little need for business to intervene actively or systematically in budgeting; the issues which most concern it are settled, and the remainder — incremental adjustments in growth rates of agencies or items — can safely be left to politicians and bureaucrats.

There are, however, dangers in remaining aloof. The early 1970s saw a definite if small increase in the level of over-all government expenditures, and in 1974 there was a more pronounced shift — whether temporary or permanent — away from public investment and toward social welfare. Business protest was minimal or absent. Perhaps the absence of participation by business leaders in decisions which would seem to run against their long-term interests can be explained by statesmanship; some may have become convinced that such steps were in the national interest, at least for the time being. On the other hand, one suspects too that nonparticipation had become customary. Businessmen were not in the habit of examining the expenditure budget process with the attention given to, say, tax policy or MITI's views on export-import priorities. The boundary expectations attached to their role in budgeting were extremely limited. For the same reason, it is quite possible too that any heavy-handed

48. The classic explication is Peter Bachrach and Morton S. Baratz, *Power and Poverty* (New York: Oxford University Press, 1970).

attempts to apply pressure would have been resented and rejected by other participants.

# Conclusions

Leaving businessmen aside, it is clear that these leaders play active roles in budgeting, and that other participants (and observers of budgeting) perceive them as important. How may we compare these roles and assess their significance?

An easy first question is to ask how many functions these leaders perform in budgeting. At one extreme, Cabinet ministers most often simply represent the interests of their organizations. The formal powers of the Cabinet are sufficient to offer the occasional ambitious and interested minister a base for attempts to achieve influence over some aspect of budgeting, but such occasions have been so rare they may be safely treated as exceptions. At the other extreme is the prime minister, whose participation in budgeting is quite varied; the LDP leadership and the finance minister occupy a middle position.

Second, when several functions are performed, to what extent do they contradict each other? In other words, when an individual must play more than one role, do these roles conflict, or do they reinforce each other?[49] This problem is usually not acute for Cabinet ministers unless they wish to play a larger game which risks a sacrifice in their ability to obtain budgets for their organizations—more often, however, as Kōno Ichirō demonstrated on several occasions, threats of large-scale interventions are likely to be helpful in increasing budget payoffs to one's own ministry. Finance ministers have sometimes had difficulties in combining their roles as politicians (particularly when contending for the party presidency) and as representatives of the Ministry of Finance. Prime ministers find that their ability to manage the process successfully, by serving as the protector of the rules of the game and mediating among disputants, may depend on their remaining above the fray by not pushing particular programs or policies too enthusiastically. Perhaps the most obvious role conflict faces the LDP leadership, who on the one hand is expected to ably represent the wishes of party members, and on the other must repress those demands so that a sensible budget may be compiled in an orderly fashion.

Third, how much of each participant's behavior is constrained and how much open to his individual discretion; or put another way, to what

49. This is of course a classic role theory question, and is discussed in a bureaucratic politics context by Graham Allison in his famous article "Conceptual Models and the Cuban Missile Crisis," conveniently excerpted in a volume which contributed substantially to my thinking on these subjects: Morton H. Halperin and Arnold Kanter, eds., *Readings in American Foreign Policy: A Bureaucratic Perspective* (Boston: Little, Brown, and Company, 1973).

extent can an analyst predict behavior simply by knowing an individual's organizational position? Organization theory predicts that the behavior (and even opinions) of those lower in a hierarchy is more likely to be organizationally determined, but there will be considerable variation on this dimension among those at higher levels.[50] Again, Cabinet ministers provide the easiest example; nearly all their budgeting behavior is quite predictable. Majority party leaders have varied somewhat along the "representation-responsibility" continuum, but otherwise seem to follow routines — in particular, it is surprising that interventions to support specific programs of personal interest occur so infrequently on the part of those in formal leadership positions (though more commonly by faction leaders or members of the Executive Board, as noted in the previous chapter), given their rather substantial potential influence.

Finance ministers present the clearest example of role socialization: examples of unorthodox behavior, such as calling for higher rather than lower spending and generally being overresponsive to LDP demands, seem to come most often early in an individual's term of office. The public statements and actions of more experienced ministers rarely deviate much from Finance Ministry orthodoxy,. Any deviations, by new or old incumbents, are usually quickly followed by anonymous expressions of concern from MOF officials showing up in newspaper stories. This role is thus rather tightly defined, even if the definitions are sometimes violated.[51]

The budgeting role which is most ambiguous, and therefore allows its occupant to bring his individual objectives and talents most into play, is that of prime minister. The choices he makes about which of his several functions to emphasize, and about how much energy he will devote to budgeting, cannot be easily predicted, and can have important effects on the budget process and the size and contents of the budget. However, all of his choices have costs, and as Tanaka discovered after the 1973 budget when he received a fair share of the blame for inflation, these can be considerable. Most prime ministers seem to play a safer hand in the budgetary game.

Finally, we may ask how much difference these leadership roles can make in budgeting. Must one spend much time studying individuals to understand how the budget system works?[52] The answer to this question

50. See the editors' introduction in *ibid.*, pp. 7-9, and for some empirical findings for an American agency, Robert Axelrod, "Bureaucratic Decisionmaking in the Military Assistance Program," *ibid.*, pp. 154-172.

51. Incidentally, lower level Finance Ministry officials have occasionally propelled themselves into the "leadership," in the sense of making an individual impact in budgeting, by going beyond their normal role boundaries. The most spectacular example is Murakami Kōtarō, Budget Bureau director during the "break fiscal rigidification campaign."

52. This question is equivalent to asking if Allison's "organizational process model" is suffient to account for budgeting decisions, or if prediction is improved by also taking the "bureaucratic politics model" into account. See Allison, "Conceptual Models," *passim.*

must be rather uncertain: the role of the individual in the processes of history is a problem which is not going to be settled here. Clearly the internal processes of institutions and their relationships with each other are the primary determinants of budgeting. The fact that these processes and relationships are usually stable accounts for the slowness of changes in budgets (as measured by shares). Still, new things happen sometimes, and budgets do change at the margins. Looking over the record of twenty-one years of budgeting, one gets an impression that it is at times of change that the leaders described in this chapter become more prominent and more likely to transcend customary role expectations. Tanaka as prime minister in 1973 and Fukuda as finance minister in 1974 are major examples — different individuals would not have behaved in the same way at those junctures, and their actions did shape the budget.[53] The rather obvious point here, I suppose, is that a focus on organizations is appropriate and adequate when explaining stability, which certainly characterizes most budgeting most of the time; but when one tries to account for changes, at least some consideration must also be given to the objectives, skills and personalities of individual leaders.

53. Fukuda was pursuing orthodox MOF objectives in cutting the 1974 budget, but his activist stance vis-à-vis other participants and even Budget Bureau officials was quite unusual.

# 7

# Revival Negotiations

THE MINISTRY OF FINANCE draft budget is released in mid-December or early January every year. Up until this point, the line ministries have formulated their requests, explained them to the Budget Bureau, and answered questions. The LDP divisions have participated in shaping requests and contributed to the party's official Budget Compilation Policy document. The finance minister, after consultations with party and government leaders, has decided the size of the total budget, and may have worked out some of the thorniest expenditure problems. The Budget Bureau has managed to come up with provisional decisions on budgets for nearly all the thousands of governmental programs. The stage is set for the most hectic and well publicized period in the budget process: the revival negotiations, *fukkatsu sesshō*, literally "resurrection" negotiations in which ministry requests are "brought back from the dead."

Appeals procedures are common in budget systems. In the United States, when an agency's request is denied by the Office of Management and Budget, it can appeal to the president, or when by the House Appropriations Committee, to the Senate Appropriations Committee.[1] French agencies appeal decisions by the budget division successively to the finance minister, the prime minister and the president.[2] Appeals in Great Britain are discussed in long meetings of the full Cabinet.[3] From a systems point of view, appeals reduce decision-making costs by forcing the

1. Aaron Wildavsky, *The Politics of the Budgetary Process* (Boston: Little, Brown and Company, 1964), pp. 35-37, 58; Richard F. Fenno, Jr., *The Power of the Purse: Appropriations Politics in Congress* (Boston: Little, Brown and Company, 1966), esp. chaps. 10-11.

2. Guy Lord, *The French Budgetary Process* (Berkeley and Los Angeles: University of California Press, 1973), pp. 40-43.

3. Hugh Heclo and Aaron Wildavsky, *The Private Government of Public Money* (Berkeley and Los Angeles: University of California Press, 1974), pp. 188-197.

requesting side to eliminate, in effect, some of its demands — the budgeting authority is spared exhaustive research on newly requested programs or large increases if it makes only tentative decisions on most of them in the first round and worries seriously only about those strongly rerequested. Providing for appeals also serves to bleed off some of the political tensions which always accompany budgeting, allowing the process to appear one of compromise rather than of unilateral decision.

While sharing such general characteristics, the Japanese appeals process is distinctive in several respects. First, appeals are made to the authority responsible for the original cuts: the Ministry of Finance must approve virtually all additions to the budget, and it is nearly impossible to re-appeal to the Cabinet or prime minister. Second, the majority party has an important and quite institutionalized role. Third, the process is relatively open, and indeed receives enormous publicity. Fourth, the various stages of the negotiations have become very standardized, even ritualized; deviations from the script are rare. Finally, although little in the way of comprehensive setting of priorities occurs, the ministries do compete for shares of a relatively fixed (if not always known) pot of additional money. These points will become more clear in the discussion below. After a description of the process on the government and party sides, including the significance of the reform which occurred in 1968, we will consider the goals and strategies of the participants and ask how important the revival negotiations are in the Japanese budget process as a whole.

# The Governmental Process

The revival negotiations are basically a microbudgeting process, and proceed under the same decision-making principles that govern budget compilation generally: do the easiest and smallest problems first and save the hardest and biggest for later; do the easiest and smallest at the lower levels so the higher levels are left with as few problems as possible. In earlier years, when LDP politics were more turbulent and the budgeting system had not altogether settled down, the negotiations could drag on for quite a long time. From 1954 to 1961 they averaged over thirteen days, and in 1960, a disastrous year for the Ministry of Finance, they consumed a full three weeks. Since 1961, however, they have taken only about a week, and the order of proceedings has also become quite regular.

The process begins when the Ministry of Finance draft is reported to the Cabinet, in the form of budget figures for each of the Important Items.[4] Shortly thereafter the detailed draft of each ministry's budget is

4. Appendix A is a table of the complete Important Item budget for 1973, including both the MOF draft and government draft figures so that changes during the revival negotiations may be discerned.

"shown" (*naiji*) and explained to the ministry accounting division director by the examiner — the participants in this and the other meetings are shown on Table 10. The director takes this draft back to his ministry and discusses it with the bureau directors, who in turn explain their portions to their division chiefs; suggestions about which reductions or denials should be appealed, and for how much, then quickly are filtered back through the ministerial hierarchy for final decision at the top. Brief discussions will also be held with the corresponding LDP Policy Affairs Research Council division, which will have seen a copy of the draft. All this takes only a day or so.

The real negotiations begin on the day following the "showing." It appears that the Budget Bureau representatives at the early stages are implicitly or explicitly allowed to grant appeals up to a certain amount — scattered press accounts leave an impression that in the first two days ¥ 1-3 billion (on the order of $5 million) will be spread among all the ministries, and perhaps ¥ 15 billion or so on the third day. These are rather small amounts; the early meetings are more important for clarifying issues than actually making allocations. It is at the vice-ministerial level that more substantial sums are negotiated, although even here announcements of decisions reached may often be postponed until the Cabinet-level meetings, when the minister can pick up political points.

The sessions up to and including the vice-ministerial level are often referred to as "administrative" (*jimu*) negotiations, while the Cabinet and party leadership sessions are called "policy" (*seisaku*) or "political" (*seiji*) negotiations. In earlier years, the final discussions with the LDP were largely devoted to matters which could not be solved at lower levels, but today virtually all such disputes are wrapped up at most by the end of the Cabinet negotiations. The party leadership negotiations mainly treat matters which have been designated in advance by agreement between the LDP leadership and the finance minister.

Year-to-year variations in the revival negotiations process do not affect this basic pattern very much. The length of the later stages will vary depending upon the political situation and the strategy being followed by the Ministry of Finance; sessions with individual Cabinet ministers may take from an hour or so up to half a day; the final party-government negotiations, which nearly always begin in the late evening, sometimes have lasted until midmorning of the following day, although in the 1970s a trend toward much shorter sessions, perhaps two or three hours, could be observed. Also, finance ministers differ in their propensity to hold informal negotiating sessions outside of the formal process. Some will try to work out everything in advance with the concerned ministers and the LDP leadership, so the regular sessions do no more than ratify; others focus on one or two problems or simply let nature take its course. In the 1973

## TABLE 10
### TYPICAL STAGES OF REVIVAL NEGOTIATIONS

| Day | Name | Finance Ministry Participants | Line Ministry Participants | LDP Participants | Normal Duration | Notes |
|-----|------|-------------------------------|----------------------------|------------------|-----------------|-------|
| 0 | *Naiji* | Examiner Investigators (Chief Clerks) | Acctng Div Dir Staff | | 4–5 hours | Explanations, not negotiations. |
| 1–2 | *Kachō Sesshō* | Investigators Chief Clerks | Div Dir Staff | | 2–3 hours each | Quite detailed. |
| 3 | *Kyokuchō Sesshō* | Examiner (Investigator) | Acctng Div Dir (Bureau Dir) (Div Dirs) [Dep Vice-Min] | | 1 day | Investigator may discuss matters in his specialty. |
| 4–5 | *Jikan Sesshō* | BB Vice-Director Examiner Investigators | Vice-Minister Dep Vice-Min Acctng Div Dir (Bur Dir) | | Several hours each | Examiner occasionally talks, investigators not. |
| 5–6 | *Daijin Sesshō* | Finance Minister Vice-Minister Dep Vice-Min BB Director BB Vice-Dir Examiner [Investigator] | Minister | PARC Chmn [Vice-Chmn] | ½ to 2 hours each | Held in Finance Minister's office. |
| 6–7 | *Seiji Sesshō* | Finance Minister [BB Director] | (Minister) | Sec-Gen Exec Coun Chmn PARC Chmn | 2–8 hours total | Chief Cabinet Secretary also participates. Held at Prime Minister's residence at night. |

NOTES: Inset = takes secondary role.    ( ) = official responsible for matter immediately under discussion will be present.    [ ] = occasionally present.

SOURCE: Interview with a Budget Bureau investigator, June 1974, supplemented with other interviews and published materials.

negotiations, Finance Minister Aichi Kiichi was said to be so eager to avoid all-night negotiations that he gave in on nearly everything the LDP wanted in advance.[5]

Such is the formal process. But it is difficult to impart to a reader in a country where budgeting is normally considered a dry, technical exercise quite the air of turmoil and festivity that accompanies the revival negotiations in Japan. Interest groups schedule mass meetings and send groups of delegates waving banners through the streets to promote highways or pensions. Politicians and even ministries rent suites in nearby hotels (the Akasaka Prince is the favorite) to be at the center of tactical planning sessions. The LDP headquarters building becomes so jammed with petitioners that no one can reach the elevators. Dietmen receive three or four times the usual number of visitors in their offices.[6] Newspapers run several articles in each edition on how the negotiations are proceeding, including human interest stories about battling petitioners and embattled bureaucrats. In the Budget Bureau, examiners are staying up all night and catnapping on cots in the hallways the next morning. Delivery trucks from restaurants are seen arriving around the clock. Everyone complains of the pressure, deplores the irrationality of it all, and apparently enjoys himself.

*The 1968 Reform.* — Where does the Finance Ministry obtain the funds to grant appeals? They cannot come from raising taxes, expanding the bond issue, or revising revenue estimates upwards, because since 1958 the MOF has held to a principle that the total amount for the budget set in the Ministry of Finance draft would not be raised.[7] This basic strategy was adopted because the MOF feared that the pressures developed during revival negotiations might threaten macrobudgeting decisions. On the other hand, funds could not be transferred from one spending ministry to another once the draft budget had been announced; the loser would not stand for it. Therefore, until 1968, the Finance Ministry employed a devious strategy called "hidden resources" (*kakushi zaigen*). An amount of money known to MOF officials, but kept secret from other participants, was stashed away in budget accounts which were either under the jurisdiction of the Finance Ministry itself or were impossible to detect in the Important Item budget breakdown published for the MOF draft (primarily in the Miscellaneous account, although National Debt and other categories were also frequently used). When pressures were particularly intense, the MOF would use up all of these funds and perhaps even draw upon other

5. NKS, January 16, 1973.
6. A monthly breakdown of visitors for 1968-69 was supplied by the Secretariat of the House of Representatives.
7. As is seen in Column B of Table 11, below, the single exception is in 1961, occasioned by a last minute hike in the gasoline tax to expand highway construction expenditures.

somewhat flexible resources it controlled. In years when Dietmen turned out to be more passive than expected, some of the money could be saved and turned into a handy reserve.

Table 11 lists some estimates of my own for the amounts of these "hidden resources" (Column D). The sums grew to be rather substantial, up to the equivalent of over 500 million dollars in 1966 and 1967. Keeping the total secret had not proven to be an effective device in holding down expenditures; indeed, because it was difficult to convince the spenders that available funds had actually been used up, they tended to keep pressing for more indefinitely. The Ministry of Finance was also frequently criticized for emplying such underhanded methods. Accordingly, as part of the "break fiscal rigidity movement" in the 1968 budget process, a new system was adopted.

Instead of "hidden resources," appeals would now be met with "open resources" (*kōkai zaigen*, literally "open-to-the-public resources"). The reform had two aspects. First, each ministry would be given a certain sum, perhaps in the range of ¥10 billion or so, as "Secretariat Adjustment Expenses" (*kanbō chōseihi*). These were to be allocated among ministry programs essentially at the discretion of the minister's staff. Second, an additional, larger amount was actually listed in the MOF draft as "Adjustment Expenses" for "policy" or "political" expenditures, to be allocated at either the Cabinet or party-level negotiations.[8] These amounts (Column C of Table 11) ranged in size from the equivalent of about 150 to 500 million dollars. MOF officials hoped that the LDP and ministries would believe this amount to be all there was available, and hence would devote their energies to deciding how it would be divided up, rather than increasing the total. However, the reform was not costless: under the earlier system, the MOF retained considerable authority over the allocation of funds, but now the money for supplements was in effect to be handed over to spending ministry officials (in the case of Secretariat Adjustment Expenses) or to the LDP leadership.[9]

Although this reform was hailed with considerable fanfare by both MOF officials and budget observers in 1968, there is some reason to doubt that it really represented much of a change. Even prior to 1968, as indicated in chapter 3, the MOF had increasingly been relegating decisions on individual programs to spending ministry officials, and this trend had been particularly evident in the revival negotiations. That the party leadership would have the predominant role in the final decisions was also

8. In 1968-1973 this item was labeled *Chōseihi,* but in 1974 it was called *Ryūhohi,* "withheld expenses."

9. That the MOF gave up a significant amount of its power here is argued forcibly in Nihon Keizai Shinbunsha, ed., *Yosan wa Dare no Mono ka* ("The Budget: Whose is it?") (Tokyo: Nihon Keizai Shinbunsha, 1971), pp. 63-64.

TABLE 11

BUDGET SUPPLEMENTS DURING REVIVAL NEGOTIATIONS

(Units: 100 Million Yen; Percent)

| Budget Year | A Initial Budget (Gov. Dr.) | B Change in Total | C Policy Adjustment Expenses | D Transfers From Other Imp. Items | E Total Supps., Imp. Item Accting. (C + D) | F Percentage Increment (E/A) | G Transfers From Other Ministries | H Total Supps., Min. Accting. (C + G) | I Percentage Increment (H/A) |
|---|---|---|---|---|---|---|---|---|---|
| 1955 | 9,996 | 9 | | 288 | 288 | 2.9 | | | |
| 1956 | 10,349 | 53 | | 297 | 297 | 2.9 | | | |
| 1957 | 11,375 | 39 | | 224 | 224 | 2.0 | | | |
| 1958 | 13,121 | 0 | | 247 | 247 | 1.9 | | | |
| 1959 | 14,192 | 0 | | 163 | 163 | 1.1 | | | |
| 1960 | 15,696 | 0 | | 206 | 206 | 1.3 | | | |
| 1961 | 19,528 | 154 | | 588 | 588 | 3.0 | | | |
| 1962 | 24,268 | 0 | | 645 | 645 | 2.7 | | | |
| 1963 | 28,500 | -58 | | 896 | 896 | 3.1 | | | |
| 1964 | 32,554 | -113 | | 901 | 901 | 2.8 | | | |
| 1965 | 36,581 | 0 | | 1119 | 1119 | 3.1 | | | |
| 1966 | 43,143 | 0 | | 1721 | 1721 | 4.0 | | | |
| 1967 | 49,509 | -475 | | 1605 | 1605 | 3.2 | | | |
| 1968 | 58,186 | 0 | 470 | 11 | 481 | 0.8 | | | |
| 1969 | 67,396 | 0 | 560 | 304 | 864 | 1.3 | 31 | 592 | 0.9 |
| 1970 | 79,498 | 0 | 650 | 102 | 752 | 0.9 | 120 | 770 | 1.0 |
| 1971 | 94,143 | -12 | 1060 | 10 | 1070 | 1.1 | 101 | 1161 | 1.2 |

| 1972 | 114,705 | 0 | 1100 | 202 | 1302 | 1.1 | 47 | 1147 | 1.0 |
| 1973 | 142,841 | 0 | 1500 | 472 | 1972 | 1.4 | 808 | 2308 | 1.6 |
| 1974 | 170,994 | 0 | 500 | 860 | 1360 | 0.8 | | | |

NOTES: Column D was calculated by comparing the Important Item classification for the MOF draft and the government draft. The amounts subtracted from all items reduced, and the amounts added to all items which gained, were totalled; after adjustments for any changes in the total, the two sums were identical. This is the "net" amount transferred during revival negotiations; it excludes additions and subtractions within the same item, which are doubtlessly quite significant at least for the Miscellaneous item, and means that these figures are underestimated to some degree. The same calculation was performed on the ministry breakdown for 1969–1973 (Column G), the only years it was published for the MOF draft, as an alternative aggregation which may be somewhat more valid.

SOURCES: Contemporary newspapers; documents provided by the MOF; *Zaisei Tōkei*, 1974, pp. 189–203.

not a particularly new notion. In this sense, the 1968 reform might be seen as formalizing an existing state of affairs. Moreover, when one examines the budget process after 1968, it is unclear to what extent the reform was actually implemented. Even for 1969 and 1970, officials of some spending ministries said in interviews that they had received no explicit Secretariat Adjustment Expenses, and newspaper accounts showed that the MOF continued to dole out tiny increments for ministry programs at each of the administrative stages of the revival negotiations. Furthermore, Columns D and G of Table 11 indicate that supplements were granted above the announced Policy Adjustment Expenses, sometimes in substantial amounts. These were drawn from the same old sources (mainly the Miscellaneous items under the MOF's jurisdiction) and were covered by the same old secrecy.

But even if the 1968 change did not amount to much procedurally, it appears to be quite important substantively. Whether actually caused by the reform or simply a product of increased MOF tenacity, clearly the amounts granted during the revival negotiations declined sharply from 1968, at least in percentage terms.[10] Since restraining expenditures was a more important objective for MOF officials than projecting an image of rational decision making, the initiation of the "open resources" system can unquestionably be counted as a Ministry of Finance success.

# The Party Process

In chapter 5 it was pointed out that the LDP's pre-MOF draft Budget Compilation Policy, though produced in an elaborate process and given wide publicity, actually has little influence on budgeting. The party's participation in the revival negotiations is different: its recommendations (*fukkatsu sesshō no jūten kōmoku*) are drawn up hurriedly and are not very elegant, but some of them at least are taken quite seriously by other participants. This process offers some good indications of what the LDP is and is not capable of doing in Japanese decision making.

*Divisions.*—Immediately after the Ministry of Finance draft budget is explained to a ministry, a copy is sent over to the appropriate Policy Affairs Research Council division. The forms used show the name of the program, the amount budgeted in the previous year, the request, and the amount granted by the MOF; a blank column for rerequests is included, and

10. See Columns F and I. Since any Secretariat Adjustment Expenses which were included within items listed in the MOF draft would not be included in the calculation of supplements, the figures for 1968 and thereafter may be underestimated somewhat disproportionately. However, the differentials are surely large enough to be substantially significant even allowing for this discrepancy.

division leaders will consult with ministry officials on these amounts. During the week of negotiations the division may meet every day. Consultations with ministry officials on strategy and tactics continue, and in many cases division members help in coordinating the activities of clientele groups seeking to apply pressure on party leaders and the MOF.

The divisions all also mark up copies of budget forms to pass up through the party hierarchy, as the raw materials for the recommendations made by the LDP as a whole.[11] Rather than making specific monetary recommendations, each program is marked with an A, B or C to indicate the degree of divisional concern. Grading standards differ to some extent among divisions (as they do among college professors)—in 1970, several gave no C grades whatsoever, and in two cases (Construction and Home Affairs) only one B was given, all other items receiving an A. In the materials available, out of a possible 435 items, the distribution was: A, 230; B, 122; C, 23; and not marked, 39.[12]

*The Policy Deliberation Commission.* —On the third day of the revival negotiations, the PARC Policy Deliberation Commission meets to review these divisional recommendations. In 1970, this meeting began at 10 A.M. on January 27 in a crowded and overheated conference room in the LDP headquarters building; though scheduled to adjourn at 4 P.M., everyone ran late and the talking dragged on until late at night. The hearings were divided into seventeen segments, including one for each of the fifteen divisions then established, scheduled for 10, 15 or 20 minutes each.[13] In each segment representatives of the division and any PARC special committees and investigatory commissions in that policy area talked about the highlights of their budget suggestions. When each oral presentation was concluded, the Commission immediately discussed its own recommendations briefly and marked up the budget forms. No time was allotted for discussions of the budget as a whole.

The Deliberation Commission's marking system differed from that of the divisions. Instead of ABCs it awarded four grades. The highest is called

11. A set of these documents prepared by ten divisions during the 1970 revival period was given to me by an interest group representative present at the Policy Deliberation Commission hearings (described below). See chap. 2, n. 9, and for more detail App. II of my dissertation, "Contemporary Japanese Budget Politics" (Columbia University, 1973).

12. The forms are broken down by ministry, major category, program, and subprogram. The figure of 435 was calculated by counting all the items given a divisional grade which were not further divided into subitems receiving grades; the 39 unmarked items are subitems under unmarked items which also included marked subitems.

13. The segments receiving twenty minutes were Social Affairs, Agriculture and Forestry, Commerce and Industry, Transportation, and Construction; fifteen minutes—Judicial Affairs, Foreign Affairs, Educational Affairs, and Local Administration; ten minutes—Cabinet Affairs, National Defense, Financial, Labor Affairs, Fisheries, Communications, and Science and Technology (which was not represented by a division). Several "Miscellaneous" groups each received five minutes.

*marusei*, a circle with the character for *sei* inside, representing (according to informants) either *seisaku*, "policy" or *seiji*, "politics." The others, in order, are a double circle, a circle, and a check mark. The distribution of these marks, in the materials available, is as follows: *marusei*, 39; double circle, 83; circle, 85; check, 49; none, 74.[14]

Cross-tabulating allows us to see how the Commission treated the recommendations from the divisions (see Table 12). It is clear that the Commission regards the *marusei* and double circle as equivalent to the divisional A and the check as roughly equivalent to B, while the circle is used for both A and B. No items graded B or C by the divisions were upgraded to either a *marusei* or double circle by the Commission: clearly, programs which had been rated relatively low by the divisions were not picked up for special attention by the Commission. On the other hand, the Commission did pick and choose to some extent among the divisional A-rated items (nearly two-thirds of the total), ignoring or check-rating about a tenth of them and giving another quarter only a B, so something like a winnowing-out process did occur.

Actually, although these differentiations are interesting in demonstrating, contrary to opinions sometimes heard in Japan, that LDP bodies are capable of making decisions, it is questionable whether the ratings from double circle through check mark have much real impact in budgeting. These detailed lists are sent to the Ministry of Finance as reference materials, and may be brought up in ministry-MOF negotiations, but it is only with the *marusei* items that the LDP takes a direct hand. This mark itself means that the item should be taken up at the "political" level, the Cabinet or government-party negotiations. In 1970, about one-fifth of the 191 programs given an A by the divisions were further indulged with a *marusei* by the Commission. Why were these chosen rather than others?

*The Recommendations.* — While it is impossible to analyze each of these party budget choices in detail, we can look over some of the characteristics of the list. To begin with, the distribution of *marusei* programs among ministries is quite uneven: Agriculture and Forestry (including Fisheries) had twelve; Transport, nine; Construction and MITI, four each; Home Affairs, three; Labor, Health and Welfare, and the Prime Minister's Office, two; Education, one; and the EPA, none.[15] The LDP unsurprisingly has a disproportionate interest in agriculture, fishing, and construction projects (just over half the items are for public works). Twelve of the thirty-nine are newly proposed programs, and another is a

14. This total of 331 is less than the total of divisional marks because some Commission ratings covered more than one divisional mark.

15. It should be noted that for the Ministry of Construction, these four items comprised exactly 80 percent of its 1970 budget.

TABLE 12
PARC Priorities at Two Levels
of Decision Making
(Unit: Item)

| Divisional Grade | A | B | C | Total |
|---|---|---|---|---|
| **Commission Grade** | | | | |
| *Marusei* | 39 | 0 | 0 | 39 |
| Double Circle | 82 | 0 | 0 | 82 |
| Circle | 47 | 34 | 1 | 82 |
| Check | 9 | 32 | 0 | 41 |
| None | 14 | 37 | 5 | 56 |
| Total | 191 | 103 | 6 | 300 |

NOTE: Totals differ from those for these grades in text because (1) some illegible items were eliminated; (2) Commission grades with no corresponding division grades are not included; and (3) in some cases, several subitems were grouped and their divisional grades averaged when the Commission had marked only the item.

SOURCE: Unpublished LDP documents.

more than ten-fold expansion of an old program—as basic incrementalist doctrines predict, it is major changes which draw notice. Revealing the fragmented operation of the Commission, several of these items overlap: four actually call for the creation of quite similar new five-year plans for seashore construction, requested by four ministries anxious to expand in this area; pension plans for farmers were requested by both the Agriculture and Welfare Ministries, and both proposals were given a *marusei*; programs for aiding subway construction from both Home Affairs and Transport were included. Clearly the Commission just took each segment one by one, paying no attention to its own earlier or later discussions. It is therefore easy for contradictory items to receive endorsements—for example, on subway construction aid, the two ministries were proposing fundamentally different solutions to the same problems.[16] By simply writing a *marusei* on both requests, the Commission passed up its chance to choose between the two plans. Such diffidence is due both to the complexity of the issues involved and to the fact that each division will strongly back the claims of its ministry and resent a decision against its interests.

16. Cf. NKS, January 8, 1970, evening.

Finally, some noncharacteristics of this list are interesting. Three of the five items which appeared in the Basic Policy section of the Budget Compilation Program, therefore nominally identified as the highest priorities of the LDP, were pollution, traffic safety and price stabilization measures. These were not mentioned, even tangentially, in the appeals recommendations, presumably because they are not the objects of specific interest group or constituency pressures on the party. Note moreover that other possible budget matters of great public interest are not included; that the arrangement of items is not determined by priority or popularity, but simply by the order of witnesses before the Commission; and that each is designated only with a brief title, written in budget language incomprehensible to the average newspaper reader. All these points suggest that, unlike the Budget Compilation Program, the revival recommendations are not intended for public consumption, but are aimed directly at influencing other budget participants. This point, in turn, helps explain why these recommendations need not be quite so "balanced" as the Budget Compilation Program and other LDP policy pronouncements. The Commission does pick and choose, and its *marusei* endorsement actually are an accurate summary of the LDP's true interests in the budget for a given year.

*The Executive Council.* — The next stop for the revival negotiation recommendations is the Executive Council, the body authorized to make party decisions. Its deliberations, held on the same or the following day, are much briefer than those of the Commission. In 1970, the Council tidied up the list of recommendations, reducing them from thirty-nine to thirty-two by amalgamating some overlapping items (although the two contradictory subway construction items were left separate and intact).[17] No subjects were completely eliminated and no new items were added to this list, which became the LDP revival negotiations official plan. However, the Council also prepared a separate list of twelve additional items, apparently given a lower priority since they were mentioned only as an afterthought in newspaper stories.[18]

More generally, as indicated in chapter 5, it is because the Executive Council represents a slightly different aggregation of interests than the Policy Deliberation Commission that it frequently adds a few items to the recommendations and occasionally may even drop one or two. The number of "policy level" items recommended varies considerably from year

17. See NKS, January 28, 1970, evening. The four seashore construction proposals were reduced to two.
18. NKS, January 29, 1970. Among the nine of these which could be found in the LDP document mentioned above, seven had received a double-circle, one a circle, and one no mark in the Commission deliberations.

to year: for example, for the expansive "restructuring the archipelago" 1973 budget, thirty-five were chosen, while for the more stringent 1974 budget the Commission selected only eight and the Council added five more.[19] All these recommendations, of course, are for the establishment or expansion of programs, not their abolishment or reduction. Only one exception was encountered: in 1968, the reforms in revival negotiations instigated by the Ministry of Finance seemed to reduce the amount of money available to fill LDP requests, and the Executive Council response, in its official recommendations, was to call for "rearguing" (i.e., reducing) two items already approved in the MOF draft to allow more funds for party-supported programs. This violation of the customary rules of the game was greeted rather stiffly by MOF officials — one said "there cannot be a reduction of a budget figure that has already been examined and approved," and indeed at least one of the programs in question was actually granted more funds in later negotiations.[20] In all other years the utmost expression of LDP disapproval of a program within this process was to ignore its existence.

*Implementation.* — The Executive Council can make policy, but it is too large and diverse a body to handle the flexible (and sometimes unpleasant) decisions necessary when actually conducting negotiations. Accordingly, it details the PARC chairman to attend all the Cabinet-level negotiations, and afterward hears his report on which LDP recommendations have been approved. Sometimes a joint meeting of the Executive Council and the Policy Deliberation Commission is convened to hear this report, and sometimes the finance minister or even MOF permanent officials come over late in the negotiations to discuss remaining issues. The Executive Council then formally delegates its decision-making authority to the party leadership, the "big three" or "big four." This practice dates back to the very first budget compiled under the unified LDP, that for 1956, when after the Policy Deliberation Commission had actually succeeded in formulating a "responsible" — that is, realistically low — proposal for the entire budget, individual Dietmen pursuing favorite projects which had been left out forced repudiation of the draft. It became

19. Respectively, NKS, January 13, 1973, and NKS, December 26 and 27, 1973. The Council's additions in 1974 were actually just more detailed descriptions of the Commission's eight items. Sometimes quite elaborate lists are prepared — that for 1961 divided the recommendations into five classifications: AS, January 10, 1961.

20. Both items were rather special cases: unemployment compensation for seasonal workers, at a time when unions were actively trying to enroll such workers; and new academic departments for national universities, which had irritated the LDP with their soft handling of student rebellions. However, since other items in other years had similar political liabilities but were not singled out for reductions, it seems safe to say that this action was mainly produced by party peevishness toward the MOF. AS, January 9, morning and evening, and 10, 1968.

obvious that the more democratic party organs could not withstand such pressures, and in the end the leadership had to be authorized to make the final decisions. Difficulties in controlling the rank and file continued — in 1961, a combined Executive Council-Policy Deliberation Commission meeting refused for a time to delegate decisions to the "big three," and in several years large meetings of all divisional chairmen or even the entire party Diet membership had to be called to allow a venting of resentments.[21] However, in spite of, or more likely because of, the intensity of demands from below, final responsibility for LDP budget policy continued to be given over to the leaders.

Throughout most of the revival period the leadership devotes much of its attention to procedural matters, in cooperation with the finance minister and sometimes the prime minister. In earlier years there had been no clear and accepted ideas of what sorts of problems would be handled at various levels, how these problems should be identified, and who would meet with whom. Many meetings were held among various party leadership bodies and individuals, the finance minister and other MOF officials, and the prime minister and his representatives, confusing and extending the process; at worst, budget problems thought to be settled were reopened for more negotiations and, inevitably, more funds. However, things had settled down by the mid-1960s; in particular, the principle became established that nearly all items left over from the administrative-level negotiations would be settled in the Cabinet-level sessions, so that the final talks between the LDP leadership and the finance minister could be devoted almost entirely to a selected portion of the LDP's *marusei* recommendations. Some of these receive a first go-around by their sponsoring Cabinet ministers, while others are introduced for the first time by the party; but in either case the agenda is usually determined well before the meeting. Most often about six major items are taken up. Those that reappear quite frequently are public works allocations and war-related pensions, along with any newly proposed governmental agencies or corporations and the determination of final total figures for ministry five-year plans; other topics in recent years have included health insurance, agricultural programs, railroad construction projects and fare structure, free school textbooks and lunches, and various types of aid to local governments. All are items of great interest to the LDP.

The final negotiations have lasted anywhere from one to nearly ten hours, with a decreasing trend over time, and nearly always begin late at night. They take place in a small room at the prime minister's official residence, across the street from the Diet Building; in a nearby, larger room Finance Ministry officials — sometimes down to the level of a chief

---

21. AS, January 19, 1961. In 1966 one of these meetings resulted in expanding the official list of recommendations from 45 to 171. AS, January 11, 1966.

clerk, if his specialty is being discussed — wait along with officials from the ministry responsible for the question at issue, to figure out the administrative and financial implications of any new proposals that might develop. In between, the halls are thronged with reporters, photographers, and occasionally petitioners who push their way in for a bit. Present for the negotiations themselves are the finance minister, the three (or four) LDP leaders, the chief Cabinet secretary, and one Cabinet minister; the Budget Bureau director or an official from the requesting ministry may be called in to answer specific questions.

When the finance minister and the party leaders have come to a meeting of minds on how the remaining funds should be divided up, a special Cabinet meeting is called, even in the early hours of the morning, to nail down the deal by approving a sketchy outline of the government draft. Later, after MOF officials have had a chance to get the numbers properly arranged, the Cabinet meets again for formal passage, and the budget is ready to be sent to the Diet. Cabinet members never try to reopen a problem at this stage. In the past, when the negotiators could not reach agreement on some particularly difficult problem, the prime minister would be called in to make the final decision, but this practice became rare in the 1960s and was not revived even by Tanaka. However, sometimes issues for which the gap between MOF and LDP positions is too wide to be bridged at a single meeting are postponed for further negotiation after the budget is finished; some small administrative or "research" expenditures may be granted to signify the program is alive.

LDP participation in revival negotiations thus involves all levels of the party, from the top leadership down to members of the PARC divisions — indeed, even backbenchers as individuals may be active in supporting their own favorite projects. The wishes of the politicians are made known to the Ministry of Finance officials directly in the policy-level negotiations, indirectly via the spending ministries in administrative negotiations, and, more diffusely but with as much impact, through the press and word of mouth. However, here as in the processes described in chapter 5, the party clearly is not able to impose a comprehensive program on the budget as a whole. The very way in which its recommendations are formulated prevents consideration of "national goals" or the merits of competing policies; instead, as we have observed, overlapping or even contradictory proposals are likely to receive simultaneous endorsements. Attention is given almost exclusively to particular budget items backed by important clientele organizations or groups of party members.

# Strategies and Tactics

In the preceding five chapters we discussed in some detail the ends sought by the major budgeting participants and the means they adopt to reach them. All these considerations apply as well to the revival negotiations period. Still, because this brief, intense conclusion to the budget process throws more general budget patterns into a sharper light, and also introduces some wrinkles of its own, the strategies and tactics typically found here are worth a brief discussion.

*Ministries.* — A ministry's basic objectives in budgeting, it will be recalled, are to increase its own resources, implement the program preferences of its officials in distinction to those of other participants, and satisfy clientele groups. How does it seek to achieve these ends in revival negotiations?

First of all, it asks for reconsideration of virtually all cuts. Only for those few items which received the entire original request will the MOF's offer be accepted. In a substantial number of cases — some 40 percent of the 1970 Ministry of Health and Welfare items we have looked at previously — either the same amount as the original summer request or slightly more will be requested on appeal.[22] A little better than half the cases in this sample had their original requests shaved up to 25 percent. Naturally, those programs (basically the largest ones) for which the original request had been relatively small were shaved less at this stage.[23]

The most interesting aspect of this decision is that — so far as statistical analysis of this small sample of items can reveal — the amount granted in the MOF draft seems to make no difference whatsoever. Not only are all the rerequests calculated using the original request as a base, but the amount of the adjustment apparently has no relationship with the amount the MOF cut off the original request, or added to the current year's budget. If the ministry takes "signals" from the MOF into account when making its strategic choices at this stage, it does so on an individual case-by-case basis, not in any systematic way.

An example of the complexity of how signals are sent and received is the variety of uses of the "full-scale rerequest" (*zenmen fukkatsu*). According to budget participants there are four possible reasons for rerequesting the same amount as in the original request: the program in question might be meaningless unless fully financed; such a request as a tactic might offer the best chance for receiving more money; the ministry might wish to express its annoyance at the degree of MOF cuts in its budget; a symbolic demonstration of commitment to some clientele group

22. According to a Welfare Ministry budgeting official, when the rerequest exceeds the original request, the reason is nearly always technical or administrative, although occasionally heavy political pressures might be responsible. The data discussed here were described in chap. 2, n. 9.

23. The average percentage drop from original request to rerequest for the thirteen programs for which increases of under 40 percent had been originally requested was 4.2 percent; for the thirty-eight with requests over 40 percent it was 13 percent.

might be desired. Some feeling for the interplay of strategies and tactics in revival negotiations is conveyed in this lengthy excerpt from a 1970 interview with an Accounting Division director:

For "political budgets," backed up by some interest group, if we reduce our demand along the way it causes problems for us — we can't convince the interest group that we have done our best. So at the extreme, the demand may go all the way to the ministerial negotiations untouched. For example, on a given program, we might have originally asked for a billion yen, even though we think that half that would be enough. But because we would hear from the group if we said this, we just keep asking for a billion at the bureau director, vice-ministerial and ministerial negotiations, and say "no good" to all the MOF's suggestions. Then in the end, maybe we will get ¥ 500 million, but our supporters will have been satisfied.

. . . another case in which a "full-scale rerequest" is employed is a new program, say where we asked for ¥ 1 billion. We might think that the MOF is predisposed to approve the program, but only at a level of perhaps ¥ 400 million. They will give us a zero in the MOF draft, fearing that if they allowed ¥ 400 million right off, we would put pressure on them to increase that. But unless we change our own basic concept (*kangaekata*) of the program, we will ask for the full ¥ 1 billion again . . . .

But if they really plan to grant ¥ 400 million in the end, they will offer ¥ 200 million. Then we will see that our request of ¥ 1 billion is really too far away from MOF thinking, and will come down to ¥ 500 million — perhaps by stretching the implementation of the program out. In the vice-ministerial or ministerial negotiations, both sides will talk it over and decide a figure. MOF will say, "isn't ¥ 400 million enough?" and we will say, "we have to have ¥ 500 million" — in the end, since the MOF holds the purse strings, we are likely to conclude that we can make it with ¥ 400 million, and agree.

Actually, the final scene might as likely involve "splitting the difference" or "horse trading," a concession here for an advantage on another program. Such bargaining behavior is said to be typical of appeals negotiations meetings.[24]

As the official quoted above went on to say, "it gets to be kind of a game," and indeed sports metaphors — *sumō* or baseball — abound in journalistic accounts of revival negotiations. But what are the stakes for a ministry? It appears from the discussion in chapter 4 that a rough "framework" for each ministry's (or Important Item's) budget is established before the MOF draft, and so it seems unlikely that the total amount it will receive will be increased very much during at least the administrative level of the revival negotiations. Moreover, it has already been emphasized that more and more the Ministry of Finance has been inclined to leave ministry

24. Indeed, it is thought by many participants to be prototypical "Japanese" (*Nihonteki*) behavior — at least until they are informed that American budgeters behave in much the same fashion.

officials with the largest voice in choices among programs, as symbolized by the 1968 reforms. Of course, these are general observations while budget decisions are specific and usually taken on the margin, so there will be many occasions where a ministry and the MOF will disagree and argue about how quickly some item should grow, or more likely about whether or not a newly proposed program should be approved. Still, a ministry's first two budget objectives would not seem to provide much reason for determined battling. One is led to believe, then, that its major stakes in the revival negotiations lie in the third area, impressing and satisfying clientele groups.

*Party.* —Conservative politicians are, of course, at least as likely to play to the galleries as are ministry officials. Examples abound each year of grandiose promises and spectacular assaults on MOF defenses, motivated less by expectations of success than by the hope that an interest group will be impressed with the sincerity of the LDP, and will be inclined to blame the finance bureaucrats for the smaller than hoped for sum they actually receive. Still, as we have seen, the party does have real interests to pursue in the revival negotiations. The extent to which its wishes will be fulfilled varies from year to year depending on the economic situation and the overall political balance, as well as the strategy being followed by the finance minister, but the LDP's general strategy is to attempt to maximize the amount of money left for the party-government negotiations. Since 1968 this has meant arguing against using "adjustment resources," and therefore making too many decisions, in lower-level negotiations. Here is found another example of conflict of interest between the party leadership and the rank and file — LDP backbenchers supporting programs which are unlikely to find their way into the final negotiations prefer to have more resources made available earlier on. The leadership often tries to limit individual Dietman initiative in favor of organized efforts where its preferences will predominate: for example, before the MOF draft of the 1972 budget, the Executive Council announced a policy that Dietmen should not petition individually at the Ministry of Finance (Chairman Nakasone Yasuhiro said such behavior is "unsightly"), and that all requests should be channeled through party headquarters. It also called for a shorter "administrative" negotiations period and more time for the "political" level.[25]

Though the normal budgeting pattern is for the LDP to back up proposals initiated by the ministries, some demands are actually supported much more strongly by the party than by their ministerial sponsors. The LDP will take the lead in obtaining budgets for these programs, which usually represent direct payoffs to some large interest group. Such

25. NKS, December 24, 1971, evening.

demands often appear for the first time in the revival negotiations, sometimes as late as the government-party negotiations; this pattern first appeared in the early 1960s and was resented from the start by the Ministry of Finance. The advantage to the party, of course, is that the Budget Bureau does not have a chance to prepare a detailed defense, and the program does not have to compete with others for limited funds in the budget review stage. In the field of agriculture these requests even have a special name: *akafun*. Some say this is short for *akafundoshi*, a red loin cloth, meaning that the requests "come in nearly naked," while another explanation is that the term derives from the red paper such demands are printed on. Whatever the etymology, the term and the practice were well known in the mid-1960s.[26] A budget examiner once remarked of such late-appearing requests that "in the evening, you think you hear a distant bird singing, and then when the New Year dawns it comes swooping down."[27]

Whoever's goals it might be pursuing, the LDP's chief resource in the revival negotiations is its potential for creating confusion and delay. Besides believing in the traditional bureaucratic virtue of orderly decision making, MOF officials fear that once budgeting gets even slightly out of hand, the entire process will fall apart and the treasury will be pillaged. The tactic of disrupting the process for budgetary gain was actually carried out much more frequently in earlier years than recently, but the threat can still be an effective means for wringing concessions — for example, in 1971 the LDP gained a new tax on automobiles to provide funds for transportation construction against determined MOF opposition by threatening disruptions of the budget process, including a possible Dietmen's Bill, at a time when Finance officials were eager to get the budget wrapped up before the end of the year.[28] The budget, of course, must pass both the Cabinet and the Diet, and this ultimate power of the LDP is always kept in mind at the Ministry of Finance.

*Ministry of Finance.* — Over the years the MOF has developed means for coping with spending pressures from the majority party. Very often it will cooperate in keeping discussions with a ministry secret, allowing its spokesmen to make public statements in favor of party-backed programs while actually agreeing to relatively small allocations. It would seem that another rational strategy for coping with highly political items would be to underbudget them in the MOF draft, so that more could be added on in response to strong appeals; two interviewed officials (one from the MOF, one from an LDP-supported ministry) indicated such maneuvers were commonly employed. However, asked about this point, others in the MOF

---

26. From the series "Yosan to Atsuryoku," YS, December 5, 1965.
27. AS, January 14, 1966. Also see AS, February 27, 1967, evening.
28. Nihon Keizai Shinbunsha, *Yosan wa Dare no Mono ka*, pp. 110-113.

said that most frequently budgeters will simply devote more study to such items, so that they will be able to argue more effectively.

Apart from filtering political influence, the Finance Ministry's major interest in revival microbudgeting is to force the ministry into deciding its own priorities. If a ministry, for reasons of its own, tries to submit full-scale rerequests for all or nearly all of its budget, the MOF may simply decline to accept them until some choices have been made. When several new programs are proposed, the vice-minister or minister will be asked to select the one or two he wants most; in no case will a ministry be allowed to divide its "Secretariat Adjustment Expenses" among many new, small programs, since the MOF knows all will grow in time. Also older programs may have to be sacrificed to create new ones.

But while budgeters do pay attention to all these hundreds of small issues throughout the negotiations, it is threats to the overall budget framework which excite their serious interest. The MOF's intent is to protect its strategy of not raising the total set in the MOF draft: each year the finance minister, the prime minister and even the LDP leaders state this principle with some solemnity and frequency throughout the negotiating period. Therefore, when pressures turn out to be more intense than expected, the MOF must accommodate them with subterfuge or side-payments outside the General Account. For example, a common expedient is the substitution of interest-subsidized loans for direct budget grants, drawing upon Fiscal Investment and Loan Program trust funds rather than tax revenues. Similarly, some items can be switched to Special Accounts. Sometimes expenditures are transferred backward, by writing them into a supplement to the current year's budget rather than the one under preparation.[29] The curious aspect of such devices is that while the budget total is ostensibly being protected in the name of fiscal restraint so that the economy will not be overly stimulated by too much governmental expenditure, in reality bookkeeping transfers from the General Account to some other form of spending are meaningless in fiscal terms, in most cases just as stimulatory. In fact, increasing expenditures in the current rather than the following year has an even more immediate effect on the economy. Still, Finance officials reason, perhaps correctly, that an image of restraint is more important than its reality, and the size of the General Account (and the MOF's reputation for guarding it) is the major element of that image.

As a general rule of thumb, the Ministry of Finance wishes to avoid expensive commitments and precedents for the future: it is wary of "camel's nose" research allocations, large total projected figures for ministry five-year plans, and the establishment of new governmental

---

29. SS, January 14, 1957. Supplementary Budgets are often passed late in the fiscal year, which ends in March.

organizations (which have a tendency to expand and tie up budgets in personnel costs). However, all of these guidelines are likely to be sacrificed to avoid raising the total in a particular year. Preferring the bird in the hand, the MOF will grant a larger five-year plan in exchange for a lower first-year allocation, or will accept a sizable program if its start-up date can be postponed until half or more of the fiscal year has passed. Nearly every year the finance minister (often backed up by the prime minister) will proclaim an absolute prohibition against approval of new government agencies or corporations, but late in revival negotiations these become attractive ploys to deflect pressure away from immediate spending—the 1965 budget process was one of the most restricted by a shortage of funds, but despite the usual stricture sixteen new organizations, an unprecedented number, were finally approved by Finance Minister Tanaka.

The strategy which the Ministry of Finance uses to greatest effect in the revival negotiations is the art of the deft, small concession. Over and over again, threats against the budget schedule, the size of the total budget, and even the position of the MOF itself (as when Kōno Ichirō proposed to move the Budget Bureau to Cabinet control) have been averted with well-placed cash payoffs—not bribes to individuals, but budget grants for favored organizations or programs. Timing is the key: the concession must be made early enough to prevent a build-up of pressure, but late enough to settle the issue at hand.[30] Pertinent instances could be cited for nearly every year, so we will be content with one. In the last budget process covered here, that for 1974, Finance Minister Fukuda Takeo had to deflate expectations sharply: even in mid-fall everyone had expected a budget anywhere from 22 to 25 percent larger than the previous year, but after the oil crisis his goal was to hold its growth below 20 percent. One prong of his attack was the direct one, to convince the LDP that the times required restraint and therefore, for example, policy-level "adjustment expenses" would have to be limited to ¥50 billion (the lowest figure since 1968; they had been ¥150 billion in the previous year). But Fukuda was shrewd enough to know that however much agreement in principle he might secure from Dietmen and officials of the spending ministries, when actual negotiations began their self-interests would come forth. Accordingly, he tucked away an extra-large sum in "hidden resources" and distributed small budgetary benefits much more liberally than usual through the several stages of the revival period.[31] This

30. A cautionary example: when the LDP was particularly keen on aid to small business in the 1961 budget process, MITI was granted its full request for this program in the MOF draft; the party immediately turned to demanding even more in the revival negotiations. AS, January 19, 1961, evening.

31. As Table 11 reveals, since 1968 the officially announced "policy adjustment expenses" had exceeded "transfers from other items" by large margins, but in 1974 this relationship was reversed, and the "hidden" amount was by far the largest since 1967 despite the shortage of funds.

two-pronged tactic was completely successful: the 1974 negotiations were among the smoothest for the MOF in the entire period.

# Conclusions

How important are the revival negotiations? Are important decisions made during this period, or is it but sound and fury signifying nothing? We can examine this question at various levels, but it is well to begin by asking how much money actually changes hands. A glance back to Table 11 reveals that before 1968, up to 4 percent of the General Account was allocated during revival negotiations; afterward the figure was closer to 1 percent. These are of course rather small proportions of the total budget.

On the other hand, the fundamental fact about budgeting is that most expenditures are more or less obligatory, so it may be more interesting to know what proportion of the funds over which the Ministry of Finance (or anyone else) has some control is allocated during this period. The problem of which expenditures are actually obligatory and which are, for example, simply continued out of habit is a difficult one, but it will be recalled from the discussion of expenditure estimating in chapter 4 that in most years Japanese budgeters tend to take the budget from the previous year as a given, and then add to it "natural expenditure increases"—items such as scheduled salary increases, interest on the national debt, the formula allocation to local governments, and so forth. A rudimentary estimate of the amount available each year for discretionary or "policy" spending may be found by subtracting the "natural expenditure increase" from the increase in the total budget. Table 13 compares these figures with the amounts estimated to be transferred during the revival negotiations.

Column C on Table 13 indicates that prior to 1968, from two-fifths to three-fifths of all "policy" expenditures were allocated subsequent to the MOF draft. From 1968 on, the proportion is about one-quarter or one-fifth.[32] One should also take into consideration that the "natural expenditure increase" is a quite conservative estimate of obligatory expenditures—the MOF commonly also thinks in terms of a looser category of "seminatural" increases which it knows it will have to make even if not obliged by law, and in some years these expenses may eat up nearly all of the formally discretionary funds available. In other words, a very high proportion of budget decisions that represent real choices, allocations not simply duplicating those of the previous year or otherwise compelled, are accounted for by the revival negotiations period.

32. Note that the similar and rather low figures for 1973 and 1974 do not indicate the budget processes in those years were identical. *Both* the margin for discretionary expenditures and the amount provided for revival negotiations were usually high in 1973, and unusually low in 1974.

TABLE 13
"POLICY" EXPENDITURES AND
REVIVAL NEGOTIATIONS
(Units: 100 Million Yen; Percent)

| Budget Year | A "Policy" Expenditures[a] | B Revival Transfers[b] | C B/A (%) |
|---|---|---|---|
| 1964 | 2261 | 901 | 39.8 |
| 1965 | 1872 | 1119 | 60.0 |
| 1966 | 4156 | 1721 | 41.4 |
| 1967 | 2657 | 1605 | 60.4 |
| 1968 | 1896 | 481 | 25.4 |
| 1969 | 2256 | 591 | 26.2 |
| 1970 | 2962 | 770 | 26.0 |
| 1971 | 4346 | 1161 | 27.0 |
| 1972 | 6634[c] | 1147 | 17.0 |
| 1973 | 10664 | 2308 | 22.0 |
| 1974 | 6153 | 1360 | 22.0 |

NOTES: [a]Increase in budget less "natural expenditure increase." For 1971-74 this is based on MOF estimates during the process, so figures are approximate.

[b]Where available based on the ministry, rather than the Important Item accounting, as it is judged more likely to be accurate.

[c]Based on inferences from other data and possibly inaccurate.

SOURCES: Column A—Table 4, Column D. Column B—Table 11, Column D (1964-68, 1974), Column H (1969-73).

From this perspective, the revival negotiations appear to be quite important. But important with regard to what? To take up the three arenas of budgeting once again, it is clear that the basic macrobudgeting decisions are nearly always made before the release of the MOF draft. Indeed, it was to insulate its most vital concerns from the pressures of the revival negotiations period that the Finance Ministry established the principle that the size of the General Account would not be raised. At the level of integration too, it would appear that the Finance Ministry normally has a reasonably clear idea of outcomes before the beginning of revival negotiations. The areas on which most political pressures will bear can be predicted and discounted: note that for the restrictive 1974 budget, Finance Minister Fukuda announced specifically that public works expenditure would be held to the same amount budgeted in 1973; in the MOF draft this budget was reduced by about 1 percent, and then the supplement added in the final party-government negotiations brought it to an amount very close (within about $100,000) to the previous year's budget.[33] Obviously in this case, and perhaps generally in 1974, the Finance Ministry had correctly anticipated and adjusted for the pressures of the revival negotiations.

Still, political processes cannot always be forecast with such precision: in 1970, for instance, the Ministry of Finance had hoped to keep growth in the fiscally sensitive public works category to 17 percent, only 1 percent over forecast GNP growth; but when the LDP divied up the "policy adjustment expenditures" in the final session, much more than expected wound up in construction projects, and to the MOF's dismay the public works category actually rose by 18 percent. It seems to be the case that Finance officials do formulate rough targets for key budget categories, and to some extent discount MOF draft allocations in advance to allow for politically pressured additions in the revival negotiations, but the margin of error is probably rather wide.[34]

If this analysis is correct, the revival negotiations have little more than a marginal impact on decisions at the macrobudgeting or integration level. If they are important, then, they are important in microbudgeting, in determining which new proposals will be accepted or rejected, which old programs will grow swiftly and which lag behind. This observation is consistent with the discussion of the pre-MOF-draft microbudgeting process in chapter 3, where it was pointed out that Budget Bureau examiners frequently will simply postpone their more difficult problems so that preferences of the spending ministry and the party may be taken into account.

Some sense of the nature of microbudgeting decisions at this stage may be gained by a final examination of the 1970 Ministry of Health and Welfare budget statistics discussed at several junctures above.[35] First, we may observe that decisions on new programs are in fact left until revival negotiations—of the eleven items newly proposed, just one was approved in the MOF draft, but seven more were allowed by the time of the government draft. Second, we may again divide the sample between items for which the ministry requested a 40 percent or less increase—the larger

33. See NKS, December 18, 1973, and the tables in NKS, December 22, evening, and 30, 1973.

34. Cf. Nihon Keizai Shinbunsha, *Yosan wa Dare no Mono ka*, p. 106.

35. It should be kept in mind that the procedures for extracting this sample do not allow imputations of typicality—to other ministries and other years, and even within the Ministry of Health and Welfare budget. Since LDP documents were relied upon, programs with greater political flavor are probably overrepresented. However, in my own view, observed differences between types of items or decisions (if not the proportions of those types) are real.

and more routine programs — and the larger number of smaller programs for which more than 40 percent increases were requested. One difference between the two groups is dramatic: the amount added on during revival negotiations (i.e., percentage increase from MOF draft to government draft) for the "great expectations" group averaged 49.5 percent; for the "modest expectations" group only 3.1 percent.[36] Taking the full rise from the 1969 to the 1970 budget into account, the former "great expectations" group received over three-quarters of their increments during revival negotiations; the latter group just one-fifth. This period is indeed the occasion for adding on relatively sizable sums and for making at least some distinctions among programs.

Third, we can get a hint of how these decisions are made through a regression analysis of the forty cases for which we have necessary data. One interesting finding is that the amount rerequested by the ministry has little or no systematic influence on the amount awarded in the government draft — the MOF seems to base its decision on either the amount of the MOF draft or the previous year's budget.[37] Recall that the Welfare Ministry did not take the amount of the MOF draft into account in deciding how much to ask on appeal — taken together, these two findings leave an impression of boxers sparring in different rings: in this peculiar game, neither side seems to pay any attention to signals from the other, or at least to signals conveyed through budget figures.

That another sort of signal is important is indicated by an alternative partitioning of the sample. It turns out that six "priority" items were treated very differently from the others during revival negotiations. Three of these were the only three continuing programs mentioned just after the MOF draft by the Welfare Ministry as its major appeals objectives.[38] Another two represented sewer construction projects, the only two Welfare Ministry programs to receive the *marusei* designation in the LDP's revival negotiations recommendations.[39] The final item of this group, while apparently not publicly singled out in advance, was concerned with programs for *burakumin* (former outcasts), one of the most sensitive policy areas in Japanese politics.[40] These six items were not particularly

36. Because of missing data, the numbers of cases used here are only twenty-four and seven respectively, but this difference is too large to be easily dismissed.

37. The 1969 budget and MOF draft amounts are so highly correlated that picking between them is difficult. The conclusion about lack of effect of rerequests is based on multiple regression and analysis of residuals.

38. The other three so mentioned were new programs, all of which were approved.

39. Both were held over until the final negotiating session.

40. The six items were identified through statistical manipulations, not in advance. If I had begun with a hypothesis that "priority" items would be treated differently, I probably would have separated out the first five items but not the sixth. Incidentally, LDP priorities as expressed by PARC divisional A, B, C ratings had no predictive power on government draft budget decisions.

distinctive in terms of budgeting decisions earlier in the process, but at least five of them were identified as high-priority programs by either the ministry or the LDP immediately after the MOF draft.

How differently were these six treated? For the other thirty-four cases for which we have necessary data, the amount of the government draft is well specified by the following regression equation:

$$\text{Government draft} = 1.06 \, (\text{MOF draft}) + ¥ \, 106 \text{ million}$$

Pearson's r for this group is .975, so about 95 percent of the variance is explained.[41] For the six "priority" items, on the other hand, 99.7 percent of the variance (r = .9985) is explained with this equation:

$$\text{Government draft} = 1.10 \, (\text{MOF draft}) + ¥ \, 392 \text{ million}$$

In plain language, the more "normal" items were handled by giving them about ¥100 million ($350,000) plus 6 percent of their MOF draft amount, while the "priority" items—those few (15 percent of this sample) especially called to the attention of the Finance Ministry—were granted about ¥400 million plus 10 percent of their MOF draft amount.

Of course, further research is needed to discover if similar decision-making patterns are characteristic of other ministries and other years. But on the basis of this analysis, a good case can be made for the importance of the revival negotiations as a microbudgeting decision-making process. New information from party and line ministry is employed by the MOF to pick and choose among programs; some new proposals are accepted and others rejected; some old programs are allowed to grow faster than others.

There are indications, however, that this process has a significance even beyond that of separating out some proportion of budget decisions. Compare, for example, the rather straightforward accounts above of how the negotiations proceed with this description by Sahashi Shigeru, once vice-minister of MITI:

Like cutting your own throat, you reduce your request each time and resubmit it to negotiations, till finally at the bitter end, after hearing the almost shrieking pleas from the ministry, the MOF will approve a part. Both offense and defense go at it night and day; it becomes a battle of physical strength.[42]

Newspapers and magazine articles often take a similar tone, highlighting the bitterness of budgetary battles, "trial by exhaustion" as meetings drag on into the night, and dirty tricks played by one side or the other. Ministry negotiators and LDP Dietmen stress how hard they fight for their programs, Finance officials tell of their desperate defense of fiscal probity. Participants and journalists alike delight, albeit from a disapproving stance, in portraying the negotiations as high drama.

---

41. The three largest items were excluded from this regression because they tend to inflate correlation coefficients artificially.

42. Interview in *Asahi Jaanaru* 9, 48 (November 19, 1967), 108-110.

Thomas J. Anton, writing of budgeting in the American states, has observed that "what is at stake . . . is not so much the distribution of resources as the distribution of symbolic satisfaction among the involved actors and the audiences which observe their stylized behavior."[43] Surely these more extreme aspects of the revival negotiations must be seen as symbolic outputs — indeed, politicians, officials and reporters who wish to appear cynical and knowing will frequently laugh at the process, and characterize it as ritual or an *omatusuri*, a festival.

Why such symbols? Three overlapping explanations suggest themselves. First, as noted above, each participant wishes to demonstrate to his clientele that he is doing everything possible for a particular program. Here even the Budget Bureau sees itself as serving a clientele, the "general public" concerned with government economy, as opposed to special interests.

Second, beyond such finely calculated strategies, we observe more generally that the behavior displayed in these negotiations accords with images the participants like to hold of themselves. LDP members make weighty decisions on national policy; officials of the line ministries go all-out for their vital programs; MOF budgeters doughtily withstand intense pressures to defend the sanctity of the public purse. All emerge satisfied with the roles they have played.

Finally, it seems too that all enjoy the festival. The budget process is long, difficult, often tedious and often tense; each participant does have real interests, and they have real conflicts with each other. Like a ritualistic Japanese student snake-dance demonstration, the revival negotiations allow the months-long ordeal to end with a bang, not a whimper. In the midst of publicity and turmoil, everyone has a chance to express his desires and fight for them. In the end, agreement is reached, the budget is ratified, the examiners go off for a holiday, and soon all must begin thinking about the next budget.

43. Thomas J. Anton, "Roles and Symbols in the Determination of State Expenditures," in *Politics, Programs and Budgets: A Reader in Governmental Budgeting,* ed. James W. Davis, Jr. (Englewood Cliffs, N.J.: Prentice-Hall, 1969), p. 129.

# 8

# Other Budgets

WITH THE APPROVAL of the government draft by the Cabinet, our account of the budget process has been completed. However, it is unrealistic to view the General Account budget in isolation. If one defines budgeting in a broader sense as the allocation of the resources available to the government, it is evident that several other decision-making processes must also be taken into account. These include Supplementary Budgets, the various Special Accounts and government corporations, the Fiscal Investment and Loan Program, and a number of long-range planning efforts. While it was impossible to investigate these subjects in the detail they deserve, I can suggest a few aspects of their relationship to the politics of budgeting.

Before beginning this task, some words about the remainder of the formal budget process are in order. Following passage by the Cabinet, the budget is sent to the House of Representatives for debate and passage (first in the Budget Committee and then by the full House) and then to the House of Councillors. Under Article 60 of the Constitution, if the Upper House does not pass the budget, or if it amends it and cannot secure the agreement of the Lower House to its changes, the budget as passed by the Lower House becomes law after thirty days. With the single exception of 1972, when a combination of government mishandling and opposition unity led to small reductions in defense spending, the budget has not been amended in the Diet since 1955 (that is, since the formation of the Liberal Democratic Party and its assumption of legislative control). Indeed, as in other parliamentary regimes, the debate on the budget usually does not concentrate on expenditures as such, but provides a forum for opposition attacks on the full range of governmental policy.

When the administrative budget process becomes delayed beyond the new year, as has happened frequently, there will often be insufficient time to complete Diet action before the beginning of the fiscal year on April 1.

In such cases a Provisional Budget (*Zantei Yosan*) must be compiled and enacted to cover the gap until passage of the Main Budget (*Hon'yosan*), most often by simply continuing the spending patterns of the previous budget. Recently these have lasted for as short a period as ten days, though in earlier years they sometimes covered over six months; Provisional Budgets were required in 1955, 1967-68, 1970, and 1972-74. Provisional Budgets do not occasion major political disputes, but since they present certain technical and policy problems for the Ministry of Finance they are an additional incentive for getting the budget process finished on schedule.

For budget execution (*shikkō*), each ministry prepares quarterly plans for payments and liabilities that are approved by the Finance Ministry, which orders the Bank of Japan to disburse funds. The amounts to be expended in each quarter, particularly for public works, are often adjusted by the MOF in response to short-range fiscal policy considerations. After the close of the fiscal year, the MOF prepares the Budget Settlement (*Kessan*) which is sent to the Diet along with the report of the Board of Audit.[1]

# Supplementary Budgets

The annual practice of passing Supplementary Budgets is of considerably more than just technical interest. All countries, of course, make provision in their budgetary system for adjusting the initial budget in the light of actual experience, since for administrative, financial or macroeconomic reasons the original estimates may become inappropriate. Rather than passing piecemeal supplementary appropriations for individual items, the Japanese prepare one to three comprehensive Supplementary Budgets every year. Most often, particularly when only one is needed, the supplements come in December or January (that is, nine or ten months into the fiscal year), but when warranted they have also been passed in the fall or as early as July, or as late as February.[2] While consistent breakdowns of Supplementary Budgets are not routinely published in the documents relied upon in this study, Table 14 provides data from various sources for the years in which they were available.

It will be observed that the size of Supplementary Budgets, in absolute amounts (Column B, the sum of all supplements for each year) and as a proportion of the total budget (Column C), vary considerably from year to year. Column D, Natural Revenue Surplus, is the difference between the

1. *The Budget in Brief* always includes a brief account of the formal process in English. For more detail, see Kōno Kazuyoshi, *Yosan Seido* ("The Budget System") (Tokyo: Gakuyō Shobō, 1976).

2. For dates of legislative action on all budgets from 1892 to 1968, see Ōkurashō Hyakunenshi Henshūshitsu, ed., *Ōkurashō Hyakunenshi* ("Ministry of Finance One Hundred Year History") III (Tokyo: Ōkura Zaimu Kyōkai, 1969), pp. 164-189.

TABLE 14
SUPPLEMENTARY BUDGETS
(Units: 100 Million Yen; Percent)

| Fiscal Year | A Total Budget | B Supp. Budget | C B/A (%) | D Natural Revenue Surplus | E B/D (%) | F Disaster Reclamation | G Foodstuff Control Spec. Acc. | H Salary Increases | I Local Allocation | J Other | K Savings | L Total Additions |
|---|---|---|---|---|---|---|---|---|---|---|---|---|
| 1955 | 10133 | 218 | 2.2 | | | 0 | 67 | 0 | 181 | 107 | 130 | 355 |
| 1956 | 10897 | 547 | 5.0 | | | 0 | 34 | 0 | 110 | 403 | 0 | 547 |
| 1957 | 11846 | 471 | 4.0 | 1183 | 39.8 | 0 | 310 | 0 | 78 | 83 | 0 | 471 |
| 1958 | 13330 | 210 | 1.6 | 296 | 70.9 | 97 | 0 | 0 | 0 | 113 | 0 | 210 |
| 1959 | 15121 | 928 | 6.1 | 1362 | 68.1 | 411 | 18 | 0 | 104 | 471 | 76 | 1004 |
| 1960 | 17652 | 1955 | 11.1 | 3062 | 63.9 | 290 | 209 | 214 | 452 | 790 | 0 | 1955 |
| 1961 | 21074 | 1546 | 7.3 | 3965 | 39.0 | 450 | 300 | 184 | 341 | 271 | 0 | 1546 |
| 1962 | 25631 | 1262 | 5.3 | 1935 | 70.4 | 134 | 0 | 220 | 394 | 615 | 0 | 1363 |
| 1963 | 30568 | 2068 | 6.8 | 2529 | 81.8 | 315 | 250 | 262 | 446 | 806 | 11 | 2079 |
| 1964 | 33405 | 851 | 2.5 | 814 | 104.5 | 188 | 60 | 392 | 159 | 265 | 213 | 1064 |
| 1965 | 37447 | 866 | 2.3 | | | 166 | 209 | 353 | 0 | 900 | 761 | 1628 |
| 1966 | 44771 | 1629 | 3.6 | | | 114 | 810 | 322 | 377 | 370 | 364 | 1993 |
| 1967 | 52034 | 2525 | 4.9 | | | 147 | 1180 | 545 | 749 | 393 | 489 | 3014 |
| 1968 | 59173 | 987 | 1.7 | | | 0 | 370 | 0 | 736 | 174 | 293 | 1280 |
| 1969[a] | 69309 | 1913 | 2.8 | | | | 560 | 567 | 994 | | 567 | 2480 |
| 1970[a] | 82131 | 2633 | 3.2 | | | | 238 | 1240 | | | | |
| 1971[a] | 96590 | 2447 | 2.5 | | | | | | | | | |
| 1972[a] | 121189 | 6513 | 5.4 | | | 1083 | | 1133 | 656 | | 1094 | 7607 |
| 1973[a] | 152726 | 9885 | 6.5 | | | | 2999 | 2170 | 4240 | | 2132 | 12017 |
| 1974 | 191981 | 20987 | 10.9 | | | 856 | 3076 | 7211 | 5152[b] | 3719 | 1699 | 22686 |

NOTES:   [a]Data are incomplete or unavailable.          [b]Does not include special allocation of 2691.

SOURCES: A–B. *Zaisei Tōkei*, 1974, 190–202; *Asahi Nenkan*, 1975, p. 323.
D–E. Saitō Kazumi, "Kokusai to Keiki Seisaku" ("National Bonds and Counter-Cyclical Policy"), *Fainansu* 6, 7 (October 1970), 4.
F–L. 1955–1967: NKS, October 8, 1968.
1968:     *Maninchi Nenkan*, 1970, p. 241.
1969:     (G.I) NKS, March 2, 1970; (H,K,L) *Kuni no Yosan*, 1970, pp. 902–907.
1970:     *Mainichi Nenkan*, 1971, p. 196.
1972:     *Asahi Nenkan*, 1973, p. 325.
1973:     *Ibid.*, 1974, p. 302.
1974:     *Ibid.*, 1975, p. 323.

forecasts of tax and other revenues at the time of drawing up the initial budget and either actual tax collections or more definitive forecasts made when well into the fiscal year.[3] This surplus is the source of revenue for Supplementary Budgets, and indeed its size is an important factor in determining how large the supplement will be.

Columns F through J list the major expenditure items for the supplement. Included in Column J, as well as many miscellaneous administrative items, are certain large expenditures that vary from year to year, including contributions to governmental investment programs and to the World Bank, support for agriculture, additions to Reserves, and others. The Local Allocation, Column I, is obligatory, a predetermined percentage of the important national taxes. When these run ahead of forecasts, local governments must get their proportional shares (although the payment may legally be delayed). In some years, notably 1974, special allocations are added to this figure. Column F, Disaster Rehabilitation, is primarily public works to rebuild after typhoons and earthquakes, which of course cannot be predicted accurately at the time of the original budget.

Column G is the supplement from tax revenues of the deficit in the Foodstuffs Control Special Account, for the rice (as well as other agricultural products) price support system.[4] Without going into this complicated policy area in detail, it may be noted that the chief factors which determine the size of the deficit are (1) the price paid by the government to rice producers, well above world prices; (2) the lower price for selling to consumers; (3) the balance of production and consumption, which brought rice surpluses beginning in the 1960s; and (4) the amount of "old rice" from previous harvests which must be stored or disposed of. Increased production and declining consumption of rice in the 1960s had enlarged the deficit in this Special Account to ¥456 billion in 1970, 5.6 percent of the General Account, stimulating attempts to reform the system by providing incentives to farmers to cut back production. These reforms had some effect on the deficit in the next two years, its proportion of the General Account sinking to 4.9 percent in 1971 and 4.4 percent in 1972; but in 1973 and 1974 this figure had risen again to 5.3 percent—in 1974, for the first time, the total General Account supplement to the Special Account exceeded one trillion yen (about $3.5 billion).[5]

3. Actually, in Japan the same term, *shizen zōshū*, is used for this surplus and for the "natural revenue increase" from one fiscal year to the next, as described in chap. 4. Different translations are adopted here to avoid confusion.

4. A discerning study of problems and process in this area is Michael W. Donnelly, "Setting the Price of Rice: A Study in Political Decision Making," in *Policymaking in Contemporary Japan*, ed. T. J. Pempel (Ithaca, N.Y.: Cornell University Press, forthcoming).

5. Data from Japan, Ministry of Finance, Budget Bureau, Research Division, *Zaisei Tōkei* ("Fiscal Statistics") (Tokyo: Ministry of Finance Printing Bureau, 1974), pp. 199-202, and *Asahi Nenkan*, 1975, p. 323. These figures do not include the "side payments" offered to farmers as compensation for the reforms.

Given this record, it is unsurprising that the Ministry of Finance regarded rice as perhaps its biggest budget headache, but virtually throughout the period of this study its attempts to reduce agricultural expenditures have been stymied by well organized interest groups; moreover, rural overrepresentation in the Diet and particularly within the Liberal Democratic Party multiplies the effectiveness of political pressures in this area. The procedural problem for the MOF is that the key annual decisions which determine the deficit, namely the adjustments in the producers' and consumers' rice prices, are made in the summer or early fall after deliberations by the Rice Price Council (Beika Shingikai), and the necessary allocations are subsequently drawn from the Supplementary Budget. That is, despite their enormous impact on the budget, these pricing decisions are beyond direct MOF control (although Finance officials are of course active participants in the negotiations), and the rice support program need not compete with other governmental programs for its funds. Worse still, the size of the "natural revenue surplus" is generally known at the time rice prices are decided; when funds are seen to be available, the Finance Ministry loses its most compelling arguments against spending. In recent years inflation has both increased agricultural production costs and the resistance of consumers to higher prices, complicating the dilemma further.

Somewhat similar is the process leading to the annual increases in the salaries of government employees. This decision, usually made in August, follows the recommendations from the National Personnel Authority, which is based upon wage patterns in private industry.[6] The Finance Ministry will take the lead in arguing that the recommendation should not be implemented in full, but again, its position is considerably weakened in years when the "natural revenue surplus" can provide a large Supplementary Budget. The amounts devoted to the yearly salary increment are listed in Column H; the impact of inflation may be observed in the figures for the 1970s.

To complete our inspection of Table 14, Column K represents deductions from initial program budgets taken at the time of the supplement. These result either from Finance Ministry orders to cut back on spending, as a means to reduce fiscal stimulation of the economy, or from earlier overestimates of expenditure needs or underspending for a variety of administrative reasons. In earlier years the MOF had waited for the Budget Settlement to adjust its figures, but from the mid-1960s it began to pick up these savings during the fiscal year so they could be applied to programs requiring additional expenditures. Thus, the aggregate of new expenditures (Column L) less these savings will equal the

6. See Katō Hisabumi, *Jinjiin* ("The National Personnel Authority") (Tokyo: Rōdō Junposha, 1966).

addition to the total supplement (Column B), except for small accounting discrepancies.

The process leading to the passage of the Supplementary Budget usually does not occasion much turmoil at the microbudgeting level, since its more controversial elements, rice prices and the salary hike, have already been decided; most often the remaining items are less political in character. The chief exceptions occur when the current year's supplement becomes drawn into the politics of the main budget for the following year, which of course is being compiled at the same time. For example, in 1972, Prime Minister Tanaka used the supplement as the opening wedge in an attempt to break down Finance Ministry defenses around the 1973 budget. In macrobudgeting, the supplement tended to have a procyclical effect until 1965, since it would be larger when the economy was booming, and smaller when a slowdown diminished the "natural revenue surplus." After deficit financing became possible, economic stimulation could be provided by increasing the bond sale above the estimates in the initial budget, as happened in 1965 (when bonds were first issued), 1971 and 1972. Unhappily for the MOF, however, it has proven more difficult to reduce supplements in years when revenues are strong.[7]

The Ministry of Finance has tended to hold Supplementary Budgets in low regard not only because they tend to be stimulatory in a macro-economic sense, but also because of their contribution to the growth of fixed expenditures. In particular, the yearly rice and salary allocations make up a substantial portion of the yearly increment to the total budget, but the MOF's leverage over them is low. It is for this reason that the "comprehensive budgeting principle" (sōgō yosan shugi) became an important element of the ministry's "break fiscal rigidification movement" in 1968. The term "comprehensive" may have been chosen simply because it was a popular piece of jargon being attached to many new governmental ideas at the time; in any case, it did not refer to the "principle of comprehensiveness" of classical budgetary theory, which holds that all financial activities of government be included within a single account.[8] In Japan, comprehensive budgeting referred to the elimination of supplementary budgets, by including all of its normal components in the regular budget passed before the beginning of the fiscal year. Thus the 1968 initial budget included provisions for government employee salary increases (which in effect specified the percentage raise in advance) and a much larger than usual Reserves item to cover disaster expenses and other

7. Surplus revenues not allocated by a Supplementary Budget, along with unspent budgeted funds, are divided between a carry-over to a later budget and redemption of the national debt; both are deflationary in effect.

8. See Jesse Burkhead, *Government Budgeting* (New York: John Wiley and Sons, 1965), p. 107. This principle is observed no more in Japan than elsewhere.

unanticipated developments; for rice, the full amount of the estimated deficit under current conditions was budgeted and informal agreement was secured that the consumer price would be raised to compensate for any hikes in the producers' price.[9] In other words, these key decisions were brought back into the regular budget process, where they could be made along with all other budgetary decisions.

Comprehensive budgeting failed: in an immediate sense, because an unusually good rice harvest forced higher than estimated government purchases in 1968; and in a deeper sense, along with the other "movement" reforms, because the Finance Ministry simply lacked sufficient power to dominate these decision processes. However, "comprehensive budgeting" remained as a slogan, and the amounts added in mid-year supplements were kept down to a relatively low level until Tanaka's influence came to be felt in 1972. By 1974, inflation was forcing enormous allocations to salaries and local governments and the Supplementary Budget was pushed to near-record levels. For the near future, at least, further attempts at reform by the Finance Ministry seem unlikely.

# Special Accounts and Government Corporations

According to the official government description, Special Accounts (*Tokubetsu Kaikei*) are "established by law when the Government carries out specific projects, administers and manages specific funds, or when it becomes necessary to administer revenue and expenditures separately from the general revenue and expenditures."[10] As well as receiving support from tax revenues (directly or as transfers from the General Account), these accounts variously draw upon enterprise receipts, interest from loans, the sale of bonds and other sources to finance their operations. Special Accounts come and go: there were thirty in 1954 and forty-one in 1974; since 1947 all in all there have been seventy-four in existence.[11]

Jesse Burkhead remarks of the American equivalent of Special Accounts that "invariably, earmarking and segregation of this type represent an attempt, not to introduce an improved pattern of fiscal management, but to protect and isolate the beneficiaries of specific government programs."[12] This statement holds just as true for Japanese budgeting. Ministries know that even though the Finance Ministry reviews (and the Diet must pass) these budgets, expenditures from revenues that

---

9. See the discussion of the "break fiscal rigidification movement" in the next chap.
10. *The Budget in Brief,* 1973, pp. 57-58.
11. Calculated from *Zaisei Tōkei,* 1974, pp. 79-101.
12. Burkhead. *Government Budgeting,* p. 283.

are not part of the normal General Account competition are scrutinized much less rigorously, and indeed, even when transfers from the General Account are required, the fact that they are smaller than if all support for the program came from this source means they are easier to obtain. Perhaps even more significantly, the establishment of a Special Account also implies a highly valued commitment for continued support. For example, strong ministry and party pressures were mobilized to establish the Flood Control Special Account (finally approved in 1960, with the help of a great typhoon in 1959). This account did not draw on earmarked tax revenues, large user fees or borrowing; it was supported almost completely by General Account allocations plus support from the local governments where its projects are undertaken (a form of financing that does not normally require special handling). It is clear that its attractiveness to the Ministry of Construction was not administrative convenience, but the provision of a "foothold" in the budget that would bring more appropriations for such projects in the future than would be likely through normal budget processes.[13]

Government corporations are more difficult to define, since this rubric encompasses a bewildering variety of purposes, financial arrangements, forms of organization and names.[14] They number about 110, up from 41 in 1956. Each has some sort of formal affiliation with a ministry. The budgets of fourteen of the government corporations must be passed by the Diet, while the others are simply reviewed by the ministry in charge and the Finance Ministry; some are supported by the General Account and, to a much greater extent, the Fiscal Investment and Loan Program.

Although the normal operations of these governmental corporations are outside our scope, they are established (and occasionally disestablished) as an important part of the budgetary process. Nearly every summer the finance minister, usually seconded by the prime minister, will gravely announce that no new governmental organizations (including ordinary bureaus, Special Accounts, government corporations and so forth) can be approved this year, and the prohibition is frequently repeated as budgeting proceeds throughout the fall. Nonetheless, the ministries always request many new bodies, and in most years several such requests are granted, frequently at the very end of the revival negotiations. From the line ministry point of view, such corporations often represent highly satisfactory payoffs to a specific clientele group. Also, the executive level of public corporations is usually staffed by retired ex-officials from the responsible

13. Cf. NKS, January 1, 1960.
14. Some of the categories are *kōsha, kōdan, jigyōdan, kōko, ginkō, kinko* and *tokushu gaisha*; many of these defy rational translation. An excellent short discussion in English is Administrative Management Agency, "Government Corporations," in *White Papers of Japan*, 1970-71, pp. 277-286. See also Katō Hiroshi, *Nihon no Kōsha, Kōdan* ("Japan's Public Corporations") (Tokyo: Nihon Keizai Shinbunsha, 1970).

ministry, who receive notoriously high salaries and benefits—it is commonly alleged that greed is often a primary motive for their establishment.[15]

In general, the Ministry of Finance opposes the establishment of new organizations both because they add to administrative costs and because they tend to violate the principle, close to the heart of budgeters everywhere, that all government expenditures should be weighed together on a regular basis so that the priorities of the nation may be clearly decided. However, the MOF frequently allows short-term advantage to overwhelm principles—approving new organizations is often seen as an inexpensive means of satisfying intense pressures from ministries or the party in lieu of budget allocations, since such bodies often do not require large General Account expenditures at least in the first year. As noted above, for 1965, when the Finance Ministry had to cope with extremely low revenue forecasts, a record total of sixteen new organizations was approved. Still more cleverly, sometimes a new Special Account or governmental corporation will allow diversion of some small revenue source which hitherto had been included in the General Account, bringing down the nominal size of the total budget and allowing Finance officials to claim, for example, that budget growth is below GNP growth.

The enormous growth of special and separate budgetary accounts in the postwar period has undoubtedly contributed to "fiscal rigidification," making the MOF's tasks of managing public finance and responding to economic fluctuations and new public needs more difficult. It also helps confound any outside analyst (let alone the general public) attempting to understand trends in Japanese policy priorities. In these regards Japan is clearly not unique: such devices are found in the budgeting systems of all industrial nations.

# The Fiscal Investment and Loan Program

Although commonly referred to as "the other budget" in Japan, the important Fiscal Investment and Loan Program (FILP; *Zaisei Tōyūshi Keikaku,* or "Zaitō" for short) is not treated in the main body of our discussion above because it is not financed through taxes and does not support the ordinary business of government.[16] Its funds come from

15. Chalmers Johnson, "The Employment of Retired Government Bureaucrats in Japanese Big Business," *Asian Survey* 14, 11 (November 1974), 953-965.

16. Moreover, since it receives relatively little publicity, I was not aware of the great importance of the FILP until well along in my research. A good introduction, along with much technical information, is Ebisawa Michichika, *Zaisei Tōyūshi no Hanashi* ("Talking About the FILP") Tokyo: Nihon Keizai Shinbunsha, 1966).

governmental pension and other trust funds, the postal savings and insurance funds, bond issues and other borrowing, and a tiny portion from the General Account; they go as investments and loans to Special Accounts, many government corporations (largely for relending) and local governments. By functional division, the largest recipients of FILP funds in the 1974 plan were in the fields of housing (19.7 percent of the total), "living environment facilities" (16.4), small and medium business (15.5), transport and communications (13.6), export promotion (8.8) and highways (8.7). Since the amounts involved are large, generally a little under half the General Account or nearly ¥8 trillion (over $27 billion) in total planned for 1974, it will be appreciated that the FILP provides a significant portion of Japanese investment in economic development and social overhead.[17]

As a macrobudgeting process, the size of the FILP is determined each year simultaneously with the General Account, with fiscal policy effects taken into account. However, during revival negotiations its total is allowed to rise to finance appeals allocations instead of relying upon "hidden resources." The growth rate of the FILP has tended to parallel that of the General Account, though with year to year variations; from 1964 to 1974 it grew by a factor of 5.5 while the General Account grew by a factor of 5.2 (during this period the ratio of FILP to GNP rose from 4.2 to 6.0 percent).[18] The microbudgeting process too appears somewhat similar to that for the regular budget—spending ministries submit requests which are cut, and they then appeal reductions during the revival negotiations period— but it is handled by the MOF's Financial Bureau (Rizaikyoku) rather than the Budget Bureau. Little is known about the politics involved. It seems likely that private firms and economic interest groups involve themselves in this process much more heavily than in budgeting, and the LDP's role is less clear-cut although doubtless quite important. The FILP bears a family resemblance to capital budgeting schemes in other countries, but has many unique features and may be more significant in an economic sense than most; it is an excellent topic for future research.

One additional relationship to General Account budgeting should be noted. The Budget Bureau tends to regard the FILP, along with Special Accounts and government corporations, as another means for satisfying ministry or party demands without expending ordinary budget funds. In some cases, direct provision of investment funds is sufficient; in others, an organization may be granted FILP funds at no or low interest, which it is then allowed to lend at higher interest rates and apply the "profits" to running expenses. Such devices are rather common in times of fiscal

17. Data from *Zaisei Tōkei,* 1974, p. 295.
18. *Ibid.,* p. 41.

stringency, particularly when political pressures during revival negotiations become more intense than expected, and the MOF is hard pressed to protect its announced General Account total.

# Planning

A budget is a limited (in scope and time) sort of plan, specifying actions for a future period, so it is natural that budgeting finds itself in competition with other sorts of planning. The four kinds of planning which are regularly carried out in Japan — short-range economic forecasts, macro-economic indicative planning, administrative program projections, and regional development planning — each bear on public expenditures, and so must overlap with budgeting; to the extent plans determine governmental behavior, the importance of budgeting would be correspondingly diminished.[19] In theory, all these plans are supposed to be coordinated. Long-range macroeconomic planning establishes an economic framework for national level (and then various subnational level) comprehensive development plans, which in turn determine the projects included in individual ministry five-year plans; at the same time, yearly economic forecasts are compiled on the basis of the macroeconomic plans and influence the budget, which implements ministry-proposed projects.[20] Reality falls rather short of this ideal.

The relationship — a weak one — between the Economic Planning Agency's short-run forecasts and budgeting has already been discussed in the section on macrobudgeting in chapter 4. Longer-run macroeconomic planning can also be disposed of rather quickly: ever since the Occupation period, the Economic Council of the Economic Planning Agency has been formulating indicative plans which predicted the shape of the Japanese economy five (in one case ten) years ahead.[21] These plans have become

19. For a brief general discussion, see Aaron Wildavsky, *Budgeting: A Comparative Theory of Budgetary Processes* (Boston: Little, Brown and Company, 1975), pp. 253-260.

20. See the flow chart on p. 253 of "Regional Economic Planning," *White Papers of Japan,* 1972-1973, pp. 249-254. Part II of this edition of the *White Papers,* "Economic and Social Transition in Postwar Japan, 1945-73," pp. 183-379, is an excellent compendium of articles, documents and statistics on various aspects of planning, including translations of the most important plans.

21. Informative and rather critical articles on Japanese planning in English include Shigeto Tsuru, "Formal Planning Divorced from Action: Japan," in *Planning Economic Development,* ed. Everett E. Hagen (Homewood, Ill: Richard D. Irwin, 1963), pp. 119-149; Shuntaro Shishido, "Japanese Experience with Long-Term Economic Planning" and Tsunehiko Watanabe, "National Planning and Economic Growth," both in *Quantitative Planning of Economic Policy,* ed. Bert G. Hickman (Washington, D.C.: The Brookings Institution, 1965), pp. 212-232, 233-251; and particularly Tsunehiko Watanabe, "National Planning and Economic Development: A Critical Review of the Japanese Experience," *Economics and Planning* (March 1970).

more sophisticated, with econometric modelling used since 1965, but not necessarily more accurate. Each plan has missed significantly in its most fundamental projection, that for the real growth of GNP, although the direction of error was reversed with the New Economic Social Development Plan of 1970: previously, growth had been underestimated, but in the 1970 and 1973 plans growth was seriously overestimated.[22] Since the Japanese political system does not allow direct controls by government over such key economic factors as private investment and consumption, it is unsurprising that targets have not always been attained, but more interesting is the point that even the government sector has not been forecasted accurately. The growth rate of government consumption expenditures has typically run below planned levels, and that for government investment substantially above.[23] That is to say, Japanese economic planning is merely "indicative" for the government as well as the private sector.

The reason why performance diverges so much from plan even in the areas presumably under the government's control is that plans are drawn up by the Economic Planning Agency and budgets by the Ministry of Finance. The latter is clearly the stronger of the two in any game of bureaucratic politics. The MOF, careful to protect its own prerogatives, has been successful in preventing the EPA from specifying year-by-year spending totals in its plans; only targets for the final year or cumulative amounts over the entire period are included. Moreover, even these figures, and for example the sectoral distribution of public investment estimated in the plan, do not appear to be taken seriously by the Budget Bureau. In short, nonenforceable forecasts in a national income accounts framework do not impinge very much on the actual yearly budget process.[24]

In principle, developmental or land use planning should bear directly upon budgeting because of its close connection with public works. As well as a number of plans specific to individual regions, the chief examples in Japan have been the 1962 Comprehensive National Development Plan and the 1969 New Comprehensive National Development Plan, prepared by the Development Bureau of the Economic Planning Agency.[25] These plans

22. See the table "Footsteps of the Government's Economic Plans," in *The Japan Economic Journal* (April 8, 1975), 11.

23. However, in the 1967-69 period government consumption too ran one point above the planned level. See Table 21-17, "Comparison of Planned Figures and Actual Performance," *White Papers of Japan*, 1972-73, p. 239. More generally, see Watanabe, "Critical Review."

24. Watanabe, in "Critical Review," argues that it is budgeting which impinges on planning: projections have been distorted under MOF pressure so that revenues can be deliberately underestimated.

25. At time of writing a third plan was under preparation, with the responsibility assigned to the new National Land Agency.

are aimed at forecasting and influencing regional balances of population, industry, agriculture, recreation and so forth. Their goals are supposed to be implemented through coordination of various public policies, particularly in the construction of transportation networks, industrial facilities and housing; but as with macroeconomic planning, actual target figures for governmental outputs, either physical or monetary, are not included on a year-to-year basis. Although the Transport and Construction Ministries have important voices in drawing up these plans, the Ministry of Finance is not a major participant and does not take them very much into account in budgeting. In a 1970 interview, a budget examiner remarked of Development Bureau officials that

they do not have a lot of influence, you might say 'minor' . . . the role of that Bureau is to represent the various areas of the country, so they have a close relationship with local governments and local interest groups. Even though they do make up a national plan, generally speaking they tend to spread projects out evenly among all the regions . . . We [in the Finance Ministry] have a more national perspective.

In general, the MOF does not take seriously any plan that it does not have a major role in preparing. An interesting case in this regard is the land use plan for Hokkaido, which is part of the Comprehensive National Development Plan, but uniquely includes monetary estimates for public works expenditure. According to an Economic Planning Agency informant, this plan is negotiated primarily between the Hokkaido Development Agency and the Finance Ministry, and so examiners do consult it when reviewing Development Agency and line ministry requests for public works in that region. (It might be noted that such numbers may be included in the Hokkaido portion of the plan alone because, according to a highly-placed official, the Hokkaido Development Agency is a true "sacred cow" in Japanese budgeting, having great political power.)

It was in the late 1950s that planning of various sorts first became popular in Japan. The device was attractive to line ministries as a budgeting strategy for a number of good reasons. First, if a plan could be devised that determined expenditures on a particular program for the next, say, five years and if the Cabinet would enforce its implementation, that program would be exempt from the annual budgetary competition. Second, the Finance Ministry might have some influence over the total size of the plan, but since plans are reported to the Cabinet directly by the sponsoring ministry, the MOF would not have authority over the final decision. Third, in any debate the MOF's usual argument that revenue shortages preclude large spending increases would be obviated because believable five-year revenue projections are never available. Unsurprisingly, nearly all ministries quickly jumped on the planning bandwagon—

by the 1960 budget process, MOF officials were complaining that even the National Police Agency had come up with a full-scale plan to justify a request for more police cars. Each newly proposed plan was opposed by the Finance Ministry on the general grounds that planning freezes expenditure patterns and thereby prevents fiscal flexibility, as well as for various specific reasons. However, plans were viewed as important objectives by the ministries and their LDP supporters, who prevailed to the extent that, by the late 1960s, nearly the entire public works budget (about one-fifth of the General Account) was covered by Cabinet-approved five-year plans.

Several ministries at first attempted to include year-by-year spending totals in their plans, hoping to take care of five years' worth of budget debates at once (or better, to set what would in effect become minimum budget figures, allowing all their energies to be devoted to obtaining even more each year). However, the MOF managed to limit the official plans to no more detail than estimates of expenditures aggregated over the full five years. Each new plan or revision brought a great debate over its total size, in which the LDP was commonly even more enthusiastic than the requesting ministry. For example, in the 1970 budget process, the Ministry of Construction had originally planned to spend ¥ 10 trillion for highway construction over five years, but the party wanted ¥ 11-12 trillion and so argued the requested figure up to ¥ 10.7 trillion. The Finance Ministry then said it would allow no more than ¥ 10 trillion. Finally, it was decided after long negotiations to split the difference at ¥ 10.35 trillion.[26]

Despite the intense interest they generate, five-year-plan expenditure targets are partly fictional. Because plans do not specify yearly spending, the Finance Ministry does not feel compelled to implement them faithfully; indeed, the normal pattern is for a ministry to request a budget that is in line with the five-year plan—any request for more would be immediately rejected by the MOF on grounds that it is outside the plan—and then see it routinely cut in the regular budgetary process. After three or four years of such behavior, enormous allocations would be required to bring the plan to completion (that is, spend all the planned funds). Accordingly, so as not to violate a Cabinet directive openly by falling short on a specified target, the plan will usually be revised at that point. A new one is begun, with spending totals which are appropriately higher, given economic growth. For example, the highway plan passed in 1970 was the sixth, the fifth having run only three years; its total expenditure was about 60 percent higher than the projected five-year expenditure under the fifth plan. Table 15 lists the period for each major plan, the total target figure, what percentage was to be accomplished by

26. AS, August 14, 1969; September 4, 1969, evening, January 10, 1970 and January 31, 1970, evening.

## TABLE 15
### Public Works Five-Year Plans in 1974
(Units: Billion Yen; Percent)

| Name | Period | Planned Spending Total | Percent Accomplished 1973 | Percent Accomplished 1974 | Average Yearly Accomplishment to 1974 |
|------|--------|------------------------|---------------------------|---------------------------|----------------------------------------|
| Flood Control | 1972–76 | 3000 | 33.3 | 49.9 | 16.6 |
| Forestry Conservation | 1972–76 | 460 | 32.7 | 48.8 | 16.3 |
| Seashore | 1970–74 | 320 | 61.4 | 81.3 | 16.3 |
| Highways (free) | 1973–77 | 9340 | 15.0 | 29.9 | 15.0 |
| (toll) | | 4960 | 14.3 | 28.3 | 14.2 |
| Ports and Harbors | 1971–75 | 1550 | 48.2 | 65.6 | 16.4 |
| Fishing Harbors | 1973–77 | 680 | 10.4 | 21.1 | 10.5 |
| Sewerage Improvement | 1971–75 | 1587 | 57.4 | 76.7 | 19.2 |
| Urban Parks | 1972–76 | 320 | 28.8 | 47.0 | 15.7 |
| Disposal of Waste Matter | 1972–74[a] | 362 | 57.7 | 80.4 | 20.1 |
| Land Development | 1973–82[b] | 11200 | 5.5 | 10.9 | 5.5 |
| Public Housing | 1971–75 | 3.8 million units | 55.0 | 67.7 | 16.9 |

NOTES: [a]Four-year plan.     [b]Ten-year plan.

SOURCE: Calculated from tables in *Kuni no Yosan*, 1973, pp. 293–94; 1974, 292–93.

the end of 1973 and 1974, and the average percentage accomplished in each year.[27] These figures indicate rather clearly that the Finance Ministry almost never grants sufficient funds to live up to the letter of these public works plans.

The degree to which five-year plans are influential in budgeting does of course vary. At one extreme a number of less formal plans, not passed by the Cabinet, are probably useful only for internal purposes and are virtually ignored by the Finance Ministry. On the other hand, the Defense Buildup Plans are usually observed most scrupulously. Although not different in character from other plans, the matters treated in defense plans are highly controversial and must be handled gingerly by the government; accordingly, long negotiations among the Defense Agency, the Economic Planning Agency, the Foreign Ministry and the Ministry of Finance are required before each plan is passed by the National Defense

27. The average yearly percentage accomplished tends to be higher later rather than earlier in each plan, partly because actual inflation runs well ahead of the figures used in the plans; the money is worth less as years pass. Note also the differential impact of the 1974 controls of public works on these plans.

Council and the Cabinet. Budgeters are most wary of upsetting a consensus so laboriously reached. The accomplishment percentage of defense plans therefore tends to be unusually high: for example, after the 1970 initial budget, the Third Defense Buildup Plan was 73.8 percent fulfilled, and the Finance Ministry had already agreed that it would be 99 percent fulfilled in the following year's budget.[28]

Cynical observers of the Japanese budgetary scene, particularly those in the Finance Ministry itself, often allege that ministry five-year plans are nothing more than political gimmicks, their sole purpose being to put more pressure on the Budget Bureau for spending. Line ministry officials are sometimes a bit defensive about such charges. In an interview, an Accounting Division director from a ministry with several five-year plans said "it is not true that plans are merely devices for getting money . . . but of course that aspect is there too." Plans can have other functions, including helping the ministry itself in deciding what to do (and in what order) within a given category of public works. Helpful for this purpose are the "back-data," which set forth details of the plan down to the individual project level, and are not submitted to the Cabinet (nor to the MOF at budget time) except as reference materials.

Potentially an even more important function of planning might be coordination: among the various types of public works, between public finance and the rest of the national economy, and between governmental projects and the anticipated direction of population change and industrial development in specific regions. In practice, however, although mechanisms for coordinating the various plans exist, they have not been effective, mainly because the patterns of political pressure bearing on each planning activity (including budgeting) are different, and the pressures for integrating the plans are weak. The lack of specificity in the language of the plans, and the fact that each plan often covers a different period of years, tend to obscure what in many cases are real contradictions among them — for example, the total spending called for in ministry-developed and Cabinet-approved five-year plans for public works in the period from 1964 through 1968 was ¥24 trillion, while the Economic Planning Agency's Medium-Term Economic Plan for the same period, also approved by the Cabinet, anticipated only ¥16.8 trillion for public investment (a national income account category that also includes nonplanned activities).[29] Because the EPA has not been able to discharge its theoretical

28. Cf. AS, January 19 and NKS, February 5, 1970. Many discussions of the contents of defense plans are available; see for example "The Evolution of Japan's Defense Plans," *Japan Interpreter* 8, 2 (Spring 1972), 214-18; Japan Defense Agency, "Japan's Fourth Five-Year Defense Plan," *Survival* 15 (July-August 1973), 184-87; and Makoto Momoi, "Japan's Defense Policies in the 1970's," in *Japan and Australia in the 1970's,* ed. J.A.A. Stockwin (Sydney: Angus and Robertson, 1972).

29. NKS, December 16, 1964. Actual public investment for this period totalled ¥19.7 trillion. *Zaisei Tōkei,* 1970, p. 297.

responsibility for coordination, the task of *de facto* adjustment or arbitration falls by default to the annual budget process. To the extent that the various plans are mutually contradictory, the Finance Ministry is nearly free to disregard them all.

Still, the enormous pressures generated by the LDP when overall spending totals for the various public works plans are being debated indicates their importance is more than symbolic. Even if the Finance Ministry is able to disregard the details of a given five-year plan, Cabinet approval represents a consensus and commitment which cannot be altogether ignored. Moreover, budgeters by inclination are likely to be somewhat impressed by the sort of "rational" expenditure proposals which emerge from the planning process; and the fact that the MOF does participate in formulation, even if not to the same extent as in annual budgeting, means that plans are likely to be palatable at least as a basis for discussion. Program planning thus remains a worthwhile budgeting strategy from the line ministry point of view.

On the other hand, the more comprehensive forms of planning, whether based on national income accounting or land use forecasts, have yet to make a major impact; as will be seen in chapter 9, the various attempts through the years to institutionalize a longer-range perspective in budgeting, including Prime Minister Tanaka's scheme to "restructure the archipelago" via massive government investment, have all fallen well short of success. The inability of the planners to control budgeting is probably not unrelated to their broader failure to predict the future accurately or to direct the economy as a whole. These problems are not unique to Japan—as Aaron Wildavsky remarks, implementation of planners' goals depends on their

ability to ensure that the public sector moves consistently toward plan objectives; governmental resources must be directed toward this end, and not diverted away from plan purposes. If the plan is to be meaningful, then it must be reflected in the budget. If the plan goes one way and the budget another, the plan is ignored. That is why planners strive to influence budget allocations.

But they have failed. Why? Because planners need knowledge and power and they cannot get either.[30]

# Conclusion

This chapter has reviewed in rather cursory fashion a number of topics which deserve more adequate attention, but which are tangential to the main General Account budget process. All of these "other budgets"

---

30. Wildavsky, *Budgeting,* p. 258.

complicate budgeting, making public expenditures harder for the Ministry of Finance to grasp and control. That is, each represents an alternative to the main budget for the bureaucrat or politician seeking more funds; each increases the repertoire of strategies for the spending side, and thus works to the detriment of the institution which must try to control spending. Of course, on many occasions the Finance Ministry has also been able to use this briar-patch of budgetary intricacy to escape some dire predicaments.

While the origin, expansion and maintenance of each of these devices can be seen as resulting from specific circumstances of the time, in a deeper sense they are inevitable. Modern industrial societies and economies are very complex, requiring many kinds of special treatment by government, and moreover generating involuted webs of political pushes and pulls which naturally, over time, produce institutional patterns that cannot be neat and orderly. It is the scope and complexity of the tasks of government which bring managers to seek new methods of coordination, notably planning. Unfortunately, as often as not the contrivances designed to bring governmental management back under control only add to the confusion.

# 9

# The Budgeting System:
# 1954-1974

THE DISCUSSION to this point has treated the Japanese budget process in a rather timeless way. Most descriptions have referred to the period around 1970, and only in a few cases have I tried to show how specific patterns have changed over time. This approach is appropriate because Japanese budgeting has not undergone massive revolution since the amalgamation of conservative parties in 1955. Most of the analysis is nearly as applicable to the late 1950s as to 1970. However, a dynamic account of the past twenty years of budgeting is worth undertaking, for three reasons. First, the system has evolved over time—in particular, it has adapted to the intrusion of the majority party in budgeting, as well as to changes in economic and administrative conditions. Second, the process differs from year to year in response to fluctuations in the economic and political situations; many stresses and strains are revealed only when external constraints are varied. Third, a more specific narrative based primarily on contemporary newspaper articles, which reflect the way budget participants view events, can bring to the reader a more vivid sense of what Japanese budget politics looks like from the inside. The important budget indicators listed in Table 16, on p. 266 below, can serve as a reference throughout the chapter.[1]

1. This chapter is based primarily on newspaper clipping files, supplemented by interviews and secondary materials. As with all research methods, my approach has inherent biases of which the reader should be aware: some published items may have been missed by the staff of the Newspaper Clipping Room of the National Diet Library; any subterranean goings-on, such as secret conferences or highly classified documents, would never have reached the newspapers; and one cannot escape the tendency of newspapermen to play up the immediate, vivid, and political at the expense of the slow-moving, dull, and administrative. Still, I am confident the material is complete and accurate enough to justify the conclusions reached.

The periodization employed is my own, and is designed to highlight the most significant change-points: the formation of the LDP; the acceleration of growth under Ikeda; abandonment of the balanced budget principle; the "break fiscal rigidification movement"; and finally, Tanaka's positivist policies followed by the retrenchment of 1974. Periods in between these times of innovation are seen as more placid, when the system was adjusting to new relationships. The narrative throughout is devoted to politics; matters of administrative management or economic policy are touched upon only as necessary, and the substance of public policy is hardly discussed at all. In a sense, the chapter is an attempt to answer the following question: "To what extent in various years has the Ministry of Finance 'distorted' the budget (in terms of total size and allocation patterns) from what it would prefer in the absence of outside pressures?" The question is fundamentally unanswerable, since no one can know what the MOF would prefer in such a utopia, but posing it allows a look at the fundamentals of Japanese budgetary politics.

# The Formation of the
# Liberal Democratic Party (1954-1960)

The November 1955 unification of the Liberal and Democratic parties to form the Liberal Democrats marked, in Masumi Junnosuke's words, the formation of the contemporary Japanese political system.[2] To understand the impact of this on budgeting, we must briefly examine the earlier period. How were budgets compiled before a majority party controlled the Diet?

Looking back from twenty years later at the 1954 and 1955 budget processes, one is struck by a fact not at all obvious at the time: before the advent of the LDP, budgeting was almost completely dominated by the Ministry of Finance. The point may be illustrated by comparing the two years. During the time when the 1954 budget was being compiled, economic prospects seemed relatively gloomy. The Cabinet was controlled by the experienced Liberal Party, which had had the upper hand since 1949. Both party politicians and governmental bureaucrats were dominated, to an extent not again seen in Japan, by the "one-man rule" of Prime Minister Yoshida Shigeru; Yoshida's power and his propensity to intervene in budgeting on behalf of fiscal conservatism are well illustrated by his order in December 1953 that all ministries cut back their budget requests, already long submitted to the MOF, by 10 percent across-the-board. Negotiations with the Democratic Party after submission to the Diet

---

2. Masumi Junnosuke, *Gendai Nihon no Seiji Taisei* ("The Political System of Contemporary Japan") (Tokyo: Iwanami Shoten, 1969), p. 195.

proceeded smoothly, with relatively small concessions sufficient to secure its approval of the budget, even though the total was actually lower than the post-supplement budget of the previous year.

The 1955 process, in contrast, was much more turbulent: Yoshida had been replaced by Hatoyama Ichirō, and the Democratic Party, new to power and with policy ideas of its own, controlled the Cabinet but not the Diet; conservative politics was highly factionalized and ridden with strife.[3] The economy was looking up, leading to hopes for stronger revenues. After the release of the Finance Ministry draft, the Democratic Party Executive Council formally resolved that

the budget draft submitted by the MOF will not be changed in working-level negotiations. All amendments of this draft will be made at the direction of the party. The allocation of new funds among ministries, within the limits of the party directive, will be decided by discussion among party organs, appropriate members of legislative committees and ministers.[4]

While it soon became clear, as the MOF pointed out, that the party was unable to deal with the 3,000 or so expenditure items then under consideration, the fact that the Democrats had disdained the "responsible" role taken by the Liberals when in power, in favor of an aggressive posture seemingly more appropriate for an opposition party, led to an unusually long (seventeen days) revival negotiation; sizable concessions were necessary to obtain Cabinet approval. Thereafter, despite the vehement protests from the Ministry of Finance, the budget draft became an object of contention between the two conservative parties, which could not get together and negotiate a compromise until June.

In short, if we were to follow the line of analysis developed in earlier chapters we might conclude that while conditions favored a relatively restrained budget for 1954, all factors would seem to preduct greatly expanded spending in 1955. The actual results, however, were to the contrary: the 1955 budget was actually reduced (by 0.8 percent) from even the initial budget of the previous year, the only time that happened in our entire period. Despite the dramatic increase in political pressures, the Finance Ministry was able to achieve its quite restrictive objectives for the 1955 budget. Its autonomy and power in this early, pre-LDP period were evidently impressive.

Contemporary evaluations by those concerned about Japan's fiscal health were not as sanguine. Many were dismayed to see political parties taking charge of final budgetary decisions, beyond the reach of MOF control — Finance Minister Ichimanda nearly resigned after this slight.

3. The party and factional politics of this period were extraordinarily complex: see Haruhiro Fukui, *Party in Power: The Liberal Democratic Party in Policy-Making* (Berkeley and Los Angeles: University of California Press, 1970), pp. 44-50, for a good short account.

4. AS, April 8, 1955.

Indeed, it was widely believed in government and business circles that conservative party fragmentation was the critical problem of budgeting. In September 1955, spokesmen for big business were noting that the budget system as then constituted, allowing easy Diet amendments, produced only popular spending programs and therefore bad budgets. Party unification would be necessary to create a strong administration, able to preserve the balanced budget and keep spending down (particularly on unproductive programs such as agricultural supports and veterans' benefits). Finance Ministry officials too hoped that a strong majority party would eliminate legislative amendments and pursue rational and consistent policies, allowing cuts in the many *sōbanateki* ("all-around tips"; roughly, pork-barrel) public works and grants-in-aid items.[5]

*Entry of the New Party.*—Though knowledgeable Japanese realized that control of the Diet by a majority party would affect budgeting, no consensus existed on precisely what pattern would emerge. Four possibilities were being discussed in the early days of the Liberal Democrats.

First, Finance Minister Ichimanda Hisato believed that the Ministry of Finance could rid budgeting of its political flavor by independently compiling a "budget that makes sense" and presenting it to the people for their approval. MOF officials certainly hoped that this lofty concept could be realized, and they emphasized the legal "budget compilation authority" of the ministry.[6]

Second, the Economic Planning Agency asserted that budgeting should be subordinated to economic policy making; its director said "it is necessary that next year's budget be amalgamated with the six-year economic plan, and EPA views will have to be included. If possible, the Budget Bureau should soon be absorbed into the EPA."[7] The agency's Economic Council included a recommendation in its official report that the budget should be set at 15.4 percent of forecasted national income, amounting to a figure higher than that desired by the Finance Ministry.

The third alternative was that budgeting might simply be taken over by the new party. Immediately after unification, the LDP's first Policy Affairs Research Council chairman, Mizuta Mikio, told Finance Minister Ichimanda:

(1) the opinions of the party will have priority in budget compilation; (2) the Budget Compilation Basic Policy and Important Programs will be decided by the Deliberation Council to be established within the party, and will be implemented

5. TS, September 18 and November 16, 1955; MNS, September 20, 1955.
6. The intention to prepare an "independent" budget draft lasted well into the fall. YS, August 9 and October 15, 1955.
7. NKS, August 6; AS, August 14; and MNS, August 24, 1955.

before the government budget draft; (3) fiscal and monetary policies will be closely tied to the five-year economic plan.[8]

This economic plan too was to be developed with full party participation. A PARC spokesman was later quoted as saying, "With the new party cabinet, the budget is not simply to be handled administratively by the bureaucrats. In order that party obligations may be fully included, the PARC should take leadership authority [shudōken] in budget compilation."[9]

The fourth and most radical suggestion came from the Cabinet, or more particularly from the LDP strongman with most influence on that body, Kōno Ichirō. As Director of the Administrative Management Agency, Kōno proposed that the Budget Bureau be transferred from the Ministry of Finance to direct Cabinet control, so that the comprehensive and ambitious plans of the new government would not be undercut by fiscal conservatism. Others advised more modestly that a Cabinet-level committee should pass a set of budget guidelines each year which would be binding on the MOF.

Although the Finance Ministry lacked the power to realize Ichimanda's ideal of independent budgeting, it certainly would not passively watch its budgeting prerogatives stripped away. To counter the threat from the EPA, the MOF appointed a Financial Discussion Council (Zaisei Kondankai), informal at first, which in only three weeks managed to come up with an interim report endorsing a low budget figure.[10] Further reports and energetic lobbying efforts throughout the fall finally established the principle that yearly budget figures would not be included in economic plans or other EPA products. The ministry's other perils, however, could not be confronted so openly, nor with quite so much success.

Finance Ministry officials chose to deal first with the LDP organization rather than the influential Cabinet leaders. For November and December of 1956, a tacit compromise seemed operative: LDP participation would be allowed along the lines of Mizuta's guidelines, on condition that the party would behave "responsibly." The Finance Ministry consulted with Liberal Democratic leaders and made concessions on several revenue matters; the LDP in turn endorsed several ministry positions, including a ¥ 1.03 trillion ceiling on the 1956 budget. It seemed that a working

    8. NKS, November 17, 1955.
    9. TS, December 12, 1955.
    10. Mizuta Mikio jibed, "this Council is a publicity organ, set up simply as an agent by the MOF—a 'cloak of invisibility' for the bureaucrats. If they want to draw up their own policies and challenge the party, let them! After unification, those fellows dancing in the shadows can all be fired!" YS, October 16, 1955. For MOF strategies, see Hayashi Yoshio, Zaiseiron ("Public Finance") (Tokyo: Chikuma Shobō, 1968), pp. 176-181.

relationship might be developing which would become an important precedent for future budgeting.

However, the precedent which eventually became established was quite different. The compromise began to fall apart at two Cabinet-level meetings called to approve a basic budget policy in late December, when Kōno (as Agriculture Minister) turned the discussion from generalities to specifics, and together with his colleagues forced the addition of several new priority items. A week later, as Finance Minister Ichimanda tried to explain the MOF draft to the Cabinet, Kōno interrupted to complain about the disposition of sugar import duty revenues, encouraging other ministers to chime in with complaints about cuts in their requests. Shaken, the finance minister and chief Cabinet secretary promised more discussions. The Cabinet appeared to be taking the budget away from the MOF. However, it was the LDP organization which proved most able to take advantage of the situation: a big Policy Affairs Research Council meeting was immediately convened, and it decided to force direct MOF-LDP negotiations. Over the next three weeks, Finance Ministry offers of additional funds were repeatedly rejected by the party, which demanded more and more. In the end, the government draft totalled nearly ¥5 billion over the ceiling previously endorsed by the Liberal Democrats.

In its first budget year the LDP had clearly demonstrated both its power and its impotence: the party could disrupt budgeting and force the MOF into embarrassing defeats, but quite obviously it did not have the ability to take over the budgetary system. Budgeting requires making decisions and sticking to them, and the LDP did neither very well. Time and time again the leadership was compelled to repudiate promises when forced by rank-and-file pressures into making ever more extreme spending demands. At one point the Construction Division of the PARC, led by Tanaka Kakuei, had even walked out of an important meeting after hearing the leadership's budget plan. The final addition of almost ¥1 billion granted by the MOF was universally recognized as the LDP secretary-general's "pocket money," or "intraparty adjustment expenses" (tōnai chōseihi)—money for the party leadership to parcel out among small constituency-oriented projects, the only means available to cool down the strong demands from LDP Dietmen.

The problem facing the LDP was clearly seen by one of its staff experts, Kita Kazuo, writing just after the 1956 budget had been approved by the Cabinet. He said that it was appropriate for a national party to make budget policy, with the PARC divisions sending their budget recommendations up to the party leadership. The leadership then has to cut these to a reasonable size, one that matches the maximum revenue the MOF can provide. "If they were not cut, there would be doubts about what the party was stressing, and moreover, the meanings of the party's advising the cabinet on budget compilation would be lost. Budgeting would continue to be routinized, equalized, often plundered, and bureaucratic. . . ."[11] Despite this perception, the LDP never could devise an enforceable mechanism for budget-cutting, and it is largely for that reason that it never succeeded in imposing a coherent set of positive policies through the budget, let alone taking control of the process.

Perhaps it might be said as well that the behavior of the Ministry of Finance in the 1956 budget process actually encouraged this fragmented pattern of attacks by the LDP. The MOF could draw upon impressive strategic resources: a near monopoly over financial information, the undiminished strength of the "sound fiscal policy" ideology developed during the Occupation, the presence of allies within even the LDP leadership (MOF alumnus Fukuda Takeo was an active PARC vice-chairman). However, it chose not to make a public stand, preferring not to duel openly with the LDP on the basis of its "budget compilation authority." The MOF opted instead for a behind-the-scenes approach and for tactics rather than strategy. In both the earlier cooperative stage and the later more conflictual period of the 1956 budget process, piecemeal concessions were offered whenever it appeared that a temporary advantage could be secured.[12] The immediate result was simply that the 1956 budget turned out somewhat larger than intended. However, more significantly, the role expectations engendered in this first year of majority party budgeting would persist, and would condition budgetary decision making throughout our period.

## Adjustment

Budget processes from 1957 to 1960 generally followed the pattern established in 1956. Once approved by the Cabinet, the budget draft was not changed in the Diet in response to opposition party demands. The immense formal power of the Cabinet was sometimes translated into gains for individually influential members, but not into an authoritative institutional voice. The MOF's major antagonist continued to be the Liberal Democratic Party; the variations of conflict in those four years illustrate nicely the nature of the relationship between the two powers.

If our dependent variable in this account is the extent to which the Finance Ministry is forced to "distort" the budget, its only clear-cut victory would appear to be in 1959, when the growth rate of the budget was relatively low and the process quite placid. In 1957, as in 1956, a last

11. MNS, January 24, 1956.
12. The best example is the large agriculture allocation which converted Kōno Ichirō from the MOF's chief critic to an effective supporter. AS, January 14, and MNS, January 20, 1956.

minute intervention by Agriculture Minister Kōno disrupted the revival negotiations period, forcing the establishment of a new rice-pricing system highly advantageous to farmers, as well as leaving openings for LDP Dietmen to pursue their own special interests. In 1958 the PARC was insufficiently disciplined to produce a coherent set of demands, and the revival period was again protracted and required large MOF concessions to terminate. It is noteworthy that the PARC was most effective, in an organizational sense, in the 1959 process; when the MOF had its greatest success. Under the leadership of Fukuda Takeo, it produced highly competent budget analyses throughout the fall, allowing an orderly sequence of negotiations culminating in the passage of the government draft before the end of the year (the first time this MOF goal had been accomplished since 1952).[13]

Most of the 1960 process was equally smooth, and Finance Minister Satō hoped for as big a success as in 1959, but he had failed to take sufficient account of the disruptive potential of LDP factionalism. Throughout the budget period factional maneuvers which would culminate in the removal of Prime Minister Kishi were intensifying; despite many concessions to party demands at the MOF draft stage, the temptation for the antimainstream factions to use budgeting as a weapon against both the prime minister and his brother and ally Finance Minister Satō was irresistible.[14] At the very last moment before the government draft was to be passed, Satō was forced to apologize publicly to the PARC for "ignoring" its demands, and not only were the few questions left unsettled at that point thrown into extended negotiations, but even agreements already supposedly reached became unstuck. The revival negotiations period for 1960 wound up lasting twenty-one days, the longest ever. In the final stages, Satō appeared to hand over much of his decision-making authority to the party leadership, but neither this group nor the prime minister was able to control the awakened enthusiasm of the LDP backbenchers. New funds allocated during the negotiations amounted to some ¥ 20 billion, double the figure the MOF had apparently intended to hand out — all observers called the budget a major defeat for the Finance Ministry.

Throughout the period, such variables as the experience and political clout of the finance minister, the extent to which he was supported by the prime minister, organizational discipline within the LDP and the degree of factional strife, the presence or absence of powerful politicians in the Cabinet, and the economic situation all affected the amount of pressure

13. See NKS and AS, November 30, 1958; for an MOF view, AS, December 14, 1958.
14. For a full account of the inter- and intraparty politics of the period, see George R. Packard, *Protest in Tokyo: The Security Treaty Crisis of 1960* (Princeton, N.J.: Princeton University Press, 1966).

which would bear upon the Ministry of Finance during budgeting. With regard to longer-term trends, clearly party unification had increased the MOF's vulnerability to such pressure. But how much were budgets really distorted? Last-minute disruptions, those tamed with "intraparty adjustment expenses," perhaps caused the unanticipated addition of some ¥ 5-10 billion ($25 million or so), under 1 percent of the budget, in some years. The Finance Ministry's reactions by anticipation are of course harder to gauge, but overall, one is impressed that the basic framework of Japanese finance seems not greatly altered during this period. Budget growth ran behind GNP growth in every year but one (see Table 16, Column F), and the possibility of deficit financing had barely been seriously mentioned. Though forced to concede over specifics (the rice-price system comes to mind), and indeed to resort more often than it liked to its repertoire of tactical maneuvers against the majority party, the Finance Ministry in the late 1950s was still managing to maintain the upper hand.

# Ikeda and High Growth (1961-65)

If the 1955 conservative party unification was a major turning point in budget process, 1960, when Ikeda Hayato came to power, signified a turning point in budget substance. Ikeda entered office in the summer of 1960, in the aftermath of the security treaty riots and the fall of Kishi, with an explicit commitment to dedicate his administration to domestic rather than foreign policy. The domestic policy he chose was economic growth. From the "recession" in 1958 (nominal growth of GNP was only 4.8 percent), the economy had recovered strongly. Nominal growth in 1959 had been 15.5 percent and in 1960 it would rise to 19.1 percent, the greatest boom then on record. Although many voices, including members of the antimainstream LDP factions, were calling for restraint to avoid overheating of the economy, Ikeda's response to these trends was expansionist. He sought to build a consensus behind the "Income Doubling Plan," a scheme to achieve an average 7.2 percent growth rate and thereby double Japan's gross national product in ten years.

*Economic Management.* —Implicit in Ikeda's policy was a view of the Finance Ministry, which he had served as civil servant and minister, that was well articulated by Shimomura Osamu, his chief economic advisor:

The behavior of the Ministry of Finance bureaucrats prior to the establishment of the Ikeda Cabinet had wrongfully over-restricted the forces which should have expanded the private economy. This had been a strong minus factor against growth. Under the Ikeda Administration, the 'finance bureaucrats' ultimately matured to the point where they were removing obstacles to the growth of the private economy.[15]

A budget affects economic growth directly in two ways: by altering the pattern of resource allocation, and by stimulating or restricting aggregate demand. Most of the 1960 policy shift was a change in attitude toward demand management. The issue was sharpened by the "dollar-defense" policies adopted by the United States that year, which directly threatened Japanese exports and to some also presaged a general international slowdown. Many counseled traditionally that fiscal policy should be restrictive, to tone down the Japanese economy (since rapid growth would produce demand for imports that would quickly unbalance the international payments account). Ikeda's solution, however, was to compensate for the drop in international demand by stimulating consumer demand through governmental expenditures. The result was that the 1961 budget was expanded at a record pace—it was 24.4 percent higher than the initial budget of the previous year. It should be noted here, with reference to the discussion of Japanese fiscal policy in chapter 4, that stimulation in the Keynesian sense is not meant. Deficit spending was not a part of the plan, and indeed the official forecasts of the total government sector in the national income accounts predicted substantially higher revenues than expenditures. Rather, the budget was "positive" in that it was scheduled to grow faster than the Gross National Product. More generally, as expressed by Chief Cabinet Secretary Ōhira Masayoshi, for the first time the budget was seen as "marching in step with," rather than lagging behind, the economic growth potential of the country.[16]

It is a measure of how quickly attitudes had changed that deficit spending was actually considered in the early stages of the budget process for 1961. Just after his appointment as finance minister, Mizuta Mikio mentioned the possibility of issuing bonds under the auspices of the Road Improvement Special Account. Although these would not be used to make up a General Account deficit, and thus were not "national bonds" in a narrow sense, the repayment would nonetheless be from tax revenues and thus violate the old taboo. Even some within the MOF were sympathetic to this suggestion, arguing that more flexibility for economic regulation would be gained, and voices in the LDP and the business world called for bonds to finance needed investment in public works. Marshalled against this proposal were various technical (taking funds away from private business) and emotional (reminders of wartime inflation) arguments, but the objection that carried the most weight in the final negative verdict was

15. Cited in Suzuki Yukio, *Keizai Kanryō* ("Economic Bureaucrats") (Tokyo: Nihon Keizai Shinbunsha, 1969), p. 149. Shimomura, an economist, had at this time retired from the MOF to become a bank executive.

16. AS, December 24, 1960, evening.

that of the Budget Bureau: abolishing this traditional ceiling or "brake" (*hadome*) on expenditures would lead to even more intense pressures for higher spending, which the MOF would be powerless to resist.[17]

If bonds could not be used to finance Ikeda's positive policies, sufficient tax revenues would have to be found. Early in the summer, the MOF indicated that new revenues would amount to about ¥250 billion, representing about 16 percent growth. By the end of the process, however, it had moved to a position that about ¥450 billion would be available for new purposes. Much was made of the point that "full" revenue estimates were being used, on the explicit instructions of the prime minister.[18] The talk of deficit financing certainly encouraged the MOF's flexibility on this point.

*The Culture of Growth.* — In contrast to this macrobudgeting shift, the pattern of allocation of expenditures through the General Account changed only marginally in the 1961 budget. The shares of the budget devoted to education, war-related pensions, defense and some other items dropped off slightly; the shares for social welfare programs, export promotion and public works (particularly highways, regarded as a key to the economic infrastructure required for growth) rose slightly.[19] In part, this stability was a product of the inherent conservatism of an incremental budget system, and because political support for some established programs that Ikeda viewed as "backward" and non-growth-oriented was strong. For example, among the "new policies" for the Cabinet announced in September was a view that the agricultural share of the population should decline, with production maintained by modernization and shifts into new crops. This pronouncement aroused suspicion among agriculturally oriented Dietmen, who held fast to the old idea of agriculture as the foundation of the country; their resentment doubled when the budget for agriculture in the MOF draft rose markedly less than did the budget as a whole. Agricultural expenditures thus became a major topic in the revival negotiations, and in the end an enormous grant was made to the Foodstuffs Control Special Account to expand rice price supports still further.

If ministry budget shares did not shift much, however, the way in which shares were perceived did alter. Agriculture again provides the example: after Ikeda's policy pronouncements in the fall, rural Dietmen—

17. See NKS, July 21, 1960; AS, July 27, 1960; and especially NKS, July 30, 1960.

18. AS, January 5, 1961, evening. As it happened the performance of the economy in fiscal year 1961 far outstripped even these predictions, with revenue growth approaching ¥600 billion above that of the previous year. The "error" of anticipated versus actual revenues was 29 percent, highest of the period studied.

19. A glance at the tables indicates that a similar conclusion is warranted for the FILP—the total size was increased substantially, but relative allocations did not change very much.

exemplifying the old consciousness—were concerned with protecting the Agriculture Ministry's "framework" or "base," the amount granted in the previous year's budget. But when the MOF draft appeared, relative growth rates had come to be seen as the crucial indicator of success: they complained that Agriculture had been unfairly treated, even though its budget had been increased some 10 percent, because the total budget had gone up a full 23 percent.[20]

This shift from a static to a more dynamic conception of interministerial "balance," as the term is employed above, was associated with a new concern for growth, and for the statistics that express growth, which had pervaded the entire budget system. This "cultural" change is immediately apparent when reading newspaper accounts of the 1961 process as compared with those of earlier years. The macrobudgeting debate, unusually active that year, was concerned with the details of economic growth and the budget's role within it, rather than simply with the amount of available revenues or the budget's effect on immediate business conditions. An example of the new orientation is the way in which the new total budget was described at the time of the MOF draft: all the newspaper headlines noted prominently that it was 23 percent higher than that of the previous year, and this figure (and its adjustment to 24.4 percent with the government draft) was much discussed by participants. In previous years not only had this statistic not appeared in headlines, but it was difficult to find even in the most detailed journalistic budget analyses.

The obsession with growth, and with economic planning, had a further effect. As noted by a *Sankei Shinbun* reporter in a symposium on the 1961 budget,

The Ikeda Cabinet's way of expressing economic policy in figures has made the role of the Economic Planning Agency more important, and has made its presence felt. Therefore, it has more frequent chances to make strong statements.[21]

Among the strong statements was that of EPA Director Sakomizu Hisatsune, to a meeting of his agency officials in August, 1960:

The authority for compiling the national budget lies with the Ministry of Finance, but the Economic Planning Agency, which is the agency for comprehensive coordination of policy, should set the standards. Using the Economic Forecast, we should hypothesize the shape of next year's economy. Particularly since next year is the first year of the Income Doubling Plan, and because adjusting the balance among tax cut, social welfare and public works policies has become a problem, we should first construct a National Economic Budget that would include all

---

20. NKS, September 10, 1960, and AS, January 8, 1961. The 10 percent figure excludes the rice price subsidy; after the government draft, it turned out that the Agriculture Ministry's budget including the subsidy grew by 44.4 percent.

21. SS, January 15, 1961.

these factors. Next, the EPA should put forth its own views on what policies are needed to accomplish the objectives set by the National Economic Budget, along with their expenditure implications. The prime minister should then adjust the budget in response to these views.[22]

As in 1956, the EPA was threatening budget predominance, though even its own officials tended to stress that the suggestion was a private opinion of their chief — they doubted if the agency was suited for this role, on grounds of "technique, ability and authority."[23] In any case, by a month later the "comprehensive plan" had been watered down to a simple expansion of the Economic Forecast into a full National Income Accounts prediction, including the government sector, which would be somewhat more binding on budget makers than earlier. Even this limited aim was not to be accomplished: when the Economic Forecast was approved by the Cabinet on December 27, the government sector had again been left out and, as in other years, once the budget had been passed the EPA indicated that an appropriately revised forecast would then be resubmitted.

*Party Intervention.* —Again as in 1956, the more significant threat to Finance Ministry control came not from the EPA, but from the LDP. A journalist commented after the 1961 budget process had been concluded,

never before has there been so much of an "LDP budget" as this. The "budget compilation authority" is clearly vested in the government by the Finance Law, but this year for the first time the lead in budget compilations from start to finish has been taken by the LDP.[24]

While a little overstated, the observation correctly indicates the extensive degree to which the majority party had become influential.

Actually, through most of the fall, the party had been unusually quiet, perhaps because no one knew enough economics to argue with Ikeda.[25] The PARC had hoped to "adjust opinions" among the divisions in time for pre-MOF draft negotiations but was unable to do so, and decided instead to wait for the draft and then offer reactions. Perhaps in fact it was because the party's intervention was so late that it turned out to be so disruptive. When the divisions finally began work, their appeal requests were very large, and a group of PARC officials who met to boil these down on January 8 found the task impossible. Instead, they decided to send the raw demands directly to the MOF, accompanied only by an informal (that is, lacking Executive Council endorsement) five-tiered statement of

22. NKS, August 5, 1960, evening.
23. NKS, August 6, 1960; also see AS, August 8, 1960. It will be recalled that the EPA is largely managed by posted officials from the MOF and MITI; organizational esprit was not well developed.
24. AS, January 19, 1961, evening.
25. AS, December 28, 1960.

priorities. The MOF dealt with this document as best it could, distributing small increments among ministries in the three revised drafts it released in the early stages of revival negotiations, and initiating discussions on the harder points among top-level ministry and party leaders. But apparently there was insufficient time: the government draft had to be postponed for two days, and the Dietmen began taking advantage of the disarray. For example, on January 16 the Agriculture and Forestry Division of the PARC, which had long since formulated its "final" position, met again and came up with an additional ¥25 billion in requests, and on January 17, a combined Executive Council — PARC Deliberation Council meeting even openly refused to take the conventional step of handing responsibility for the final settlement to the party leadership. Only after another round of negotiations was this permission granted and the budget finished. This rank-and-file rebellion had results: the amount added to budget items in the revival negotiations was over twice the size of the previous record, and the 1960 Supplementary Budget — another source of funds to satisfy party demands — also was more than twice the size of any precedents.

While the LDP had not "taken over" budgeting in any structural sense, it is clear that the party's influence had grown. Compared with earlier years, the Finance Ministry left many more questions unsolved at the MOF draft stage, LDP participation in working out solutions to these questions was more extensive, and the LDP rank and file put more intense pressure on its leaders. On the last point, it is worth noting that Finance Minister Mizuta had considerable experience as Chairman of the Policy Affairs Research Council, and the new PARC chairman, Fukuda Takeo, was an MOF "old boy" — the two cooperated closely, and journalists were joking that the real budget headquarters was in the Akasaka Prince Hotel, where Fukuda maintained his private offices. Such strong pressure for spending from the party leadership has a touch of irony, when it is recalled that Fukuda and the others had been, at least in theory, rather opposed to Ikeda's "positive" approach to fiscal policy.[26] It is likely therefore that the positive attitude of the LDP leadership had been motivated more by pressure from below than by inner conviction.

Within the LDP, a structural shift that had begun some time ago became obvious in 1961.[27] A reporter covering the LDP, asked what the main feature of the budget battles for that year had been, replied:

26. For example, the party's Budget Compilation Program for that year had included the rather restrictive statement, "fiscal policy should not overstimulate the economy," while the Cabinet-passed Basic Policy, written within the MOF, had noted only that "the balanced budget will be preserved" — that is, simply no deficit financing. Pointed out in AS, December 28, 1960.

27. Earlier examples include the interest group–LDP cooperation in raising war-related pensions in 1958, and the coalition of twenty-four agriculture groups with Ministry of Agriculture and Forestry officials and LDP Dietmen to capture a tithe of the budget in 1959. See AS, January 19, 1958, and January 1, 1959, and YS, January 28, 1959.

In an ordinary year, budget demands come from the party factions, but this time there were almost none of these. Agriculture, local finance, military pensions . . . the problems which bother the party are in most cases being pushed by 'connected Dietmen' (*kankei giin*) on a superfactional basis.[28]

Suzuki Yukio, then a staff reporter for the *Nihon Keizai Shinbun,* also noted that interest groups were particularly active, and the group-ministry-division (or other LDP group) alliances had become exceedingly close.[29] The degree of "back-up" for ministerial budgets by party groups was unprecedented: one story had it that the agriculture minister was pushed back into the finance minister's office three times by Dietmen during the final negotiations, each time after he thought he had successfully concluded an agreement.

*Ikeda.* —It is of course not surprising that the LDP should press for higher expenditures; this is its accepted role within the budgetary system. The question of how the MOF was induced to accept party demands to such an extent—or even more significantly, why it proposed such an enormous budget even before major party pressure had been brought to bear—requires additional attention. Part of the explanation lies in structural factors. As we have seen, MOF officials have an easier time in budgeting when led by a strong minister and backed up effectively by the prime minister. These leaders are expected to reiterate the virtues of sound fiscal practice, endorse the position of the Budget Bureau on specific questions, and work to hold down pressures from the party and the ministries. In 1961, however, Finance Minister Mizuta leaned rather to the expansionist side on fiscal matters, a perspective perhaps stemming from his many years as a pillar of the PARC. The role of the prime minister was still more important. Not only was Ikeda an expansionist, but he had a far more activist conception of his office with respect to domestic policy in general and the budget in particular than any prime minister since Yoshida and until Tanaka. Throughout the budget process, he met frequently with participants inside and outside the MOF, and spoke in specific terms on budget issues small and large. This effort was supported by his personal knowledge of economics and his skillful use of advisors like Shimomura, providing a theoretical rationale for his positive policy line.

This turnabout of role on the part of both the finance minister and the prime minister, coupled with the high revenue forecasts resulting from rapid economic growth, meant that MOF officials would have faced a difficult struggle if they had attempted to push through a "neutral" or deflationary budget in 1961. In fact, they did not try, no doubt partly because they recognized this strategic picture, but also in large measure

28. SS, January 15, 1961.
29. NKS, January 13, 1961.

because many within the ministry had been won over to the prime minister's position. Ikeda, of course, had strong ties with the MOF: his career as a Finance official was capped by service as vice-minister in 1947-48, and after election to the Diet he served as its minister in 1949-52 and again in 1957. He knew the policies, procedures and personnel of the ministry intimately, and in turn was highly respected by the officials.[30] It is apparent that Ikeda's arguments were extremely influential inside the MOF, many officials agreeing with him that the budget should be used to maintain demand and build the economic base for growth, and that fuller revenue estimates and a less critical attitude toward requests were warranted.[31]

One final remark on the 1961 budget: at the very beginning of the process, the MOF for the first time imposed a limit on budget requests. Each ministry was permitted to ask for only 50 percent more money than it had actually received in the previous year. Several resentful ministries submitted requests well over this limit, but these were returned by the MOF. This small but significant move by the MOF to transfer some of its work (and therefore some of its decision-making authority) to other participants presaged a long-term strategy which would become more apparent in the late 1960s.

## Adjustment

The period from 1962 to 1965 essentially continued the pattern set in 1961. Budgets were significantly larger than in the 1950s and "ran ahead" of the economy (in the sense that budget growth exceeded GNP growth), but continued to be financed without recourse to bond sales (until the 1965 Supplement). The MOF attitude toward pressures from the LDP was relatively soft; it is notable that the amounts allocated during the revival negotiations period, when party influences are at a peak, were notably higher for this period than earlier.[32] Moreover, the tone of relations between these two organizations was quite harmonious and cooperative. One contributing factor was the role taken by the ex-MOF officials in the LDP leadership during the period (including Maeo Shigesaburō, Aichi Kiichi and Fukuda Takeo), as well as the sympathies and personal styles of Finance Ministers Mizuta (1961-62) and Tanaka (1963-65). Both were basically expansionists, identified with the party organization, and their

30. Ikeda was greeted by officials on his return as Finance Minister in 1956 with this speech: "The minister has accumulated more and more political influence and has accomplished much as a man. The ministry is pleased to welcome his smiling face again." SS, January 10, 1957.

31. Cf. Suzuki, *Keizai Kanryō*, p. 148; NKS and AS, January 5, 1961, morning and evening. Similarly, in the following year Ikeda was said to be personally responsible for obtaining MOF agreement to raise revenue estimates considerably. AS, November 23, 1961.

32. See the discussion in chap. 7 and Table 11.

style was to consult widely and often. The fact that Prime Minister Ikeda had gained in personal popularity and was running the government and party with confidence and skill was also significant. In retrospect, however, the key factor in accounting for the lack of tension in budgeting during this period may have been the more peaceful mood in the broader Japanese political arena, perhaps a reaction to the turbulence of 1960, and a reflection of an emerging consensus on economic growth as a national goal.

Reflecting this harmony, there were no major alterations in budget structure, process or "culture" in these four years. Prime Minister Ikeda continued to take a more active role than normal, maintaining an overall expansionist tone and intervening with the MOF, the EPA and other participants to achieve particular goals. Within the LDP, factions again played a minor role in comparison with the PARC divisions and their alliances with ministries and interest groups, and pressures from below did not get out of hand.

# The Fiscal Crisis (1965-67)

The summer of 1965, overlapping with the compilation period for the 1966 budget, was called by a Budget Bureau official the busiest season in budget history.[33] It marked another turning point in Japanese budgeting: the advent of deficit financing. The possibility of financing part of the General Account by issuing bonds, rather than solely from tax revenues, had been brought up repeatedly and increasingly in earlier years, but memories of wartime inflation combined with strong Finance Ministry opposition, based particularly on its conviction that the balanced-budget restriction was the only effective "brake" against skyrocketing expenditures, had always been sufficient to avert a lapse from fiscal austerity.

It had been apparent while the 1965 budget was being prepared that the nation was again falling into a recession. The small size of the revenue forecast had allowed a budget only 12.4 percent higher than that of the previous year, the lowest growth rate of the 1960s, and by the beginning of the fiscal year, MOF officials had started to worry that even the relatively low forecasted revenues would not be forthcoming: tax collections even for 1964 had fallen a bit short of expectations, and expenditures for that year had to be cut back slightly. When this pessimism was seen to be realistic after the spring tax collections, the Finance Ministry's initial response was similar: it imposed a 10 percent cutback (*ryūho*) of expenditures on all governmental agencies in June 1965.

While temporarily solving the revenue shortfall problem, this move obviously ran directly counter to the needs of a declining economy. The only

33. Funago Masamichi, "Yosan Hensei no Butaiura" ("Behind the Scenes at Budget Compilation"), *Fainansu* 1, 4 (March 1966), 25.

concession to urgent demands from businessmen that the government take positive action had been a loosening of monetary policy; the Cabinet had discussed an expansion of General Account and FILP spending in April, but had deferred decision because of the lack of funds.[34] Although the topic of deficit financing was brought up again and again, the prime minister had said in February that issuing bonds was not currently being considered and would not be at least until 1968, and this policy was reaffirmed by Finance Minister Tanaka as late as May. In June, however, Fukuda Takeo was appointed finance minister, and in his first press conference said, "without talking about timing, I think that at some point we will have to change our policy regarding the issuance of bonds."[35] Although nominally addressed to Japan's long-range economic problems rather than the immediate crisis, his statement touched off still more speculation; within the Finance Ministry discussions began on how a bond policy could be implemented technically if one were to be adopted.

On July 27, the Cabinet-level Economic Policy Conference finally decided to move positively to pull Japan out of recession by removing spending restrictions and ordering an expansion of FILP expenditures — this step made deficit financing inevitable, and within weeks it was decided that bonds would be issued to support both the 1965 and (since economic conditions could not be expected to change quickly) 1966 budgets. The "balanced budget" principle, the keystone of Japanese postwar fiscal policy, finally had been broken.

In taking this decision, three considerations were relevant: structural changes in the Japanese economy, which to many observers meant that the high-growth leadership role taken by private investment in the early 1960s must be supplemented by a stronger government role; the need for pump-priming to pull Japan out of recession; and the revenue shortfall. Although the first two problems were not ignored by MOF officials, their primary motive in approving the issuance of bonds was the shortfall, which was already causing extreme practical difficulties before the fiscal year was half over. This was because a lack of funds could not be ignored, and could be met only by cutting back substantially on expenditures or raising taxes — both as politically unfeasible as economically foolish — or else by finding funds elsewhere, through borrowing. That such administrative and short-run concerns were dominant is indicated by the course of MOF actions while the 1965 budget was still in effect: restraints on expenditures were maintained well after formal decisions to expand had been taken, no immediate tax cut or expansion in public works were ordered, and

34. Ōkurashō Hyakunenshi Henshūshitsu, ed., *Ōkurashō Hyakunenshi* ("Ministry of Finance One Hundred Year History") II (Tokyo: Ōkura Zaimu Kyōkai, 1969), p. 308.

35. AS, June 4, 1965.

Supplementary Budgets were unusually small. The bond issue itself did not come until mid-January, six months after it had been deemed necessary, and even then was of minimum size. The change in fiscal policy therefore had very little impact on the economy in fiscal 1965.[36]

Therefore, although 1965 was the precedent-breaking year, 1966 stands as the first year of, in Fukuda's phrase, the "new era of public finance" (*zaisei shinjidai*), when deficit financing would be used as a positive tool for economic regulation rather than simply as an emergency expedient. The policy switch meant that even after the decision to issue bonds had been taken, at the start of the normal compilation period, many new and difficult problems remained. Some of these were technical — interest rates, methods of marketing, and so forth — but the question of how large the bond issue should be was central to the budget process and obviously complicated the macrobudgeting task of setting the size of the total budget. The traditional revenue criterion could no longer be automatically applied. As for microbudgeting, in the past the MOF had often replied to LDP and ministry demands by saying simply that no funds remained (so another program would have to be cut); now, a more complicated logic that the economic dangers of an increment to the bond issue outweighed the benefits of the proposed program became necessary. This problem, widely discussed during the 1966 budget process, was perceived as the loss of a "brake" on expenditures, and a corresponding need to find a new brake was felt.

Two rationales were chosen by the MOF. The first was the difficulty of marketing government bonds, because the required institutions were undeveloped and unprepared. Resistance from banks and brokers, and from businesses also seeking funds once recovery began, were cited as related factors. The second argument was that under Article 4 of the Finance Law, bonds or direct borrowing could cover only that portion of the General Account devoted to public works, investment, and governmental loans.[37] The second point established a ceiling on bond financing; the first provided an argument for keeping the amount as low as possible within that ceiling.

Having decided on this course, the Ministry of Finance faced a communications problem. The rationale for its broad change in policy had to be demonstrated; the agreement of banks, other financial institutions,

36. Helpful brief accounts of the fiscal policy of the period include Fujita Sei, "Antei Seichō to Zaisei" ("Stable Growth and Public Finance") in *Zaiseigaku* (2): *Nihon no Zaisei* ("Public Finance (2): Public Finance of Japan"), ed. Okuma Ichirō et al. (Tokyo: Yūhikaku, 1970), pp. 278-285; and Endō Shōkichi, "Fuisukaru Porishii to Yosan Seido" ("Fiscal Policy and the Budget System"), *Ekonomisuto* 43, 55 (December 28, 1965), 39-43.

37. See Sugimura Shōsaburō, *Zaiseihō* ("Finance Law") (Tokyo: Yūhikaku, 1959), pp. 42-47.

and business firms whose cooperation would be necessary to make the new
program work had to be secured; all budget participants had to be
impressed with the importance of the two "brakes." More immediately,
LDP pressure for an extremely large bond issue needed countering.
Available for these purposes were the MOF's various public advisory
bodies, particularly the Fiscal Systems Council (*Zaisei Seido Shingikai*).
This Council, appointed by the finance minister and representing various
private interests, had been greatly expanded in the spring of 1965, and
with the MOF's internal movement of opinion toward deficit financing, a
new chairman (Kobayashi Ataru) who favored this policy was appointed in
the summer. In fact, Kobayashi and many other Zaishin members actually
favored a more expansionist bond policy than the MOF's plan, but their
disagreement proved not to be a major problem for the officials. A council
member commented afterward:

From beginning to end, we met at Budget Bureau Director Tanimura's 'pace.'
From the point of view of one like myself, who favored a full ¥ 1 trillion bond
issue, the bureaucrats seemed set on establishing the 'brakes' of construction
bonds [*kensetsu kokusai*, the Article 4 point] and marketing problems. These
bureaucrats really have a knack of getting the other guy to agree to what they
want. We cannot disagree on details face-to-face; in response to the arguments of
the officials, the members can talk only from their own experience. The problems
of fiscal systems are too much for an amateur to handle.[38]

Similarly, when the Monetary System Investigative Council (*Kinyū Seido
Chōsakai*) seemed to take a more obstructionist position, reflecting the
doubts of the banks, Yamagiwa Masamichi was appointed chairman — an
MOF official was quoted as saying afterward, "Yamagiwa is our 'great
senior [*daisenpai*; i.e., an eminent former MOF official] and has been
Governor of the Bank of Japan. He got those opinions together in short
order for us." [39] The favorable reports from these and other Councils were
helpful to the MOF in overcoming objections to the new policy line. Of
course, as pointed out in chapter 4, the two new "brakes" were not as useful
in setting budget totals as the balanced budget principle had been.

Except for the question of bonds, the budget process as such for 1966
was not very eventful. Finance Minister Fukuda consulted extensively with
LDP officials before the MOF draft, making a key compromise for a larger
bond issue and tax cut than earlier expected, and then handled the appeals
negotiations skillfully; he managed to prevent the establishment of any new
organizations for the first time in years.[40] The budget was large, up 17.9

38. Quoted in Kuno Mantarō, "Kōsai Hakkō to Yottsu no Shingikai" ("The Issuance of
Bonds and the Four Councils"), *Ekonomisuto* 43, 53 (December 14, 1965), 48-50.
39. *Ibid.*
40. See a reporters' round-table discussion, "Yosan Hensei no Uraomote" ("Behind the
Scenes of Budget Compilation"), *Fainansu* 1, 3 (February 1966), 63-68.

percent from the 1965 initial budget (the highest growth since 1962), but unlike the 1961 case, the temptations of an expensionist policy did not bring an explosion of political demands.

## Adjustment

The most notable event of the budget process for the following year was a nonevent. For at least a decade the primary object of the Finance Ministry's macrobudgeting strategies had been to prevent deficit financing, and MOF officials had acceded to the issuance of bonds for 1965 and 1966 reluctantly and only because Japan was faced with a true financial crisis. By the time the 1967 budget was being compiled, the emergency was clearly past—nominal GNP growth in fiscal 1966 amounted to 17.2 percent—and in fact economists were again most concerned about the balance of payments and overheating. Nonetheless, no suggestion was advanced that the budget be balanced once again (let alone made to run a compensatory surplus). Deficit financing was a *fait accompli*: all apparently agreed that bond sales were now a normal and accepted portion of the revenue mix, and indeed would continue to be so indefinitely. The question thus became not whether bonds would be issued, but simply how much.

Debate even on this problem was quieted early in the 1967 budget process when the Finance Ministry announced a long-term principle designed to satisfy both expansionists and fiscal conservatives. Because "social capital" in Japan is underdeveloped and tax revenues cannot be expected to meet the need, it said, deficit financing must be continued and indeed must be expanded in absolute terms, at least for the following year. On the other hand, bonds tend to be stimulatory and relying on them too much is unhealthy, so the "bond dependence ratio," the proportion of the General Account covered by deficit financing, will be reduced each year. The ratio for 1966 had been 16.9 percent, but ths should be reduced to around the 14 percent level in five years and about 10 percent by 1976.[41]

The LDP was again unusually cooperative in 1967, even though an election was called in the midst of the process. Its Basic Policy read like an MOF document: it emphasized the danger of overheating, called for administrative economies, and set ceilings for the size of the total budget and the bond issue. Important factors here may have been that the MOF allowed the budget to grow at a respectable rate (14.8 percent over the 1966 initial budget) despite the perceived need to slow the economy down, and that Fukuda Takeo had moved from the Finance Ministry to be secretary-general of the party. However, cooperation at the higher levels

41. Finance Minister Fukuda Takeo at a press conference, AS, October 27, 1966. His prediction turned out to be grossly inaccurate, in that the ratio soon dropped well below the expected level but later rose again: see Table 16, Column I.

did not prevent the development of rank-and-file pressures which brought substantial transfers and five newly approved governmental organizations in the revival negotiations.

## Trends

Two developments in this period presaged the dramatic events of 1968. First, the Finance Ministry had become increasingly concerned about the problem of "fiscal rigidification," the increasing share of government spending used up by fixed expenditures. In the 1967 budget process it began some hesitating moves to combat the problem. In the summer, all ministries were asked to submit "budget cut requests" (*gengaku yōkyū*) along with their ordinary requests for funds. These specified reductions in current programs, and the MOF threatened to deduct arbitrary amounts from the requests if the ministry suggestions were unsatisfactory. While the "budget cut requests" proved to total only about ¥ 41 billion, they may have demonstrated the seriousness of the Finance Ministry's concern over fixed expenses.[42] More directly, there was another attempt to reduce the enormous rice subsidy, which by 1966 had risen to about ¥ 213 billion (about $700 million) or 4.8 percent of the entire General Account. The MOF's strategy was to specify a hike in the consumer price for rice in the budget draft, large enough (at 14.4 percent) to cover most of the anticipated additional deficit. This reform was carried over the protests of many within the LDP, even though one election was approaching (for the Upper House), and in the Lower House election just completed it had been promised that the consumer rice price would not be raised "for the time being."[43] Again, the attack on the rice subsidy was probably significant more as a symbol, that the MOF was willing to take on even the LDP to attack rigidity, than for its substantive effect.

The second development was the increased willingness of the Finance Ministry to use publicity as a weapon in its skirmishes with ministries, interest groups and the party. When the amount and nature of the first bond issue was being hotly discussed in 1965, the MOF skillfully manipulated the reports of the four deliberation councils under its control to gain support for its point of view among the general public and, more importantly, within the governmental, financial and business elite. The

42. AS, March 31 and September 6, evening, 1966. Note that the earliest expression of this concern I encountered was in an analysis by Ōuchi Tsutomu, the Tokyo University economist, of the 1960 budget. MNS, January 14, 1960.

43. AS, January 31 and February 12, 19, 20 and 27, 1967. As it happened, the consumer's price was raised by nearly 15 percent later in fiscal year 1967, but the government's purchase price was also raised by over 9 percent, which along with a large increase in the rice surplus (which must be stored) meant a supplement of ¥ 118 billion had to be added at the end of the year. The share of the total General Account thus remained about the same as in 1966.

simultaneous intensive economy drive against grants-in-aid and administrative expenses, which as pointed out in chapter 4 had much more symbolic than real intent, was another example of the calculated use of public relations. Finally, not coincidentally, it was in December 1965 that the first issue of the semi-official Ministry of Finance monthly organ *Fainansu* appeared, in a glossy format and filled with declarations of MOF opinions on budgetary and other matters. The ministry was paying more attention than it ever had before to the need for "mood-building" (*muudozukuri*), creating a positive climate of public opinion for its policies. The traditional approach of the Ministry of Finance had been well expressed by Morinaga Teiichirō, vice-minister in 1957-59. "The MOF should in no case take the initiative and publicize its new policies," he said, "our job is to receive requests passively."[44] The reversal of these strictures against initiative and publicity began in 1965-67 and culminated in 1968.

# The "Break Fiscal Rigidification Movement" and Its Aftermath (1968-72)

The words "break fiscal rigidification movement" (*zaisei kōchokuka dakai undō*) were to be seen on front pages of Japanese newspapers throughout the fall of 1968. They represented a systematic and sustained attempt by the Ministry of Finance to regain its control over budgeting. While the attempt ultimately failed, it is worth exploring in some detail as far and away the extreme example during our period of MOF sustained activism.

*The Problem.*—Murakami Kotarō, then serving as Budget Bureau director, spearheaded the movement. In a published interview, he explained the MOF's dilemma as follows:

I think I would like to start by setting forth what I mean by fiscal rigidification. As the words imply, the various items which make up the budget gradually come to lose the quality of expansion and contraction, and flexibility declines. Further, the inherent pressures for an item to expand are strong, and we can now see that we are getting into a situation where this cannot be controlled. . . . Then another thing—when one looks ahead at the course of the Japanese economy, there is a probability that with increasing rigidification, we will have to face a crisis in the near future. I think we are now gradually coming to the point where it becomes clear that we cannot return to the high growth era of the 30s [i.e., the Shōwa 30s, the decade beginning in 1955], and that it is extremely dangerous to expect that possibility. In this way, our growth rate is becoming blunted. The growth of revenues for public use has to decline, but what will happen to the

44. Quoted by Suzuki Yukio, "Ōkura Kanryō no Shisō" ("The Thought of MOF Bureaucrats"), *Chūō Kōron* 81, 2 (February 1966), 106-123.

demand-pressure for expenditures? Won't it continue, on the opposite course? So far as I can see, this inertia which was built up in the old high-growth period is getting stronger every year. So on the one hand, fiscal demand-pressure is on an upward trend, and on the other, economic growth—which provides the revenue—will be blunted. We will have to face the problem of bringing these two trends together. It is then that the problem even of bankruptcy may become a reality. [45]

As Murakami implies, the "inertia" of fiscal rigidification is the direct product of high-growth budgeting. In the 1960s expectations of high growth became institutionalized in budgetary decision making. Each year many new programs were authorized, usually at low initial levels, in the expectation that future resources would be sufficient for them to grow. Five-year expenditure plans covered a wider and wider range of government activities; while not binding on the Finance Ministry, these plans could not be altogether ignored, and their expenditure projections presupposed continued prosperity. Government employees and those receiving benefits from the Treasury grew accustomed to large annual increases in their incomes, eventually coming to see them as a matter of right. Interest groups and their allies within the LDP became sensitive to any suggestions that their particular policy sectors might be viewed less favorably than any other, and stood ready to defend against declines in their shares. However rapidly revenues increased, then, a larger and larger proportion of the annual increment came to be "frozen," used up by expenditures which to greater or lesser degree were obligatory.

This pattern led the Finance Ministry into a vicious circle. High budget growth encouraged expectations among ministries, clienteles and politicians that major expansions and new programs would be possible, even though rigidification might have sharply reduced the amount of truly discretionary funds available. Worse still, such expectations continued even into low revenue years. Since Ministry of Finance officials share with their counterparts around the world a tendency to worry more about immediate problems than long-range considerations, they were tempted to adopt dubious fiscal devices: for example, the MOF often would grant new programs with no accompanying General Account funds, by providing loan financing through the FILP or earmarked funds through a Special

45. Murakami Kōtarō, "Zaisei no Atarashii Hōkō" ("The New Direction of Public Finance"), *Kōken* (November 1967), quoted in an analysis by Amano Hajime, "Ōkurashō Kanryō" ("Ministry of Finance Bureaucrats"), *Chūō Kōron* 84, 10 (October 1969), 244. Good discussions of the movement may also be found in Suzuki, *Keizai Kanryō,* pp. 181-191; Ōkurashō Hyakunenshi II, pp. 310-16 and 322-23; and Nihon Keizai Shinbunsha, ed., *Yosan wa Dare no Mono ka* ("The Budget: Whose is it?") (Tokyo: Nihon Keizai Shinbunsha, 1971), pp. 61-67. For an interesting semi-official MOF view, see the memorandum of the Fiscal Systems Council, "Zaisei no Kōchokuka Keikō ni tsuite" ("Concerning the Fiscal Rigidification Trend in Public Finance"), reprinted in *Fainansu* 3, 7 (October 1967), 71-73.

Account; or it might give only "research" costs, which inevitably would lead to a report calling for more money within a year or two; or a new agency or government-affiliated corporation might be approved.[46] Or expenditure hikes might be carefully scheduled: in 1965, a rise in pensions was timed to start so that it would cost only ¥5.3 billion in the first year, but fully ¥41 billion in the next. Rigidification, then, may be seen as an unintended consequence of adaption to the environment of high economic growth — adaption by the Ministry of Finance no less than by the LDP and other budget participants.

*Motives.* — These rigidity factors had been apparent for some time, and indeed the Finance Ministry had frequently pointed them out. Whey did they receive such concentrated attention in the 1968 process? The first reason is the gloomy vision of Japan's growth potential generally held at the time. Second, for reasons that are not entirely clear, the "natural expenditure increase," the rise in fixed expenses from one year to the next, increased markedly in the 1968 budget. Only about ¥150 billion was held to be available for "new" expenditures in 1968, down from ¥266 billion in 1967 and ¥416 billion in 1966; the 1968 natural increase alone would force budget growth of 13.7 percent. The major elements of the increase were the local allocation (¥240 billion); salary raises already determined (¥110 billion); social welfare items, particularly pensions and medical expenses (¥100 billion); and bond redemption expenses (¥100 billion).[47]

A third possible reason for the MOF's unusual campaign in 1968 is the unusual personalities of its top officials at the time: Tanimura Hiroshi, the vice-minister, and particularly Budget Bureau Chief Murakami Kōtarō. Murakami had been the best-known budget examiner of the postwar period, and the subject of many anecdotes illustrating his cleverness and stubborn behavior that were frequently retold within the Budget Bureau. Where the MOF in past battles had tended to act defensively and passively, Murakami was perhaps predisposed to go on the offensive.

The campaign first reached the public eye on September 14, 1967, when Murakami and Tanimura personally called on the prime minister — permission from the finance minister had been obtained, but such a visit at the initiative of a permanent official was by no means standard operating procedure. They explained the problems of rigidity to Satō and asked his assistance. This step was both preceded and followed by a great many informal meetings with LDP figures and by talks with newspapermen

46. Among the sixteen new organizations created in the lean budget year of 1965 was the New Airport Construction Company, given an allocation of just one-half billion yen though it was realized that construction costs would eventually come to over ¥200 billion. NKS, December 28, 1964.

47. See Table 4, above, and AS, September 15 and 27, 1967.

which produced detailed accounts of the Finance position in print, accompanied by a raft of editorials pointing up the fiscal crisis.[48] Interviews with MOF officials and discussions by scholars appeared in magazines throughout the fall. The Fiscal Systems Council discussed the problem thoroughly and its report was given wide circulation. In all, this was a public relations campaign conducted with great skill, far exceeding in scope the MOF's effort two years before when it had successfully put forward a new point of view on deficit financing.

*Objectives.* — The movement may be seen as having two major goals: in the long term, solving the problems of fiscal rigidification by reducing the proportion of fixed expenses in the budget; and for the 1968 budget itself, holding spending pressures down sufficiently to assure the "restraining model" (*yokusei-gata*) budget seen as economically necessary by the MOF. It was marked by two innovations in the budget process itself: "comprehensive budgeting," the elimination of Supplementary Budgets by including all expenditures in the initial budget; and a change from "hidden resources" to "open resources" in the appeals negotiations. These have already been discussed in chapters 7 and 8. The following additional policies aimed specifically at various aspects of the budget were proposed at the same time, associated with the MOF's antirigidification campaign or with the somewhat parallel "Miyazawa plan" of Miyazawa Kiichi, then director-general of the Economic Planning Agency, which emphasized the problem of inflation (always stressed by the EPA) as well as controlling public expenditures. Most of these share long-term and short-term implications in varying proportions.[49]

1. Total size — since no supplement will be passed, the relevant budgetary growth rate figure for 1968 is growth over the postsupplement 1967 budget. This figure should be below projected GNP growth, and the budget can then be called "restrictive."
2. Bonds — both the absolute amount and the dependence ratio of the bond issue should be reduced, in 1968 and afterward.
3. Taxes — there should be no effective tax cut in 1968 (i.e., any reductions should be compensated by hikes elsewhere), and Japan's comparatively low ratio of taxes to National Income should be reevaluated.
4. Rice — no supplement later in the year is allowed, but only the current deficit will be budgeted. Either the producer's price will not be raised (Miyazawa), or the consumer's price will "slide," enough to cover the new deficit (MOF).

48. Eg., all in September, 1967: MNS, the 11th; TS, 18th; SS, 21st; AS, 22nd; NKS, 27th; and YS, 29th.

49. As well as the sources cited above, see AS, September 27, November 11 and December 30, 1967, and January 6, 1968; NKS, September 27, October 14 and 15, and December 30, 1967, and January 18, 1968.

5. Local finance—the local allocation rate (then at 32 percent of tax revenues) should be reduced; if this is impossible, funds should be "borrowed" from the allocation for national purposes, and the balance of functions between the two levels reexamined.

6. Personnel expenses—salary raises for public employees will be specified in the initial budget, and will be only enough to cover the forecast rise in the cost of living.

7. "Livelihood support" (welfare)—limited to the increase in public employees' wages.

8. Unemployment compensation—cut back to eliminate payments to seasonal workers.

9. Public works—growth should be restricted to the forecast growth rate of GNP.

10. Medical insurance, railroad fares, university tution, etc.—the principle will be established that the user of services will bear more of its costs, rather than the taxpayer (opposed by Miyazawa).

11. Administrative expenses—not only will proposals for new agencies and governmental corporations not be approved, but the size of the governmental apparatus will be reduced. (The prime minister initially suggested lopping off one bureau from each ministry, but after resistance the policy became one of eliminating 5 percent of government employees each year for three years.)

*Reactions.*—Many participants not only complained about the reforms which impinged directly on their interests, but resented the new, activist role assumed by the Ministry of Finance. Sahashi Shigeru, who had resigned the previous year as vice-minister of MITI and had as strong a personality as Murakami, dismissed the entire rigidity concept: "That's simply a Budget Bureau 'campaign.' They really do it skillfully, using the newspapers and business magazines—MITI can't hold a candle to them."[50] Many in the LDP agreed, with remarks about the BB's "tactics," and objections to the MOF "monopolizing" the budget process with its own ideas. However, no concerted opposition could be mounted. For one thing, Prime Minister Satō, who was backing the campaign, held even more than his usual degree of control over both the party and Cabinet that year, and the factional scene was quiet. Second, Fukuda Takeo and Ōhira Masayoshi, MOF "old boys" and strong supporters of the movement were in the key party posts (secretary-general and PARC chairman). Their aid was considerable, as was recognized in the classic budgeting joke that "this year, Fukuda was the finance minister, Ōhira the vice-minister, and Mizuta just the parliamentary vice-minister."[51] The MOF also showed considerable skill in sweetening the final budget with small concessions.[52]

50. Interview, *Asahi Jaanaru,* 108-110. Also see AS, September 15 and December 25, 1967.

51. AS, January 13, 1968.

52. Fukuda called the result a "Chinese dinner" budget—not many ingredients but lots of taste. NKS, January 18, 1968, evening.

However, beyond these political factors, the key to the lack of effective resistance was probably that most among LDP and other participants were simply convinced by the MOF's arguments. They agreed that the economic situation was difficult in both the short and long run, and that fixed expenditures were rising too quickly and threatened the structure of public finance.

*Assessment.* —How successful was the Finance Ministry's campaign? From an immediate perspective, several achievements can be noted. The principle of avoiding Supplementary Budgets seemed to be established, with provision for salary raises and the handling of rice prices included in the initial budget. Although budget growth was fairly high by contemporary standards, 17.5 percent over the 1967 initial budget, on the MOF's new standard it was only 11.8 percent over the 1967 post-Supplementary Budget, a figure below anticipated GNP growth and probably as low as possible given high fixed expenditure growth. There was no net tax cut for the first time since 1960, and the bond issue was reduced to a projected ¥640 billion from ¥800 billion in 1967 (a drop in the "dependence ratio" from 16.2 to 10.1 percent). Although the local allocation rate was not reduced, ¥45 billion was "borrowed" back from this account. Public works growth was held to the lowest figure since 1958 (and relative to the total growth of the budget, the lowest figure until 1974). Some progress was made in increasing the beneficiary's proportion of the costs of services. Administrative cutbacks were ordered. With these accomplishments on the record, it was generally agreed at the time that the MOF had managed its most successful year since the era of the "one trillion yen budget."[53]

Somewhat later, however, the achievement appeared dimmer. The 1968 pay raise for government employees was covered by the sum initially budgeted, and after the government's purchase price for rice was hiked by 5.9 percent in August, the selling price was raised 8.9 percent in October, enough to cover the newly created deficit. However, the weather was unfortunately good, the harvest large, and the amount of rice purchased by the government and unsold ran well ahead of expectations—the amount of old rice in storage rose almost five times in 1968.[54] The required additional funds plus a larger than anticipated deficit in the medical insurance system forced a Supplementary Budget late in the fiscal year. Even though it was much smaller than usual (just 1.7 percent of the initial budget, compared with an average of 5.5 percent from 1960 to 1967), the principle of comprehensive budgeting had been broken before ever being established, and the MOF had lost credibility.

53. See stories in all newspapers, January 13-18, 1968.
54. Japan, Ministry of Agriculture and Forestry, "White Paper on Agriculture," in *White Papers of Japan*, 1969-70, pp. 255-59.

Moreover, from a still longer range perspective, it is clear that the impact of the "break fiscal rigidification movement" was almost entirely limited to 1968. The budget was kept small, even below GNP real growth — since the MOF viewed fiscal restraint as particularly important in 1968, the significance of this success in terms of its policy goals should not be understated, but it is no more than a matter of one year's fiscal policy. At the start of the campaign, MOF spokesmen had talked rather grandly of systemic changes to soften rigidity, but there was little in the program as implemented that offered much hope for lasting effect. Typical is the treatment of the local finance problem. The proportion of the three major taxes (income, corporation, and liquor) that went automatically into the local government allocation had risen steadily over the years, and in the late 1960s it seemed that local and prefectural finances were in more comfortable shape than those of the national government. However, the MOF's attempt to cut the local share permanently from 32 to 30 percent failed, and instead it borrowed ¥45 billion with repayment promised.[55] Thus the problems of 1968 were alleviated, but no enforceable precedent for the future was set; certainly there was no fundamental reevaluation of the balance of administrative functions between the two levels. Similar observations could be made about the rice price system, medical insurance, public works and other budget problems.

The causes of the longer-term failure are not hard to find. "Fiscal rigidity" is not primarily a budget problem, it is a problem of the Japanese governmental system (or, arguably, the entire political or even social system). As a Finance Ministry official put it in 1969, it stems from "the deep-rooted rigidity of customs, and these customs are none other than the rigid thought patterns held by the men who make up and operate the system."[56] As well as such psychological or "cultural" aspects of rigidity, the basic power relationships which govern all political processes, including budgeting, cannot be ignored, and indeed cannot be overcome by administrative devices alone.

The Ministry of Finance was aware of these problems at the outset, and knew that a single year's campaign would not assure its long-term objectives. The budget for 1968 was seen as the start of an effort to last several years. Ironically, the success of Japanese economic policy, of which fiscal policy is a part, helped to undermine the MOF's own interests by maintaining growth at similar levels to the 1955-64 period (average real growth per year for fiscal years 1955-1964 was 10.0 percent; for 1965-1972, 10.4 percent). The crisis foreseen by Murakami was the intersection of

55. This was about 4 percent of the allocation. Similar borrowings occurred in 1969-1970. See the discussion in MNS, February 13, 1970.

56. Matoba Junzō, "Zaisei Kōchokuka Dakai Daini Nenme no Kadai" ("Topics in the Second Year of Breaking Fiscal Rigidification"), *Fainansu* 4, 11 (February 1969), 2-6.

rising fixed expenditures and slowing growth of revenues; the force of his argument was lost when revenues continued strong, and a surplus that could cover both fixed and new expenditures became available at least for the moment. Indeed, it was the strong economic recovery of 1968 itself which made a Supplementary Budget possible and immediately undermined the credibility of the antirigidification movement.

## *Adjustment*

Not only did the movement fail; seen in retrospect, from the Ministry of Finance point of view it probably can be called counterproductive. Earlier lower-key trends which seemed to point toward increasing MOF control over fixed expenditures were swept away in the reaction to the movement, and the influence of the majority party reached new heights.

When the 1969 budget process began in the summer of 1968, the reformist enthusiasm of the Finance officials was still high; they hoped that a tax cut could again be avoided, the producer's rice price could actually be reduced, the local allocation tax rate permanently lowered, and a Supplementary Budget prevented. The Fiscal Systems Council again looked into rigidification and possible solutions and produced two long reports.[57] Later in the fall, however, it had become obvious that a supplement to the 1968 budget would have to be passed and moreover that the LDP was not as disposed to fall in with the MOF's plans.

In part, problems with the party arose because the political situation had changed. A general election was expected soon. Intraparty struggles had been at a minimum in 1968, but a contested LDP presidential election occurred in the middle of the 1969 process; and the Maeo faction, including Ōhira Masayoshi, had moved into the active antimainstream, attacking the administration's fiscal policy and calling for a larger budget.[58] Even after the election, Finance Minister Fukuda and Secretary-General Tanaka were already contenders for the post-Satō premiership, and a certain rivalry over who could do more favors for party members developed. As another complication, while in 1968 the party "big three" had been dominated by Fukuda and Ōhira (both then acting as cooperative MOF alumni), all three officers in 1969 were "party men" (i.e., not "ex-bureaucrats) with expansionary tendencies. Finally, the MOF's tough attitude and active proselytizing in 1968 had irritated many politicians; particularly when the dire revenue predictions failed to materialize, they entered the 1969 competition with renewed vigor. Whatever the influence of these various factors might have been, party spokesmen took out after

57. See *Fainansu* 4, 9-11 (December 1968; January and February 1969), including the article by Matoba cited above.
58. NKS, October 13, 1968. Again as during the 1961 budget process, factional considerations outweighed the natural sympathies of ex-MOF officials.

the MOF soon after the LDP presidential election: Nemoto Ryūtarō, the new PARC chairman, proclaimed that, in contrast to the earlier pattern of LDP intervention only at the last stage, this year the leadership would get together with the finance minister and the ministers responsible for major problems and work things out before the MOF draft.[59] Discussions of this sort did take place and in fact most party desires were accommodated in the MOF draft. As a result, the revival negotiations passed rather peacefully; but the budget was also relatively large at 15.8 percent above the 1968 initial budget (the "comprehensive budgeting" formula of comparing with the previous year's post-Supplementary Budget had been tacitly abandoned), considering that the "break fiscal rigification movement" had succeeded in holding down the natural expenditure increase, if only for one year. Analysts agreed afterward that this had indeed been a "party leadership" budget, and a disappointing one from the point of view of MOF officials.

A similar pattern persisted in the 1970 and 1971 budget processes. The budget growth rate was high and growing: 17.9 percent in 1970 and 18.4 percent in 1971, the result of increasing inflation, the inexorable rise of the natural expenditure increase, and continued passivity in the face of demands from the party. With Prime Minister Satō's announcement that his fourth term as LDP president would be his last, political attention in both years was focused on the rivals for his succession, Fukuda and Tanaka, serving in the crucial posts of finance minister and LDP secretary-general. Since it was a common assumption that LDP Dietmen (the main electors of the party president) are swayed above all else by budget money for their favorite projects, the two politicians competed to see who could take most credit for providing such grants—or at least, so ran the explanation for large budgets offered by observing newspapermen.[60] In both 1970 and 1971, the finance minister consulted extensively with other ministries and the party before the MOF draft was released; with major problems worked out in advance, the revival negotiations tended to be quite smooth.

For the 1972 budget, economic conditions were deteriorating—real GNP growth for fiscal 1971 was just 6.6 percent, the lowest since 1965—but the economic picture was complicated by the second "Nixon shock," the August 1971 devaluation of the dollar. Japanese economists and officials were uncertain about the effects of this event, which had been followed by revaluation of the yen, on Japan's international and domestic economic prospects. Compilation of the budget for 1972 therefore began in a cloud of economic ambiguity, a cloud soon agitated by the political turbulence of the closing days of Satō's long tenure as prime minister.

59. NKS, December 9, 1968, evening.
60. E.g., NKS, January 30, 1970.

Under such conditions, a large budget may have been inevitable—from the very beginning of the process the new Finance Minister, Mizuta Mikio, was talking of an "economic stimulation" (*keiki shigeki-gata*) budget—but two points indicate that the Finance Ministry had been induced by a new variation in an old threat to set the budget total at a figure much higher than its true preference. First, although it is normal for the MOF to start with a low estimate of the budget in the fall and then increase it gradually to accommodate pressures, for 1972 the slope of this curve was unprecedentedly steep: from ¥11.10 trillion as late as November 30; going up to ¥11.15, ¥11.2, ¥11.3 and then ¥11.4 through December; ending up with the announcement of ¥11.47 trillion on New Year's Eve. In terms of growth over the 1971 budget, this shift was from 18.1 percent to 21.8 percent.[61] Second, the year-to-year growth in public works expenditures was the highest to date of the postwar period, 29.0 percent.

The threat that produced this rapid movement was the Finance Ministry's old nightmare, deficit spending, in a new guise. In 1965, the taboo against financing the General Account by selling bonds had been broken, but then and ever since deficit financing had been held in check by the "brake" of Article 4 of the Finance Law: bonds could cover only the investment portion of government spending. For 1972, the projected amount of this investment portion was too small to permit a bond issue big enough to bring the budget up to the size demanded by business and LDP leaders calling for pump-priming. Accordingly, pressure for repeal of this article became intense, particularly from party faction leaders (Ōhira, Miki, Nakasone) maneuvering for advantage in the coming LDP presidential election.[62] MOF officials naturally were dismayed by the prospect of losing this last institutional check on the LDP's free-spending tendencies, and responded, as they had in the past, with short-run concessions to protect their position in the longer run. That is, by revising their early growth rate forecasts and therefore revenue expectations upward, and by expanding the public works budget enough to allow a bond issue of ¥1.95 trillion under the Article 4 formula, it became possible to construct a budget large enough to satisfy the LDP and still avoid a revision of the Finance Law.[63]

## Trends

The 1968-1972 period saw the Finance Ministry taking a more active stance toward its steadily growing financial and political difficulties than it

61. See the analysis in NKS, January 5, 1972, evening.
62. Many asked for a ¥2.5 trillion bond issue, while the MOF early on saw ¥1.5 trillion as the limit which could be accommodated within Article 4 restrictions. See AS, October 9, evening, November 28 and 30; NKS December 13, evening, 17 and 19, 1971.
63. AS, December 14, 1971. For the MOF's fears of losing a "brake", see Yamamoto Masao, *Keizai Kanryō no Jittai* ("The Reality of the Economic Bureaucrats") (Tokyo: Mainichi Shinbunsha, 1972), pp. 238-39.

had thought proper or possible in earlier years. After the failure of its frontal attack, the break fiscal rigidification movement, it tried to impose the virtues of scientific rationality by importing program budgeting techniques. As noted in chapter 4, PPBS stimulated considerable discussion but had remarkably little effect on actual budgeting. As the 1970s began, Finance officials drew on traditional tenets of fiscal conservatism to attack their most intractable spending problems — the "three k's" of rice, health insurance and railroads — via "structural reform" and the "benefit principle." Befitting the more modest size of these efforts, their failure was less spectacular.

Why should the MOF been so frustrated in reaching even modest goals? While some of the reasons may have been specific to this period, two basic factors of a sort which had been significant since the 1950s seem to explain many of the MOF's difficulties. First, the impending departure of Prime Minister Sato meant on the one hand that factional politics were turbulent, which always increases political demands upon the budget, and on the other that the personal effectiveness of the prime minister in controlling party pressures was seriously diminished. The fact that Finance Ministers Fukuda and Mizuta were themselves drawn into the intraparty maelstrom left MOF officials even more exposed. Second, the economy failed to cooperate. The growth rate was high, from 16 to 18 percent in nominal terms for each fiscal year from 1968 to 1972 except in 1971, which saw a "recession" (nominal growth was 11.2 percent, real growth 6.6 percent). That is, in most years government revenues grew so quickly that Finance officials were not able to argue convincingly that spending would have to be cut back to avoid a financial crisis, while in the single exceptional year the falloff in business conditions was sharp enough to bring irresistible demands for pump-priming. For the most part, 1968-1972 (or actually to 1973, though for somewhat different reasons) was the period when the Ministry of Finance was most dominated by the Liberal Democratic Party and the inexorable growth of government spending. The comment of an anonymous MOF official about the 1970 budget appropriately summarizes this entire period: "Rather than looking forward to the 1970s, this budget is stained with the grime of the 60s, and reveals a fiscal system which has not been able to move."[64]

# Tanaka and Fukuda (1973-74)

The last two budget years to be examined contrast admirably with each other, and throw several of the themes of this chapter into sharp relief. An expansionary budget strongly influenced by the most activist prime

64. AS, February 1, 1970.

minister in years was followed by a restrictive budget sternly dominated by
the Ministry of Finance — or perhaps by the finance minister himself.

Even before his election as LDP president, and hence prime minister,
in July 1972, Tanaka Kakuei had called for an enormous 1973 budget:
¥ 15 trillion, 31 percent larger than 1972. Though the demand was partly
a tactical ploy, Tanaka's enthusiasm was genuine and may be ascribed to
three factors. First, the Japanese economy appeared not yet recovered from
its slump, and a large balance of payments surplus was drawing
international pressure for another revaluation of the yen.[65] Second, for
some twenty years Tanaka had consistently been a spokesman for high
government spending in general and public works programs in particular.
Third, this was a new administration, with an image of dynamism and a
sense of mission — Tanaka said he would "respond to the dreams of the era"
and change the shape of Japanese society.[66] His widely publicized "Plan for
Remodeling the Japanese Archipelago" was at once the most comprehensive, the most radical and the most detailed program authoritatively put
forward in Japan since Occupation days. Criticizing the earlier "passive
fiscal approach," Tanaka wrote in the first pages of his book that
"remodeling is to serve as the forerunner of the future, and naturally
requires colossal capital outlays for such projects as improving the entire
transportation network . . . an enormous amount of money will be
required for remodeling."[67] Much of it would have to come from the
budget.

Tanaka chose as his finance minister a ranking member of his own
faction, Ueki Kōshirō, who although an ex-MOF bureaucrat — he had been
a Budget Bureau director during the war — was known primarily as a
stalwart of the LDP Policy Affairs Research Council. Ueki's first official act
was to announce that the MOF would relax a long-standing restrictive
budgeting rule: the limitation on the amount ministries could request was
raised from 25 to 30 percent above the previous year's budget, to allow
room for items connected with the Cabinet's new plans. Moreover,
ministries would be given an extra month to formulate new requests.
According to press reports, MOF officials thought that Tanaka's ¥ 15
trillion budget would be impossible — the prime minister himself later
agreed — but conceded that budget growth would be very high, and that

65. Traditionally it has been held that recessions enlarge balance of payments surpluses
and high growth reduces them, although the record after 1965 in Japan does not support the
latter proposition (probably because the yen was undervalued). For a review of the economics
literature on this relationship, see Lawrence B. Krause and Sueo Sekiguchi, "Japan and the
World Economy," in *Asia's New Giant: How the Japanese Economy Works,* eds. Hugh
Patrick and Henry Rosovsky (Washington, D.C.: The Brookings Institution, 1976), pp.
404-407.

66. NKS, July 10, 1972. Tanaka's budgeting style is examined in chap. 6.

67. Kakuei Tanaka, *Building a New Japan: A Plan for Restructuring the Japanese
Archipelago,* trans. of *Nippon Rettō Kaizō-ron* (Tokyo: Simul Press, 1973), pp. 6-7.

the government share of national income would have to rise in order for Japan to overcome its backwardness in social capital and social welfare.[68]

The Finance Ministry bureaucracy seemed entirely on the defensive for 1973, trying to salvage what it could in a decidedly unfavorable policy climate. The first major skirmish came over the 1972 Supplementary Budget. In August the MOF said ¥180 billion would be an appropriate size for the supplement, and then in September raised its estimate to ¥300 billion (already quite large—the previous record supplement, in 1970, had been ¥263 billion). But Tanaka employed the same tactic as in demanding an outrageous ¥15 trillion for the 1973 main budget: he requested five times the MOF's figure, ¥1.5 trillion. After intense MOF-LDP meetings in October, the result was a compromise at ¥651 million. Although on paper this figure appears closer to the Finance Ministry's position, in reality everyone knew the finance bureaucrats had been completely vanquished—indeed, adding in the FILP supplement and other non-General Account expenditures, on a "project" (jigyō) base government spending did rise by about ¥1.5 trillion.

Throughout the course of the main budget process, Tanaka continued to make strongly expansionary pronouncements, and endorsed a great many specific programs of his own devising or proposed by the spending ministries (which saw his remodeling plan as the best chiyansu in years for major expansions of their programs). The Liberal Democrats too were naturally eager to press the advantage. From as early as August a series of party conferences were held to discuss the budget, and it was proclaimed that instead of allowing the Finance Ministry to squeeze LDP requests into its revenue framework, the party would first determine what should be done, and the MOF would then contrive a revenue plan to fit. Such brave dicta had been heard before, but in the climate of the early Tanaka administration they carried unusual weight, and the party continued quite active through the early fall until the attention of its members was distracted by preparations for a general election in December. Finance Minister Ueki found himself in a difficult position, and his statements were ambivalent: at times he played the normal role of voicing the permanent officials' objections to spending proposals, but at other times he actively supported Tanaka's plans. In September, testifying before the House of Councillors Budget Committee, he even said that he "preferred to avoid it, but if political conditions warrant it would be possible to issue deficit bonds"—the first time a Finance Minister had ever admitted that such a dire event might come to pass.[69]

---

68. At the same time, perhaps as the sort of psychological strategy described in chap. 4, they promised a strong attack on the "three K's," NKS, July 9, 25, and 25, evening, 1972.

69. The reference is to an amount above the Article 4 limitation. See NKS, September 20, 1972.

The response by MOF officials — at least as revealed in the press — was unprecedentedly passive. Other than some complaints about the difficulty of reviewing such large requests, and dour discussions of the revenue picture, they made few comments on budgeting issues. In previous years, from midsummer to December, Finance Ministry estimates of the size of the budget would periodically appear; these were more often leaks than official policy statements, and their size usually was determined more by tactical considerations than disinterested forecasting, but they did serve to counter larger party estimates and help structure the long macrobudgeting decision process. But for the 1973 budget, the MOF was quiet until December 18, when the ministry's preparations were virtually complete. Certainly an important factor inhibiting officials was that under such intense spending pressure, including a new threat of deficit finance, and with their usual allies either gone over to the other side (the prime minister) or undependable (the finance minister), they feared that enunciating any figure appreciably lower than the amounts being mentioned elsewhere would invite drastic retaliation. Though their worries about where the money would come from were obvious in newspaper accounts, even on this topic the officials appeared to be trying to avoid sounding too pessimistic.[70]

However, an alternative to this "strategic" explanation is also worth considering. In 1965, when bond financing was introduced, and more particularly earlier still in 1960, when Ikeda's Income Doubling Plan first came to the fore, not only had the Ministry of Finance bowed to economic necessity or political trends in relaxing old strictures, but had itself undergone something of an ideological transformation. Influential groups within the ministry had come to believe, in each case, that a larger role for government finance in the economy was not only inevitable but desirable. In 1961, this view amounted to seeing the budget as an instrument which should facilitate rather than hinder growth; in 1965, to favoring more active use of fiscal (rather than just monetary) policy in regulating economic conditions. In 1973 it was proposed that the government take the lead in reshaping the Japanese economy, emphasizing social over private investment and catching up with Western welfare systems. At a broad level of generality, such ideas had been around for some time, and in fact had constituted the official policy of the Satō government from its beginning as well as (in a somewhat different form) a campaign slogan for Fukuda Takeo. But until the advent of Tanaka, they had not directly and unequivocally been brought to bear on the budget.

The permanent officials of the Ministry of Finance had not actively opposed this positive conception of public finance on policy grounds — they knew that battles over abstractions are unproductive and dangerous — and of course budget growth had been increasing since 1968. However, most of

70. See for example NKS, September 19 and 26, October 8 and December 9, 1972.

this expansion may be accounted for, as argued above, by the rise in the natural expenditure increase and increasingly intrusive political factors. Most of the time, at least, the MOF apparently tried to hold budgets down and had given in only when necessary. Still, there had been hints of a new attitude: particularly during the process leading to the antirecession 1972 budget, two notions could be discerned in many discussions of budget problems by Finance officials.[71] One is "structural reform of public finance," which as noted usually referred to solutions of the "three k's" and other fiscal rigidity dilemmas, but which from time to time appeared in a more general and positive-sounding context—some in the ministry were said to view 1972 as the year of the first "world reformation" budget (the term used, *yonaoshi*, has quite an evocative ring). The other is "fiscal leadership" (*zaisei shudō*), a notion that public finance should take the leading role in the regulation of aggregate demand and then, again by extension, in allocating national resources between the public and private sectors.

These slogans, heard increasingly during the 1973 process, perhaps indicate that Finance officials were not unanimously or unambiguously opposed to Tanaka's positive budget ideas. It is difficult to know the extent to which this partial "conversion" was due to intellectual conviction, to a desire for renewed Finance influence and prestige (as the leader in "fiscal leadership"), or to individual calculations of loyalty and self-interest— Tanaka retained close ties with many officials from his days as finance minister, ties which he had been careful to maintain; moreover, since in 1972 he appeared to be settling into the premiership for a long stay, it could be anticipated that he would wield considerable influence over the career paths of ministry officials for some time to come. Under such circumstances, it would not be surprising to find MOF officials dividing into a "progressive" Tanaka faction and a group of more traditional Fukuda supporters, and in fact several interviews in 1974 did give some indication that such a split had occurred. In any event, Ministry of Finance policy positions throughout the 1973 process were much more positive than ever before: in November, it was reported that the ministry's three major budget objectives were (1) to change the direction of resource allocation from "manufacturing first" to "public welfare first"; (2) to balance the international accounts (through economic expansion)—both implying larger budgets—and then, last and clearly least, (3) to control inflation by not overstimulating the economy. Either the Finance bureaucrats had become believers, or they had just decided to relax and enjoy it.[72]

71. Most often in newspaper stories setting forth their views without direct attribution: see, e.g., NKS, December 9, 1971, and January 5, 1972, evening.

72. See NKS, November 11, 1972, and for an elaborate MOF justification of high spending even in an economic boom, NKS, November 7, 1972. Budgeting authorities elsewhere have been known to undergo a "philosophical change . . . the negative role of the

In November and early December, the Budget Bureau continued its technical budget review while LDP Dietmen campaigned for election, as always promising new public works projects and other budgetary benefits. Following the election a new Cabinet was appointed on December 22, and on the following day the new finance minister, Aichi Kiichi, reaffirmed the positive policy line. In an interview with the *Nihon Keizai Shinbun*, he mentioned a number of specific program expansions which would be included in the budget, and said that the current economic recovery would allow a big budget without strain (in the early fall, conversely, the sluggishness of the economy had been the pretext for expanding government spending.[73] Aichi met with the other Cabinet ministers and party leaders to work out budget problems, and — another radical departure from past practice — approved many specific program initiatives from the ministries for inclusion in the MOF draft. This innovation was openly recognized as a reversal of the MOF's well established rule of thumb called "zero review," that all new proposals should be rejected in the MOF draft and approved, if at all, only during revival negotiations.[74]

As expected, the budget turned out to be enormous: ¥14.28 trillion, up 24.6 percent from 1972. In assessing the various influences which inflated the total, the fact that public works expenditures grew by 32.2 percent might be attributed either to Tanaka's comprehensive restructuring plan or to traditional LDP pressures — Tanaka and the MOF said it was the first; more cynical journalists emphasized the second. However, it may also be noted that war-related pensions, which since 1964 had grown an average of only 12 percent annually, were pushed up by 26.8 percent. This program has always been regarded as one of the LDP's favorite special-interest payoffs, and its expansion in 1973 — it was increased in the revival negotiations even beyond its supporters' hopes — indicates rather clearly that the traditional sort of highly fragmented demands from the LDP organization and groups of Dietmen were a major factor which accounts for the budget's great size. Party influence had been growing for some

---

Bureau [of the Budget in the United States] has become less important, at least in relative terms . . . we're supposed to give pretty serious consideration to alternative and better ways of accomplishing an objective which the President or an agency head or a member of the majority party in Congress thinks is a desirable objective." Former budget examiner Phillip S. Hughes, quoted by Martha Derthick, *Uncontrollable Spending for Social Service Grants* (Washington, D.C.: The Brookings Institution, 1976), p. 85. Initiation of the Program Analysis and Review system in Great Britain may signify a similar trend away from strict financial controls and toward a more programmatic and positive approach for the Treasury: see Hugh Heclo and Aaron Wildavsky, *The Private Government of Public Money* (Berkeley and Los Angeles: University of California Press, 1974), pp. 385-88.

73. NKS, December 24, 1974. Traditionally, of course, the MOF had always claimed that a strong economy requires fiscal restraint while a slowdown does not allow enough revenues for expansion.

74. NKS, January 7, 16, 1973.

time, but observers agreed that LDP power had made a quantum jump in 1973.[75] What of restructuring the archipelago? Expenditures which appeared related to the plan did rise sharply, of course; according to a later MOF accounting, they amounted to ¥ 3.48 trillion in the General and Special Accounts, a rise of 30.7 percent over spending for these items in 1972.[76] But except for the rhetoric early in the budget process and during the election campaign, there was little evidence that anything like a comprehensive, top-down plan that would shape the pattern of public expenditures to correspond to national priorities had actually had any influence in budgeting. Such comprehensive planning is immensely difficult; one need not question Tanaka's sincerity or good intentions in launching an idea he could not implement. But in retrospect, the major real effect of the plan seems to have been simply to provide a justification for high spending, allowing the Liberal Democrats and even the MOF to throw a cloak of virtue and high purpose over a budget which, in the final analysis, was little more than the largest pork-barrel in the history of Japanese public finance.

The revenues to cover such a large budget came from a fuller than normal natural tax increase estimate (raised by abut ¥ 300 billion over the course of the fall) and a ¥ 2.34 trillion bond issue. That is, 16.4 percent of the General Account was financed by bonds. The figure is not unprecedentedly high, since this "dependence ratio" had reached 16.9 percent in 1966 and 17.0 percent in 1972, except in that the previous records had been set in times of economic slowdown, while at the end of the 1973 budget process the economy was booming — GNP was rising at a 15 to 20 percent annual rate, and the Economic Planning Agency was warning that an "inflationary psychology" was growing.[77] After the MOF draft, Aichi asserted that the budget was not *really* inflationary, since growth in the goods and services accounts was not higher than estimated GNP growth (due to the high proportion of transfer payments), and apparently also because the MOF had "tried as hard as it could to keep the size of the General Account down and avoid encouraging an inflationary mood."[78] His claims were not entirely credible.

*The 1974 Budget.* In fact, with heavy government expenditures and deficit financing piled on top of existing economic trends, inflation

---

75. NKS, January 16, 1973. Note that the pattern of revival negotiations decisions in 1973 may be seen in Appendix A, which gives both MOF and government draft figures for the Important Item breakdown.

76. NKS, January 27, 1973.

77. The EPA's monthly report issued on January 12: NKS, January 12, 1973, evening.

78. To a group of businessmen on January 9, in NKS, January 10, 1973, evening. See also the analysis in NKS, January 8, 1973, evening.

increased mightily; in 1973, the consumer price index rose well into double digits. Many were calling it a "fiscal inflation," and Aichi, reverting to a more traditional role for a finance minister, criticized the idea of "fiscal leadership" of the economy and called for restraint in spending and, particularly, a reduction in deficit financing for the 1974 budget.[79] Even Tanaka himself turned a little cautious, agreeing that both budget growth and the bond dependence ratio should be kept below 1973 figures.[80] The MOF's limitation on budget requests was initially returned to its usual level of 25 percent of the previous year's budget.[81] Into September, even the LDP's Policy Deliberation Council managed to maintain a conservative tone, and the MOF was talking of a ¥17 trillion budget, which would represent just 19 percent growth over 1973.[82]

However, Prime Minister Tanaka again began coming up with new ideas — for example, in mid-September he called in the MOF vice-minister and the BB director to talk about buying up old farm land for new university campuses — and others in the ministries and the LDP followed suit. By early October the MOF had to concede that many new programs would be established and the budget would have to be ¥17.3 trillion or more (at least 21 percent growth). After moving toward a Supplementary Budget just short of ¥1 trillion — much larger, absolutely and relatively, than even the giant supplement of 1973 — by November 3 the Finance Ministry estimate of the 1974 budget had risen to ¥17.43 trillion (22 percent growth) with every prospect that, as usual, it would keep on rising.[83]

But then . . . someone has defined the "postindustrial society" as Japan without oil. When the Arab countries announced an embargo on petroleum shipments in November, Japan — importing nearly all its oil from the Middle East — was thrown into confusion. Although no one could predict the ultimate effects of the energy crisis, it did appear, first, that industrial production would be curtailed as the supply of oil was reduced (or could not grow unless the supply of oil grew); second, that the costs of buying needed oil would quickly transform Japan's balance-of-payments surplus problem into a deficit problem; and third, that the higher domestic prices that would have to be charged for petroleum-related products would contribute to the already rapid inflation. The implications

79. NKS, June 5 and July 3, 1973.
80. NKS, July 29, 1974.
81. It was then discovered that just natural expenditure increases in welfare programs forced by the expansion of 1973 would bring the Ministry of Health and Welfare's requests over the limitation, so some flexibility had to be allowed.
82. For the LDP, NKS, September 7, 1973. For the MOF, see NKS, August 10 and September 1, 1973.
83. NKS, September 21, October 3, November 3, 12 and 27, 1973. A guess that it might have gone nearly to the previous year's 24.6 percent growth would not be unreasonable.

for public finance would seem to be that resource-consuming public works should be cut back, that revenues might be short, and that aggregate demand would have to be controlled to avoid stimulating inflation and aggravating international payments difficulties.

By a curious stroke of fate, it was just at this point that the weak and expansion-oriented finance minister, Aichi Kiichi, fell ill and died. In the midst of the crisis Tanaka turned to Fukuda Takeo: his chief party rival, a fiscal conservative, the most skillful compiler of budgets in Japan, and a man who had been publicly critical of Tanaka's and Aichi's policies for over a year. Fukuda accepted the post of finance minister on November 26 after two days of talks with Tanaka, during which the prime minister promised that Fukuda started with a clean slate and would not be bound by any promises made by Aichi, that economic policy would be changed to emphasize price stability, and (apparently) that Tanaka would refrain from interfering in budgeting matters.[84] Fukuda immediately announced that even though the various plans and programs requested for the 1974 budget were good ideas in themselves, they nonetheless fueled inflation; hence, all programs, except those having "close connections with the people's lives"—that is, social welfare—would be reexamined.[85]

There followed a period of forty days unique in the annals of Japanese budgeting. Conflicts between a finance minister and the bureaucrats of the Budget Bureau had not been unknown, but never before had it been the minister, backed up by the prime minister and even the LDP, calling for lower and lower budgets, and the bureau officials trying to keep the total up. At the start newspaper reports said that the BB was aiming at a target of 23 percent growth, or ¥17.57 trillion, while Fukuda wanted to keep growth down to about 20 percent. On December 6, Vice-Minister Aizawa Hideyuki told the weekly Vice-Ministers' Conference that the MOF would be cutting back on large scale projects—the space program, ocean development, new airplanes—and would hold public works to a nominal growth rate of 10-15 percent (which in real terms meant negative growth); such economies would keep the budget somewhat under the 23 percent growth figure. By a week later, Fukuda had met twice with Tanaka and the new LDP Policy Affairs Research Council chairman, Mizuta Mikio, and amidst talk of "economic emergency" a formal pledge of party support for budget cutting was obtained. MOF officials, under pressure from Fukuda, began work on reducing the announced amount of the tax cut and said that growth in the Fiscal Investment and Loan Program would be held below 20 percent. But the Budget Bureau officials were having great difficulty in cutting ministry requests; on December 16, they reported to

84. Except perhaps with regard to the size of the tax cut. From interviews with MOF leaders in 1974 and NKS, November 11, 1973.
85. *Ibid.*, and a November 26 interview with Fukuda in NKS, November 27, 1973.

the finance minister that they had succeeded only in bringing the total down to ¥17.6 trillion (23 percent growth), and Fukuda told them to go back and try again until they reached ¥17.4 trillion (21 percent). Then on the very next day, Fukuda met again with the party leadership to announce that the total would actually be kept below ¥17.3 trillion, and that public works would be held to even a *nominal* growth rate of zero, meaning a cutback of nearly one-third in actual construction. The LDP agreed, incorporating the MOF's restrictive principles in its formal Budget Compilation Program, and even proclaiming (at a top-level government-party conference on the nineteenth) that "it is not merely a matter of 'endorsing the general argument while opposing the specifics'"—*sōron sansei kakuron hantai*, a good characterization of the normal LDP posture in periods when restrictive budgets seem necessary—rather, "we will cooperate in all aspects."[86]

Fukuda's strategy, in his almost nonstop series of meetings with party and government leaders, apparently was not only to convince them of the logic of his position and prevent later interventions, but also to build a consensus at the top that would increase his real authority over the only participants still resisting, if passively, his pressure for lower and lower budget figures—the Budget Bureau officials themselves. On December 20, he visited the prime minister (who was recovering from an illness in the hospital) and had him endorse a budget growth figure of around 20 percent—a notch lower—as well as tighter restrictions on the FILP and the amount of the bond issue than were then expected. Later that day, he held a session with representatives of the four opposition parties, afterward announcing that all had agreed on the critical nature of the economic situation. By the time of the formal Finance Ministry Budget Conference the next evening, Fukuda's ceiling had been brought down to ¥17.1 trillion, or a growth rate of only 19.7 percent from 1973.

In other words, the total of the MOF draft, ¥17.0994, represented a reduction of 2.7 percentage points of growth from the figure regarded by the specialists in the Budget Bureau as the bare minimum less than a month earlier. This reduction is both impressively large and impressively small: large in revealing that even a November MOF budget estimate, which in a more normal year would rise substantially before the final decision, contained nearly one-half trillion yen (about $1.5 billion) that could somehow still be cut despite the BB's reputation for stringency; small in reminding us of the narrowness of margins within which budgetary decision making takes place.

It would, however, be going too far to infer that the BB's reluctance to cut the budget as deeply as demanded by Fukuda was a result of some

86. NKS, December 19, 20, 1974. The account above is based on NKS articles throughout November and December.

earlier conversion to an ideology of free spending. Undoubtedly, most MOF officials agreed that a restrictive budget was desirable. Their problems were administrative — facing great stacks of ministerial budget requests and justifications, they could not cope with the thousands of individual decisions required to bring the budgetary totals gradually down. Years of comfortable budgeting had taken away the knack.

If the bureaucrats of the Budget Bureau had willy-nilly returned to a role of earlier days in microbudgeting, so, more deliberately, had Fukuda Takeo in planning his tactics for the revival negotiations. In recent years, most finance ministers had adopted a strategy of extensive prenegotiations with ministry and party leaders, working out compromises (or surrenders) on most difficult budgetary issues in advance of the MOF draft so that the revival negotiations period might be as peaceful as possible; a large amount of "adjustment expenses" was also openly set aside for the LDP to dispose of on the last day. Fukuda's early consultations were not negotiations, and did not include the spending ministries; they were aimed at proselytizing for economy and damping the spending instincts of politicians and bureaucrats in advance. He even requested, in the December 7 Cabinet meeting, that ministry officials refrain from contacts with interest groups, including appearances at conventions. While no such attempts could be completely effective — Dietmen still had constituencies, and many ministries were greatly disturbed by the cutbacks — Fukuda's attempts to insure restraint were remarkably successful. Ministry appeals were muted, and the LDP leadership put a heavy lid on rank-and-file demands: when Amano Kōsei, the chairman of the PARC Construction Division, said to a meeting of the Executive Council midway through the appeals negotiations, "Since we too are appropriately holding down our demands for this budget, there should be an official party decision that the government will not be allowed to make a large scale deferment of public works expenditures," Chairman Suzuki Zenko blandly responded, "This important opinion will be taken into account," and then immediately after the meeting said "Impossible!"[87] There was no party opposition to the MOF's reducing adjustment expenses to just ¥ 50 billion (one-third to one-half of recent precedents), nor any party attempt to take advantage of the brightening economic situation when the oil-producing nations relaxed their restrictions on exports to Japan on Christmas Day.

Whatever spending pressures that were not controlled by Fukuda's skillful exploitation of the current economic mood were absorbed by another old-fashioned Finance Ministry tactic — timely concessions. Earlier in December, after initially taking an opposing position, Fukuda had agreed to go along with Prime Minister Tanaka's promise of a ¥ 2 trillion tax cut, and with the party's urgent request that railroad fares and other

87. NKS, December 28, 1974.

public fees not be hiked immediately. During the revival negotiations themselves, "Secretariat Adjustment Expenses," the amounts of which were kept concealed, were used much as "secret resources" had been before the 1968 reforms; they were doled out, a little at a time, to meet the most urgent ministry or PARC division appeals. Despite earlier MOF avowals, several new governmental organizations were also approved late in the process (one reportedly as a reward to Prime Minister Tanaka for not requesting anything else).[88] Such concessions helped prevent a dangerous buildup of resentment against MOF behavior which was, by recent standards, clearly highhanded. There was no excitement over the final party-government negotiations — Fukuda apparently had already figured out the ultimate results almost to the last yen, and in any case, as a Dietman remarked, "50 billion yen is hardly worth staying up late for."[89] Perhaps for the first time ever, the revival negotiations were finished up some twelve hours ahead of schedule, at 10 o'clock on the evening of December 28.

# Conclusions

Our concern in this chapter has been the degree to which the Ministry of Finance has been forced to "distort" budgets, to do other than what it would prefer in the absence of external pressures. Since such ideal preferences cannot be known, we have no way to assign values of a "distortion index" to each year and explain its variation. However, drawing on the more impressionistic evidence developed above, it is possible to speculate, at least, about some cause-and-effect relationships.

A few clues are provided by a senior MOF official interviewed in 1974. Asked about that year's rather distinctive budget process, he said,

. . . we need some sort of political leadership, which can be achieved either through very strong personal characteristics of the leader, or by a unanimous consensus caused by certain unusual circumstances. Otherwise, so far as the political balance of power is concerned, it is rather difficult for the prime minister to control the various voices from the party and to make an "idealistic" budget. And the finance minister is still weaker than the prime minister.

The key is the "political balance of power" between savers — basically the Finance Ministry — and the forces for spending. What factors influence year-to-year shifts in this balance of power?

The first factor is the economic situation. In the years of balanced budgeting the MOF found itself in its most difficult straits when the economy was booming and in need of restraint; spending demands were

88. *Ibid.*
89. NKS, December 25, 1973.

then heightened by the awareness of available revenues. After 1965, however, times of moderate recession or their immediate aftermaths were just as dangerous, since politicians could then argue that pump-priming through increased deficit financing is desirable. Economic conditions can be positively helpful to Finance officials only in a few cases, the "certain unusual circumstances" when all or nearly all participants can be convinced that conditions are truly grave and do require restraint. The best recent examples are 1968 and 1974, though both also remind us that such a consensus must be encouraged by active MOF proselytizing (or more generally, that economics is mediated by politics in its impact on the behavior of budget participants).

The second factor is the political situation. To some extent, the loudness of "the various voices within the party" is increased when an election (to either house of the Diet, or even the Comprehensive Local Elections) is impending, although as indicated above this point tends to be overemphasized by journalists. More important is intraparty politics: pressure from the LDP on the budget will increase when factional politics heat up, most often because of an impending possible vacancy in the post of LDP president. However, even in such times it is rare for particular factions as such to demand more spending on individual programs (although at times debates between faction leaders on macrobudgeting policy have been significant). Rather, the heightening of intraparty political tensions seems to stimulate Dietmen to be more assertive in all areas. When candidates for the presidency are competing for the favor of electors, as in the latter part of the Satō administration, pressures on the budget are intensified still further.

Weighed on the other side of the balance are the "personal characteristics" — skill, unity, strength — of budgeting leaders, primarily the prime minister and finance minister, and secondarily the formal LDP leadership. As emphasized in chapter 6, an important role of the top leadership is to restrain demands from the LDP; if this role is performed ineffectually, because of inexperience, squabbling or political weakness, MOF officials will be relatively unprotected. When the leaders become spenders, as in 1973, budgeters are nearly helpless. In 1974, the personal strength and skill of Fukuda, backed up by the LDP leadership and of course aided by a widespread sense of crisis, were the major factors in rolling back the size of the budget.

*Change in Budget Indicators.* — It is possible to observe some reflections of these factors in the budget statistics recorded in Table 16. For example, the high growth rates in the initial budgets of 1961-62 and 1973 are clearly related to strong positive interventions into budgeting by Prime Ministers Ikeda and Tanaka. A major Finance Ministry attack on spending came in 1968, the success of which is indicated by the relatively low 13.7 growth rate of the final budget for that year. However, the limitations of this line of analysis are illustrated by the other major case of a real (and in a sense successful) attempt to cut expenditures, that of 1974. The burden of the obligatory expenditure increase meant that despite Fukuda's most extreme efforts, including cutting back public works expenditures to zero growth, the initial budget that year still had to grow 19.7 percent, one of the highest figures of the period. The difficulty here is that although budget growth is the most obvious surrogate for our hypothetical "distortion index," it is affected by too many other factors (given the limited number of cases) to allow many inferences about the short-run effects of the variables we have considered.

However, longer-term trends are more readily observed in this table. For example, budgets were being held nearly constant in the period immediately preceding the conservative party amalgamation, and then from 1956 began to rise. A new plateau was attained in 1961 (or, more precisely, beginning with the 1960 Supplementary Budget), the result of Ikeda's high-growth policies and the eagerness of the ministries and Dietmen to grasp the opportunities it provided. The marked increase in the growth rate of the initial budget during the latter years of Satō's administration is particular striking, as consistent with the argument in the previous chapter that majority party influence was rising during that period.[90] Another indicator of LDP predominance in this period is the relationship between public works and social security spending: as pointed out in chapter 5, conservative politicians desire constituency-pleasing public works projects above all else, and certainly above the more diffuse benefits of increases in social welfare programs. Averaging figures from Columns G and H, we observe that during the Ikeda administration (1961-64), social security growth averaged 24.6 percent and public works 22.1 percent per year; this differential was more pronounced in the early years of Satō's regime (1965-70), when social security growth averaged 17.6 and public works 14.3 percent. But when LDP influence was at its height in 1971 and 1972, the relationship was reversed—public works growth averaged 23.6 percent, and social security 20.0 percent. (The dramatic difference between "Tanaka's year" of 1973 and "Fukuda's year" of 1974 may be read directly from the Table.)

90. Note also Column F, a rough index of the relationship between the initial budget and economic growth. The mean for the period of greater party (or prime ministerial) influence since 1961 is +2 percentage points, compared with -5 for the earlier seven years. A similar index based on EPA annual growth forecasts would be more relevant to actual decision making, but these forecasts are not sufficiently independent of tactical budgetary politics considerations for such an index to be valid.

Column I represents the proportion of deficit finance foreseen at the time of drawing up the annual budget. The fact that this column exists at all well expresses the trend toward an increasing role for the budget in economic regulation; before bonds were first sold under the 1965 Supplementary Budget, it was difficult to stimulate the economy very much by increasing governmental expenditures. The large anticipated bond issues of 1966-67 and 1972 clearly were aimed at pulling Japan out of economic slumps. That of 1973 was not, and therefore contributed substantially to the double-digit inflation which occurred later that year. Finally, the average "change-in-share" figures in Column J indicate, for example, the relative stability through the 1967-70 period of Satō's tight control, with the amount of fluctuation increasing in the 1970s—particularly in 1973, with Tanaka's activism, and then in 1974 when Fukuda forced real changes in priorities as a response to economic crisis.

*The Evolution of the Budgetary System.*—However imprecise these statistics, they allow us to state with some confidence that despite the basic continuity of budgetary institutions in Japan, the relationship among institutions have changed over time in significant ways. Turning back for one final glance at the system's history, let us look now at these changes from the viewpoint of the Ministry of Finance as it reacts to and attempts to deal with alterations in its environment: in particular, to the expansion and increasing complexity of government, the greater economic role for public finance in a time of rapid growth, and the development of the Liberal Democratic Party.

Early hopes to the contrary, the newly established LDP entered the budget arena not in the character of a sober, responsible governing party, but rather, despite its control of the Cabinet, in the style of the fractious pre-1955 minority conservative parties. Largely because it lacked the internal cohesion to discipline its own members, the party repeatedly failed to produce any sort of comprehensive and implementable budget plans. Instead it generated long lists of demands for specific spending programs which totalled to amounts well beyond realistic possibility. Impossible demands are easier to deal with than possible demands; that the LDP should choose this role meant that the Ministry of Finance could get by simply with tactical adjustments, continuing to follow the same basic strategy in pursuing its interests that it had before the conservative amalgamation. That is, it could play one element within the party against another, handle each demand one by one, concede where it must to bleed off pressure, and resist wherever it could. The ministry could afford to be tactically flexible because its strategy was solid: few participants were willing to challenge the ideology of "sound" fiscal policy and the balanced

## TABLE 16
### Budget Indicators, 1954-1974
### (Unit: Percent)

| Fiscal Year | A Prime Minister & Finance Minister | B Budget (initial) | C Budget (final) | D GNP (nominal) | E GNP (real) | F Difference (B − D) | G Social Security | H Public Works | I Bond Ratio | J Change in Share |
|---|---|---|---|---|---|---|---|---|---|---|
| 1954 | Yoshida/Ogasawara | 3.5 | −2.7 | 4.0 | 2.3 | −0.5 | | | | |
| 1955 | Hatoyama/Ichimanda | −0.8 | 1.3 | 13.3 | 11.3 | −14.1 | | | | |
| 1956 | Hatoyama/Ichimanda | 4.4 | 7.5 | 12.3 | 6.7 | −7.9 | | | | 2.8 |
| 1957 | Ishibashi/Ikeda | 9.9 | 8.7 | 13.0 | 8.2 | −3.1 | | | | 4.1 |
| 1958 | Kishi/Ichimanda | 15.4 | 12.5 | 4.8 | 5.7 | 10.6 | | | | 6.6 |
| 1959 | Kishi/Satō | 8.2 | 13.4 | 15.5 | 11.7 | −7.3 | | | | 4.2 |
| 1960 | Kishi/Satō | 10.6 | 16.7 | 19.1 | 13.3 | −8.5 | 21.4 | 18.5 | | —[a] |
| 1961 | Ikeda/Mizuta | 24.4 | 19.4 | 22.5 | 14.4 | 1.9 | 36.6 | 24.6 | | 4.4 |
| 1962 | Ikeda/Mizuta | 24.3 | 21.6 | 9.1 | 5.7 | 15.2 | 20.3 | 28.9 | | 5.1 |
| 1963 | Ikeda/Tanaka | 17.4 | 19.3 | 18.2 | 12.9 | −0.8 | 22.4 | 14.3 | | 2.5 |
| 1964 | Ikeda/Tanaka | 14.2 | 9.3 | 15.9 | 10.8 | −1.7 | 19.2 | 20.5 | | 3.3 |
| 1965 | Satō/Tanaka | 12.4 | 12.1 | 10.6 | 5.4 | 1.8 | 19.9 | 15.7 | | 2.8 |
| 1966 | Satō/Fukuda | 17.9 | 19.6 | 17.2 | 11.8 | 0.7 | 20.3 | 18.9 | 16.9 | 4.0 |
| 1967 | Satō/Mizuta | 14.8[b] | 16.2 | 17.9 | 13.4 | −3.1 | 15.7 | 14.3 | 16.2 | 2.4 |
| 1968 | Satō/Mizuta | 17.5[c] | 13.7 | 17.8 | 13.6 | −0.3 | 13.1 | 7.0 | 10.1 | 1.8 |
| 1969 | Satō/Fukuda | 15.8 | 17.1 | 18.0 | 12.4 | −2.2 | 16.1 | 12.8 | 7.2 | 2.7 |
| 1970 | Satō/Fukuda | 17.9 | 18.5 | 16.3 | 9.3 | 1.6 | 20.5 | 17.3 | 5.4 | 1.2 |
| 1971 | Satō/Fukuda | 18.4 | 17.6 | 11.2 | 6.6 | 7.2 | 17.8 | 18.1 | 4.5 | 3.0 |
| 1972 | Satō/Mizuta | 21.8 | 18.7 | 17.3 | 11.0 | 4.5 | 22.1 | 29.0 | 17.0 | 3.8 |
| 1973 | Tanaka/Aichi | 24.6 | 26.0 | 22.0 | 6.4 | 2.6 | 28.8 | 32.2 | 16.4 | 4.2 |
| 1974 | Tanaka/Fukuda | 19.7 | 25.7 | 17.9 | −0.2 | 1.8 | 36.7 | 0.0 | 12.6 | 5.4 |

NOTES: Columns B–H are year-to-year growth rate figures, the amount minus the previous year's amount, divided by that amount, times 100. All data refer to the fiscal year, April 1–March 31.

aNot available because the Local Allocation Tax expenditure item was transferred from the Prime Minister's Office to the newly established Ministry of Home Affairs in 1960, skewing the average.

bWould be nearly 16 percent if the new Coal Mining Industry Special Account had not been separated out.

cSince as part of the "break fiscal rigidification movement" several items usually covered by Supplementary Budgets were here included in the initial budget, this growth figure is not strictly comparable to those of other years, and Column C is more valid.

SOURCES: A. In office at time of government draft. *Ōkurashō Jīnmeiroku*, app., p. 3.

B. Initial budget as passed by Diet. *Zaisei Tōkei*, 1970, pp. 28–29; 1974, pp. 28–29.

C. Budget as passed by Diet after all supplements. *Ibid.*, 1970, pp. 32–33; 1974, pp. 32–33.

D–E. Real GNP is in 1965 prices, except 1973–74 is in 1970 prices. *Ibid.*, 1970, pp. 302–303; 1974, pp. 322–23; Nihon Ginkō, *Keizai Tōkei Geppō* ("Economic Statistics Monthly Report") No. 349 (April, 1976), p. 168.

G–H. Initial budget basis; data are adjusted for constancy over time in two separate series, but there are no significant differences between the two. Adjusted data were not available for period before 1960. *Ibid.*, 1970, pp. 28–29; 1974, pp. 28–29.

I. The proportion of the General Account financed by bond revenues, as estimated at the time of the government draft. In most cases the amount was reduced later in the year. Contemporary newspaper accounts.

J. Calculated by the same method as in Table 7, except that scores for all eighteen (seventeen before 1961) organizational units (ministry breakdown) are weighted by share and averaged. 1956–1970: Official audit figures for postsupplementary budgets, compiled by Steven R. Reed for the Interuniversity Consortium for Political and Social Research. 1971–73: Postsupplement budget figures; 1974: Initial budget figures—both from *Zaisei Tōkei*, 1974, pp. 65–66.

budget. New requests could be granted only within the yearly revenue surplus generated by modest economic growth. The MOF was thus in a strong position thrugh the 1950s, although in 1959, when the 1960 budget process became entangled in factional battling, it was reminded that its bulwarks against party influence were not impregnable.

It was the 1961 budget, the first under Ikeda's Income Doubling Plan, which thrust the Finance Ministry into a new and more dangerous game. From now on high economic growth, and therefore large yearly revenue increments, would be presumed by budget participants; moreover, public finance would be expected to play a facilitating rather than restraining role in the economy. It is noteworthy that even the enormous size of the 1961 budget did not satisfy the Liberal Democrats. Groups of politicians, now beginning to work closely with spending ministries and clientele groups, continued to press for more and more spending on particularistic programs — the MOF's capitulation on the rice subsidy is a case in point. The balanced budget principle, which Finance officials regarded as their last-ditch defense, actually became a liability in the first half of the sixties, in that the LDP could use the threat of deficit financing to force the MOF into making concessions — even increased expenditures, which could be paid for only by inflating tax revenue estimates. This defensive strategy was inherently unstable: when the economy slumped in 1965, the inevitable revenue shortfall compelled the government to go into the red. Moreover, the MOF's enlarged responsibility for pulling Japan out of recession meant that bond sales had to be continued in the 1966 budget, and became an accepted part of the government's financial resources.

The Finance officials had lost a vital "brake" on expenditures; they could no longer maintain that all demands must be covered by tax revenues. Without a convincing ceiling in the macrobudgeting sphere, it became more and more difficult to defend microbudgeting decisions against penetration by the line ministry-interest group-PARC division alliances. Powerful enough when seeking new spending, these alliances had become nearly invincible in protecting old programs, so that the MOF was almost helpless against the inexorable rise in fixed expenditures engendered by the enlargement of government since the early 60s. Faced with stronger and stronger demands, the Finance Ministry had fewer resources to meet them. In this untenable position, it became apparent that the ministry's traditionally passive stance in budget politics would no longer suffice. The MOF would have to go on the offensive.

The result was the "break fiscal rigidification movement" of 1968, which significantly if uncharacteristically was led by permanent Finance officials, particularly Budget Bureau Director Murakami. This campaign may be regarded as a truly creative (if ultimately futile) attempt by an organization to protect and even advance its most vital interests in an increasingly uncomfortable environment. The Liberal Democrats could not be banished from budgeting, and the Japanese government could not be returned to a simpler era where its activities could be effectively monitored and controlled by a few budget examiners. Unable to regain its earlier dominance of microbudgeting, the MOF in effect withdrew from this field, handing a large proportion of specific program decisions over to the spending ministries (through "Secretariat Adjustment Expenses") or even the LDP leadership ("Policy Adjustment Expenses"). That is to say, as concluded in chapter 7, the bulk of "policy" or "new" expenditures are allocated during the revival negotiations period, and in 1968 the Finance Ministry explicitly gave the dominant voice in these allocations to the ministries and party. Similar in intention was the reduction in the ministry request limitation from 30 to 25 percent above the previous year's budget. While resented by line ministry bureaucrats (it gave them more work and reduced their ability to pay off interest groups with fictitious budget demands), this reform was actually a forced transfer of decision-making authority, since many choices among programs would now have to be made before submission of requests by line ministry officials, instead of afterward by the Budget Bureau.

This renunciation of influence in microbudgeting is related to all three of the long-term trends noted above. First, it was a response to complexity. Programs were becoming ever more numerous and difficult to understand, and budgeters increasingly had to defer to the specialized expertise of line ministry officials; MOF influence in microbudgeting was eroding anyway. Second, although officials in the MOF had always remained more aloof from the LDP than those in other ministries, the effects of politically active finance ministers, the numbers of MOF alumnae among LDP Dietmen, and the more general trend toward increasing party influence in government affairs all thrust politicians and Finance bureaucrats into closer relationships and thereby threatened MOF autonomy. So long as decisions of interest to LDP Dietmen — usually microbudgeting matters — were being made within the MOF, politicians would try to insert themselves into internal Finance Ministry policy arguments, jurisdictional disputes and even personnel decisions. As observed in chapter 4, protection of its autonomy is the MOF's most valued organizational interest, and the 1968 reforms were designed to keep the LDP at arm's length — as a journalist pointed out in an interview, "under the new system, when a budget examiner is asked a favor by a Dietman during revival negotiations, he can now simply tell him to go over and talk to the ministry secretariat." Or, if the request were a large one, he could be reminded that a substantial sum had already been set aside for the party and he should speak to his secretary-general.

The third motivation was that cutting back on old tasks would allow the Finance Ministry to concentrate its energies on fulfilling its ever more demanding role in economic regulation. To do so, it needed a firmer grip on macrobudgeting, particularly on total government spending. The "comprehensive budgeting" reform of 1968 was an attempt to increase MOF control over two spending decisions which have considerable impact on the size of the budget — rice prices and government employee wage hikes — by bringing them back into the regular annual budget process, where they would have to compete with other uses for funds (these matters previously had been decided in the summer, by mechanisms over which the Finance Minister had limited influence, and were heavily influenced by the amount of money which had become available for Supplementary Budgets). "Comprehensive budgeting" was thus an attempt to *extend* MOF control. Similarly, the remaining elements of the "break fiscal rigidification movement" were primarily aimed at increasing the MOF's ability to restrain various fixed expenditures. Only if these could be controlled would Finance officials have any financial margin to allow flexibility in deciding the size of the total budget; otherwise, all the money available would be eaten up by unavoidable expenditures and the total budget would quite likely be larger than economically desirable.

The Finance Ministry's intention in 1968, then, was to withdraw from the sectors of budgeting less vital to its interests and where in fact it had already been losing ground, so that it could increase its authority over macrobudgeting policy making.[91] The attempt failed, in part because the ministry simply lacked sufficient power to attack the basic causes of rising fixed expenditures. Only for a brief interlude did the LDP accept the MOF argument that Japan was headed for a revenue crisis. The ministry attempted other, more modest reforms with similar objectives after 1968, but these were even less successful in reversing expenditure growth and the increasing politicization of budgeting. Perhaps because all the short-term variables were tilted against the Finance Ministry in the early 1970s — the economic situation did not discourage spending, intraparty factional politics was active (with the finance minister a leading participant), and the prime minister either a weak supporter or a strong opponent — the budgets of the period were large and dominated by the LDP.

Largest and most dominated of all was the 1973 budget. Its growth rate of 24.6 percent was the record for the entire period. Although the new prime minister claimed that, for the first time, governmental resource allocation was being subordinated to a comprehensive "vision" of national development, the 1973 budget was in reality the culmination of the trend toward increasing majority party penetration of the budgetary process — truly a *sōbanateki*, "tips-for-all" budget. Tanaka breached the Finance

---

91. Cf. a somewhat similar trend in the British Treasury: "Macro-analysis of the economy is tending to overwhelm micro-analysis of policies, if only because so many political administrators feel more confident with the former than the latter." Heclo and Wildavsky, *Private Government*, p. 383.

Ministry's macrobudgeting defenses, and the line ministry-PARC division-interest group alliances were quick to rush in. As a result, the economy was badly overstimulated, and the many programs created or expanded in 1973 meant that the following year's budget would have to grow enormously simply to take care of the "natural expenditure increase." In other words, precisely those fears expressed by MOF officials back in 1968 had come to pass.

Finally, we may ask how the 1974 budget should be regarded. Was it the beginning of a new era, or merely a pause in the long-term decline of the Ministry of Finance? Certainly it is true that only extraordinary economic and political conditions allowed the severe cutbacks in the budget draft which occurred late in the process. Moreover, the fact that the Budget Bureau had to be forced into budget-cutting by the finance minister indicates how comfortable even MOF bureaucrats had become in the high-growth environment. Still, the Liberal Democrats (and even Tanaka) had been silenced, and the budget was most drastically restrained in the sector normally of most party interest, public works. The message that in a modern mixed-capitalist system government spending must be regulated by economic policy was presented to budget participants with new force. For their part, Finance officials perhaps were reminded of the home truth that macrobudgeting cannot be separated from microbudgeting: unless budgeters are willing to resist pressures to expand individual programs, the size of the total budget cannot be held in check.

More fundamentally, there were indications in 1974 that Japan was reaching a turning point, that the years of double-digit economic growth had ended, and perhaps that the Liberal Democrats would be unable to maintain their political hegemony much longer. Were such basic parameters of governmental politics to change, the budgetary system too would necessarily be altered. But such considerations lead us beyond the purposes of the present discussion, which have been to identify and explain fluctuations and trends in budgeting over the past twenty years, and into speculations more properly reserved for the final chapter.

# 10

# Conclusion

HAVING SCRUTINIZED the Japanese budgetary system close up, we may now step back a pace to see how it looks in a broader context — or rather, two broader contexts. First, how does Japanese budgeting compare with that of other countries? Second, how does it fit into the broader Japanese political structure and process? These questions are best approached with references to the "typical" period of contemporary Japanese budgeting, the decade of the 1960s. This accomplished, we may attempt a brief evaluation of more recent changes and even think a little about the future.

## *Japanese* Budget Politics

Comparing large and complicated decision-making systems cross-nationally is extraordinarily difficult. To discover how distinctive the important elements of Japan's budgetary system appear in international perspective, a logical place to begin is with microbudgeting and what we might call the "Wildavsky model."[1] It can be summarized as follows:

1. Budgeting is historical. Much of the budget for a given year is obligatory, and even for the remainder alterations are marginal. Budget participants usually give attention only to change.
2. Budgeting is specialized and fragmented. The budget is broken down into parts, each handled by specialized organs; there is little formal coordination among them. Each participant usually adheres to his own role (e.g., spender, cutter, appeals court).
3. Budgeting tends to be nonprogrammatic. Because comparing and judging policies on their merits are so difficult, participants employ rules of thumb

---

1. I.e., an abstraction and oversimplification of Wildavsky's empirical observations of American and other budgeting, summarized from many passages in *The Politics of the Budgetary Process* (Boston: Little, Brown and Company, 1964) and *Budgeting: A Comparative Theory of Budgetary Processes* (Boston: Little, Brown and Company, 1975).

which focus on administrative aspects of problems. Simultaneous means-end analysis, and indeed much attention to ends at all, is avoided.

4. Budgeting is sequential and repetitive. Since the process is repeated every year, problems can be solved little by little. Within each yearly process, amenable problems are solved at each stage, with others left for later.

5. Budgeting functions to minimize conflict. Stable role behavior brings stable expectations among participants, who usually share an interest in getting the work done. Anticipated reactions by other participants are fundamental criteria for decisions.

If this list may be taken as an accurate description of "normal" budgeting practices, how well does it apply to Japan?

As should be quite clear by now, the first generalization to be made is that the model seems to fit very well. It would not be too much of an exaggeration to maintain that a reader seeking an understanding of the politics of Japanese budgeting would do better to read Wildavsky than most of the available Japanese materials on the subject. In fact, it is possible to argue that Japanese budgeting is even more "incrementalist" than the American process.

For example, with regard to "historical" budgeting, though both systems use the previous year's budget as a base Japanese budgets are cut less frequently. Also, Japanese examiners are more passive than their American counterparts, almost never making on-site visits and rarely seeking information beyond established ministry-dominated channels. There are few evaluations of past performance, except on the most legalistic or technical level. Further, it is taken for granted that nearly all budgets will go up a bit each year, at least enough to compensate for inflation, so even changes from the previous year do not necessarily draw attention. All in all, it appears that a program's chances of growing incrementally from year to year without much interference are much better in Japan than in the United States.

On the second point, fragmentation and specialization, Japan appears less similar to the United States and closer, perhaps, to the British pattern. The concentration of budgeting functions within the Finance Ministry would seem to permit a greater degree of coordination, and in fact the balance of revenues and expenditures and similarly crucial macrobudgeting matters are kept under tight MOF control. However, for the allocation of expenditures the principle of specialization is well respected in the Budget Bureau. Examiners rarely participate in decisions on other policy areas, and intersectoral comparisons are quite rare. That is to say, although in formal terms the Finance Ministry would seem to be in a good position to make "comprehensive" budget decisions, in practice the process is quite fragmented.

Third, Japanese participants often strive to eliminate programmatic considerations from budgeting. As well as the many examples cited in chapter 3, we note that policy-based criticism is even more effectively screened out in Japan than in the United States, where House Appropriations Subcommittees have sometimes included Congressmen on opposite sides of an agency's policy questions, and the full Committee, House floor, Senate Committee and Conference stages offer further points of access for objections on policy grounds.[2] The president may himself intervene or be represented by the Office of Management and Budget. In Britain, more difficult issues come to the attention of the prime minister and even the full Cabinet, where ministry proposals are sometimes severely criticized.[3] The Japanese process is more insulated and bureaucratized. Policy suggestions from the finance minister during MOF budget review, and from other Cabinet ministers during both the ministerial internal process and in the penultimate appeals negotiations, are generally not too significant. The internal Liberal Democratic Party process, while more influential, tends to be dominated by enthusiasts. The final government-party negotiations take up only a small portion of the budget. The point is that in the Japanese microbudgeting process there is little participation by potentially hostile "outsiders," with diverse clienteles tending to produce differing interests and points of view. Such restricted participation encourages routinization and the reduction of policy disputes to technical problems.

Fourth, the sequential and repetitive nature of budgeting appears to be even more characteristic of Japan than elsewhere. The degree to which a repeated "filtering" process has become formalized is notable. First, in its own budget process, each ministry must cut large portions of its proposals to stay within the 25-percent request limitation. The "Standard Budget" process in the summer then gets the most routine items out of the way (though more so in the earlier than the later years of this period), and much of the remainder is handled in the Budget Bureau's "Miscellaneous Category Bureau Meetings" in October. Simultaneously, efforts are made to isolate the difficult areas among the "Important Item" budgets for systematic treatment during November. Some tentative judgments are reached here, but many difficulties, such as new program proposals, are put over until the revival negotiations stage. Even within that final process, there is a rather careful determination of which leftover problems will be treated at each level of negotiations, so that when the last government-party sessions are reached, only a small number of decisions (often about six) remain on the table. This is the time sequence; structurally speaking, lower-level officials take care of all they can, using up most of the available funds, leaving the most "difficult" problems for progressively higher levels.

2. Cf. Richard F. Fenno, Jr., *Power of the Purse: Appropriations Politics in Congress* (Boston: Little Brown and Company, 1966), pp. 136-149.

3. Hugh Heclo and Aaron Wildavsky, *The Private Government of Public Money* (Berkeley and Los Angeles: University of California Press, 1974), pp. 129-197.

This pattern is, of course, a highly efficient means of getting through a huge workload. Inevitably, it also prevents higher, policy-level officials from having much influence over the bulk of budgetary decision making.

This filtering process, and the other mechanisms mentioned here, all help to minimize conflict in the system. Moreover, each participant adheres closely to his own role; mutual expectations of appropriate behavior become very strong, sometimes to the point of ossification into ritual. Each understands and adjusts his own behavior to the interests of others. In general, all the central participants—excluding perhaps those LDP Dietmen who identify very closely with a particular interest group's demands—perceive their interests better achieved through cooperation than disruption, and have aided in keeping the budget process moving along each year.

One generalization suggested by these observations is that the Japanese budgetary system seems more routinized, less programmatic, more likely to produce the same old decisions year after year than even the budgetary systems of the West. Indeed, this impression is strengthened when one considers such distinctively Japanese elements as the norm of "balance," which works against change, or the unusual degree of penetration by the majority party organization into the budget system. As observed in chapter 5, the net effect of LDP participation has actually been to increase inertia, by inhibiting attacks on "backward-looking" expenditures.

How do these considerations affect what the government does? In chapter 1, it was shown that allocation patterns have shifted less over the decade of the 1960s in Japan than in the United States (and elsewhere), and chapter 4 included data demonstrating that year-to-year fluctuations are smaller in Japan. So we find on the one hand that many structural and procedural elements of the Japanese budgeting system tend toward inertia or stability, and on the other that the outputs of that system seem to be unusually stable. Would we be justified in inferring that the former causes the latter? Perhaps so; certainly it would be foolish to deny any relationship. Yet the entire story seems not to be told here. Examining the application of the "Wildavsky model" to Japanese budgeting, one is struck most of all by how well it fits; similarities with budgeting elsewhere clearly outweigh differences. The fact is that the fundamental nature of the budgetary problem—scarcity combined with complexity—determines most budgetary behavior. If this proposition is true, and if Japanese budgeting is basically as similar to that elsewhere as we have claimed, it would seem illogical to maintain that major differences in policy outputs are caused by characteristics of the budgetary system, narrowly defined— that is, differences in relationships between spenders and cutters, in the strategies and calculations commonly employed, even in "personality" traits of budgeters.

Where, then, should we look? We should, I suggest, see how the budget process fits into the larger political process. What are the connections between the budgetary system and its environment, and how might these relate to public policy outputs?

In most countries budgeting is considered too important to be left entirely to budgeters. Many decisions having important financial implications will be made outside the budgetary system, with only the details left over for budget officers, examiners, and accountants. Guy Lord observes of France that "the development of budgetary expenditure follows patterns that are often beyond the reach of even the most sophisticated budget machinery. . . . in budgetary matters the Minister of Finances is often in the position of one who has to pay for decisions made or agreements reached outside his sphere of direct influence" — that is, in Parlement under the Fourth Republic and by the President in the Fifth.[4] In Great Britain, important questions of how the country's resources should be distributed are subject to great Cabinet debates. John P. Crecine's research on American budgeting indicates that the larger changes in an agency's budget level usually occur in between, rather than during, the annual budget processes, as a result of presidential or Congressional action.[5] Indeed, the fact that new programs in the American government are begun through the authorization process, involving the legislative rather than appropriations committees and in general quite a different frame of reference than budgeting, indicates that an understanding of the budgetary process as such is not sufficient to comprehend sources of change in American budgetary outputs.

Support for this argument may be found in Table 1, which compared the change in budget shares over ten years of the major policy areas in Japan and the United States. The crucial reason for the less stable appearance of the American budget is that a few large programs saw their expenditures doubled (the space program), almost tripled (education), or even sextupled (health), in terms of shares. It is clear that these great expansions did not arise from within the budgetary process — as a result of, say, a particularly clever strategy on the part of some bureau chief, a momentary lapse by an OMB examiner, or a deft intervention by some subcommittee chairman eager to see a new project located in his district. No, the decisions to expand these programs came from outside, in these cases as explicit presidential decisions: Kennedy's to reach the moon, and Johnson's to declare war on poverty.

4. Guy Lord, *The French Budgetary Process* (Berkeley and Los Angeles: University of California Press, 1973), pp. 190-92.

5. Lectures at the Institute for Public Policy Studies, University of Michigan, November, 1975.

From what quarters in Japan might such large-scale interventions have come? Institutions which might be possibilities in other countries — the legislature, the Cabinet, a unified bureaucratic elite, even organized big business — were for many reasons fundamentally unable to take such a role in Japan; if policies were going to be imposed on budgeting, they would have to have been imposed by the Liberal Democrats or the prime minister. But the LDP, as we have seen in chapter 5, has been good at microbudgeting and at protecting the status quo at the integration level, but not good at making and carrying out comprehensive policy. The prime minister, with a few exceptions, has defined his role as achieving "harmony" rather than formulating and implementing major domestic initiatives. Thus, *no one* has intervened. Budgeting has been left to budgeters. We observe on the Japan half of Table 1 that the shares of no categories have changed mightily, and those showing most change are administrative rather than policy matters.[6] The budgetary system has been allowed to function with relative autonomy, to run untended — leaving budgeters alone to this extent in *any* country would result in stable outputs.

Our problem then is to account for budgeting autonomy or (to use the term applied in chapter 1) "budget primacy," the tendency for budgeting to dominate or encroach on other arenas of government.[7] In the words of Itō Daiichi quoted above, why is it that, in Japan, "the rules of the budgetary compilation process have . . . come to substitute for the rules of policy decision-making"?[8]

# Japanese Budget *Politics*

Inevitably, the possible answers are many. One is that competitive processes, or competitive institutions, seem not to work as conveniently or effectively as budgeting: in the various nonbudgetary arenas, rules of the game are not as well institutionalized and procedural wrangling may drag on for months.[9] Budgeting imposes an attractive "logic of the deadline," in Itō's words, and no one need wonder about who should participate, when meetings should be held, what is open for discussion, and where the

---

6. The items which show the greatest change are "external affairs," which are postwar reparation expenditures set by long-term treaties, and interest on the national debt. Neither is subject to "decisions" in any real sense.

7. For example, recall the principle that all proposals requiring expenditures, however trivial an aspect of their overall importance, normally must first be granted a budget within the regular routine before "authorization" legislation may be introduced.

8. Itō Daiichi, "The Bureaucracy: Its Attitudes and Behavior," *The Developing Economies* 6, 4 (December 1968), 455.

9. Though I know of no comparative research, reading case studies from several countries leaves an impression that even relatively noncontroversial issues take far longer to be resolved in Japan than elsewhere.

ultimate decision-making authority lies.[10] Even beyond its pragmatic advantage, somehow in Japan budgeting seems regarded as more legitimate than alternative processes: participants are more likely to accept its outcomes as just, or at least as inevitable. We note the appeal of ways to reach decisions which at least appear to be "rational"; the historic prestige of the Japanese bureaucracy and, accordingly, bureaucratic style;[11] and the peculiarities of Japanese culture which tend to inhibit taking strong positions and to favor consensus-building — for which budgeting is well suited — as a decision-making procedure.[12] These various causes are difficult to evaluate, beyond observing that a given set of objective circumstances is likely to allow a *range* of responses — in this case, styles of decision making — and the alternative which emerges will probably be the one most congruent with existing social patterns and cultural preferences.[13]

However, let us for now concentrate on the objective circumstances. One which has been important in the development of "budget primacy" is the degree of consensus within the Japanese governmental system on social goals — notably, the priority of rapid economic growth in a mixed-capitalist framework — and in a broad way even on the policy implications of those goals. Moreover, amplifying the substantial degree of agreement on policy, for quite a long period most in the elite believed that the results of their policies were quite satisfactory, and they saw little need to alter them in any fundamental way. The disputes which arose within the governmental system were accordingly over means rather than ends, were arguments about policy adjustments at the margin or forms of implementation. Policy consensus tends to favor budgeting over other arenas. Marginal issues are much more amenable to budgetary resolution than are more fundamental conflicts. They flow almost naturally through well-worn channels, and participants are likely to be satisfied with solutions which add a little larger increment to one policy area and a little smaller one to another.

These remarks about consensus are intended to pertain to the governmental system — the elite — and not necessarily to the Japanese

10. "The Bureaucracy", p. 456.

11. This theme is well developed by Tsuji Kiyoaki, *Nihon Kanryōsei no Kenkyū* (rev. ed.; Tokyo: Tokyo Daigaku Shuppankai, 1969).

12. E.g., for an argument that cultural predilections make bureaucratic disputes difficult to solve by direct methods, see Ide Yoshinori, "Gyōsei Kokka to Tekunokurashii" ("The Administrative State and Technocracy") in *Gendai Nihon no Seiji* ("Politics in Modern Japan"), eds. Inoki Masamichi and Kamikawa Nobuhiko (Tokyo: Ushio Shuppansha, 1969), pp. 276-303.

13. See Robert E. Cole, "The Theory of Institutionalization: Permanent Employment and Cultural Change in Japan," *Economic Development and Cultural Change* 20, 1 (October 1971), 47-70, for the interplay between economic circumstances and tradition (or "neo-tradition") in the evolution of organizational forms.

political system as a whole. In Japan as everywhere, direct participation in decision making is monopolized by a tiny portion of the citizenry, and it is relationships within the elite that determine both the methods by which issues are settled and their outcomes. However, as a general principle of democracy, one expects groups in the larger society to work through various mechanisms to influence the elite, in particular such factors as its composition, how its members behave, and especially the agenda of problems which the governmental system must handle. Most of these mechanisms — free elections, politicial parties, an independent press, organized interest groups — are quite active in Japan. One may then ask whether this stable consensus within the governmental system, which partially explains budget primacy, is the result of consensus in Japanese society? Or are dissenters excluded or ignored? Or do people simply not care about governmental policy?

All three explanations would seem to apply. First, many people do not care sufficiently: although knowledge about politics and policy matters in Japan compares favorably with other nations, the inclination toward active participation, particularly with regard to matters which transcend the interests of the local community, appears less at least than in the United States.[14] Second, many are excluded. Radical students and the like are of course ignored almost everywhere; more to the point is that large sectors of the population which in other countries have been continuously or alternately represented in the elite, notably organized labor, have been denied much influence by the twenty-year rule of the Liberal Democrats. The rural bias in the electoral system, still more pronounced in the composition of the LDP, has meant that other groups — urban residents, "consumers," white-collar workers — have also been severely underrepresented.

However, as a third point, it would be misleading to see this exclusionary pattern as the sole cause of elite consensus. Certainly through most of the period, a majority — perhaps a large majority — agreed with the government's emphasis on economic growth, and was satisfied enough with performance to see little need for basic changes in policy. Accordingly, many were content to leave the necessary marginal adjustments up to the elite. Interest groups were active, but they typically aimed at obtaining limited benefits for their own memberships. Further, evidence from newspapers of the mid-1950s to the late 1960s indicates that the array of pressure groups visiting Tokyo, holding demonstrations and being deplored in editorials seems hardly to have changed at all. That is, although Japanese society did make demands upon government, those

14. Bradley M. Richardson, *The Political Culture of Japan* (Berkeley and Los Angeles: University of California Press, 1974), pp. 44-45, 96, 124-47.

demands were narrow and easily satisfied, and the *pattern* of demands was surprisingly stable over time.

How do these facts about mass political behavior affect decision-making patterns within the governmental system? First, in terms of elite composition Japanese governmental politics has been continuously dominated by a group representing a limited spectrum of interests. The stability of rule itself is an important point: in other countries alternation of parties or executives (even when they are not very divergent ideologically) has introduced new faces and new ideas, and frequently has brought shifts in policy significant enough to show up in budget statistics.[15] The Japanese governmental system for many years has been made up of the same people, or the same sorts of people, who have gotten used to each others' habits and preferences—no small explanation of a tendency toward routinization of decision-making processes and budget primacy. Second, while the interests of social groups might affect the behavior of elite members, Japanese politicians tend to perceive voters as animated almost solely by particularistic, pork-barrel desires rather than by concern over issues of broad social policy.

Finally, and probably most significantly, the agenda of problems presented by society to government has been narrow in scope—or rather, the agenda accepted as legitimate within the governmental system has been narrow in scope. In part because of the exclusion of large segments of society from direct participation, during this period Japan has been racked by several disputes which have divided the public, brought legislative proceedings to a halt, and occasioned large-scale demonstrations in the streets.[16] Such disputes are not reflected in divisions within the governmental system, which would lead to real policy debate and presumably a compromise solution; instead, they become confrontations *between* the governmental system and the forces of the opposition, in the public arena and in the Diet. One might then visualize *two* political agendas as operating, one made up of these great ideological issues, not regarded as serious alternatives within the governmental system, and the other of incremental additions or marginal adjustments to policy: it is the "middle range" of policy problems in between, such as questions of defense versus

15. Davis, Dempster and Wildavsky found for the United States that changes in partisanship of Congress or the presidency are the single major cause of shift points; their research is summarized in Wildavsky, *Budgeting,* chaps. 2-3 and esp. p. 45. An imaginative analysis of budgetary statistics in other countries is Valerie Bunce, "Elite Succession, Petrification, and Policy Innovation in Communist Systems: An Empirical Assessment," *Comparative Political Studies* 9, 1 (April 1976).

16. The issues have usually been either of foreign policy—the U.S.-Japan Security Treaty, the Japan-Korea Friendship Treaty—or of the extent of central government control, for example, over elementary and higher education, police organization, and the right of public employees to strike.

welfare versus education versus other broad areas, which seems to have been relatively neglected in Japan.[17]

To summarize, a general agreement on goals and satisfaction with governmental performance in Japanese society, assisted by a political structure which tends to exclude dissent, has both narrowed the range of issues on the effective political agenda, and has produced a governmental elite, quite stable over time, characterized by an even higher degree of basic consensus. As a result, domestic policy making has largely consisted of incremental additions and marginal adjustments, matters easily handled through budgeting; moreover, the budgeting system seems to hold some natural advantages over alternative decision-making processes in Japan. Thus, compared with other countries, a larger proportion of the business of government is handled through the budgeting system, and participants are more likely to allow budgeting to follow its natural course.

Underlying every facet of this analysis is the dominant fact of postwar Japanese politics: high economic growth. At the level of mass political behavior, a constant rise in personal incomes increases popular optimism and satisfaction. The ever-expanding pie means that disputes among social groups over the size of individual slices are softened.[18] Growing revenues allow taxes to be cut every year even while the flow of government benefits is increased. All these factors attenuate demands on and dissatisfactions with the government, contributing to elite continuity and to the narrowness of the political agenda with which the elites must deal. At the elite level, similar considerations pertain to relationships within the governmental system. Battles among policy "subgovernments" are typically resolved by each getting a share of the revenue increment; the lower levels of tension associated with positive-sum rather than zero-sum games encourage routinized rather than more confrontational decision processes. In these several ways, high growth is favorable to a takeover of policy making by budgeting; in all likelihood, indeed, "budget primacy" could not endure in a low-growth environment.

What are the effects of growth within the budgeting system itself? When sizable new revenues are available for allocation every year, there is

17. Note my first agenda corresponds roughly to Lowi's "redistributional" sector and my second to his "distributional" sector. Theodore J. Lowi, "American Business, Public Policy, Case-Studies, and Political Theory," *World Politics* 16 (July 1964), 677-715. A tripartite typology of public policy more nearly parallel to the one implicit here is that of T.J. Pempel, "Patterns of Policymaking: Higher Education," in *Policymaking in Contemporary Japan,* ed. Pempel (Ithaca: Cornell University Press, forthcoming).

18. See Richard Rose and Derek Unwin, "Social Cohesion, Political Parties and Strains in Regimes," *Comparative Political Studies* 2, 2 (April 1969), 39; W. Runciman, *Relative Deprivation and Social Injustice* (London: Routledge and Kegan Paul, 1966); and Robert A. Dahl and Charles Lindblom, *Politics, Economics and Welfare* (New York: Harper & Bros., 1953).

less need for the Ministry of Finance to take on the most unpleasant and politically most difficult task of budgeting, that of cutting back or abolishing existing programs which appear outmoded or wasteful. Sufficient slack is provided to indulge demands from powerful interest groups and the majority party even while programs seen as more vital to national needs are allowed to expand rapidly. Decisions become easier because opportunity costs are perceived as being low — choosing to give money to one item is not seen as precluding the simultaneous pursuit of other values. We might suggest, in fact, that however deeply the characteristically Japanese budgeting norm of "balance" may be rooted in traditional value structure, it is able to flourish and grow only in the confortable environment provided by that most modern phenomenon, rapid economic growth.

# Japanese *Budget* Politics

Having seen how the functions of Japanese budgeting have been shaped by broader socioeconomic and political factors, it is appropriate now to turn ourselves about and ask about the *effects* of budget primacy. What difference does it make that such a high proportion of governmental decisions are channelled through the budgetary system?[19]

First, Japanese political style, or tone, has been affected. People come to see decision making as a game played behind closed doors, among few participants, following an esoteric set of rules. The budget process tends to transform arguments over broad conceptions of policy into arguments over details, battles of principle into horsetrading, ideals into yen. Policy issues are decided either by the application of dry technical criteria, or by one side's tactical superiority over the other. Politicians and their more active constituents are seen as narrow-minded, selfish, out for immediate gain. The public as a whole has no role; individuals or groups can make their needs heard only by more or less humbly "petitioning" a direct participant. Such images of the political process pervade even the elite, and are amplified and broadcast through newspaper reporting — the budget process is given broad and intensive coverage each year, very much from an "insider" viewpoint.[20] One must conclude that the net effect on popular

19. Imputing causal relationships here is a bit speculative: to some extent the effects of budget primacy are also direct effects of the *causes* of budget primacy outlined above.

20. One reason is the system of press clubs attached to each ministry, breeding great intimacy. See Nathaniel B. Thayer, "Competition and Conformity: An Inquiry into the Structure of the Japanese Newspapers", in *Modern Japanese Organization and Decision Making*, ed. Ezra Vogel (Berkeley and Los Angeles: University of California Press, 1975), pp. 284-303, esp. 296-300.

perceptions of government can only reinforce traditional tendencies toward a "subject" political culture, oriented to the outputs rather than inputs of government, passive and deferential.[21]

Second, the primacy of the budgetary mode of decision making confers differential advantages and disadvantages on members of the governmental system, compared with other ways of making decisions — the effective political structure is affected. To take our major participants in turn, within ministries the central organs (vice-minister, deputy vice-minister, Secretariat, Accounting Division) are strengthened vis-à-vis the bureaus because budget requests and rerequests are decided at that level; bureaus are less able to attempt end-runs around their parent organizations than in, say, the United States. However, within the LDP the effect of budget primacy is the opposite of centralization: specialized ministry-level Policy Affairs Research Council divisions are more influential in budgetary matters; the generalized aggregating bodies (Policy Deliberation Commission, Executive Council) are faced with the choice of either passing divisional demands along without much modification or taking on the enormous task of "comprehensive" budgetary decision making — inevitably they choose the former, and thereby relinquish their potential influence. Hence the party's impact on policy, while substantial, is quite fragmented. Similarly, the nature of budgeting tends to inhibit most prime ministers from taking a very influential direct role.

The greatest advantages obviously accrue to the Ministry of Finance. Budget primacy means that a high proportion of decisions, compared with other nations, are made within the arena where the Finance Ministry is the leading actor. Formally, MOF power rests on such jealously guarded principles as the rule that all budget appeals must go to the finance ministry (not, as in other systems, to the president or Cabinet), or that the budget total set in the MOF draft will not be raised. Less formally, the fact that policy disputes come to be structured along financial and administrative lines clearly favors the peculiar expertise of the budget examiner. As we observed in chapter 8, the Finance Ministry has reacted sharply to all threats against its supervisory position in the Japanese governmental structure, the primary source of status for its officials.

The irony of the Finance Ministry's high position, of course, is that the MOF stands so delicately balanced on the peak of the Japanese governmental structure that a sudden move in any direction would cause it to fall. That is to say, the ministry can maintain its power (or its reputation for power) only by refraining from using it; if Finance officials were to

21. See Gabriel A. Almond and Sidney Verba, *The Civic Culture* (Boston: Little, Brown and Company, 1965), pp. 16-18 and chap. 7); also Richardson, *Political Culture,* especially the conclusions.

attempt, say, a major transfer of funds from one ministry or policy area to another, not only would opposition sufficient to veto the move quickly arise, but generalized pressures would mount and probably threaten the framework for the entire budget. The Finance Ministry has some freedom of maneuver, as was seen in the 1968 "break fiscal rigidification movement," but as the retreat of 1969 illustrates its scope is quite limited. Indeed, one suspects that if the ministry had persevered in any of its attempts at reform, calls for transfer of the budgeting function to the Cabinet would have been renewed and perhaps even carried out. It must be remembered that the Ministry of Finance lacks the institutional links to the president of the American OMB, or the stature in the unwritten constitution of the British Treasury. The MOF's real power is less than appears on the surface.

Third, what has been the effect of budget primacy on public policy? Governmental outputs (as measured by budget shares) have been extremely stable in Japan throughout most of our period. The possible reasons for stability encompass nearly all the points mentioned in this chapter, but once again, dominance by budgeting rather than some other, more dynamic decision making arena seems particularly important. That so much of the policy-making flow is directed through the budgeting system has meant that pretty much the same old decisions get made year after year. Such stability presumably means that some "outmoded" programs receive more funds than they would in a more dynamic system, although it can be difficult to specify the impact on particular policy areas. For example, if the Japanese budget were less "balanced," it seems unlikely that growth in the defense sector would have so closely approximated budget (and GNP) growth; but whether the military would thereby have received more or less funds is hard to say.

At a more abstract level, however, a budget-dominated decision-making system is less likely to be responsive to its changing environment than one less devoted to routinization and incrementalism. As Allen Schick observes (of American state budgeting):

A routinized decisional process tends to establish its own internal success indicators. . . . These perceptions are only indirectly related to the uses to which the budget process is put, the quality of budget choice, or the results of public service. A routinized outlook, therefore, induces insulation from the winds of change that blow outside.[22]

Once times begin to change, the existing set of policy outputs becomes more irrelevant to real needs, and dissatisfaction will mount. If the inertia

22. Allen Schick, *Budget Innovation in the States* (Washington, D.C.: The Brookings Institution, 1971), p. 207.

developed over time in the decision-making system prevents a quick and effective response to strong objections to existing policy, it should follow that the decision-making system itself will come under attack, and finally be changed or even radically reformed. Although a few examples of marginal adjustments from 1955 to the early 1970s may be found, by and large the system maintained itself without great modification in this period. However, at time of writing, it appears that fundamental shifts may be occurring in Japan. Indications that these shifts will be reflected in governmental policies—the budget—and perhaps even in the budgeting decision-making system began to appear in 1973.

# *Contemporary* Japanese
# Budget Politics

By the mid-1970s, Japanese politics and policy—so comfortable, so stable, perhaps so dull for so long—were entering a transition. New pressures were falling on the governmental system from its environments. Resource constraints stimulated inflation and led to a sharp drop in economic growth. Long continuing voting trends had brought the Liberal Democrats to the brink of losing their majority. Citizens' movements arose around the country to oppose pollution and industrial expansion. Demands grew louder that the "gaps" in welfare programs and social facilities between Japan and the West must be narrowed. Consensus on national priorities was clearly breaking down.

Precursors of these shifts were apparent even in the late 1960s, but the budgetary system was sufficiently insulated from outside winds of change not to take much notice. Budget examiners mentioned with some amusement during interviews in 1970 that local petition groups no longer seemed as eager for more dams and factories, but there was little sense of the impending end of an era, and as we have seen budget allocations remained quite stable. Probably one should see the accession of Tanaka in 1972 as the first important sign of change. His "restructuring the archipelago" plan, however disastrous in effect, did represent a large-scale response to recent social and economic trends, and did have a major impact on budgeting and policy outputs. Still, it was economic troubles— particularly the revenue crisis—in the following two years which seem to have jarred Japanese decision makers into perceiving that life will not go on as before.

Clearly it would be foolish to make definitive-sounding statements about the implications of these trends, but some cautious speculations may be offered. In terms of public policy outputs, it does seem safe to predict that the budget growth rate, along with GNP growth, will be lower than in the 1960s, but it is likely that the government share of GNP (and therefore the tax plus social security burden) will have to be higher to meet new demands. The trend toward a larger share of the budget going to the welfare policy area will continue, if only because of impending demographic shifts. Depending upon domestic and international political conditions, support for agriculture and perhaps defense may fall relatively. Government investment for economic growth will probably drop, but that for "quality of life" probably rise.

One is much less confident about assessing trends in mass political behavior. Are citizens' movements a trivial fad, or are they but a surface manifestation of long-term shifts in popular attitudes toward more social awareness and a propensity toward activism? What of the trends toward apathy and cynicism, especially among urban educated youth? We cannot say, but if the analysis in the preceding sections is accurate it would seem that a slowdown in growth, a less rapidly expanding pie, will lead to greater perceptions of different interests and increased conflict among social groups. If so, and if party politicians have their wits about them, political discourse should become a bit more issue-oriented and substantive; that is, the "middle range" of the political agenda mentioned above, lying in between ideological confrontation and pork-barrel distributions of benefits, will become somewhat more popular.[23]

What of the effects of these environmental changes on the budgetary process, our primary subject? Radical and impossible-to-forecast changes could occur if, for example, the Cabinet were to be taken over by a progressive coalition, but this prospect seems distant at best. More likely in the short or medium term is that the Liberal Democrats will simply acquire one or two smaller parties as junior coalition partners by offering minor Cabinet posts and policy payoffs.[24] In this case, the Finance Ministry presumably would have to deal with more than a single party headquarters during revival negotiations, and conceivably the budget would again be subject to marginal amendments in the Diet. Such developments might weaken the Finance Ministry's control over budgeting, but on the other hand, as in the mid-1950s, its chances of playing one party against another would increase. Moreover, as in the 1974 budget, inflation and other economic problems, which seem likely to continue indefinitely, will

23. However, there is likely to be a considerable time-lag, as Robert Putnam suggests in *The Beliefs of Politicans* (New Haven: Yale University Press, 1973), pp. 147-49.

24. Perhaps the next most likely possibility is a breakup of the LDP, with its "left" wing joining with others to form a majority center party; one would guess here that continuity of structure, personnel and policy would still be sufficient to maintain budgeting without a total shakeup.

increase the weight of macrobudgeting considerations and accordingly strengthen the hand of the Finance Ministry. It is probable too that the complexities of coalition balancing and the real difficulties of current policy problems will tend to inhibit prime ministers from attempting to emulate Tanaka's large-scale interventions into budgeting very soon. On the other hand, the long-neglected Cabinet may become a more important forum for policy development if other parties come to be represented.

Such would seem to be likely short-term effects of current political, social and economic trends on the structure of the Japanese budgeting system — they are significant, but not revolutionary, in their implications. However, at a more general level, some additional current tendencies which are more independent of transitory economic ups and downs or the details of political shifts may be discerned. The Japanese governmental system is loosening, moving a few notches closer to a more pluralist and activist model of political process.[25] Representatives of new interests will find new channels into the policy process; their objectives and even their political styles will be different. More conflict over national priorities will develop. The distribution of power within the system will ebb and flow more rapidly. It is possible that even the political leadership, particularly the prime minister, will see a more active policy role as a key to mobilizing popular support. Japanese politics will become more open, more fluid, more interesting.

Under such conditions, we would expect "budget primacy" to decline. More decisions will be made outside the budgetary arena, with budgeters left only to cope with their results. Even within the budget process itself disputes will become more programmatic, less ritualistic; rules of thumb will not be applied as automatically, "balance" norms will become less pervasive. It follows that budgetary outputs will be affected as well: ministries will see their budget shares fluctuating more from year to year. Again, signs of all these trends could be found in the mid-1970s, and unless they represent merely a brief transition to a new stable equilibrium, which seems unlikely, the tempo of change should accelerate.

But yet the study of budgeting, like the practice of budgeting, tends to inculcate an outlook of cautious cynicism, a disinclination to believe that things ever change much. Whatever may be happening in Japan today, one remains reasonably confident that the model of the budgetary system we have outlined here will still be applicable ten years from now. Ministries will still devise strategies to expand their programs. Politicians will still add

25. For a similar prognosis see Margaret McKean, "Pollution and Policy-Making," in *Policymaking in Contemporary Japan*, ed. Pempel. The essays in this volume provide an excellent overview of the variety of policy-making patterns which can be found in Japan.

up budgets in terms of votes. The Budget Bureau director ten years hence is probably a working budget examiner today, already well steeped in the traditions of the Ministry of Finance. Every year, nearly the entire budget will be identical with the previous year's document. Some new utopian budget reform will be talked about but will be indiscernible in the actual process. Change does occur in Japanese budgeting, but it occurs incrementally, on the margin; balance is preserved.

# Appendix A

# The 1973 Japanese Budget (Important Item Breakdown)

| Item | MOF Draft (¥ Billion) | Government Draft (¥ Billion) | Net Addition (Percent) | Dollar Equivalent ($ Billion) | Share (Percent) | Growth (Percent) |
|---|---|---|---|---|---|---|
| Social Security | | | | | | |
| Public Assistance | 352 | 356 | 1.0 | 1.19 | 2.49 | 14.7 |
| Social Welfare | 321 | 322 | 0.4 | 1.07 | 2.26 | 65.3 |
| Social Insurance | 1119 | 1120 | 0.5 | 3.73 | 7.84 | 32.0 |
| Public Health Service | 197 | 200 | 1.2 | 0.67 | 1.40 | 10.1 |
| Measures for the Unemployed | 116 | 117 | 1.1 | 0.39 | 0.82 | 9.7 |
| Total | (2106) | (2115) | 0.4 | (7.05) | (14.80) | 28.8 |
| Education and Science | | | | | | |
| Compulsory Education | 713 | 727 | 2.0 | 2.42 | 5.09 | 17.3 |
| National Schools Special Account | 374 | 383 | 2.5 | 1.28 | 2.68 | 16.4 |
| Promotion of Science and Technology | 205 | 210 | 2.4 | 0.70 | 1.47 | 24.6 |
| Public School Facilities | 102 | 112 | 9.3 | 0.37 | 0.78 | 46.9 |
| School Education Assistance | 108 | 113 | 5.4 | 0.38 | 0.79 | 27.8 |
| Loan Scholarships | 25 | 25 | 0.0 | 0.08 | 0.18 | 12.1 |
| Total | (1527) | (1570) | 2.9 | (5.23) | (10.99) | 20.4 |
| National Debt | 701 | 705 | 0.6 | 2.35 | 4.93 | 54.7 |

| | | | | | |
|---|---|---|---|---|---|
| **Pensions, etc.** | | | | | |
| Civil Servants | 41 | 43 | 5.3 | 0.14 | 0.30 | 11.8 |
| War-related Pensions | 364 | 383 | 5.3 | 1.28 | 2.68 | 27.9 |
| Administration | 5 | 5 | 0.0 | 0.02 | 0.03 | 13.6 |
| Aid to Bereaved, etc. | 39 | 41 | 5.3 | 0.17 | 0.29 | 36.3 |
| Total | (448) | (472) | 5.3 | (1.90) | (3.31) | 26.8 |
| Local Allocation Tax | 2781 | 2781 | 0.0 | 9.27 | 19.47 | 20.9 |
| Special Grants to Okinawa | 39 | 39 | 0.0 | 0.11 | 0.27 | 6.3 |
| National Defense | 935 | 935 | 0.0 | 3.64 | 6.55 | 16.9 |
| **Public Works** | | | | | |
| Erosion and Flood Control | 423 | 443 | 4.8 | 1.48 | 3.10 | 28.3 |
| Road Improvements | 1013 | 1039 | 2.6 | 3.41 | 7.27 | 22.1 |
| Harbors, Ports, Airports | 224 | 235 | 4.8 | 0.78 | 1.64 | 26.1 |
| Housing | 199 | 203 | 2.0 | 0.68 | 1.42 | 35.1 |
| Public Service Facilities | 214 | 226 | 5.7 | 0.75 | 1.58 | 61.4 |
| Agriculture | 331 | 345 | 4.1 | 1.15 | 2.41 | 25.1 |
| Forest Roads, Industrial Water Supply | 67 | 71 | 6.3 | 0.24 | 0.50 | 26.7 |

| | | | | | |
|---|---|---|---|---|---|
| Adjustment Works | 11 | 14 | 29.5 | 0.05 | 0.10 | 67.6 |
| Disaster Reconstruction | 265 | 265 | 0.0 | 0.88 | 1.86 | 95.7 |
| Total | (2746) | (2841) | 3.4 | (9.39) | (19.89) | 41.1 |
| Economic Cooperation | 121 | 129 | 6.4 | 0.43 | 0.90 | 11.7 |
| Measures for Small Business | 78 | 80 | 3.1 | 0.32 | 0.56 | 15.1 |
| Foodstuffs Control Special Account | 541 | 541 | 0.0 | 1.80 | 3.79 | 3.9 |
| Industrial Investment Special Account | 63 | 76 | 20.7 | 0.25 | 0.53 | 8.8 |
| Miscellaneous | 1818 | 1771 | -2.6 | 5.90 | 12.40 | 21.9 |
| Reserves | 230 | 230 | 0.0 | 0.77 | 1.61 | 27.8 |
| Policy Adjustment Expenses | 150 | — | — | — | — | — |
| Grand Total | 14284 | 14284 | 0.0 | 47.61 | 100.01 | 24.6 |

NOTES: Columns may not add exactly because all calculations were performed at the million yen level and then rounded. Dollar equivalents are at the rate $1 = 300 yen. The final column is the growth rate from the 1972 initial budget (government draft). Brief explanations of items will be found in *The Budget in Brief*. It should be kept in mind that the 1973 budget was atypical, strongly influenced by Prime Minister Tanaka's plan to restructure the Japanese archipelago and other expansionist tendencies.

SOURCES: Calculated from tables in NKS, January 8 and December 22, 1973, evening editions; *Zaisei Tōkei*, 1974, pp. 201–202; English titles adapted from *The Budget in Brief*, 1973, pp. 71–73.

# Appendix B

# Japanese Budget Forms and Classification

Although this is a study of budget politics, not budgetary technicalities, a brief discussion of budget classifications and forms may be helpful to other scholars wishing to investigate the Japanese system, as well as shedding some light on the modes of decision making inherent in the process, since classifications and forms make up the language that budget participants must think in most of the time.[1]

It is easiest to begin with the breakdowns of expenditure shown on the official budget documents submitted to the Diet for passage.[2] In decreasing order of size, the categories are:

(1) Jurisdiction (*Shokan*): there are eighteen that collectively cover all General Account expenditures—the Imperial Household, Diet, Courts, Board of Audit, Cabinet, Prime Minister's Office, and the twelve ministries.

(2) Organization (*Soshiki*): agencies (*chō*), institutes, bureaus whose work is somehow separate from the main work of the ministry, sometimes councils and committees, and other units. Each jurisdiction has one organization called the "home office" (usually, *honshō*), which includes the ministry-level staff, plus the departments and bureaus (and divisions underneath them) that perform the main work of the ministry. This unit is

---

1. For a good general discussion of classification systems, see Jesse Burkhead, *Government Budgeting* (New York: John Wiley and Sons, 1965), chaps. 6-8. For Japanese budget forms, see Hayashi Yoshio, *Zaiseiron* ("Public Finance") (Tokyo: Chikuma Shobō, 1968), pp. 114-138, as well as Kōno Kazuyoshi, *Yosan Seido* ("The Budget System") (Tokyo: Gakuyō Shobō, 1976), esp. chap. 3.

2. Reference will be made to the General Account only. The submission to the Diet is published as (for 1970) "Shōwa 45 Nendo Ippan Kaikei Yosan", and later as "Ippan Kaikei Yosansho (Shōwa 45 Nendo)," both compiled by the Budget Bureau and published by the MOF Printing Bureau.

not further subdivided on an organizational basis (except for administrative expenses) in published official budget documents, making it impossible, for example, to compare bureau-level expenditure changes with those in the United States. The entire General Account had ninety-seven such organizations in 1970.

(3) Item (*Kō*): the subdivision of organizations—some will have twenty, others only one—that might be considered a "program." However, the level of generality varies enormously. In 1970, for example, one item covered all flood control projects (a total of almost $500 million), while another was just disaster recovery aid for local agricultural institutions (about $7,000). There are 422 Items in the General Account and so in 1970 the average size was somewhat under ¥20 billion (about $65 million).

(4) Subitem (*Jikō*): a further specification of the item, so it might be considered a subprogram, but often quite large. Some items have only one subitem, covering its entire budget, but others have ten or more. Although not included in the official documents, subitems can be further subdivided into mid-level (*chūjikō*) and small (*shōjikō*) subitems. These are all essentially "program-based" classifications.

(5) Line-item (*Moku*) and detailed line-item (*Moku no saibun*): subdivisions not of the subitem, but of the item, shown on separate tables in the official documents; an object-of-expenditure classification, such as expenses for personnel, purchase of supplies, and so forth. Many line-items are grants-in-aid (*hojokin*) or transfers to other accounts (such as Special Accounts).

(6) Unit price (*Tanka*) and Quantity (*Inzū*): while not shown on the official documents, these are the building-blocks of each line-item. Quantity is the number of units (stamps, men, buildings); unit price is what each costs; multiplied, they produce the line-item. The determination of unit prices, particularly when they cannot be decided by market conditions, is extremely complicated. Elaborate charts that specify the object to be purchased or constructed in great detail, and then vary the price by region, are required for many sections of the budget. Unit prices are proposed by ministries in the budget process, and reviewed and reduced by the Ministry of Finance—indeed, a common MOF cost-cutting strategy is to set stringent unit prices (for a precedent applying to other items or later years) and then make concessions on the quantity side.

This format, with the possible exception of the subitem level, may be seen as primarily useful in the "control" function of budgeting ensuring that expenditures are made legally and for the purposes specified.[3] But

3. Further administrative detail is provided in the most complete published budget compilation, entitled "Shōwa 45 Nendo Yosan" edited by the Zaisei Chōsakai (in reality, by Budget Bureau officials) and published by Keiyū Kyōkai. Explanations of a single ministry's budget here may run over 250 pages. Incidentally, a comparable audit document—"Shōwa

because budgeting has other functions as well, additional classification schemes are required.

In particular, this official breakdown is not an effective way to explain government activities in various policy areas to interested citizens, legislators, or even those who participate in the budget process itself.[4] For this purpose, the most widely known of the several classification systems is the Important Item (*Jūyō* or *Shuyō Keihi*) classification, which is the basis for *Kuni no Yosan*, the semi-official detailed explanation of the budget each year.[5] Unlike its operational equivalent in the United States, the functional budget, this breakdown includes both broad policy areas (education, welfare) and specific and relatively small programs (measures for the coal mining industry, agricultural insurance).[6] That is, rather than being a "rational" classification, the Important Items are those which at some time the MOF has seen as worth emphasizing. The list thus changes marginally from year to year, as does the internal composition of some of the items.[7] However, because this breakdown is considered the primary reference to the budget, the MOF has also devised a more standardized list, which compares expenditures using these categories with constant definitions over the most recent seven years, and back to the 1934-36 period.[8] The Important Item classification is based on the subitem level, with each subitem classified into a single Important Item. Budget items (*Kō*), on the other hand, might be split into several Important Items.

Completely unofficial, but similar to the Important Item classification in character, are the individual formats used by each ministry to describe its own budget to the public, worth mentioning here because such documents are used within the LDP budget review process, and perhaps even occasionally at the Finance Ministry. These divide the expenditures of the ministry into whatever classifications will show its activities in the best light, and accordingly change a good deal from year to year. They are easily available to researchers, who afterward have a difficult time matching them up to other classification systems. An example is the Ministry of Health and Welfare budget outline used for various analyses in

45 Nendo Kessan"—is published about one year following the close of each fiscal year under the same auspices.

4. On this point, see Fujii Makoto, "Puroguramu Sutorakucha Ron" ("A Study of Program Structure"), *Fainansu* 6, 7 (October 1970), 66-71.

5. *Kuni no Yosan*, compiled by the Zaisei Chōsakai, published by Dōyū Shobō.

6. Note too that it classifies public works separately rather than under the functions they are to perform. See Burkhead, *Government Budgeting*, pp. 113-125.

7. Cf. Tables 21-22 in Japan, Ministry of Finance, Budget Bureau, Research Division, *Zaisei Tōkei* ("Fiscal Statistics") (Tokyo: Ministry of Finance Printing Bureau), 1974, pp. 186-217.

8. *Ibid.*, respectively, Table 23, pp. 218-221 and Table 36, pp. 271-72.

the text above.[9] It is organized programmatically, with five major headings, each with four to seven subheads followed by lists of several programs — none of these are the same as any of the official titles, and even the amounts given often do not correspond. As one minor case, the popular day care center (*hoikujo*) program is given a subhead of its own and five program items in the ministry document, while in *Kuni no Yosan* it is buried, with scant space, in a long list of small miscellaneous items (and is not to be found at all in the official documents, even the appendices). Further, the budget figures in these two classificatiions are not equal, though of similar magnitude, and the programs are explained differently. Such are the initial problems of doing policy analysis in Japan.

The other classification commonly encountered is Jurisdictional (*Shokanbetsu*), assigning all expenditures to one of the eighteen ministry-level jurisdictions.[10] Except for those that are themselves jurisdictions, independently budgeted agencies, common in the United States, are lacking; any organ which spends government funds must receive them under the auspices of one of these jurisdictions, a factor which contributes to the dominance of "subgovernments" defined by ministry spheres of responsibility in the Japanese governmental system. Categories and definitions for this classification do not shift as rapidly as for the Important Item breakdown, but several jurisdictions include large funds which fluctuate for economic or other nonbudgetary reasons, so longitudinal analysis is difficult. (Such funds include General Account contributions to the Industrial Investment Special Account, payment of the national debt, and so forth.)

For comparisons both over time and with other countries, the Functional (*Mokutekibetsu*) classification is most useful.[11] It has twelve categories, and the MOF has broken these down into detailed programs with constant definitions over a ten-year period, as well as for comparisons with the 1934-36 period.[12] This classification is based on item (*Kō*) level units. While useful for analysis, the Functional breakdown is not a "real" budget classification, in the sense that it is not used as a basis for making decisions during budgeting (unlike the three above), but is simply an *ex post facto* rearrangement of figures. Similar in this regard is the Economic Character (*Keizai Seishitsu*) or National Income Accounts classification, which assigns expenditures depending on whether or not they are included

9. "Shōwa 45 Nendo Kōseishō Shokan Yosan'an no Gaiyō" ("Outline of the Fiscal Year 1970 Ministry of Health and Welfare Budget Draft") (Mimeo: February 4, 1970).

10. Seventeen from 1953 to 1960. See *Zaisei Tōkei*, 1974, Tables 5-6, pp. 62-71.

11. Japanese and American functional budgets are compared in Table 1, above.

12. In *Zaisei Tōkei*, 1974, see respectively Tables 24-25 and notes on pp. 222-27, and Table 37, pp. 273-74.

in the Government Purchases of Goods and Services Account, and are consumption or investment expenditures and so forth.

The final major classification indicates what the money buys, under two systems. The Line-Item (*Mokubetsu*) classification is the more detailed, with each line-item classified into one of twenty-five categories. The more generalized Object-of-Expenditure (*Shitobetsu*) breakdown is also based on the line-item, but uses only eight categories (personnel, regular and other; travel; supplies; facilities; grants-in-aid; transfers to other accounts; and other).[13] These breakdowns are the most stable over time in categorization and definition, and are easily comparable cross-nationally, but unfortunately yield little information of interest to the analyst.

Many of these classifications are indicated for each expenditure at the line-item level by a complicated coding system. As a random example, the following is the full code number for a grant-in-aid to pay fees in connection with part-time or correspondence schools, budgeted at about $1 million in 1970: 10-007-15071-215-16.[14] These figures mean:

(1) "10"—the jurisdiction, Ministry of Education.

(2) "007"—the (arbitrary) number of the item (*Kō*) within the jurisdiction.

(3) "15"—the "promotion of education" category in the Important Item classification.

(4) "071"—the "school education expenses" category in the Functional classification.

(5) "2"—not an expenditure which may be paid for by deficit finance, instead of ordinary revenues.[15]

(6) "1"—included within the goods and services account, in the Economic Character classification.

(7) "5"—a grant-in-aid, the Object-of-Expenditure classification.

(8) "16"—a cross-reference to an earlier coding system.

A Budget Bureau Examiner does not, of course, have to keep all these categorizations in mind while reviewing a ministry's budget requests. Many of the technicalities are handled by specialists. Still, this discussion is a reminder of the inevitably complex nature of budgeting, which helps to explain why the MOF sometimes appears preoccupied with administrative questions at the expense of policy.

13. For these two see *ibid.*, Tables 27-28, pp. 229-241.

14. "Shōwa 45 Nendo Ippan Kaikei Yosan." The item is on p. 335 and an explanation of the coding system is on pp. 647-49.

15. Under the Finance Law; see the section on initiating deficit financing in 1965-66 in chap. 9.

# Appendix C

# Bibliographic Note

Sources drawn upon in this study have been cited in footnotes, but a few of the most useful materials may be described briefly here. First, on budgeting in general, the basic text and reference volume is Jesse Burkhead, *Government Budgeting* (New York: John Wiley and Sons, 1965). Seminal in the study of budget politics are Aaron Wildavsky, *The Politics of the Budgetary Process* (Boston: Little, Brown and Company, 1964) and Richard F. Fenno, Jr., *The Power of the Purse: Appropriations Politics in Congress* (Boston: Little, Brown and Company, 1966). A summary of much budget politics research and a provocative first stab at cross-level and cross-national comparison is Wildavsky's *Budgeting: A Comparative Theory of Budgetary Processes* (Boston: Little, Brown and Company, 1975).

Among classic works by political scientists on the Japanese governmental system are Oka Yoshitake, ed., *Gendai Nihon no Seiji Katei* (Tokyo: Iwanami Shoten, 1958); Tsuji Kiyoaki, *Nihon Kanryōsei no Kenkyū* (rev. ed.; Tokyo: Tokyo Daigaku Shuppankai, 1969); Masumi Junnosuke, *Gendai Nihon no Seiji Taisei* (Tokyo: Iwanami Shoten, 1966); and the collection of articles in Nihon Seiji Gakkai, ed., *Gendai Nihon no Seitō to Kanryō* (Tokyo: Iwanami Shoten, 1967). Somewhat more recent is Inoki Masamichi and Kamikawa Nobuhiko, eds., *Gendai Nihon no Seiji: Bunseki to Tenbō*, Nihon no Shōrai, Vol. II (Tokyo: Ushio Shuppansha, 1969). More narrowly, the most helpful reference on Japanese administrative practice was Okabe Shirō, *Gyōsei Kanri* (Tokyo: Yūhikaku, 1967). Two books in English should be noted, both devoted to the LDP: Nathaniel B. Thayer, *How the Conservatives Rule Japan* (Princeton: Princeton University Press, 1969) and Haruhiro Fukui, *Party in Power* (Berkeley and Los Angeles: University of California Press, 1970). Many leading Japanese specialists including Ide Yoshinori, Kojima Akira and Itō Daiichi contributed fine articles to a festschrift in honor of Tsuji Kiyoaki,

*Gendai Gyōsei to Kanryōsei,* ed. Taniūchi Ken et al (2 vols.; Tokyo: Tokyo Daigaku Shuppankai, 1974).

Partly filling the gaps left by political scientists in our knowledge of Japanese political process is a genre of books and articles aimed at a general audience but treating topics rarely encountered in American journalism. By academic standards these works sometimes seem overly given to fuzzy generalization (particularly about "power elites"), but they often provide detailed descriptions of institutions and relationships unavailable elsewhere, as well as entertaining anecdotes and the possibility of insights into how Japanese participants view their own politics. Some are produced by teams of reporters, notably Nihon Keizai Shinbunsha, ed., *Yosan wa Dare no Mono ka* (Tokyo: Nihon Keizai Shinbunsha, 1971); Asahi Shinbunsha, ed., *Jimintō: Hoshu Kenryoku no Kōzō* (Tokyo: Asahi Shinbunsha, 1970); and Asahi Shinbun Keizaibu, *Keizai Seisaku no Butaiura* (Tokyo: Asahi Shinbunsha, 1974). One of the best books among many by individual journalists and *hyōronka* is Suzuki Yukio's *Keizai Kanryō* (Tokyo: Nihon Keizai Shinbunsha, 1969). Honda Yasuharu's amusing *Nihon Neokanryō ron* (Tokyo: Kōdansha, 1975) and the biography *Ikeda Hayato* by Shioguchi Kiichi (Tokyo: Asahi Shinbunsha, 1975) are worth at least a look, as are various magazine articles by Amano Hajime and Kusayanagi Daizō. Some works by professional economists are also aimed at a broad readership; helpful for pre-1955 budgeting is Endō Shōkichi, ed., *Yosan* (Tokyo: Yuhikaku, 1959), while Yamamoto Masao's *Keizai Kanryō no Jittai* (Tokyo: Mainichi Shinbunsha, 1972) is both recent and detailed.

Japanese specialists on public finance often take an institutional approach of interest to political scientists; for the present study Hayashi Yoshio, *Zaiseiron* (Tokyo: Chikuma Shobō, 1968) was invaluable, and Okuma Ichirō et al., eds., *Zaiseigaku (2): Nihon no Zaisei* (Tokyo: Yūhikaku, 1970) should also be noted. A good historical treatment in English is Koichi Emi, *Government Fiscal Activity and Economic Growth in Japan: 1868-1960,* Hitotsubashi University Institute of Economic Research Economic Research Monographs, No. 6 (Tokyo: Kinokuniya, 1963). Two superb sources of historical statistics and much other information are Emi and Shionoya Yuichi, eds., *Zaisei Shishutsu,* Vol. VII of *Chōki Keizai Tōkei,* eds. Ohkawa Kazushi, Shinohara Miyohei and Umemura Mataji (Tokyo: Tōyō Keizai Shinpōsha, 1966); and Ōkurashō Hyakunenshi Henshūshitsu, ed., *Ōkurashō Hyakunenshi* (3 vols., Tokyo: Ōkura Zaimu Kyōkai, 1969).

Official budget documents have been described in Appendix B, but the most useful official or semi-official annual publications should be mentioned here. *Zaisei Tōkei* is compiled by the Research Section of the

Budget Bureau and published by the Ministry of Finance Printing Bureau; as well as some 300 pages of Japanese fiscal statistics, it includes brief cross-national comparisons. The entire Budget Bureau contributes to *Kuni no Yosan,* titularly edited by the Zaisei Chōsakai and published by Dōyū Shobō; it runs nearly 1000 pages each year and is the authoritative source for detailed budget information at the program level. Popular annuals on the budget in Japanese are *Yosan no Hanashi,* edited by the Zaisei Chōsakai and published by Keiyū Kyōkai, and *Zusetsu Nihon no Zaisei,* edited each year by an MOF ministry-level official and published by Tōyō Keizai; *The Budget in Brief,* in English and about 75 pages, is compiled by the Budget Bureau. Most Japanese ministries and some agencies issue annual white papers; since 1969 English versions have been collected (along with other materials) in the extremely useful *White Papers of Japan,* edited and published by the Japan Institute of International Affairs. Somewhat more tangentially related to budgeting as such are the annual surveys of Japan by the Organization for Economic Co-operation and Development, and the compendium of everything one might want to know about politicians, *Kokkai Binran,* published by Nihon Seikei Shinbunsha.

The most consistently informative magazines for studies of this sort are the weekly *Ekonomisuto* and the monthly semi-official organ of the Ministry of Finance, *Fainansu.* Japanese newspapers cover budgeting and governmental decision making more generally in exhaustive detail; the *Nihon Keizai Shinbun* is outstanding, but *Asahi* and *Mainichi,* and to a lesser extent *Yomiuri, Sankei* and *Tokyo* dailies, were also drawn upon extensively. The collection of the Newspaper Clipping Room of the National Diet Library is an excellent resource for tracing the evolution of policy and process in the postwar years.

# Studies of the
# East Asian Institute

*The Ladder of Success in Imperial China,* by Ping-ti Ho. New York: Columbia University Press, 1962.

*The Chinese Inflation, 1937-1949,* by Shin-hsin Chou. New York: Columbia University Press, 1963.

*Reformer in Modern China: Chang Chien, 1853-1926,* by Samuel Chu. New York: Columbia University Press, 1965.

*Research in Japanese Sources: a Guide,* by Herschel Webb with the assistance of Marleigh Ryan. New York: Columbia University Press, 1965.

*Society and Education in Japan,* by Herbert Passin. New York: Bureau of Publications, Teachers College, Columbia University, 1965.

*Agricultural Production and Economic Development in Japan, 1873-1922,* by James I. Nakamura. Princeton: Princeton University Press, 1966.

*Japan's First Modern Novel: Ukigumo of Futabatei Shimei,* by Marleigh Ryan. New York: Columbia University Press, 1967.

*The Korean Communist Movement, 1918-1948,* by Dae-Sook Suh. Princeton: Princeton University Press, 1967.

*The First Vietnam Crisis,* by Melvin Gurtov. New York: Columbia University Press, 1967.

*Cadres, Bureaucracy, and Political Power in Communist China,* by A. Doak Barnett. New York: Columbia University Press, 1967.

*The Japanese Imperial Institution in the Tokugawa Period,* by Herschel Webb. New York: Columbia University Press, 1968.

*Higher Education and Business Recruitment in Japan,* by Koya Azumi, New York: Teachers College Press, Columbia University, 1969.

*The Communists and Chinese Peasant Rebellions: A Study in the Rewriting of Chinese History,* by James P. Harrison, Jr. New York: Atheneum, 1969.

*How the Conservatives Rule Japan,* by Nathaniel B. Thayer. Princeton: Princeton University Press, 1969.

*Aspects of Chinese Education,* edited by C. T. Hu. New York: Teachers College Press, Columbia University, 1970.

*Documents of Korean Communism, 1918-1948,* by Dae-Sook Suh. Princeton: Princeton University Press, 1970.

*Japanese Education: A Bibliography of Materials in the English Language,* by Herbert Passin. New York: Teachers College Press, Columbia University, 1970.

*Economic Development and the Labor Market in Japan,* by Koji Taira. New York: Columbia University Press, 1970.

*The Japanese Oligarchy and the Russo-Japanese War,* by Shumpei Okamoto. New York: Columbia University Press, 1970.

*Imperial Restoration in Medieval Japan,* by H. Paul Varley. New York: Columbia University Press, 1971.

*Japan's Postwar Defense Policy, 1947-1968,* by Martin E. Weinstein. New York: Columbia University Press, 1971.

*Election Campaigning Japanese Style,* by Gerald L. Curtis. New York: Columbia University Press, 1971.

*China and Russia: The "Great Game,"* by O. Edmund Clubb. New York: Columbia University Press, 1971.

*Money and Monetary Policy in Communist China,* by Katharine Huang Hsiao. New York: Columbia University Press, 1971.

*The District Magistrate in Late Imperial China,* by John R. Watt. New York: Columbia University Press, 1972.

*Law and Policy in China's Foreign Relations: A Study of Attitudes and Practice,* by James C. Hsiung. New York: Columbia University Press, 1972.

*Pearl Harbor as History: Japanese-American Relations, 1931-1941,* edited by Dorothy Borg and Shumpei Okamoto, with the assistance of Dale K. A. Finlayson. New York: Columbia University Press, 1973.

*Japanese Culture: A Short History,* by H. Paul Varley. New York: Praeger, 1973.

*Doctors in Politics: The Political Life of the Japan Medical Association,* by William E. Steslicke. New York: Praeger, 1973.

*Japan's Foreign Policy, 1868-1941: A Research Guide,* edited by James William Morley. New York: Columbia University Press, 1974.

*The Japan Teachers Union: A Radical Interest Group in Japanese Politics,* by Donald Ray Thurston. Princeton: Princeton University Press, 1973.

*Palace and Politics in Prewar Japan,* by David Anson Titus. New York: Columbia University Press, 1974.

*The Idea of China: Essays in Geographic Myth and Theory,* by Andrew March. Devon, England: David and Charles, 1974.

*Science and Technology in the Development of Modern China: An Annotated Bibliography,* by Genevieve C. Dean. London: Mansell Information/Publishing, 1974.

*The Origins of the Cultural Revolution. I. Contradictions Among the People, 1956-1957,* by Roderick MacFarquhar. New York: Columbia University Press, 1974.

*Shiba Kokan: Artist, Innovator, and Pioneer in the Westernization of Japan,* by Calvin L. French. Tokyo: Weatherhill, 1974.

*Rebels and Bureaucrats: China's December 9ers,* by John Israel and Donald W. Klein. Berkeley: University of California Press, 1975.

*Embassy at War,* by Harold Joyce Noble. Edited with an introduction by Frank
   Baldwin, Jr. Seattle: University of Washington Press, 1975.

*House United, House Divided: The Chinese Family in Taiwan,* by Myron L.
   Cohen. New York: Columbia University Press, 1976.

*Insei: Abdicated Sovereigns in the Politics of Late Heian Japan,* by G. Cameron
   Hurst. New York: Columbia University Press, 1976.

*Escape from Predicament: China's Cultural Orientations on the Eve of Moderniza-
   tion,* by Thomas A. Metzger. New York: Columbia University Press, 1976.

*Deterrent Diplomacy: Japan, Germany and the USSR, 1935-1940,* edited by James
   William Morley. New York: Columbia University Press, 1976.

*Tanaka Giichi and Japan's China Policy in the 1920's,* by William Morton.
   London: Dawsons, 1976.

*Cadres, Commanders, and Commissars: The Training of the Chinese Communist
   Leadership, 1920-1945,* by Jane Price. Boulder: Westview, 1976.

# Index